THE BATTLE-CRUISER HMS *RENOWN* 1916–1948

By the same Author:

NAVAL

Arctic Victory
Midway: Dauntless Victory
Battles of the Malta Striking Forces
Battleship Royal Sovereign
British Battle-Cruisers
Cruisers in Action
Destroyer Action
Destroyer Leader
Eagle's War
Fighting Flotilla
Hard Lying
Heritage of the Sea
H.M.S. Wild Swan
Into the Minefields
Midway: Dauntless Victory
Naval Warfare in the English Channel
Pedestal; the convoy that saved Malta
Royal Navy Ships' Badges
Task Force 57
The Great Ships Pass

AVIATION
Close Air Support
Fairchild-Republic A10A Thunderbolt-II
North American T-6, SNJ, Harvard and
Wirraway
Lockheed C-130 Hercules
Ship Strike!
RAF Squadron Badges
T-6: the Harvard, Texan and Wirraway
The Sea Eagles
Torpedo Bombers
Avro Lancaster
MILITARY
Massacre at Tobruk
The Royal Marines: A Pictorial History
Per Mare, Per Terram
Victoria's Victories
War in the Aegean

DIVE BOMBERS
Aichi D3A1/2 Val
Curtiss SB2C Helldiver
Dive Bomber!
Dive Bombers in Action!
Douglas SBD Dauntless
Douglas AD Skyraider
Fist from the Sky
History of Dive Bombing
Into the Assault
Jungle Dive Bombers at War
Junkers Ju87 Stuka
Luftwaffe Colours – Stuka –1
Luftwaffe Colours – Stuka – 2
Petlyakov Pe-2 Peshka
Skua! – the Royal Navy's Dive Bomber
Straight Down!
Stuka Spearhead
Stuka at War
Stukas over the Mediterranean
Stuka Squadron
Stukas over the Steppe
Vengeance

THE
BATTLE-CRUISER
HMS *RENOWN*
1916–1948

PETER C. SMITH

Pen & Sword
MARITIME

First published in Great Britain in 2008 by
PEN & SWORD MARITIME
An imprint of
Pen & Sword Books Ltd
47 Church Street
Barnsley
South Yorkshire
S70 2AS

ISBN 978 1 84415 745 7

First edition published in 1976 as *Hit First, Hit Hard*
by William Kimber, London

Typeset by Phoenix Typesetting, Auldgirth, Dumfriesshire

Printed and bound in England by CPI UK

Pen & Sword Books Ltd incorporates the Imprints of Pen & Sword Aviation, Pen
& Sword Maritime, Pen & Sword Military, Wharncliffe Local History, Pen &
Sword Select, Pen & Sword Military Classics, Leo Cooper, Remember When,
Seaforth Publishing and Frontline Publishing

For a complete list of Pen & Sword titles please contact
PEN & SWORD BOOKS LIMITED
47 Church Street, Barnsley, South Yorkshire, S70 2AS, England
E-mail: enquiries@pen-and-sword.co.uk
Website: www.pen-and-sword.co.uk

A complete list of all the books written by Peter C Smith can be found at:
www.dive-bombers.co.uk

Contents

`Hit First, Hit Hard and go on Hitting',
Admiral of the Fleet Sir John Fisher,
First Sea Lord, 21 October 1904 to 25 January 1910.

Foreword

by the late Vice-Admiral B.C.B. Brooke, CB, CBE, Royal Navy

I welcome Peter Smith's history of the last of the Battle-cruisers, HMS *Renown*. My own connection with this famous ship was unique. When she was commissioned for the first time in September 1916 I was on her bridge during her first seagoing trials. Many years later I was her Commanding Officer in the East during the last two years of World War II.

In my experience this great ship never failed to answer the slightest touch of wheel or engines, nor did her armament ever fail when needed.

The rapport between *Renown* and her commanders brought her to life and permeated all who served in her; indeed it became an identity. This ship thereby attained the heights of efficiency and morale, and was always found ready and anxious to 'Hit First and Hit Hard'.

Renown's last appearance on the world stage took place in Plymouth Sound in 1945 where she lay proudly wearing the standards of His Britannic Majesty and that of the President of the United States of America, 'Old Glory', a fitting symbolism of her place in history.

After this she laid down her burden, as so many great fighting ships had done before her, with supreme and immaculate dignity. The reception of the most powerful leaders of the Western World was a final tribute to her life of strenuous and unfailing service. To those who served in her she will never die and for those who follow this book will serve as fitting memorial.

Introduction

This is the story of a famous warship in peace and in war. The facts of the operations are, wherever possible, from official records and use of published material during my research has been kept to a minimum.

Renown was not just a ship – she was a family, and a close-knit family at that. Moreover it was a family that has withstood the test of time. So for the details of life as it was *really* lived aboard a British man-o-war, I hand my narrative over to the 'Renowns' themselves. It is through their eyes that the reader will see World War II and the Royal Navy as it was. They talk freely of the boredom, of the perils of VD ashore, of TB afloat, of the ever-present rats, of fear in action and of common sense and heroism too. It was not all 'blood and guts' in the Royal Navy during the last war, but a steady endurance test, punctuated with moments of intense mental and physical shock. It is none the less gallant and noble for that. If some of the myths are swept away (such as that they were eager to pit the *Renown* against the *Bismarck* – on the lower deck they were just not that stupid!) then the reality from the men themselves makes the story even more worth the while telling.

I would like to express my appreciation to the following ex-Renowns who gave up their time to talk about their old ship, who lent logbooks, photographs, scrapbooks and personal mementoes of the 'largest destroyer in the Fleet', without which this book would not have been attempted; their names, and approximate years of service and position in the ship, are given herewith in chronological order:

Admiral B.C.B. Brooke, (Midshipman 1916–17, Captain 1943–45); W.F.J. Waller, (Captain of the Fo'c'sle 1921–22); A. Duff-Steward, (Stoker, 1921–24); Eric Brand, (Navigation Officer 1927–29); L.P. Stirk, (Torpedo Rating 1934–36); Captain A.W. Gray, (Chief Engineer 1937–41); Lieutenant Commander C. McD. Stuart, (Midshipman 1939–41); Jimmy Cannon (Seaman 1939–43); Tom Oliver, (Master-at-Arms 1939–48); John M. Roche, (Seaman 1939–44); A.V. Herbert, (Signal Boy 1939–41); John C. Shattock, (QMS Royal Marines 1939–41); Charles G. Wright (CPO Stores 1939–48); Bill Cain, (Stoker Petty Officer 1939–44); Henry Shannon, (Seaman 1939–44); M.V. Holmes, (Stoker 1940–44); E.J. Smith, (Leading Steward 1940–42); Norman W. Hopwood, (Chief ERA 1941–44); D.G. Anderson, (Seaman 1941–45); Peter Elvin, (Damage Control Officer 1941–44); J.H.G. Stuart,

(Engineering Officer 1942–43); Peter Allbeury, (Walrus Pilot 1942–43); J.T.J. Dobie, (Lieutenant, RNVR. 1942–46); Maurice Balaam, (Lieutenant, RNVR. 1942–46); George H. Kennon, (Shipwright 1943–45); The Very Reverend H.M. Lloyd, (Chaplain 1943–45); Peter Churchill, (Engineering Lieutenant 1943–45); T.J. McCafferty (CPO 1945–46); Edward Walker, (Lieutenant, RNVR. 1944–46); Martin Cain, (Seaman 1944–46); and also a great many other old Renowns who have written to me and sent in information which I was unable to use due to lack of space.

To all these gallant gentlemen, my thanks and my respect. This story is their story. Thanks also to my old friends John Dominy and Edwin Walker for making available all their detailed notes on HMS *Renown,* generous assistance for any author. Also to the late Captain F.S. De Winton for valued opinions. A special thank-you to my wife, Pat, for patience and endurance.

Peter C. Smith, Riseley, Bedford.

CHAPTER ONE

The Battle-Cruisers

The warships of the sailing age were both functional and beautiful creations, easy to romanticise in print and painting. However, the coming of steam marred that and produced some of the ugliest vessels ever to sail the world's oceans. Further, in the second half of the twentieth century a similarly ugly transformation from accepted aesthetic values too place. With the standardisation of battleship types a new order of strictly stern and forbidding basics laid hold of British warships, which were, nevertheless, not without a certain grandeur. The advent of the little torpedo-boat destroyers, with their slim racing hulls, restored a little excitement to warship design, but not until the *Dreadnought* era did the larger vessels approach an awesome majesty to the sailor's eye.

With the advent of the battle-cruisers the designers and builders once more produced ships that were both sleek and powerful: the most famous of these being the *Lion* and *Tiger*. The 'Splendid Cats' was a popular term in the press for them and this conveyed the impression they made on the eye. Not surprisingly this combination of beauty, speed and apparent power caught the public imagination and the battle-cruisers became associated with all that was best with the Royal Navy in the pre-Great War era.

It was, of course, the quest for speed that resulted in their unique lines and this reflected the will of their creator, Admiral Sir John Fisher. Speed was one of Fisher's gods, striking power was another and he spurned compromises that detracted from both. It was inevitable that in initiating the battle-cruiser both would have priority over protection. This would not have mattered so much had these ships not represented such a colossal outlay of national wealth. It was unthinkable to the public, to Parliament, and even to many admirals, that such enormous vessels should shun the ultimate clash of arms: a major fleet action against the Kaiser's battleships. Yet shun them they were meant to do in the nature of their duties as laid down at the time.

When Admiral Fisher, a man of towering genius, assumed the mantle of First Sea Lord, on Trafalgar Day, 1904, he was at last able to put through many of the sweeping reforms his agile brain had deemed absolutely vital, to sweep away the Victorian cobwebs after a century without battle in time to meet what he regarded as the inevitable challenge of the new German Navy.

Many of his reforms are still praised today but others were bitterly criticised at the time. Two examples are the all big-gun battleship (the *Dreadnought* type), which was seen as throwing away an overwhelming British lead in the number of capital ships and the abolition of the light-cruiser type; a decision that was soon found wanting. But it is for the initiation of the battle-cruiser type, the project dearest to his heart, that the most lasting criticism has come.

In the 1890s when the great ships of Sir William White ruled the oceans and formed the core of the battle fleet, the most likely challenger to Britain at sea still remained the ancient one of France, with Russia a close second, Japan and America unconsidered (they hardly merited the description naval power in the nineteenth century) and Germany, still on the threshold of greatness at sea, nominally friendly. The battleships, as always, could be relied upon to defeat any combination of these powers in a straight fight but the long and vulnerable sea-lanes of the Empire were exposed to raids by powerful cruisers.

To counter such threats the armoured cruiser was evolved, and large numbers of such vessels were built in reply to each foreign cruiser-building programme. As with the battleship itself, the type rapidly grew in size and power, but always it was designed as a hunter of the commerce raider on the distant oceans and *not* as an auxiliary to the main line of battle. Nonetheless the type so increased in potential during the early years of the twentieth century as to be on a par with a second-class battleship.

With the advent of the *Dreadnought* battleship the armoured cruiser still had the same function to perform; the equivalent to the capital ship in armoured cruisers was the *Duke of Edinburgh* class, with a tonnage of 12,590 tons (larger than many old battleships still in service), an armament of 9.2-inch and 6-inch guns and a speed of 23 knots. This type was also developed, step-by-step, with the increase in battleship dimensions and power, through the *Warrior* Class (13,200 tons, 9.2-inch and 7.5-inch guns) to the *Defence* class (14,600 tons, with similar speed and gunpower). But with the coming of Fisher such (to him) half-hearted compromises were to be done away with once and for all.

In simple terms, Fisher's new concept was a vessel of battleship size, armed with the same main armaments as the latest battleships, but with the speed, or better, of the latest cruisers. Striking power and the speed to enable them to dictate the course of action was what he was striving for. This was epitomised in one of his many famous slogans:

'Hit first, hit hard and go on hitting.'

He who got in the first telling blows would win the day, he decreed, and it was with this in mind that he presented his new idea in warship construction, which he christened HMS *Uncatchable*. Indeed the first battle-cruisers were known pure and simply as 'improved armour cruisers' thus showing their simple lineal descent. It was not until they were in service that the term battleship cruiser came to be used, later giving way to the universal term, battle-cruiser.

As in the case of the *Dreadnought* herself, the battle-cruiser concept was not new, nor exclusively a British idea, let alone Fisher's sole and solitary brainchild. As the Americans had been proceeding with their own all big-gun battleships, with the *Michigan* class, so had the Japanese advanced an 'improved armour cruiser' type armed with four 12-inch guns and with a speed of 21 knots. What Fisher did was to reject the traditional British policy of allowing other nations to lead with new ideas and then outbuilding them, by producing a radical design from the outset and then using superior British shipbuilding capacity to beat them into the water. Thus when *Dreadnought* and the first of the new type armoured cruisers, the *Invincible,* appeared, all rival designs were left at the post. Indeed Germany, by now the main contender for naval supremacy, was hoodwinked, for her first 'battle-cruiser' the *Blücher* was in fact nothing more than an improved armoured cruiser, still mounting cruiser-type 8.2-inch guns when the British ships were carrying 12-inch weapons.

Although the basic task of the battle-cruisers, remained similar to that of the armoured cruiser before them, the hunting of commerce raiders in the outer oceans, their new-found power added two new duties to their role. With battleship guns on a cruiser hull they now had the capacity to act as a fast wing to the main battle fleet and thus were able, in theory, to force their way through any opposition screen and report back to the Commander-in-Chief the composition and disposition of the enemy fleet with impunity. They could also act as a reinforcing squadron to bring additional fire-power to any hard-pressed squadron once battle was joined.

However these two new functions did not mean, in Fisher's original concept of the design, that the new battle-cruisers were supposed to slug it out with battleships, unless British battleships were also engaged with the same target and drawing the fire. Such a role was *never* intended; they were simply not equipped with the armour protection to follow such a suicidal policy. It was their undoing that roles two and three became their principal *raison d' etre* once they had been so successful in role one as to rid the high seas of any further suitable targets.

To prepare a new type along the lines cast by Fisher, with big guns and a speed of 25 knots, the Committee of Design considered five alternatives, all of which presented the desired disposition of armament. This was for at least four main guns to command the fore or aft arcs with four to six for broadside firing. The 1905 programme included provision for three such vessels and these became the *Invincible* class completed in 1908.

Of 17,250 tons displacement and a length of 567 feet overall, they carried four twin 12-inch guns and a secondary armament of sixteen 4-inch guns. Their turbines rated at 41,000 hp gave them a legend speed of 25 knots and they had a complement of 784 officers and men. These three ships *(Indomitable, Inflexible* and *Invincible)* caused a furore when they first appeared; their backers proudly pointed out that they were indeed invincible, for nothing that could sink them could catch them; but their detractors pointed out that to put 12-inch guns into a hull with only cruiser type protection was to court disaster.

Fisher was elated with his brainchild and a further class was laid down, with the Empire contributing two of the ships for Imperial defence, and these became the *Indefatigable* class *(Indefatigable, Australia* and *New Zealand)* which were completed between 1911 and 1913.

However, these ships only intensified the controversy, for they mounted the same main armament and had the same speed but the design was stretched to give better arcs of fire and they were 590 feet overall on a displacement of 18,800 tons. Over this increased hull area the same weak 6 to 7-inch armour protection as on the *Invincible* class was spread, and their critics claimed that this merely increased their vulnerability as a target. Equally the claim of their invincibility was nullified by the fact that the Germans had laid down their own battle-cruisers, with equal speed but much greater protection. So now there *were* ships that could catch and sink them.

However, the German battleships and battle-cruisers always mounted guns of smaller calibre than their British equivalents and so the argument that the *Indefatigable*s could still outrange their opponents and 'Hit first' still held good.

By the time the last of these battle-cruisers had joined the fleet an even greater advance had been made with the building of the three ships of the *Lion* class. These were the battle-cruiser equivalents of the new *Orion* class battleships, which mounted the new 13.5-inch gun, and the *Lions* followed suit, carrying eight of these in four twin turrets but still retaining the sixteen 4-inch secondary armament of earlier classes. Speed was also increased and these magnificent ships had turbines developing 70,000 hp, or half as much again as the *Invincible,* to get the required two knots extra speed. Naturally dimensions increased accordingly, these ships being 700 feet overall, while the tonnage exceeded that of the battleships at 26,350 tons. These three ships, *Lion, Princess Royal* and *Queen Mary,* were completed in 1912–13 and were highly regarded. Their great size and striking power combined with their speed, again seemed to make Fisher's battle-cruiser concept a viable proposition.

They featured all centre-line turrets for the first time, a long delayed improvement. Their armour protection, however, a 9-inch deck, still lagged far behind contemporary battleships. Their speeds were claimed to be in excess of 29 knots by the popular press and, at a cost of £2,000,000 apiece, the danger of regarding them as fast battleships increased.

By now not only Germany but also other leading powers had begun to follow the British lead, and their designs showed a different line of thought. The German *Derfflinger* for example carried 12-inch side armour while the Japanese *Kongo* (designed and built in Britain incidentally) showed further improvements in design, which at once outclassed even the *Lions*. Therefore, the next British battle-cruiser design was radical in concept compared with what had gone before. This was the majestic *Tiger,* the only ship of her class, which was completed just after the outbreak of war in 1914.

Tiger displaced a record 28,500 tons and was 704 feet overall. She carried the same main armament as the *Lion* but more sensibly laid out, the awkward midships 'Q' turret being resited aft where it fired over 'Y' turret. This not only made better sense from a firepower viewpoint but strengthened the hull amidships, as it was subjected to less crosswise stress, and better arcs were obtained enabling her designer to produce a hull and upperworks combination of classic beauty. *Tiger* in fact was an aristocrat in appearance, achieving a perfect blending of line and power. She was rushed into service and, as a result, her gunnery was poor in the early engagements, especially at Dogger Bank in 1915. (The best gunnery battle-cruiser was the famed *Queen Mary* at this stage of the war.) Her 108,000 hp gave her a credited speed of no less than 29 knots, but still her main armour belt remained a paltry 9-inches.

Despite grave misgivings in many quarters the battle-cruiser was a recognised and most valued part of the fleet when war came, as Fisher had predicted, in the late summer of 1914. The battle-cruisers formed their own squadron and were first commanded by Admiral Sir Lewis Bayley, but in 1913 Admiral Sir David Beatty took over from him and became the most famous of all battle-cruiser commanders. Brave, aggressive and intelligent, he was the ideal man for such a command that was bound by its very nature to be in the forefront of the coming struggle at sea.

On assuming his new command Beatty found that no formal policy had been laid down for the operations of these new warships other than in general outline. He at once set about formulating his own from intensive training and realistic tests at sea. For example, these gigantic warships, capable of speeds far in excess of anything that had gone before, had to train their great guns on an enemy fleet, and pound it at ranges of more than 15 miles, when they might be on a converging course at speeds combining to 60 miles an hour. None of his contemporaries had ever faced the attendant problems of such high-speed, long-range duelling with the major weapons of the day. When added to the prevalent bad weather conditions for which the North Sea is famed, and with the great clouds of dense black smoke emitted from up to a hundred warships steaming flat-out, it is little wondered that accuracy was so hard to achieve.

The first test of war was not a triumphant debut for the battle-cruiser: two of the British ships on station in the Mediterranean allowed the solitary German battle-cruiser *Goeben* to slip through their hands with catastrophic results. But this was more due to the vacillation of their commander than to the ships themselves. When 'Jackie' Fisher returned to triumphant harness as First Sea Lord he soon set about, with characteristic energy, obtaining some vitality and action from the Admiralty. No better vindication for the man or his battle-cruisers could be found in the events leading up to the Battle of the Falkland Islands.

The powerful Pacific squadron of the German Admiral von Spee had defeated a pair of aged armoured cruisers of Admiral Craddock off Chile with ease and dealt the Royal Navy a damaging blow to its reputation. Fisher at once despatched the *Inflexible* and *Invincible*, under the command of Admiral Sturdee, to remedy the situation. They arrived at Port Stanley in the Falkland Islands the day before von Spee made his attack with the *Scharnhorst* and *Gneisenau* (11,600 tons, eight 9.2-inch guns, 22 knots), armoured cruisers with an enviable gunnery record. At once Admiral Sturdee gave chase and, after a long day's action, brought both the German vessels to battle and destroyed them.

It was the perfect example of the battle-cruisers being employed in the classic role Fisher had intended and it completely vindicated his ideas. In the support role too the battle-cruisers had achieved notable success at the Battle of the Bight, off Heligoland in August 1914. Here a British force of light cruisers and destroyers was heavily involved with superior German forces and was being badly knocked about. Beatty and his battle-cruisers were out in support and he unflinchingly accepted the risks of submarines and mines; he steamed his great ships into the Bight, destroying several German light cruisers with ease and extracting the British ships without further damage.

All the necessary ingredients had therefore come together in late 1914 that were to mix and result in the new *Renown*. Fisher was back in command and pressing the adoption of his long-held idea of a landing on the Baltic coast to threaten Berlin from the rear. The battle-cruiser had proved itself in two easy victories. Four new battle-ships had been cancelled, with the result that spare 15-inch gun mountings were readily available for new construction, and shipbuilding capacity was available. It only needed Fisher to blend all these ingredients into a new design and fire it with his own abundant energy, and this he now did.

For his long-cherished Baltic landing plan Fisher commenced the construction of a huge fleet of specialised craft. Heavy guns, high speed and a shallow draft were requirements for the main warships for this fleet and these ideas were transmitted into a series of battle-cruisers that were to stretch his belief that 'Speed is Armour' to the absolute limit. The *Renown* class was the first manifestation of that theory and that fleet.

It was on 19 December 1914, that the first intimation was given to the Director of Naval Construction that a new battle-cruiser design was required. The ship was to have a speed of 32 knots and be armed with six 15-inch guns, the same huge weapons mounted in the latest *Super-Dreadnoughts*, but in the usual manner of battle-cruiser design one mounting less could be carried to achieve the phenomenal speed asked for, and they were to carry six in three twin turrets, two forrard, one aft. The design was conceived as a direct result of the Falkland Island battle, and also on account of the experience gained during the actions fought on 28 August in the Bight, which had shown the immense value of very high speed with long-range powerful gunfire and a large radius of action, which qualities, in association, enabled the British ships to run down the enemy under any circumstances, with the power of enforcing or declining action as they deemed fit.

The confidential *Records of Warship Construction During the War,* written by the Director of Naval Construction (DNC) department of the Admiralty in December 1918, attributed their conception to 'the initiative of Lord Fisher, then First Sea Lord'. Naturally to achieve features of 'such magnitude' either a very large ship was required or else comparatively light armour protection had to be accepted. Not surprisingly the latter course was adopted and the *Indefatigable* was taken as a standard type for protection with a 6-inch armour belt and 7-inch barbettes.

Churchill bridled at such a prospect. He had already come out against the battle-cruiser idea; his viewpoint, as later stated, was that if high speed and heavy guns were a requirement then it was best to spend very much more money and add adequate armour as well rather than compromise. As First Lord he could, and did, refuse to obtain Cabinet sanction for the new ships. But Fisher outfoxed even the wily Churchill. This time he wrote to the C-in-C of the Grand Fleet, Admiral Jellicoe, on 23 December 1914 asking him to write back a casual letter in which the need for more battle-cruisers was pointed out.

This Jellicoe was happy to do; the Third Sea Lord also added his support to the project and, in the end, Churchill gave way and the Cabinet approval was given and on the 24th a model was made and inspected by Lord Fisher. On 21 December the dimensions for the new ships were decided but Lord Fisher asked for some modifications and these were duly incorporated. On 28 December, such was the pace at which the old Admiral worked, the DNC was informed that this model was approved and that the design should be started at once.

Fisher had argued for the particularly high speed because none of the existing British battle-cruisers had the speed to catch a 28-knot ship, which is what the German battle-cruiser *Lutzow* was believed to be capable of. This carried the day.

This battle won, Fisher went all out to get his pets to sea in the shortest possible time and went about it in his usual ruthless way. 'We must "scrap" everyone who gets in the way', he insisted. Fifteen months was the time he insisted upon from keel laying to commission! To facilitate this incredible demand it was decided by the DNC that the machinery for the *Tiger* be duplicated as much as possible, but with additional boilers. Although a lighter design of machinery to develop the power needed would have been possible, the preparation time would have exceeded Fisher's demands. With this method considerable time economy was possible as the patterns were already to hand. This was agreed to.

On the 29th Fisher interviewed the representatives from both John Brown and Company and Fairfield and orders were placed there and then for the two ships, the work to be carried out on a 'time and line' principle. John Brown and Company was chosen because the slip at Palmers (initially chosen to build the original battleship design) was too short to accommodate the longer Battle-cruiser design. However, the material for the building of the original Battleships had already been delivered to both Fairfield and Palmers and because it had been decided to use this steel for the building of the Battle-cruisers the material at Palmers was transferred to John Brown's at Clydebank forthwith.

By 21 January 1915 both firms had been supplied with enough information for them to build the midships portion of the vessels to the turn of the bilge, to prepare all the main structural drawings, and to order the greater part of the steel required for their hulls. The actual keel laying of both ships was made on 25 January, Lord Fisher's birthday. The great speed at which the new ships was rushed through over-took the more orthodox Admiralty procedures so that the official directive to begin the design was not given until 30 December 1914 and the modified contracts were not placed until March 1915.

By February 1915 however, the prints of the building drawings of the hold, plat-form and lower decks were sent to the firms and by the 28th of the same month the building drawings of the main, upper and forecastle decks were completed. By 12 April all the drawings, specifications and calculations usually made for a design were completed at the Admiralty and on 22 April the design received the formal approval of the Board of Admiralty.

The main features of the *Renown* as conceived at this point were as follows.

Length between perpendiculars:	750 feet
Length overall:	794 feet
Breadth:	90 feet
Mean draught in legend condition with 1,000 tons of oil and no reserve feed:	25 feet
Displacement at load draught:	26,500 tons
Freeboard forward:	32 feet
Freeboard amidships:	23.1 feet
Freeboard aft:	19 feet

In the extreme deep condition with about 4,000 tons of oil the draught was estimated to be about 29 feet 3 inches.

The side above water had a slope outwards intended to help towards keeping the ship dry in a seaway, and the flare forward was made very considerable to throw off the sea at high speed. Below water the shape was slightly bulged.

For machinery Brown Curtiss turbines were installed that were intended to develop 110,000 to 120,000 shp. The forty-two boilers were of the Babcock and Wilcox type and were oil burners exclusively. With this machinery it was estimated that slightly under 32 knots would be obtained in deep water (about 60 fathoms plus) at legend draught with 120,000 shp and at deep draught they were good for 31 knots. In service this was achieved and Beatty called *Renown* and *Repulse* in service with the Grand Fleet, 'The Gallopers'.

The main armament of the *Renown* was, as it was to remain throughout her long life span, six 15-inch guns (12-calibre Breech Loading (B.L.) with 20° elevation initially) in two pairs forward and one pair aft, mounted, as was now standard, on the centre line. The height above water of the three turrets was from forward to aft, A – 35 feet, B – 45 feet and X – 23 feet. Stowage was provided for 120 rounds of shell and ammunition per gun. Ahead fire was four guns, astern (not contemplated by Fisher of course) two guns, and broadside fire six guns. The acceptance of a six-gun ship was a compromise, as eight-guns broadsides were the most acceptable to gunnery conditions of the time to enable the spotting of fall of shot and grouping.

Fisher had always scorned the increase in calibre of the secondary armament on the later *Dreadnoughts*, brought about by the increasing size of the destroyer. For the *Renown* he reverted to the smaller 4-inch weapon, preferring to rely on *volume* of fire rather than weight to stop torpedo attacks. Rapid salvos *not* weight of shell, he thought, would be more viable to achieve this. This led to some argument: the weapon most suitable for this role at the time was the 4-inch quick-firing Mark V, however this was difficult to arrange for director firing, and that was another condition that Fisher considered essential. Suggestions that the Evershed bearing indicators be substituted were turned down flat. The 4-inch breech-loading Mark VIII was mooted as an alternative, but this lacked the volume of fire that Fisher envisaged necessary, even though director firing would have been possible with this type. The day was saved by the DNO who put forward a design incorporating the Mark V body with the Mark VIII breech mechanism. Further, this was to be mounted in a new triple mounting as the 4-inch breech loading Mark IX. A total of fifteen was therefore carried by each ship with an elevation of 30°, plus two single guns with 25° elevation. This total of seventeen 4-inch guns seemed impressive enough, and should in theory have swamped attacking destroyers. Unfortunately the new triple mounting was not a success. Its volume of fire was negated by the fact that it was of necessity a very heavy and sluggish mounting that required a large gun crew(thirty-two men per mounting) to operate it. For defence against air attack, which was being considered even in 1914, two 3-inch AA guns were carried. Provision was also made for two 21-inch torpedo tubes in a submerged torpedo room forward. The weight of *Renown's* main broadside was 11,520 lb.

There were two directors for the main armament fire-control, of the tripod type: one was fitted in an armoured revolving hood over the conning tower and the other in a tower at the top of the foremast. Two secondary armament directors were positioned on the foremast and on the mainmast. Each main turret had a 15-foot range-finder and an open director-sight for local control conditions.

As already noted, they were fragile ships with regard to their protection. The barbettes had a thickness of 7 inches and the conning tower 10 inches. The main armour belt was 6 inches only, with a depth of 9 feet, covering the length occupied by machinery and magazines, dropping to 4 inches thickness forward of this and 3 inches aft. In fact they were regarded as 'Tin Cans' when they arrived at Scapa with their long lines of scuttles showing just how open they were. In the aftermath of the terrible losses at Jutland their chances of survival were rated very slim indeed! The armoured bulkheads were 4 and 3 inches thick, all the armour being of KC or equivalent quality. A 1+inch H.T. side plating above this slender belt gave protection to funnels; funnel casings above the forecastle deck were of the same quality and thickness, reducing to 1 inch at the ends.

The deck armour of the *Renown* was puny: that over the citadel was 1 inch on the flat and 2 inches on the slope, while the lower decks forward and aft were 2 inches thick HT steel. The three main 15-inch turrets had 9-inch frontal armour, 7-inch on the sides, of KC or equivalent quality, with 170 lb special quality steel roof-plates. A proposal to fit longitudinal torpedo protection bulkheads was considered in March 1915, but owing again to the delay this would cause (two months was estimated) it was dropped. Torpedo net defence was part of the original plan, but this too was not finally fitted.

Underwater protection was an advance and for the first time warships were fitted with an internal bulge, forming an integral part of the ship instead of the hitherto 'tacked-on' afterthoughts. It had a maximum width of 14 feet and lay under the sloping part of the armoured deck. It consisted of an outer cellular skin covering a wide cushion of oil which was shut off from the bulk compartments by a vertical cellular skin filled with air. Plans were prepared during the course of construction to strengthen further the longitudinal bulkheads to a maximum of 2 inches, but once more the overriding question of speed of completion ruled this out. Two months again would have been required, while weight would have gone up by 700 tons and draught increased by 7 inches.

Another provision planned, but dropped, was that asked for by Fisher in January 1915, for the shipping of twenty-five Vickers Type 20 automatic mines and rails to be fitted to the quarter-deck. After Fisher's departure from the Admiralty six months later these were dropped from the design; he probably still had Baltic operations to the forefront of his mind in requesting this modification.

The turbines were housed in two engine rooms, two in each room of high-pressure on the wing shafts, and two low-pressure on the inner shaft, enclosed in the same casing. The condenser rooms were aft of the engine rooms. The large-tube boilers, with a working pressure of 235 pounds per square inch maximum, were in six boiler rooms, seven in B boiler room and three in each of the others with a total heating surface of 157,206 square feet.

Renown as first built had a total complement of 953 officers and men (increased to 967 when utilised as a flagship). Her oil fuel capacity was 4,000 tons and her deep load displacement was 30,835 tons. She was a beautiful ship in appearance, long, rangy, her upperworks turrets and masting arrangements combining with her two vertical funnels, the after one lower than the fore funnel, to give a most impressive and pleasing silhouette. She was built for speed and it showed in her every line.

Renown was launched on 4 March 1916 at a weight of 16,065 tons, and though her building time was breathtaking fears were still being expressed at the delays in her original time. Beatty was so perturbed at the comparative ratios of strength between the British battlecruiser fleet and that of the German that he felt impelled to write to the Prime Minister Asquith on 3 February complaining. Whereas, wrote Beatty, the Royal Navy had added but one battle-cruiser to their pre-war strength, the *Tiger*, the Germans had added three, *Derfflinger*, *Lutzow* and *Hindenburg*, while two more of an improved type, *Victoria Luise* and *Freya* (30,510 tons, eight 14-inch guns, 27 knots) would be completed soon with two further sisters being built. In fact we now know that *Hindenburg* was not complete, she did not join the fleet until 1917, while the four improved ships were never finished. But the concern that the British would be totally outnumbered and outclassed in this vital type of warship was worrying in the extreme. Battle-cruisers moreover, Beatty asserted, were twice as valuable to the

British, being to the Grand Fleet what Zeppelins were to the High Seas Fleet in the scouting role.

Even when *Renown* and *Repulse* joined his flag he estimated the Germans would have eight battle-cruisers to the British ten, and that these eight would match the British ships because of the superior qualities and newness. But the urgency of getting these two ships to sea was tempered after Jutland by the need to make them more fit to stand in the line of battle. In particular their pathetic deck protection could not remain unaltered in the light of the loss of the *Queen Mary, Indefatigable* and *Invincible.*

Accordingly, extra armour was added on the building slip before their completion, by the addition of 1-inch plating over the magazines. Apart from this the constructors, William Berry and E.L. Atwood, were to be congratulated for achieving wonders and these two ships were not only the fastest capital ships in the water but were built in record time; *Renown* completed on 20 September 1916. On her acceptance trials on the famous Arran course *Renown* clocked the following figures on a displacement of 27,900 tons. On the measured mile with 126,300 shp: 32.58 knots. Four hours full power trial at 123,850 shp, 32.284 knots.

Her gun trials carried out the day before were satisfactory. Accepted into the Royal Navy just twenty-one months after her keel was laid, *Renown* was already something of a legend. That legend was to grow.

CHAPTER TWO

The Tethered Giants

Since the early battles of the Great War, in which the battle-cruisers had shone so outstandingly, there had been little chance for the men of the Grand Fleet to prove their worth, and, as so often before in the long maritime history of Britain, the war at sea developed into a patient watching game. The fact that this was not unique but normal was not understood by the country as a whole, conditioned during the long years of peace to recalling only the highlights of the great decisive sea battles and forgetting the years of patient patrolling that had led up to them. An impatient press and politicians eagerly seeking positive achievements to justify their own positions were not in 1914–18 ready to accept a long wait. To the sailors too this was a period of frustration, although up to 1916 there was little outcome on either side of the North Sea.

Again only the battle-cruisers saw brief action, in 1915 at the Battle of the Dogger Bank, which Beatty dubbed a battle of lost opportunities. A raid by the German battle-cruisers was intercepted by Beatty and a long stern chase followed with every prospect of the annihilation of a greater part of the German force. Unfortunately at a critical time Beatty's flagship *Lion* received a hit, which forced her to drop out of line. A signal sent to the remaining ships to engage the enemy and finish them off was misconstrued and the whole British force instead concentrated on the already crippled *Blücher,* sending her to the bottom and allowing the rest of Hipper's hard pressed squadron to escape. It was a tragedy and not until May 1916 was another opportunity to present itself.

When the two fleets did eventually clash the outcome of the battle was equally frustrating. Despite heavy losses, especially of the battle-cruisers, three of which went up like Roman Candles with the loss of almost their entire crews, the British felt they had the High Seas Fleet in the palms of their hands as night fell on 31 May, only to have it slip away in the darkness. They returned empty-handed to a storm of criticism. It was poor return for so much patience. It was also a lesson.

Naturally the destruction of three battle-cruisers in this battle threw a great deal of doubt and suspicion on the type as a whole, and on British designs in particular. When therefore the *Renown* joined the fleet a few months later she was regarded more of a liability than an asset, her improved deck protection notwithstanding. As a good seaboat she soon proved herself. Both *Renown* and *Repulse* had in fact received extra stiffening during their construction after reports of 'panting' in the hulls of earlier *Dreadnoughts*, and her great turn of speed coupled with her 15-inch guns made her an asset to the battlecruiser fleet as a whole. But her complete lack of armour, as shown by her rows of scuttles, betrayed her weakness to a fleet that had just witnessed the appalling tragedy of *Queen Mary,* a ship of superior protection.

The *Repulse* undertook further sea trials in the Atlantic after commissioning and these led to the discovery that the construction of the two battle-cruisers had certain weaknesses forward. Although the striking flare minimised the effect of the heavy swell the deck right forward was bent and sunk inward and additional pillars were required to be fitted to strengthen this. This again was done to *Renown* but still further strengthening was required in the same area later in the war.

Another alteration was in the funnel arrangements. Originally both were built with squat funnels in the Fisher manner, but as with all ships of this era, this was found to cause great smoke difficulties, hampering fire control and making the bridge almost untenable at times. All these ships therefore had to have their funnels raised by several feet. In the case of the *Renown* it was at first thought that this might be unnecessary for her fore funnel was placed well back from the bridge. But in the event sea service showed that this was still not satisfactory and in the end both battle-cruisers had the fore funnel raised by 6 feet giving an uneven appearance that somewhat marred their earlier symmetry.

They also differed from traditional capital ships in that their decks were not wood-planked, in order to save both time and weight. Lagging was fitted under the weather decks to compensate for the lack of this insulation, but they were not cosy ships in which to serve. Some of the senior officers quarters were located forward close to the wardroom instead of traditionally aft, which made for another innovation in these two vessels.

However it was their lack of protection that most exposed them to a certain amount of scorn and derision. In October 1916, soon after they had joined the Grand Fleet, the C-in-C roundly condemned them on this point and recommended their immediate return to harbour for modifications. He proposed that extra armour be fitted to both the main deck, lower-deck and the vertical bulkheads around the lower conning tower. Should this be done then it would also be necessary to increase the thickness of the armour gratings in the trunks passing through the main-deck. With all this the DNC agreed and a total of 500 tons of protection to the crowns of the 15-inch magazines, over the engine rooms and elsewhere, was approved by the Board. The *Renown* therefore returned to Rosyth and this work was carried out by the builders. In order to compensate for this extra 1 to 2-inch plating the fuel bunkerage for the ship was reduced by a similar tonnage.

In 1917 even wider-ranging modifications were put forward to bring the two battle-cruisers up to standard. Several proposals were made in consultation with Beatty, now Commander-in-Chief of the Grand Fleet, and the Board recommended that a larger bulge with stowage of 9-inch crushing tubes be incorporated, which would increase the width of the ship to 101 feet. These covered the magazine and machinery spaces, the ends being well fined off. A new 9-inch armour belt was proposed between the main and lower decks in place of the existing 6-inch armour, which was to be removed and fitted between the main and upper decks. A new 4-inch armour bulkhead at the same level was to be worked abreast the after barbette at the end of the belt. Additional HT plating on the main deck was contemplated in the way of the magazines, to give a total thickness of 3 inches on the flat and 4 inches on the slope. The *Repulse* was so taken in hand at Portsmouth in December 1918 but the similar modifications to *Renown* were postponed. *Renown* had to wait.

All the magazines were fitted with anti-flash equipment after Jutland and this was common in all Grand Fleet ships and training scales were another wartime refinement being painted on A and Y turrets. Further wartime experience led to the replacement of eight 36-inch searchlights carried on the bridge and funnels by searchlight platforms, with searchlight towers. Carley rafts were first fitted in 1917 and other minor modifications included the fitting of a 12-foot rangefinder tower on the roof of the fore-top. All these changes required frequent visits to the dockyard and it was not too long before the canny sailors of the Grand Fleet had re-christened *Renown* and *Repulse* as *Refit* and *Repair!*

Nor were the underwater torpedo tubes a success either. The torpedo flat was forward of A barbette with single submerged tubes on either beam. It was proposed to fit eight 21-inch torpedo tubes above water with 3-inch protective mantlets in both ships. These increases would, it was calculated, increase the draught of the two ships by about 9-inches giving a rise in their tonnage displacement of 4,000 tons. Their speed would thereby come down to 30 knots. However this work was not done in *Repulse* until after the war.

A unique viewpoint of *Renown* as she then was is given by Vice-Admiral B.C.B. Brooke. Being her first officer of the watch when she ran her trials and her last captain, Basil Brooke naturally regards her as 'the most splendid ship Britain ever built.' Joining a brand new battle-cruiser in the middle of war was an exciting experience for the young midshipman, as he recalls:

> We midshipmen and sub-lieutenants were sent to live at the Adelphi Hotel in Liverpool where we were instructed in gunnery. There was a revolver range under the hotel where I made a few shillings in competitions, as one of my more useless natural arts is to shoot straight! Later we joined *Renown* at Fairfields where she was almost ready for her trials. Alec Madden and I shared a cabin immediately over the starboard screws. We could not hear one another speak when under way.

The first captain of the *Renown* was Hugh F.P. Sinclair, later to be Admiral William Hall's successor at the DNI in January 1919. Arthur Marder described him as '. . . a very strange and original character, a clever man who shone in command of men.' He was nicknamed 'Quax' Sinclair, from his nasal drawl, which was likened to the quacking of a duck! He was reputed to be the son of King Edward. Vice-Admiral Brooke recalls:

> He had all the royal gifts and was perhaps the most intelligent and revered officer in the Fleet. An able seaman would refer to his appearance as 'Too 'orrible' and really he would not have been far wrong! But he was just and usually right. Eventually I became 'Sub of the Men' and as the Captain took a pride in his junior officers, I got to know him and like him very much. He had a way of asking his officers to dinner one at a time. We used to arrive in some anxieties but were immediately put at ease and given a splendid dinner. Warmed by a little wine and our superb host we became very talkative and left thinking how well we had competed. Later it dawned that he had learned all about us and we nothing about him, and, 'He Never Forgot!'

As *Renown* commissioned in the middle of the war her crew was something of a motley collection including a fair number of reserves, pensioners and the like, but Quax Sinclair soon licked them into shape. The *Renown*'s special construction qualities were soon noted by her new crew. For example when testing a derrick to lift the ship's cutter it was found that the head of the derrick just would not stand the strain without the stiffening usually given by the teak deck, which of course *Renown* lacked. Likewise her two short funnels caused some smoke problems and with a following wind the bridge became 'intolerable'.

As to her protection Captain Brooke said:

It must be remembered that the ship was designed to overtake raiders on the shipping routes, so that she had no deck armour and very little side. When she was in a swell or heavy head sea we used to be fascinated at watching the expansion gland (scarcely the correct word) working.

After her initial working up period *Renown* joined the fleet in the Firth of Forth, lying at an anchorage below the bridge with the rest of the battle-cruisers.

'We became a very happy ship, particularly the Gunroom which included many future admirals,' recalls Vice-Admiral Brooke. Much of the credit for this transformation of course lay with her Captain and Vice-Admiral Brooke recalls a typical example of the way he worked in this regard:

I was on watch alongside in the dockyard early in the commission. The Captain, after a gruelling time, had left instructions that he was not to be disturbed until midday. We had had trouble with a fresh water valve amidships which was reported to me, so, knowing the trouble, I left the quarter deck for three minutes to close it. On my return I found an irate Captain of the Yard. Having reprimanded me for not meeting him, he asked to see the Captain. I told him very politely that he was not to be disturbed and apologised for my absence and explained the cause. He turned and went off.

In the afternoon I was leaving the ship when the Captain, holding a letter and shaking with anger, appeared. The letter from the Captain of the Dockyard reported that he had not been received by the officer on duty who had arrived ten minutes later, and had slouched up with his hands in his pockets and then become impudent, and so on. I was speechless for a moment, then told the reason for my absence. I then appealed to his reason by saying, 'You know me a little, Sir. Can you believe that I am capable of behaving in such a way?' In spite of his pent up wrath, he immediately said, 'I will write to the officer' and I heard no more. I would like to have seen my Captain's letter!

Between dockyard refits it was a weary time for the men of the battle-cruisers. They were sustained by the hope that the lessons of Jutland having been assimilated the Grand Fleet was at a high pitch of readiness, and the confidence of all concerned that they would inflict a sound drubbing on the Germans the next time they met was universal. Even so the endless waiting for their chance wore down even the hardiest of them at times, as Beatty's letters of the period reflect.

Between periodic sorties the battle-cruisers lay in the Forth, and were later joined by the rest of the fleet in 1918. This was a much more attractive berth than the bleakness of Scapa Flow, but all the same there was really little to relieve the monotony.

There were of course visits to be made to Rosyth town itself and further afield to Edinburgh which made life more tolerable than the treeless wastes of the Orkneys. Ashore facilities were made for games; football, ice hockey, rugger and the normal competition of the inter-ship regattas. Boxing and deck hockey could also be played aboard and there was a great demand for amateur theatrical shows of great scope and talent from all sections of the ship's company. But mainly it was work, work and more work. Since Beatty had moved up from command of the battle-cruisers to command of the whole Grand Fleet his place had been taken by Admiral Sir William Pakenham. Rear Admiral Pakenham, 'Paks' as he was known in the Fleet, described as an aloof patrician by Marder, was thought by Beatty to lack the flair and initiative for the high-speed decision-making that went with the job, but 'I don't know a soul who would do it better.'

Vice-Admiral Brooke recalls the time in the Forth as one of intensive training in readiness for *Der Tag*:

> My own activities were almost entirely confined to my turret, learning every nut and bolt and training my crew. These early 15-inch turrets were exceedingly well built and designed, certain anti-flash arrangement were made and, of course, minor improvements in wartime are continuous.
>
> The officers and ship's companies included reservists who had never before enjoyed the comforts of a modern ship, many of them had suffered great hardship in ships built in the seventies or even earlier.

Renown at this time formed part of the 2nd Battle Cruiser Squadron, which had already earned quite a name for itself. It was commanded at this period by Rear-Admiral Arthur F. Leveson who had taken over from Pakenham, while the 1st Battle Cruiser Squadron was commanded by Rear-Admiral Richard F. Phillimore who had relieved O. de B. Brock.

Between 1917 and 1918 also the aircraft made itself more and more known in the Fleet and at sea, and many of the big ships were fitted with flying-off platforms on their turrets following Squadron Leader Rutland's first experiments from *Repulse* in October 1917.

Renown was fitted in this manner early in 1918, with flying-off platforms built atop both B and Y turret. When at sea in company the two battle-cruisers could therefore carry between them two reconnaissance aircraft and two fighter planes. Some experimentation still remained however before these could be termed fully effective, as Admiral Brooke again recalls:

> Among other interesting episodes during the early days were our experiments in flying off aircraft. We constructed a fly path from A turret to the stem down which an aircraft was to be flown off as we steamed into the wind. The first plane dived straight into the sea and this plan was abandoned!
>
> We then erected a platform on B turret upon which we hoisted a plane by a traveller on a forestay rigged for the purpose. The difficulty here was to secure

it against wind and sea as, of course, it had fixed wings. Several flew off successfully when we were in harbour but when we took one to sea on a sweep to the
south the plane broke up; only the engine survived.

The aircraft concerned initially was the single seater Sopwith Pup fighter. Later
experiments were made with launching the heavier two-seater types and by the end
of the war over a hundred aircraft were thus employed with the Grand Fleet. This
conception of battleships and battle-cruisers carrying their own aircraft was extended
between the wars and vast sums were spent in converting ships to take hangars and
catapults for this purpose when in fact the correct way to employ these aircraft or
any other type was from their own specially built carrier. During the Second World
War the increased use of aircraft carriers in sufficient numbers made this type of ship-
borne defence redundant but in 1917 it was quite a visionary concept.

Despite the extra 2-inch armour fitted in 1916 the *Renown* and *Repulse* still failed
to enjoy the confidence of their contemporaries as fit for the line of battle; in fact they
were regarded as weak links. However the battle-cruisers that followed, still as part
of Fisher's original Baltic scheme of 1914, were to take his particular ideas to even
more extreme lengths. The next pair were the *Courageous* and *Glorious*. Much
lighter than *Renown,* they too were beautiful ships, though quite what these
unarmoured, single funnelled greyhounds were supposed to do with the Grand Fleet
was never clear. Described as 'large light cruisers' they displaced 18,600 tons and
mounted four 15-inch guns in two turrets, one forward and one aft, together with
eighteen 4-inch guns, two 3-inch AA weapons and torpedo tubes. They had a speed
of 31 knots in service and both joined the fleet early in 1917. Their half-sister was
the *Furious* and she was to be generally similar to this pair but to mount two single
gigantic 18-inch guns. In the event she was never completed thus; her light hull was
never up to the strain of firing such a monster and she could not have made steady
practice with only two such weapons at 30 knots anyway. She was completed as a
hybrid carrier with a flight deck forward and a single gun aft, and as such she was
neither fish nor fowl! Eventually the after gun was also landed and another deck
added in its place. These three beautiful misfits were quickly sized up by the lower
deck, as had *Renown* been, and they were dubbed *Curious, Outrageous* and *Spurious*
in the Grand Fleet.

Nonetheless they at least saw a limited form of action, which was denied to
Renown completely in this conflict. When America joined in the war in mid-1917
they sent a squadron of battleships to reinforce the Grand Fleet, which already had
overwhelming superiority in that class of ship. Thus the issue of battle was never in
doubt had it been joined. But with regard to the battle-cruiser situation the uncertainty continued well into the last year of the war.

For example, in a memorandum to the First Lord, Geddes, drafted in January
1918, Beatty again bewailed estimated margin of strength in this area, pointing out
that we had nine against the Germans' six which was considerable on paper, although
in *fact* this was *not* so. He considered that only the *Lion, Princess Royal* and *Tiger*
were as good as the German six, the elderly *Invincible* and *Indefatigable* class of ship
was outmoded in both speed, armour and fire power by this date, while of the newer
ships: 'The "Renown" class are insufficiently armoured, they cannot stand a
hammering.'

If the situation was therefore far from happy in 1918 the Admiralty forecasts for the future were even bleaker. Only one such ship was building in British yards – the *Hood* with eight 15-inch guns. Three sister ships had been cancelled, and *Hood* was delayed while improvements were built into her following Jutland, with the result that she could not be expected to join the Fleet before the end of the year. (In fact she was not completed until 1920.)

By comparison it was estimated in August that the German building programme would result in a ratio of nine British against six German in 1918 giving way to ten to seven in 1919 and ten to nine by 1920. Although the new British armour piercing shell was entering service and greatly improving the ships' hitting power vis-à-vis the enemy, the *Renowns* were 'dangerously liable to destruction by a single hit.' The Government turned down a plea for completing the three suspended *Hoods* on the grounds that they could not be completed before 1921 and would take up vital mercantile building capacity, which left this situation unresolved. Nor in view of this slender margin could either ship undertake the recommended reconstruction mentioned in the previous chapter.

It was just as well then perhaps that they were never to be put to the test they were all longing for. The effects of long-range gunnery by the new high-speed battle-cruisers were put to a practical test in the North Sea on 17 November 1917 when the *Courageous* and *Glorious* went into action against German cruiser forces amid the minefields of the Bight. The *Repulse* managed to get herself into the fight as well, tearing into action at top speed spitting salvos, but the results were disappointing; the battle-cruisers suffered almost as much damage as the German light cruisers they were chasing. Against the German battle-cruisers they would not have fared at all well on past form. *Renown* was denied even this limited chance to prove her merits however, and the last years of the Great War passed by without her firing a single shot in anger.

One last duty lay to her, and that in itself was an event as momentous as any major battle, and far more effective. It was the surrender of the German High Seas Fleet to Admiral Beatty's Grand Fleet on 21 November 1918. Among the great assembly of British warships, the greatest fleet in her history, 224 vessels, battleships, armoured cruisers, light cruisers and destroyers, were the eleven ships of the Battle Cruiser Fleet. The 1st Battle Cruiser Squadron now comprised the *Lion, Princess Royal, Tiger, Repulse* and *Renown,* the 2nd Battle Cruiser Squadron the veterans *Australia, New Zealand, Indomitable* and *Inflexible* while the *Courageous* and *Glorious* formed the 1st Cruiser Squadron. The Captain of *Renown* at this historic meeting was Captain A.W. Craig CB. With the scuttling of the German Battle Cruisers at Scapa Flow seven months later their work was done. The waiting was over. And with these events it seemed also that very little future faced *Renown.*

With the ending of the war there was naturally a rapid run-down of the fleet. Oliver had relieved Pakenham in command of the Battle Cruiser Force, and he, in turn, was relieved by Admiral Keyes of Zeebrugge fame, on 21 March 1919. The principal duty of the battle-cruisers at this time was to guard the surrendered German ships but the 2nd Battle Squadron took over this duty in May and the British battle-cruisers thus did not witness the final self-destruction of their old foes.

With *Renown* were the *Lion, Princess Royal* and *Tiger; Repulse* had departed for her reconstruction in December and the other ships were reduced to reserve pending their ultimate disposal for scrap, for their 12-inch guns were no longer up to modern standards. Thus reduced the Battle Cruiser Force became the solitary Battle Cruiser Squadron.

Post-war plans ensured that the new Atlantic Fleet would always have a Battle Cruiser Squadron but with the rapid scrapping programme initiated before the Washington Treaty of 1922, and the wholesale cut down resulting from that Treaty afterwards the Royal Navy was very quickly left with but four ships of this type, *Hood, Renown, Repulse* and *Tiger*. These were matched against the four Japanese *Kongos* in this period. Only the Turkish *Yavuz* (ex German *Goeben)* remained of the other nations' battle-cruisers and she was clearly by now obsolete. At Washington the Americans insisted on classifying the three British battle-cruisers in the same category as battleships, although the two types were miles apart, and thus while they ultimately were to retain a battle fleet of fifteen ships, the British were only allowed to keep twelve true battleships. In order somehow to lessen this drastic blow a great deal of thought and money was expended in bringing the *Renown* and *Repulse* up to some semblance of fighting efficiency. Between 1918 and 1921 the *Repulse* was taken in hand to enable those major modifications already itemised to be carried out. She did not again emerge from dockyard hands until January 1921 by which time 4,500 tons had been added to her displacement.

A far different refit was applied to *Renown* during this period for she was selected as the vessel to conduct representatives of the Royal Family on a series of goodwill tours throughout the Empire to cement the ties of friendship and blood in the new post-war world. For the next few years then *Renown* was to become a Royal Yacht first and a fighting ship second.

CHAPTER THREE

Royal Yacht

The first of these goodwill trips planned was that of HRH the Prince of Wales to Newfoundland, Canada and the United States. In preparation for this *Renown* was docked and underwent minor alterations.

The two aircraft flying-off platforms were removed from her turrets and extra accommodation and recreation areas were built into the ship. To facilitate this one triple 4-inch mounting was taken out completely and the deck of the mounting above was extended to form a roof over the resulting space. Extra covered spaces were formed by building various structures around the bases of the two funnels, which had the appearance of steel-built, square blockhouses. Opportunity was also taken at this time to improve fire control, the 15-foot rangefinder in Y turret being replaced by a 30-foot one, while a second 20-foot rangefinder was added to the revolving conning-tower hood.

The Admiralty acutely aware of the prestige building qualities of such a tour went to great lengths to give the *Renown* an Imperial facelift and even the Treasury, for perhaps the last time ever, cooperated with them and released extra money for the facelift. Consequently high-grade teak planking was laid over all the hitherto austere upper decks, on the quarterdeck, forecastle-deck and boat deck, giving her a post-war appearance of some grandeur. Special crews were handpicked to ensure that the image presented by the Royal Navy overseas was a correct one. The boiler brickwork was renewed as was much of the auxiliary equipment and vital repairs that had gone untended earlier were soon carried out. A special entertainment allowance was granted to the officers, and this was much required to cater for the flood of visiting dignitaries that swarmed aboard at every port of call during the next ten years.

It was therefore a highly resplendent *Renown* that sailed under the command of Captain E.A. Taylor in 1919 on the first post-war voyage to Newfoundland, Canada and the United States and this tour was a great success. In the March of 1920 the same arrangements were made for an even greater voyage to the far-flung Dominions of Australia and New Zealand. Again the event was a triumph, after visiting Auckland and Melbourne *Renown* returned home after 210 days away.

In 1921–2 the Washington Conference dominated the naval scene and at the end of it Great Britain had lost her centuries old pre-eminence at sea. Perhaps to reassure old friends abroad that the Navy was still a potent force and that the mother country had not forgotten them another tour was organised with the same care as the previous two. This time the Prince of Wales visited India, Burma, Ceylon, Singapore, Hong Kong and Japan, again embarked in *Renown*. In India the reception, away from the glitter and glamour, was surly and hostile, but in all the other countries visited his reception was as joyous as before, even in Japan where the American insistence on Britain sundering their old Treaty of Alliance had been looked upon as provocative. The Prince was able to allay many of those fears, but afterwards relations between the two great maritime nations steadily grew worse.

Two of the crew of the *Renown* for this historic voyage remember it well and it is through their eyes therefore that I shall recall it rather than from the official and press viewpoint. Naturally the sailors had a completely different view of the events, and were rather more perceptive and honest! William Waller was then a young petty officer with two years' seniority; he was Captain of the Fo'c'sle during the tour, and thus saw much of the behind the scenes activities. A. Duff-Stewart, BM, was at that time a second-class stoker. Their memories are exceptional, and their stories a delight. Duff-Stewart recalls:

> I was one of an advance party sent aboard to help get the ship ready for the Prince of Wales' tour to India and the Far East. At that time the *Renown* had forty-two boilers and I helped to clean every one! As I remember we were the first ship's company to be issued with sun helmets and they superseded Sennet hats, the old-fashioned sailor's hat like the straw boater.

Renown left Portsmouth dockyard with the Royal Standard proudly flying on 26 October 1921, after visiting Portland to shakedown and clean up ready for the Royal Party. Whilst there leave was given to the ship's company and soccer, hockey and other sports were played in preparation for the challenges they knew would follow. *Renown* was commanded by the Hon Herbert ('Jimmy') Meade. William Waller recalls:

> We had an excellent ship's company, approximately 800. Lieutenant Commander Dalrymple-Hamilton was Fo'c'sle Officer. The Prince made it an occasional practice to walk around the decks on his own and chatted to all. For his recreation he trained also. Our sailmaker on board made a bell shaped tent and it was inverted and 'Chippy', the ship's carpenter, fixed it to some boards. The gym vaulting horse was fixed with a saddle and reins and the Prince of Wales had a horse's head fitted to one end. Thus with mount and net he would sit astride the horse and hit a polo ball around the base of the tent, his coach stood on a deck outside of the area and he would call the strokes. The nets at the top of the tent would prevent any balls coming outside and one could see what was going on.

The voyage was via Gibraltar and Malta, 'the island of bells and smells', where there were official functions of all types. The younger seamen were given the ritual information on the island by the old sweats, such as 'you will never see a fat goat or a thin priest.' Then on via the Suez Canal with receptions at Port Said and Port Suez, where the Prince rode for the ship in the match against the Eastern Telegraph Company. Aden was touched, then *Renown* sped onward across the Indian Ocean to Bombay where she arrived to a reception in November.

The Prince and his staff, including his aide Lord Louis Mountbatten, left the ship at Bombay and part of the ship's company went on a *Ban ran* (guided excursion) to Agra and Delhi by train while the *Renown* went on a 'Show the flag' trip up the Persian Gulf. No rich oil sheiks then, although one local sheik – I think it was at Kuwait – brought some sheep on board as a gift. For some reason we were short of fresh meat and the mutton was useful. The heat in the Gulf was terrific and some stokers actually cooked an egg (fried) on the steel upper deck abaft the fo'c'sle, which had been planked over.

William Waller was in the party to Agra and Delhi.

At Agra we played cricket against the Kings Own Scottish Borderers and later went over the Taj Mahal and had our photographs taken in front of the pool. During the cool of the evening the natives sold the sailors wax Taj Mahals in boxes; later, when back in England and the boxes were opened it was not wax but candle grease they found and it had all melted into a single lump. I will pass over the remarks made at this discovery. I suppose it was the heat on other parts of the cruise that was the cause.

We were paid our wages in those specious days in gold sovereigns monthly. I remember that the natives who did the washing of our clothes used to look forward to pay day because of this. A laundry had been fitted up for the voyage but this was for officers only, consequently the Indians cleaned and ironed our tough duck sailor suits and brought them back next morning. Well they knew the first of the month was payday, so they came onboard in twos and threes with canvas bags of two shilling pieces (10p) and would offer us twenty-eight shillings for every golden sovereign we would sell. Sometimes one would meet a native who would offer thirty shillings per gold sovereign. These natives were called 'Dhobie Wallahs' and probably the washing job was just a cover to get on board for the money business, at least at Bombay and Ceylon.

Whilst we were at Bombay our divisional officer went with the Prince's tiger hunting party. During the hunt they wounded a tiger and it sprang onto the trunk of the elephant, which he was riding. Of course Dalrymple-Hamilton's elephant did the natural thing in the circumstances; it lowered its head to crush the tiger, pitching him out on to the ground. The tiger leapt off the elephant and landed on D-H's back but was so frightened that it immediately made off but not before it's claws tore through his shirt at the shoulder and sleeve making some nasty gashes. D-H ended up in Bangalore Hospital and when he returned aboard *Renown* everyone, including myself, asked him exactly what had happened. He confirmed that the tiger was as frightened as he was. Later when the ship's company were bathing one could see the scars on his left arm and shoulders.

While the Royal Party was touring the Indian sub-continent the *Renown* carried out an intensive visiting programme: Bundar Abbas and Bushire in Persia between 30 November and 10 December, Kuwait, Henjam (Persia), Muscat returning to Bombay. On 18 January she sailed for Colombo and visited Trincomalee as a cooling-off period after the fleshpots before again returning to Bombay on 27 February 1922. On 4 March the Royal Party was re-embarked at Karachi and course was set for the Far East.

Port Swettenham was visited on the 28th and Singapore on the 31st. On 6 April they arrived at Hong Kong and from there completed their outward journey arriving at Yokohama on 12 April having covered a distance of some 6,074 miles on the first leg.

Japan at this time proved a hospitable place for the crew of the battle-cruiser, as Duff-Stewart remembers:

> Everywhere we went we were welcomed and the ship was illuminated every night we were in harbour. The huge set piece of the Prince of Wales' feathers hung between the two funnels and looked great from ashore. In Japan we were paid out in gold sovereigns also. My pay as a stoker being 3s 6d [17½p] per day I did not get many sovereigns and that was the last time I ever saw a gold pound!

William Waller recalls:

> At Yokohama we were all given a pass printed in English, French and Japanese allowing us to travel free anywhere in Japan, including arrangements to visit Mount Fuji as far as the rail went. All was very friendly then; we were still training the Japanese Navy at the time of course!

Renown finally left Japan after visits to Osaka, Kobe, Obe Wan in the Inland Sea, Miyajima, Kure naval base and Kagoshima, destroyed by an earthquake a few days after the British party had visited it. They began their homeward journey with a visit to Manila in the Philippines on 13–15 May where they had another great welcome. Then on to Labuan in Borneo, Penang and back to Trincomalee. The beautiful islands and the sun-drenched seas made even the humblest stoker feel glad he was in 'the Andrew' for such an occasion William Waller remembers:

> You may recall the story of the Flying Fish which Nelson told his grandmother and she refused to believe him. While we were crossing the Indian Ocean, where there are heavy swells, the bows of the ship dipped down and came up beneath one; hence the fo'c'sle deck was littered with flying fish on many occasions. They are about the size of a herring and have a pair of 6-inch fins. They could be seen in shoals of about twenty just a couple of feet above the waves and they flew for about ten yards or so and then dipped into the surface. Some of our fo'c'sle sailors picked them up and asked our doctor if they were fit to eat when cooked. Our ship's cooks were not all that pleased because the tin dishes became smelly and Cooky had to clean them for other uses.

While at sea the Prince particularly wanted to witness the firing of *Renown's* main armament, but this was vetoed by Admiral Halsey, one of his prime advisers, on the grounds that had they done so all the special mouldings in the Royal apartments would have cracked and been ruined. 'However the Prince came into my Rangefinder Tower,' says William Waller, 'and I showed him the workings etc, Lieutenant Tullymarsh our gunnery officer was with him.'

The Prince, despite his voyaging in *Renown* far and wide, was *not* a good sailor!

On the way to Japan from Hong Kong going up the Straits of Formosa, the weather became very rough and the cruiser *Durban,* our escort at that time, must have found it pretty uncomfortable steaming against it at 15 knots. She was sent back to Hong Kong but the Prince pushed on to Yokohama. When we met the Prince at the south entrance to one harbour in Borneo a powerful wind came up suddenly and we prepared to lift the piquet barge aboard with the main derrick. But great difficulty was experienced owing to the swell and heavy sea running. It is not easy to put a 56 lb iron ring on to the derrick hook weighing nearly a ton, and then to lift quickly on the correct swell to avoid the slings breaking away from the boat weighing 18 tons. The derrick officer misjudged; the large derrick hook crashed the boat as the swell lifted her. About the third or fourth time we were lucky; we could hear the Prince shouting above the noise of the gale, 'Get me out of this, Halsey,' etc. etc. But then we can't all be good sailors and poor Teddy, he did feel bad!

From Trincomalee *Renown* sailed on 30 May and made her stately way back via Great Hanish Island in the Red Sea to Suez. Port Said was reached on 11 June and then the final leg home reaching Portsmouth on the 22nd after disembarking the Royal visitor the day before. In all this most successful visit had covered a grand total of 29,957 miles and was considered one of most worthwhile ever undertaken in terms of prestige and friendship.

When Lord Louis married shortly afterward he remembered his happy times in *Renown* and it was members of this crew that pulled the bridal car with dray ropes. He was never to forget her although the next time he came aboard, again in the Indian Ocean, it was a whole world away in contrast with those halcyon voyages of the 1920s. *Renown's* royal wanderings, however, were far from over yet.

After paying off in July 1922 *Renown* was finally ready for her long deferred major refit, which *Repulse* had just completed, recommissioning for a round the world cruise with the *Hood.* A vote of £979,927 was allocated for this but it would not stretch as far as it had three years earlier and *Renown* therefore had to be content with a much more limited renovation than her sister at this time. The emphasis was more on torpedo protection than shellfire.

In order to try and save money the DNC proposed in February 1922 that a new belt 9-inches thick was to be fitted and the original 6-inch belt taken out of the planned improvement. Not only was thicker armour thus proposed, but it was to be placed higher to allow for the increased draught of the ship caused by existing improvements. The main deck armour was to be increased to 4-inches over the magazines and 2-inches amidships, instead of 3-inch and 1-inch as fitted to *Repulse.* Two longitudinal splinter bulkheads were to be added on the main deck and some extra armour added to the lower deck to protect against raking fire. The crushing tubes were to be omitted from the old bulges, new bulges were added on in addition to these, outside them. Further economy was effected by using much of the 9-inch armour plate originally ordered for the Chilean battleship *Almirante Cochrane,* that was being built in a British yard, was taken over in the Great War and subsequently completed as the aircraft carrier *Eagle.*

This refit finally commenced, with some additions and modifications, in May 1923 at Portsmouth and was not finally completed until August 1926 – almost twice as long as her original building time incidentally! *Renown* thereby became the first British capital ship (the term was then in common usage for both battleships *and* battle-cruisers) to be fitted with non-cemented armour for her deck protection. The proposal to fit eight above-water tubes was *not* proceeded with in the final event but four 4-inch high angle guns replaced the old AA armament at this time and a high angle control-position was fitted on to the fore-top roof. The bridge was slightly modified and the after 36-inch searchlights taken out completely. The fore topmast was cut out giving her an unbalanced appearance, the main wireless-transmitting aerials being re-rigged to the rear on the fore-top in rearward angled bracings.

Thus re-equipped for the service as envisaged in the mid-1920s *Renown* was set to commence the second decade of her life in full fighting trim, and she rejoined the Battle Cruiser Squadron, Atlantic Fleet that same year. Her period as a *bona fide* fighting ship, however, was of brief duration for she was selected two years later to carry HRH The Duke of York on his state visit to Australia. The planned voyage was to circumnavigate the globe and repeat the very successful mission accomplished earlier by his brother, and in preparation for this *Renown* was again fitted out to serve the Royal Family. Again a special crew was selected for this voyage and her commander, Captain Norton A. Sullivan was a particularly apt choice for he had devoted himself to the study of naval history and the part that this played in the various prescribed rites. Major Hunton commanding the Royal Marines was similarly well versed. Commander N.C. Moore and Lieutenant Commander H.H.J. Hodgson 1st and (T) with John Leach (later to win fame as Captain of *Prince of Wales)* was her Gunnery Officer, Peter Dawnay, as watch keeper and Colin Buist as Equerry to Their Royal Highnesses made for a strong team.

The scene was set on 6 January 1927 at Portsmouth when the train bearing HRH Duke of York arrived and he went aboard. Taylor Darbyshire of the APA described it thus:

> As Their Royal Highnesses stepped from the train to the quay, they saw the long, low, silver-grey ship, with her bunting fluttering gaily in the breeze. They saw the crew standing in long lines from stem to quarter-deck, arms outstretched and hands crossed as they stood. In Nelson's day it took place on the footropes of the yardarms, with arms crossed and holding on to the guard-ropes, whenever the ship was manned. The new Navy has no yards to man, but they still preserve the method. As in Nelson's day, too, TRH were piped over the side by the bo'sun and his mates, because in Nelson's day distinguished visitors coming aboard were hoisted in their boat, and the bo'sun's pipe conveyed the orders. As they stepped on board they saluted the quarter-deck, as had been the custom since the quarter-deck carried a crucifix as a symbol that a King's ship was a Defender of the Faith. And, finally, there was the Royal guard drawn up along the whole broad quarter-deck itself for the clashing general salute, as royalty have ever been welcomed when they boarded one of their ships.

Renown sailed down the Solent on a cold winter by picking up her destroyer escort off St Catherine's Point and heading out to sea, and shaped course for the Canary Islands, her first port of call. The Channel was kind but the Bay of Biscay lived up to its reputation and an easterly gale soon had *Renown* rolling and awash with everything battened down. A visit to Las Palmas followed with the battle-cruiser anchored in the roadstead while the Royal Party paid visits ashore as a sort of dress rehearsal for the voyage ahead.

Leaving this fragment of Spanish territory, *Renown* turned her bows westward and crossed the broad Atlantic making her landfall on the evening of 18 January, passing through Mona Passage and into the Caribbean Sea, sailing south of Haiti and arriving at Jamaica on the 20th. Here she lay in Kingston Harbour by the cruisers *Calcutta* and *Colombo* dressed and manned and took gun salutes from Port Royal. After due ceremonial the *Renown* sailed to the Panama Canal, being met off Colon by the American battleship *Arkansas*. Pilot Osborne, the same canal pilot who had seen the *Hood* through years before, came aboard them and took control. The *Renown* was lifted through the series locks up to Gatun Lake, 85 feet above the level of the Atlantic Ocean, and a formal reception was held at Gatun lock, the Duke being met by the Governor of the Canal Zone. During her previous passage in 1920 she had lost a propeller but now all went without incident. She passed down through the Pedro Miguel lock and that at Miraflores and reached Balboar that evening where a reception was held for the President of Panama. The pilot was presented with a mono-grammed watch by the Duke to match his cufflinks received from the Prince of Wales after performing the same feat for *Renown* in the 1920 voyage.

Renown then set out across the empty Pacific Ocean, touching land again only briefly at lonely Nukuhiva. The long eventless days were brightened on 1 February when Father Neptune and his retinue came aboard as the Line was crossed and the Duke duly initiated into the mysteries of that event. This was followed by a fully-fledged cabaret laid on by the ship's company during which the Can-Can and the Sir Roger de Coverley were both performed with equal zest!

At Tai-o-hae, Nukuhiva, in the French Marquesas Islands *Renown* found the oiler *Delphinula* waiting for her and after refuelling pressed on, arriving at Suva, Fiji after a diversion to look at Samoa requested by the Duke. Next port of call was Auckland, New Zealand for a more extended stay. After that they sailed to Sydney where *Renown* anchored on the morning of 26 March under a cloudless sky, to an enor-mous welcome. She anchored in Neutral Bay, in the same spot she had rested seven years before. While the Royal Party spent a month visiting all corners of Australia the ship's company were also regally entertained, not sailing again, under lowering skies, until 14 April, arriving at Hobart, Tasmania on Easter Saturday, for a briefer visit. This tour was cut short by bad weather and *Renown* sailed on to Melbourne from where the Duke again disembarked to visit the towns of Victoria and open the first Australian parliament in the new capital of Canberra. *Renown* sailed from Port Melbourne on 12 May escorted by the cruiser *Melbourne* on the first leg of her long homeward journey. A heavy gale marked their passage across the Bight, which lasted all night, and through the next day, the battlecruiser 'taking it green' with a vengeance, her fo'c'sle awash up to 'A' turret, and speed had to be eased to avoid any further strain on her hull. *Renown* arrived at Freemantle in West Australia on the 18th and further civic functions followed the pattern set all over the world where the Royal Party had stepped ashore. This was the final port of call on the Australian sub-continent and then *Renown* set course across the Indian Ocean for Mauritius. She was unescorted for this journey for it was expected to be an easy passage. This was far from the case.

On 26 May, 1,000 miles from the nearest landfall, and almost the same distance from the nearest ship, a serious fire broke out in 'D' boiler room. Darbyshire described it thus:

Caused by an overflow of fuel-oil from one of the tanks, it was due to a mistake on the part of a stoker. The fire, which began in the most inaccessible part of the stokehold, quickly gained full control. The boiler-room had to be abandoned at once and flooded with water. The usual plan in cases where fire occurs in oil-burning ships is to cut off all air and let the fire burn itself out, but in this case the presence of a large indraught fan working on its own steam made matters all the more complicated. The Engineering Commander and his staff made superhuman efforts to reach the fan through an inferno of smoke and gas fumes and terrifying heat welling up from the flaming oil floating on the top of the water ten feet or so below the gratings. To cut the steam off at the source – the engine room – would have meant that a very valuable adjunct in keeping the flames in check would have been lost. There was nothing for it but to make dash after dash along the gratings, give the control gear a twitch or two and dash back before falling exhausted. It was done at last and the boiler-room completely sealed. There was a very real danger, however, of the flames spreading to other parts of the ship and no knowing where, if that happened, the next outbreak would occur. Indeed there was one outbreak in an adjacent boiler-room, but that was quickly got under control. The bulkheads all round the burning room and the decks above it were red-hot and blistering, and on the boys' mess deck, which was directly above the seat of the fire, the water which had been poured on to it to keep the corticine from catching alight was steaming.

Although there was little danger of an explosion in the ship's magazines the oil tanks were fairly close and had the fire spread there the *Renown* would have had to be abandoned in mid-ocean. Fortunately the fire was safely brought under control and by 10 o'clock that evening the danger was over. *Renown* had hove-to for two hours during the worst of the blaze, and the cruiser *Sydney* put towards her at once but she was not needed. The boiler-room was burnt out but there were only four casualties, none of them fatal ones. Within twenty-four hours all the damage around the fire area had been made good and *Renown* was ploughing along at 16 knots once more.

At Port Louis, Mauritius *Renown* was met by the cruiser *Effingham* and again ceremonial took over before she set her bows due north towards the Red Sea, oiling again at Great Hanish Island under an intense sun and a barren sky. This was *Renown's* third visit to the tiny island, 'a bare, desolate, volcanic patch without inhabitants and almost without vegetation', and opportunity was taken there to paint ship and refurbish her before passing through the Gates of Hell, Bab-el-Mandeb, and entering the Suez Canal and the Mediterranean Sea, for she was by this time showing outward signs of her long voyage and not infrequent bad weather. She passed through the Suez Canal under her own power in a day. Because of local unrest at the time, she did not stop at Port Said itself but anchored out in the roadstead. Here she was visited by Lord Lloyd, the High Commissioner, before steaming on to Malta. Although the bulk of the Mediterranean Fleet, *Malaya, Barham* and *Royal Sovereign,* was at this time in Egyptian waters, the *Renown* was met by the Fleet flagship, *Warspite,* and the aircraft-carrier *Eagle.* It is perhaps interesting to note in passing that when Britain found herself at war in that theatre some *thirteen* years later, it was with these self-same ships that Cunningham sailed to do battle with the Italians!

After a short stay the battle-cruiser sailed on the last part of her journey, escorted by the eight ships of the 1st Destroyer Flotilla and guided by their flotilla leader *Montrose*. Gibraltar was reached on 23 June in heavy sea fog and three blissful days of perfect weather. Here they were met by the Governor. When *Renown* sailed for home next day the combined bands of the garrison played them out to sea. This was not without a touch of humour however for as the *Renown* was about to move and sail away the hymn selected by some unconscious wit was, 'Now thank we all our God!'

And so ended *Renown's* third royal voyage and her second circumnavigation of the globe. The future monarch's visitations had been as successful as the earlier ones in cementing the bonds of Empire more firmly than ever. It was as well that this was so, for already the balmy, carefree days of the twenties were showing signs of darkening horizons, and as the years wore on into the 1930s *Renown* more and more became attuned to her proper function. A splendid Royal Yacht was once more to become a magnificent weapon of war.

CHAPTER FOUR

The Sands Run Out
– Re-birth

he Royal tour brought to its successful conclusion and the damage to her
boiler-room repaired, the *Renown* recommissioned in readiness to resume
her sterner functions as part of the Fleet. Her refit was completed at
Portsmouth and on 19 December 1927 she went out to Spithead for Christmas leave
under her new captain, Sidney R. Bailey. Her navigator for this commission was Eric
Brand and he recalls: 'I joined *Renown* as navigator in October 1927 and served in
her until she took over battle-cruiser flagship (Rear Admiral Dudley Pound) in April
1929 when I had to be relieved by a Commander (N) Benn.' About his captain he
recalls:

> Though he later gained some unfortunate notoriety, when, as ACQ his flagship
> *Hood* collided with *Renown* at sea, he was, to my mind, the perfect captain.
> Though he had never been an executive officer, (he was Beatty's flag
> commander) and never came into the wardroom, he knew everything that was
> going on in the ship. On the bridge he was ready to ask anybody around for
> their opinion on what should be done next and was not in the least afraid to
> learn something from a side-boy if he had anything to impart. He was great
> company on the bridge. I recall two remarks especially. On heavy ships ponder-
> ously doing equal speed manoeuvres: 'This is like playing polo on carthorses'.
> On another occasion a struggle was going on in the forecastle with the
> commander in the centre of a milling crowd dealing with some form of
> Paravane trouble: 'You know, Pilot, this is a time when human nature urges
> one to send a messenger to the Commander saying what is the delay? thereby
> increasing the delay!'
>   My initiation brought another classic exchange thus: at the outer Spit Buoy
> the dockyard pilot turned over to me and we had to go westward before turning
> 16 points to come east and head the stream for anchoring. I was of course
> frightened stiff. The 'stem to standard' distance in that ship was 100 yards and
> I had never handled anything bigger than a 'D' class cruiser, while Bailey had

commanded nothing bigger than a flotilla leader. The time came for me to make the turn and having been granted permission I ordered 'Port 20 (in those days), Stop Starboard, Half Astern Starboard' and the ship charged onward till it seemed the forecastle was about to hit Ryde Pier. After a bit – 'Are you doing this right Pilot?' And when I replied I had got away with it before – 'Never mind the reminiscences, are you getting away with it now?'

The spring cruise of 1928 started with an exercise on passage to Gibraltar when the three battle-cruisers (under Rear Admiral Dreyer) were dispersed and were to come in at dawn from different bearings and attack a convoy. This was done quite successfully. After a period at Gibraltar *Renown* went out for the combined fleet exercises, known that year as MU2. This was a rehearsal for operations against Japan, then far and away the likeliest enemy at sea. Singapore Dockyard was only in its early stages of building and for the purpose of the exercises was under siege by the enemy who held the seas around the island base. MU2 was to practise the forcing of the Malacca Straits against determined opposition to relieve the British garrison by defeating the blockading enemy fleet.

On their way home the Fleet rehearsed a demonstration firing by the three battle-cruisers at 25 knots for the benefit of King Amanullah of Afghanistan. 'In the event we could not fire because of low visibility but it was exhilarating driving round in the middle at that speed in those days.'

Captain Brand recalled the 'funny parties', which *Renown* produced at Gibraltar at this time, an event that was to feature also in her later life.

That was one of my many odd jobs in *Renown* but it was in 1927 that Stephen King-Hall (T) of *Repulse* first produced *The Middle Watch*, which was afterwards such a hit on the London Stage. In 1928 King-Hall also organised a cutter race manned by lieutenant commanders, any ship having an excess over the number actually rowing were to be carried in the stern sheets! Unfortunately it was stopped at the last minute on the grounds of ridiculing the officers – an absurd reason for which it was said the Flag Captain and not the C-in-C was responsible. *Nelson* of course was going to have a hell of a crowd of passengers.

In *Renown* however I was the fourth Lieutenant-Commander in seniority in the days when there was a serious surplus of that rank (the cutter race was designed by King-Hall to kill off a few of them!).

Organising the 'funny parties' often raised as much humour as the actual production.

I so well remember once, when doing this, I said, 'And what sort of thing do you do?' and got the answer, 'I sing songs, Sir, – mostly in reference to moonlight and such like'. 'Oh,' I said, 'Sentimental', to which he replied, 'Yes, Sir.' I always liked that touch, but he was no good when it came to the business.

In *Renown* we were lucky to have the square court, built for the Prince of Wales, in which we could rehearse. One time we were doing a sort of 'cod' opera using well-known tunes put to local topical words. I am not musical, regrettably, but to my mind the greatest musical feat I ever witnessed was when the bandmaster stopped the band and shouted at the small band-boy playing the double base – 'What the 'ell are you doing? You ain't playing the "Vilia" song you're 'arf way through the "Minni-bloody-Tonka".' Fancy being able to tell what a double base was really playing – Terrific!

The return to Home Waters was followed by the summer cruise of 1928 to Invergordon and Cromarty Firth, pushing up to Scapa Flow of bleak memory for the Fleet Regatta, before the fleet finally dispersed to the seaside resorts to let the public see them. *Renown* went to Lyme Regis.

> I remember it so well because nowhere in the world, in my limited experience, has a visiting man o' war been treated so well. There were picnics and parties for the sailors, and all sorts of things for the officers including a house rented as a refuge and changing rooms for them.

Then followed the autumn cruise to Invergordon and Cromarty again and then the 1929 Spring Cruise to Gibraltar in the great 'season' of the Royal Navy of pre-war days. The combined fleet anchoring together in Pollensa was still a vast concourse of warships beautifully handled and shining with efficiency, a sight to remember and treasure, and never again repeated. Thus passed the life afloat and at the end of the 1920s it seemed as if this pattern would never alter. But alter it did before many more years were to pass.

By now Britain's battle-cruisers had been reduced to three, for the faithful old *Tiger* was due to go to the breakers. She served as a seagoing gunnery ship between 1924 and 1929. In June of that year, when *Hood* paid off for a refit, the *Renown* took over as battle-cruiser flagship and the *Tiger* rejoined her companions for the last time as an active unit. She served throughout the 1929 to 1931 commission in her full capacity proudly enough, the last 13.5-inch gunned capital ship in the Royal Navy; on 30 March her day was done and she was cheered by the whole Atlantic Fleet as she took her final departure to pay off. A year later she lay in Devonport dockyard forlorn and neglected and was sold for scrapping under the Life Duration clause of the Washington Treaty. Thus passed the veteran of Dogger Bank and Jutland.

At the end of this commission, early in 1931 *Renown* found herself in the Mediterranean for combined fleet exercises. One feature of these was that the battle-cruisers were utilised to refuel their destroyer escorts at sea underway, a far from common practice at this time, but one that was to prove increasingly necessary and vital when war broke out. Experiments of this nature had started as long ago as 1917 and Captain F.S. De Winton recalls similar exercises being held on the China Station in 1927 when he was in command of the destroyer *Somme*. In 1931 he commanded the *Whirlwind* and he describes the manoeuvre as it was then carried out thus:

> The Navy had, by this time, taken the matter of oiling at sea seriously, and it was becoming a fairly regular evolution as far as I remember. My ship *Whirlwind* and my sub-divisional leader *Watchman* oiled in succession from *Renown*. Sea was about 3–4, which means a bit lumpy, and a fairly fresh westerly wind. I can't remember how many tons we took in, but the evolution was completed without difficulty. I secured roughly abreast *Renown's* deck oil valve, probably about the after funnel, though I cannot remember exactly. Rear

Admiral Pound was watching the proceedings from a seat in one of *Renown's* picket boats in its stowage.

We used hemp hawsers only and at that time the battleships and battle-cruisers did not oil more than one ship at a time. The speed of the ships was about 15 knots, which seemed to be quite satisfactory. During this exercise *Renown* topped up four destroyers in succession, probably using about 400 tons. I never oiled from stern; it may have been tried before but oiling along-side became the recognised procedure.

The next commission was notable for a series of misfortunes that overtook the *Renown*, culminating in a sensational court martial for the three senior officers of the squadron that made front-page news. Despite these incidents the *Renown* was, during this commission, as happy a ship as she had always been, as L.P. Stirk recollects:

Renown took her place in Portsmouth dockyard for a further refit, which lasted from 1931 to June 1932. This refit concentrated on re-equipping her with a new close-range anti-aircraft armament and involved the fitting of several of the new pom-pom 2-pounder guns designed to give a blanket of fire against torpedo-bombers making a close approach. Accuracy and range took a back seat in this weapon, which was meant to lay down an impenetrable curtain of exploding shells in front of the aircraft. Great things were expected from it.

Provision for two pom-pom mountings and their associate directors was made by extending the conning-tower platform aft, placing the directors themselves on the fore-top roof. It had been planned to ship a further pair of pom-poms on either beam, but insufficient mountings were available, another result of the severe cuts set in train by the Government of the day and the cut-backs from the London Treaties; so *Renown* just shipped one Mark V and a director on the starboard side. To compensate for this increased weight the two after searchlights were taken out from the after funnel before she again rejoined the Battle-cruiser Squadron.

At the end of the commission, in 1933, further slight modifications were made to *Renown*. One of the 4-inch triple mountings was taken out amidships to allow for the fitting of an aircraft catapult on the after shelter-deck to the rear of her after funnel. A little later the overdue pom-pom addition was fitted amidships to port but not the director. Two multiple 0.5-inch machine gun mountings were also added to strengthen her close range AA defence. Apart from this little else was done. Under the terms of the various treaties extra tonnage was allowed for the older ships to increase their protection but *Renown* having had the most recent additions in that line, albeit a decade before, was considered then to be among the best protected and took a lower priority.

On 4 May *Renown* again commissioned at Portsmouth under the command of Captain Henry Richard Sawbridge for the Battle-cruiser Squadron, with Bailey, now a Rear-Admiral, as commander,

She was a really happy ship from truck to keel; a happy and proud ship's company with excellent officers led by a great captain whose outstanding quality was his ability to combine discipline with understanding and humanity. I think I can safely say he was loved by all.

The usual round of exercises and ports of call followed in the Home Fleet cycle. *Renown* had suffered some superficial damage in a collision with a Finnish vessel in thick fog early in 1934 but apart from that no untoward incident marred their usual routine other than a second, minor, collision in Sheerness harbour at the beginning of January 1935, when her flagstaff was carried away. Such incidents are said to go in threes, and *Renown* unfortunately proved the truth of that old saw while off the coast of Spain at the start of the spring cruise to Gibraltar.

It was around 10.50 on 23 January 1935 and *Hood* and *Renown* were steaming a parallel course of 223° at 18 knots in readiness to conduct an inclination exercise. At 11.35 Admiral Bailey gave the orders for the exercise to commence. At that time the two ships were between 10 and 12 miles apart. Both vessels therefore put over their helms to comply, converging at pre-arranged angle, *Hood,* the flagship, steering 254° and *Renown* closing from her starboard side on 192°. The intention was for *Renown* to glide smoothly astern of the flagship as the latter turned the squadron on a new course of 180° in line ahead. What in fact happened was that at 12.21 the ships collided, the *Renown's* bows hitting the *Hood* amidships with considerable way still on despite the fact that *Renown's* engines had been ordered to full astern moments before the impact. L.P. Stirk remembers the crash:

> I was a member of the Bosun's party and had just settled myself down in our 'Caboush' after dinner, intending to have a short siesta, when a resounding crash and thud made sleep a non-starter. As is usual in an efficient ship there was no panic whatsoever, hands went to their collision stations as if they were taking part in an exercise in the full knowledge that this was the real thing. Many and humorous were the matelots' comments at the time, one of which from the Bosun's party was – 'All the bloody ocean between us and that great lumbering so-and-so has to get in our way'. Other comments were too lurid for me to repeat!

Fortunately neither ship was seriously damaged although it was a close thing. *Hood's* side armour took the shock well but the stem of *Renown* just above the waterline was crushed in badly. Both ships were able to steam and returned at once to their home ports. There were fortunately no casualties, either from the initial collision or the second glancing blow that bent her plates back.

The aftermath proved much more protracted and harrowing for the three officers who were called to face court martial proceedings at Portsmouth at the end of February. It also caused a great deal of comment and friction between the crews of the two ships, one Chatham-manned and the other Pompey; the accident increased the centuries-old rivalry between the two groups.

An Admiralty court martial takes place with due time-honoured ceremony and form. On the results of the findings of the court depended the reputations and future careers of three distinguished officers, Rear Admiral Sidney Robert Bailey, Captain Henry Richard Sawbridge and Captain F.T.B. Tower, OBE, Bailey's Chief of Staff and Captain of the *Hood.*

The Deputy-Judge-Advocate was Rear Admiral C.G. Ramsay and the President of the Court was Vice-Admiral Astley-Rushton. Vice-Admiral J.A.G. Troup, tactical expert, acted as prosecutor. Five admirals and three captains, wearing the full dress naval uniforms, dark blue frock coats with gold epaulettes, cocked hats and swords, were to judge the three men, in most cases old friends and compatriots. It was a scene of considerable tension and drama.

Admiral Bailey was the first to be tried after the court had begun with the age-old naval symbolism of court-martial flag and gun. He surrendered his sheathed sword that was placed on the table before the president with its blade pointed towards the accused. The prosecution alleged that Admiral Bailey was to blame for the collision because: 'Having ordered *Hood* to steer 254 degrees and *Renown* to close her on a course of 192 degrees, he failed to take action to prevent the development of a situation in which risk of collision between the two ships arose.'

In defence Admiral Bailey replied: 'My impression at this time was that *Renown* was carrying out the manoeuvre badly; in fact that she was making a bad shot. I have been captain of her myself, and I know she is a handy ship.'

He went on to state: 'Since the accident I have naturally gone over in my mind whether some other form of signal would have been more appropriate to my purpose, but I cannot think of one unless I had been prepared to give orders for the movements of *Renown* – in fact to command the ship myself.'

After a recess the court reached its verdict and Admiral Bailey was brought back by the Naval Provost-Marshal to hear his fate. He saw immediately that his sword had been reversed and now lay with its hilt towards him. A sure sign of acquittal.

The Judge Advocate confirmed this thus: 'The court finds that the charge against the accused is not proved. The findings are signed by all the officers of the court.'

The President then lifted the sword from the table, strode across the courtroom and handed it back to Admiral Bailey with one word, 'Congratulations'.

It was then Captain Sawbridge's turn. His report to Admiral Bailey, written two days after the accident, was read out:

> I fully realised it was the Admiral's intention to turn both ships to 180 degrees at the proper time to bring them into line on that course. *Hood* was kept continuously under observation, and at 12.18 I decided that although she had ample room and time to carry out the manoeuvre I would take the precaution of turning away.

At 12.19 he therefore ordered, 'Half speed astern both', and immediately afterwards, 'Full speed astern.' *Hood* hoisted and hauled down, to execute the signal to form single line ahead. 'Thus', said Captain Sawbridge, 'even as late as 12.20 *Hood* could have taken avoiding action by turning outwards, but apparently she did not do so.'

Lieutenant Commander G.M.S. Sitt of *Renown* had been called to give evidence for the defence and stated that when the Captain decided to hold on to his course as *Hood* appeared to be late in turning, he entirely agreed. 'I was convinced then, and still am, that *Renown* was ordered to steer that course for one reason only, and that was that when the ships got within a mile of each other *Hood* would turn to 180 and *Renown* would be able to form astern.'

Rear-Admiral Bailey was asked by Rear Admiral Troup: 'Would you expect your flagship to avoid *Renown* or *Renown* to avoid the flagship?' To which Bailey replied, 'The flagship being the guide, I should certainly not expect her to have to alter course.'

The trial continued until late in the afternoon. Lieutenant-Commander Sitt told how, when the *Hood* was seven cables away, he remarked to the Captain: 'Now is the time for *Hood* to turn to 180 degrees.' The Captain replied that as *Hood* appeared to be late in turning he would hold on to his present course to give more clearance when the *Hood* turned. At 6 cables the Captain decided to take action. At 3 cables Commander Sitt said he saw a signal going up in the *Hood,* and the Captain remarked: 'It is not much use making that signal now.'

Lieutenant Commander C.B. Hodgkinson, *Renown's* officer of the watch, said that when the ships were 6 cables apart the Captain remarked, 'I don't like this,' and ordered the wheel to starboard and the engines to be stopped. Later Hodgkinson said, 'Why doesn't the *Hood* obey the rule of the road?' The Captain then ordered 'Full speed astern.' When a collision appeared inevitable the Commander said he ordered the closing of the watertight doors.

Captain Sawbridge was asked by Captain Miles, 'Why did you not give the order "astern" at an earlier time?', to which he replied, 'I did not expect to have to go astern at all. I was absolutely certain *Hood* was turning to 180, and that when I put my wheel over she would do the same in a proper seamanlike manner, and when she saw me turn away, she would alter course.' He added that he considered his action was effective in extricating two ships from a collision when one of them did nothing to contribute towards it.

The court took an hour and twenty minutes to consider its verdict. Then Captain Sawbridge was led in. His sword lay still with its point towards him. He took his place in dead silence then the judge Advocate rose and said: 'The sentence of the Court, having found the charge against Captain Sawbridge proved, is that he shall be dismissed His Majesty's ship *Renown.*' While he spoke everyone was standing with the exception of the members of the court who remained seated wearing their cocked hats. Captain Sawbridge bowed his head to the President, and then pulled himself up sharply, and with shoulders square and head erect, walked from the room, following the Provost-Marshal. A second later the President announced, 'The court is dissolved'.

The effect of the sentence was that Captain Sawbridge was placed on half pay from midnight. Further, as an officer on half pay he was not allowed to give evidence, in anticipation that he would be called as a witness for the next day's trial of Captain Tower, he was temporarily posted to HMS *Victory.* There was no appeal against the sentence passed; only the Lords of the Admiralty had the power to alter the decision.

The trial of Captain Tower duly followed the same procedure. He stated that on the day of the accident he expected that *Renown* would fall into his wake. About two minutes before the collision he realised that the *Renown* was apparently continuing on her course and he tried to swing his own ship round. 'I began to get uneasy when the ships were about 6 cables apart', he said. 'At that time I expected *Renown* to get in astern of *Hood.*

Captain Miles then asked him. 'Why did you not take action to obey the "Rule of the Road"?' to which Captain Tower replied; 'I might have taken action in the literal interpretation of the "Rule of the Road" when the two ships were separated by 2 or 3 miles. That would have involved using the starboard helm. That I did not consider seriously for I knew it could not possibly have been defended. Later, keeping in mind the whole of the approach, I had no doubt, and had every reason to believe, that *Renown* would fall astern of me. I considered it was my duty as guide of the Fleet to continue my course and speed to the last possible moment.'

Captain Towers was acquitted by the Court.

Naturally there was much grief aboard *Renown.* P Stirk remembers: 'We on

Renown followed the Courts Martial proceeding and when the news filtered through the ship that our captain had been found guilty everything went deadly quiet and despondency settled over all of us.'

However there came a remarkable turn-about in Captain Sawbridge's fortunes. Nineteen days after he had walked down the gangplank of *Renown* for what he thought would be the last time the Board of Admiralty made a startling announcement:

Their Lordships dissent from the findings of the court martial held for the trial of Rear Admiral Bailey to the following extent: 'Rear Admiral Bailey adopted an unusual procedure in directing *Hood* and *Renown* to steer definite course to close. Since he had given that order, responsibility for the manoeuvre rested on him, and it was incumbent on him at the proper moment to make a further signal to reform his squadron. His not doing so left in doubt his final intention.

The signal for *Hood* and *Renown* to form single line ahead was made too late. For these reasons their lordships are unable to absolve Rear-Admiral Bailey from all blame.

Their lordships agree in the findings of the court martial held for the trial of Captain Sawbridge but they have decided to reduce the sentence to a severe reprimand, Captain Sawbridge will, therefore, resume command of *Renown*. Their lordships consider that Captain Tower should have taken avoiding action earlier, and to that extent they are unable to acquit him of all blame.

This announcement was naturally received aboard *Renown* with great elation. 'You will quite understand the delight on board when it was made known that the Admiralty were not satisfied and in reversing some of the decisions gave us back our Captain', says Mr Stirk. 'The pubs in Pompey did a "renowned" trade that night despite Captain Sawbridge's dignified response.'

Captain Sawbridge had stated after the original findings to two of his fellow officers that 'My conscience is clear. I reckon that I have saved the country about ten million pounds and about a thousand lives. So, whatever happens, I do not think I have anything to be ashamed of.' He had been staying aboard *Renown* though not actually in command and this had been thought by his fellow officers a favourable sign. After the decision had been changed and he had resumed command Captain Sawbridge addressed the ship's company thus: 'This is not to be a time for rejoicing, for whilst some rejoice others suffer.' It was a noble sentiment, but: 'Nevertheless rejoice we did!' remembers A.B. Stirk.

Fortunately the damage to both ships was slight and soon repaired in the dockyards. This was just as well for they were both soon urgently required for something more serious than exercises that went amiss.

On 16 July the Silver Jubilee of His Majesty King George V was marked by the traditional Review of the Fleet at Spithead and *Renown* was present in the centre of the array being illuminated overall at night. But sterner duties lay ahead.

In the summer of 1935 the nation found itself on the verge of an all-out naval war with Italy over that nation's aggression against the African state of Ethiopia. Sanctions were finally resorted to, which were completely ineffective, but for a time it seemed as if the Mediterranean Fleet would be the front-line force in a major war. Consequently hurried reinforcements were made to both ends of the Mediterranean

Sea, and from the ships in the Home Fleet (as it had been termed since the Invergordon Mutiny), the *Hood* and *Renown* were hurriedly sailed to Gibraltar together with three light cruisers and a destroyer flotilla of six ships. This imposing force arrived at the Rock on 17 September 1935 when the crisis was at its height, and shells were fused and full combat-readiness ordered.

This action was regarded as provocative by the Italians, and the British Government showing the spirit it was to display throughout the late thirties, quickly offered to withdraw them again if the Italians would withdraw one of their divisions! Not surprisingly Mussolini, sensing their irresolution, refused to do so. The addition of the two battle-cruisers was held by the C-in-C Mediterranean, Sir William Fisher, to be a 'tremendous asset' in his calculations for war, but the Admiralty were concerned, for these ships were the only vessels afloat that were capable of both catching and destroying the new German pocket battleships, three of which were by now in service, and they did not wish to risk their damage. Nor did they want losses in a war with Italy of the other big ships, for only a narrow margin existed and it was feared that Japan might take advantage to start further aggression in the Far East. So although a lot of huffing and puffing was done, the French declined to commit themselves, the British followed suit and the Italian invasion went ahead to an ultimately victorious conclusion.

There was little to be done save to rearm at a faster pace for the war that now seemed inevitable as Hitler and Mussolini continued to gobble up the smaller nations of Europe and Japan penetrated deeper into China. It was therefore decided that the *Renown* should take her place in the modernisation programme without further delay, and on 23 June 1936, with the war clouds clearly on the horizon and the international picture darkening by the day, she paid off into dockyard hands at Portsmouth at the end of the second decade of her life for a refit that was to result in a complete transformation of the old ship. After twenty years capital ships were supposed to be scrapped, but in the case of the *Renown,* she was to be so completely rebuilt, so that rather than a modernisation it was more a complete rebirth. She was in effect about to take on a new life. In September work commenced.

By now it was accepted that the role of the true battle-cruiser was over. Although her virtue of high speed was still a considerable asset, new battleships being built would nearly match it and attention was therefore concentrated on two main factors: to equip her, as far as her existing hull would allow, to withstand punishment, both from guns and the heaviest bombs then envisaged, and to provide her with modern machinery and anti-aircraft capacity to take her place in the line-of-battle in the 1940s. In the case of the *Renown* this transformation was successful beyond the highest hopes and she more than earned her keep in the years that followed. In terms of actual cost this rebuilding amounted to an expenditure of £3,088,008, only £30,000 less than her prime cost when first built; but compared with the £8,000,000 of a brand new unit it was still a bargain. Her refit took twice as long as her original building but the work involved was considerable and it was very well done. Despite the complete face-lift she received and heavy additions to her armament, upperworks and torpedo protection, the provision of a complete outfit of brand-new machinery not only enabled her to operate with only a small loss of speed, but resulted in her displacement actually being reduced from an estimated 31,520 tons in 1926 to 30,025 tons in 1939, although later the myriad of wartime additions considerably increased this once more, as we will see.

Renown's rebuilding was a complicated process. The provision of the new machinery was matched by the complete rebuilding of her superstructure above the forecastle-deck and the ship that finally emerged bore no resemblance to the lithe, sleek battle-cruiser of the 1920s that had so entranced the world.

A great tower-like bridge structure arose, a huge block of steel on the lines initiated by the *Nelson* in 1927 and improved upon in the rebuilt *Warspite*. This solid block provided ample cabin and bridge space for the personnel and a stable base for the new directors and other equipment now brought into service to serve her new armament. An integral armoured conning position was built in to the front of this structure with the main armament control tower atop and the HACS director to the rear. The compass-platform and navigating positions at the top front of this block were curved round after the fashion of the newest cruiser designs while the signal deck was extended aft behind it to the massive new tripod foremast. The fore and aft shelter decks were built out flush to the ship's sides, presenting a much higher broadside profile all-round as far aft as Y turret to enable the new secondary armament, cross-deck catapult and aircraft hangars to all be carried at a higher level and less vulnerable to the weather conditions, as well as giving the guns important clearer sky-arcs on either beam. The whole bridge was constructed much further forward of the two new funnels which effectively eliminated all the old smoke troubles in this ship. The aim was to present a modern and balanced picture of clean, firm lines and efficiency, but many mourned the passing of the rakish lines of the original *Renown*.

Because her protection had received so much attention in her earlier refits it was not deemed necessary to make sweeping changes in this direction, but she was improved to bring her into line with current thought. New non-cemented armour was fitted on decks not already covered and over the new secondary armament magazines, the new 'D' steel replacing existing deck plating in those areas. The magazine armour additions were of 4-inch thickness, that over the engine rooms 2-inches. Also, 11-inch armour replaced the longitudinal bulkheads abreast the boiler-uptakes, between the main-deck and the upper-deck and 2-inch armour added on the main-deck forward, with 3-inch aft to provide extra protection against end-on fire.

The forward barbettes remained intact but their sides were increased to 6-inches above the armour, which was still scanty but could not be further improved without an unacceptable loss of speed.

The existing 15-inch main gun turrets were lifted out of the ship and were converted to give greater range by increasing their elevation to 30 degrees, again not excessive even by the standards of the time; the battleships *Nelson* and *Rodney,* for example, had 16-inch triple-turrets whose guns could cock-up to twice that angle and could be (and were) used for long-range anti-aircraft fire! This was not deemed practicable in the case of *Renown's* mounting however.

One of her most impressive features was the new secondary armament, among the best fitted to World War II British capital ships. No less than twenty of the new 4.5-inch high-angle/low-angle guns were fitted in ten twin turrets, counter-sunk into the shelter decks, three forward and two aft on either beam, with two inch armour protection outboard. The four groups thus established each had their own director with R/F height finder known as the 'four corner system'. Under this arrangement the high-angle fire was controlled by an HACS Mark IV table and the low-angle by an AFCC Mark VII. Stops were fitted which in theory eliminated automatically the guns firing on a dead-ahead bearing for safety, but it was found with the forward groups that the massive bridge structure 'wooded' the guns while tracking round ahead giving some blind spots.

Close-range armament was harder to improve; the new automatic cannon had been rejected earlier, although vastly superior to British systems, and by the time substantial orders had finally been placed they were too late to reach *Renown* before she set off for war. In the interim she was fitted with three 8-barrelled 2-pounder pom-poms on Mark VI mountings, on a special pair of raised platforms between the funnels port and starboard and another at the rear of the after shelter deck over-looking Y turret. In addition four 0.5-inch machinegun mountings were fitted, two forward and two aft, also on the shelter-decks.

Although established as ineffective as long ago as 1917 the two submerged torpedo-tubes were now finally removed and replaced by four pairs of 18-inch Mark XI torpedo tubes along the upper deck.

This additional equipment and the provision for increased ammunition stowage for the improved secondary armament required extra space, so it was fortunate that the new machinery installed was both to take up less space and to be of greatly improved performance. Not only these factors benefited from this; in addition water-tight stability could be much improved under the new system of sub-division – a whole list of bonus spin-offs in fact.

Only four of the original six boiler rooms for example were taken by the eight Admiralty three-drum boilers which replaced the forty-two original Babcock and Wilcox boilers. Extra tanks were fitted around these for oil-fuel and water and additional bulkheads were built to the latest specifications. The funnels were shifted further aft. The Parsons single-reduction geared turbines were supplied by Cammell Lairds, and they gave her a legend speed of 29 knots with 108,000 shp. There was a small auxiliary boiler forward of A boiler room. *Renown* carried 4,613 tons of oil fuel and 244 tons of diesel fuel for the auxiliary machinery. This was completely renewed also and included new dynamos, new hydraulic and air-compressing machinery, and electro-hydraulic steering equipment; electric capstan machinery replaced the old steam driven engines and an electric bakery was installed. Boiler pressure was increased to 400 psi. Her new endurance was now 3,640 nautical miles at 10 knots speed, or 1,300 miles at 30 knots, and although her dimensions remained the same her draught came out at 26 feet (mean) 30 feet (deep load). Her crew comple-ment was increased to 1,200 officers and men in 1939.

And so the work progressed on *Renown* over those grim three years. In every ship-yard in the land there was now a hive of activity and yards that had lain deserted and men who had spent depressing futile years on the dole as defence cuts bit into their jobs now found themselves in demand as never before. Fifteen years of Governmental neglect and decay had to be made good in those three years, and it became a race against time to complete the work as the humiliation of Ethiopia was rapidly followed by the similar coups in Austria, Czechoslovakia and Albania as the Germans and Italians surged outward, sensing the weakness of the democratic powers.

Not only on *Renown* were the workers toiling against the clock as the war loomed closer and closer but on the old *Warspite,* the *Queen Elizabeth,* the *Valiant* and on the brand-new ships of Britain's rearmament programmes, the five battleships of the *King George V* class, the six carriers of the *Illustrious* class and scores of cruisers and destroyers. For many of these ships the race against the clock was lost and they were not completed until after the war had commenced. In the case of the *Renown* it was a dead-heat; never did a major warship complete in readiness for sea at such an appropriate time as this ship.

As the long job grew closer to completion so the proportion of dockyard workers dwindled and the percentage of her ship's company from advance drafts increased aboard, seeing to the final details of her elaborate facelift. More and more as 1938 gave way to 1939 did her new crew begin to find themselves familiarising themselves with the new-look *Renown*. Not a few who had known her in the 20s and 30s now found themselves lost below decks as they made their way around the rebuilt ship. There were a thousand and one checks to be made on her complex battery of machinery and always the urgency of the world headlines showed just how little time remained to them to get her ready for the combat that now seemed inevitable.

It was about the middle of July 1939 that the main part of *Renown's* sea trials was carried out at sea on the measured mile. On 10 and 11 July on the contractor's measured mile she attained a speed of 29.93 knots with 120,560 shp and at a displacement of 32,800 tons. As the course was held in shallow water it was estimated that about three-quarters of a knot could be added on to this figure, and in later trials she did in fact attain a speed of 30.1 knots with a displacement of 34,800 tons. Further trials held on 24 and 25 July confirmed that she was still a lively lady in her new guise and gunnery trials confirmed that the new secondary armament was one of the most efficient embarked in a British warship, no faults being encountered and a high rate of fire attained.

The period between her completion and her ship's company joining her was a hectic time. Henry Shannon recalls the period well:

It was about mid-summer that the main part of the crew were fallen in inside the drill-shed of HMS *Drake,* and then split up into groups, each group with a petty officer in charge. Then we were marched to the railway station alongside Royal Naval Barracks and went on board the train. I don't believe any of us younger ratings really knew what was happening except that we were going to commission HMS *Renown,* a battle-cruiser.

However we were soon all aboard for Pompey town from Guzz (Plymouth), the 'Farmers' as they called our West Country crew, or the 'Hoggie faces'. We were very well cared for on the long journey, and on arrival at Pompey dockyard we were marched down to the old carrier *Argus* that was being used as sleeping accommodation etc as she was not in commission. Her ancient flight deck was full of humps and hollows; however later on in the war we did see her again in fighting, trim.

We were all issued with commissioning cards, which contained full particulars of our allocated mess numbers, gun numbers etc and I met my old divisional officer whom I had as a boy seaman on the cruiser *Galatea.* He was now *Renown's* new gunnery officer, and he told us as we went aboard and received our card, 'You now have 24 hours to find your way round your ship and find your battle station!' Well, you can imagine, looking over at the bulk of the *Renown* was frightening to young sailors, such a big ship, and we all knew the vast amount of red tape attached to big ships in peace-time.

Next day we were on *Renown* cleaning and scrubbing and painting, and getting to know the ship in real detail. This continued for a few days and then we went out to sea for trials of all kinds, engine, gun, damage control, testing all the gear, dropping paravanes, which were trailed on either bow of the ship to cut mines. A tough week in all for breaking us all in and I had pity for some of the poor old dockyard maties, because we were told to dump everything that was not belonging to the ship, toolboxes, wheelbarrows; all the lot went overboard in Davy Jones locker, no messing, over the side and clear the decks.

John Roche had similar recollections of that period:

We commissioned HMS *Renown* in Portsmouth Dockyard in August 1939 after the completion of a lengthy refit, which involved stripping the ship down to its hull and completely rebuilding her with all new materials so she was virtually a brand new ship.

The crew arrived by train from Devonport and joined the advance party and quite a few Chatham ratings that were already on board.

As can be imagined the ship was in quite a shambles with dockyard workmen and tool boxes everywhere, but things soon took shape and it was not long before she began to look like a ship and the process of storing and ammunitioning proceeded with the utmost haste. HMS *Argus* had been used as an accommodation ship by the advance party and it was in her hangar that we first met Captain C.B. Simeon, our commanding officer, when lower deck was cleared. Addressing the assembled ship's company and referring to the refit, the Captain said that it was a case of putting new wine into an old bottle and he felt sure that it would be a good combination.

He added that war was imminent and after his experience of the Great War he told us that we should be prepared for a war lasting five or six years. Work proceeded unabated getting the ship ready for sea and it was not long before we were doing sea trials off Portsmouth.

A young gunnery rating, W. Pittendreigh, was also in this draft:

I joined the *Renown* at the end of August 1939 (on the 28th I think it was) along with several hundred other boy seamen and the remainder of the ship's company, which just about cleared Devonport Barracks. We had left our various training establishments some months before and had only been to sea doing sea-going training, which was just a day or so at a time, so this was really our first ship.

My first impression, I think, was the size and length of *Renown*. She was not big by some standards perhaps, but she looked enormous. She had been in dockyard hands for three years during which she had had an extensive refit which altered her superstructure considerably and was now completely different from her sister ship *Repulse*. She had a streamlined look about her that no other big ship had (except the *Hood* of course).

The first few days on board were chaotic to say the least; the task of trying to commission, ammunition and store a ship of this size and at the same time clear up the mess after such a long refit was formidable, and besides the ship's company doing their best to get on with it there were still hundreds of dockyard maties finishing off jobs and struggling to get their gear ashore. I can well remember when we did sail and were steaming west through the

Channel we were still just dumping boxes, crates and stuff over the side to clear the decks.

Hitler's invasion of Poland abruptly changed several million lives that September for good or evil; one of those was that of Chief Petty Officer Bill Kennelly.

My long and lasting connection with *Renown* began with one of those curious twists of fate. I had planned to finish my naval career after the first twelve years and had had a lucky break in changing ships in the Mediterranean, from the carrier *Glorious* to the cruiser *Devonshire* and later changed over to her sister ship *Norfolk, en route* to the UK with a vibration defect, arriving at Devonport in May. I was due to 'take my twelve' on 27 December and, on leave from *Norfolk* I took the opportunity of setting up and furnishing a home in Devonport for my wife and baby daughter whom I had met for the first time at Euston station on her first birthday – she didn't want to know me then!

On returning to RN Barracks I found I was on draft to *Renown* at Portsmouth where she had just completed a D2 refit. It would seem my wife and I were the only two unaware that a war was imminent as I had assured her that I'd be back in a week or two as we were a Devonport crew and would be bringing the ship around for the usual working-up trials. Little did we know that our next meeting would be years away and that we had seen the last of our new home.

Our arrival at Portsmouth was quite smooth and we eventually bedded down for the night in the old carrier *Argus,* adjacent to *Renown.* We mustered onboard next day and we were allocated our 'parts of ship'. I was the senior PO of the three allocated to the DB party, with its complement of leading-stokers and stokers. There was a chief stoker in command but as he was also in command of a boiler room steaming watch, the brunt fell on our backs. DBs (double-bottoms) as you know covers all compartments in the ship below the main decks from the forepeak to the WTCs aft of Y Magazine. I've forgotten quite how many there were but believe me we knew all about them in double-quick time, their pump and flooding systems, access doors etc and in particular the counter-flooding valves for the outer bulge compartments, just in case.

A young midshipman, Charles McDonald Stuart, joined the *Renown* on 26 August. He recorded in his midshipman's journal:

We joined the ship at Portsmouth on 26 August 1939. In order to join the ship I had travelled without ceasing for thirty-six hours, having been handed my telegram while fishing a loch only a few miles south of Cape Wrath.

Renown was our first ship as we had come fresh from our first cruise in the training ship HMS *Vindictive.*

After commissioning with a predominantly West Country ship's company we were working at full pressure until we sailed a few days later. Ammunitioning ship went on till after midnight with halts only for meals and mostly in the rain. At the same time the dockyard was hard at work finishing the ship off for sea, fighting a harder battle against time as war became more imminent. In the end hard work won and the ship sailed less than twenty-four hours before the declaration of war. Previously there were numerous requests for permission to go ashore; we dealt with a long queue of men requesting it. Their leave was restricted to the evening only and during that evening a signal came from the Admiralty 'Ship all warheads, fuse all shell, in all respects prepare for war.' That did it! No-one knew about the watertight doors, the layout of the ship or anything else for that matter. Next morning we were ordered to Scapa to work up. After putting to sea we threw everything over the side that was movable and that was being used in connection with the refit. Over went dockyard maties' tool boxes, parts of the catapult that was about to be fitted for the Walrus, wood, steel, even a couple of bicycles!

And so *Renown's* hour had come, and that of her company of over 1,000 officers and men. The veterans and the boy seamen, the officers from the Great War and the fresh faced 'Snotties' off the training ships. From now on they were to function as part of a great team and family, they were all Renowns now, uncertain of the future but proud to be in such a great ship, brand-new, full of the latest equipment and certain to be in the thick of any action going. The prepared, the unready, the calm and the frightened, *Renown* gathered them all into her vast bulk and, on the evening of 2 September, with German troops deep inside Poland and the British ultimatum steadily running out, they set off for war.

For at least one person this period meant a great deal of hard work. Tom Oliver was Master-at-Arms and the fact that *Renown* had commissioned hastily with crews drawn from all three manning ports meant a degree of chaos that he had to sort out quickly.

It was a nightmare. The immediate issue was to get all men in messes to be fed and to know where everyone was. Rum as usual in those days was a nuisance for each mess had to be allocated with rum at the issue according to the number of Grog ratings in respective messes. Having got everyone aboard the watch bill had to be made out for duty and leave purposes and it was made out in traditional port and starboard watches which in turn were split into two parts. Snags and chaos were too numerous to mention. War being in the air there was not a little restlessness and when shore leave was stopped for *bona fide* natives of Portsmouth, there that night. I did not get much rest, I can tell you, except for a bite to eat and a wash at your station with a bucket; we even had to use a bucket for toilet arrangements at each station. In fact it was eat, live, sleep and eat at your post. Water was rationed and one man would be detached to go and fetch the rations and make the tea because you had your own plate, mug, knife and spoon; tough times, but it had to be done.

Under the command of Captain C.E.B. Simeon, *Renown* sailed to take up her war station as part of the Battle-cruiser Squadron with *Hood* and *Repulse* at Scapa Flow, Rear Admiral W.J. Whitworth flying his flag in the former as commander.

For *Renown* her first voyage of World War II was very nearly her last. Along with two of the pocket battleships several German submarines were already at sea waiting for the outbreak of war. On Sunday 3 September *Renown* was ploughing northward through the Irish Sea with her two escorting destroyers *Electra* and *Escort;* 30 miles away the Donaldson liner *Athenia* was steaming on her peaceful affairs, unescorted. Lurking below the waves was the *U-30* skulking some distance south of Rockall

Bank, her commander, Lieutenant Lemp, eager to strike his first blow for the Fatherland. Slowly into his sights steamed the *Athenia* with her cargo of civilians, women and children.

Aboard *Renown* Henry Shannon recalled:

It was while we were bound for Scapa Flow on the morning of 3 September that the Captain spoke over the loudhailers to us, for we were already closed up at action stations. He told us the facts, that England was now at war with Germany and that we were all to look towards the foremast from our stations. Here was hoisted Nelson's famous signal, 'England expects that every man will do his duty', and from then we had to tighten up on everything. We more or less had to sleep at our stations, so it meant a makeshift bed of a blanket and something that you could put your head on; we used to call them 'Caulkers'. If you were resting and you had the order to stand-to it was quickly bundled up and thrown into a corner out of the way. One man had the gun telephones manned all the time; of course he used to be relieved after an hour.

'We were working up every minute and hour of the day and we were at sea when war was declared, something we all more or less realised was inevitable,' recalled W. Pittendreigh. 'It was nevertheless a bit of a shock when it came. During the passage to Scapa in addition to the normal routine, we exercised everything many times, especially gunnery control, sun drills and, of course, action stations.'

The 4.5-inch guns did not respond so well as reported for the first trials as Midshipman Stuart recorded: 'All this time we were trying hard to find out how everything worked. The HA armament, completely modern, was a source of great trouble, but it was mastered with some effort after a short while.'

When news came of the sinking of the *Athenia*, *Renown* and her destroyers were the nearest ships to the scene. The battle-cruiser naturally could not herself be risked, but her two destroyers were at once detached to rescue any survivors they could, while *Renown* plunged on north alone. It was a gamble accepted in the name of humanity, and fortunately was favoured with good luck for no other U-boat sighted the unescorted giant and she arrived safely at Scapa Flow on 4 September. Almost as soon as she had anchored there was an air raid warning, which proved to be a German reconnaissance plane. As the RAF had already made abortive attacks on German heavy ships a reply from the *Luftwaffe* was expected at any time. Meanwhile, the two destroyers reached *Athenia*, which was still afloat, at 06.00 and saved about 500 survivors from this callous and unwarranted attack, whom they landed at Princes Pier on the Clyde on the morning of the 5th.

At Scapa there was time for a brief period of relaxation, at least for part of her crew. W. Pittendreigh remembers:

In a surprisingly short time she was ship-shape and was always, to us anyway, a good ship, (a clean ship, a happy ship and, as usually followed, an efficient ship). Routine duties were as for a seaman on any ship, general care and maintenance, keeping the ship clean, painting, rigging (i.e. renewing wires and ropes, splicing etc), boats' crew. I was coxswain of the ship's 45-foot launch, probably the job I had for longer than any other, although I also cox'd the other ships' boats at different times.

I had several action stations during my five years on *Renown* but as I eventually became a gunnery rating, the majority of the time I was in a 4.5-inch gun turret and, later in the 15-inch A turret.

Entertainment, in the main, was a do-it-yourself job, especially in the first months on board when we did not even have radios on the messdecks. There was always an abundance of talent – it was surprising whom it came from sometimes – and some of the concert parties were really very good. She was also a very good ship for sport; we could always raise several good teams for any game. Cards of course were played a lot; crib and solo were probably the most popular, and every turret had at least one regular solo school. Ludo (Ukkers to us matelots) also helped to produce some fun and many arguments, while later when we went out east Mah Jong was played a lot.

John Roche had similar memories:

After arrival at Scapa we were soon engaged in all sorts of drills and practice firings and the ship soon began to look very efficient with everybody very keen. My part of the ship was the quarterdeck and my action station was the starboard after 4.5 T.S., which was down below the main deck hatch of 4-inch steel to get to it. Life soon took on a pattern of three watches and action and cruising stations and with the odd air raid over Scapa Flow there was always something exciting happening.

For the youngest members of her crew there was much to learn. A.N. Herbert joined *Renown* as a signal boy and he recalls how his duties and lessons combined during this early period:

Although at sea in action conditions, training was very much part of the scene wherever possible. This would entail manipulating a fleet of small brass ships on a chart, and the flagship would hoist a series of manoeuvring signals, which we would enact with these ships on the chart. Then at a given signal on the completion of the manoeuvres we would have to indicate the deployment of the fleet. There was very much a competitive spirit among the ships to see which could hoist the correct answer first. We would have to act as lookouts for our own fleet actions and report any incident, read and transmit semaphore and Morse (light) signals though the latter was very much on its way out at that time.

The captain would advise the yeoman of any flag signals he might want sent to the accompanying ships; he in turn would pass the message to us on the flag deck, and we in turn had to code it into flag signals and hoist them. The flags were joined together by clips top and bottom very much like a Chinese puzzle that once bent on would not come apart, but if anyone failed to bend the flags on correctly and the halliards came adrift, then the man who bent the flags had to climb the mast to retrieve the halliards; going up the mast and out on the yardarm of the *Renown* was quite something, as I remember from more than one occasion. With the sea a bit rough it took some hanging on, I can tell you. You might be scared stiff, as everyone probably was, but you daren't say no; apart from what you might get officially, I think more chaps were more scared of what their mates might say.

At Scapa the Master-at-Arms had even more problems to set straight as Tom Oliver vividly recalls:

Of course at Scapa it was day and night hard work to shake down. We found port and starboard watches were unworkable, for *Renown* had three main armament turrets and the number of men required to man the ten twin 4.5-inch turrets plus other smaller weapons required us to change the whole system into red, white and blue watches. This meant one duty watch, one standby and one off. Similarly were the degrees of readiness, 1st degree, all watches, 2nd degree, the duty and standby watches and 3rd degree, the duty watch. We were never below 3rd degree while at sea.

The alteration of watches meant the complete change of the messing system: instead of each mess being made up proportionately of port and starboard watches, there had to be separate messdecks for the colour watches so that when they came off watch they all sat down together. This eased the cooking situation in the galley. At action stations or in the 1st degree of readiness meals were arranged by turrets and other positions. These usually were made up of sandwiches, corned beef, soup etc and this was distributed to each station according to the number of men stationed there.

This alteration in messing had its advantages and disadvantages. The latter was that now shore leave was given to one watch only and on return from shore the red and blue watches, who were messed on the forrard messdeck together, would conduct their own private war. The re-organisation was still not complete for *Renown* was fitted with more short-range weapons as time went on.

On 8 September *Renown* sailed from Scapa on her first war patrol, with *Hood* (flag), the light cruisers *Belfast* and *Edinburgh* and four destroyers. The squadron left at dawn and carried out a sweep between the Faeroes and Iceland with the object of intercepting any blockade-running merchantmen hoping to sneak back to Germany by hugging the Norwegian coastline. The main fleet sailed and the area covered was between 61° and 63° North.

It was an uneventful sortie; both forces were hampered by widespread fog and the battle-cruisers found nothing but three neutral steamers, which were stopped, examined and allowed to proceed. *Renown* returned to the Flow at noon on the 12th, whereupon she embarked 2,200 tons of oil from the tanker *Belgol*.

'On completion of this patrol,' wrote Midshipman Stuart, 'we remained in Scapa for some time working up our main and secondary armament, torpedo firing and searchlights. We also devoted some time to the calibration of our direction finding apparatus.'

The whole of the period between 13th and 30th was spent inside Scapa Flow working up and *Renown* did not accompany the fleet to sea on any sorties during this period. Although no air attacks were made on the fleet at anchor at this time aerial reconnaissance was a daily happening, as Bill Kennelly remembered: 'We were enjoying a lazy evening playing cards in the mess when there was an almighty bang. The language was choice as we thought some clot had dropped the hatch on the fo'c'sle instead of lowering it gently. We soon had other ideas when action stations sounded off Red Alert.'

Meanwhile in the depths of the South Atlantic the German pocket battleship *Admiral Graf Spee* was going about her deadly work sinking isolated ships. Her sister ship was less successful in the North Atlantic but managed to slip back to Germany undetected and for a time the Admiralty thought there were two raiders still at large. Preparations were made to hunt them down and these were soon to involve the *Renown*.

CHAPTER FIVE

South Atlantic Interlude

The threat of air attack on the Fleet at Scapa still loomed large and as early as 7 September plans were put in hand to prepare an alternative fleet anchorage on the west coast of Scotland at Loch Ewe until the Flow's aerial defences could be brought up to standard. Between 12 and 15 September most of the main units of the Home Fleet proceeded to the new base where they were inspected by the First Lord, Winston Churchill, but they returned to Scapa Flow on the 21st. However on 1 October the bulk of the fleet again left for Loch Ewe leaving only the *Repulse* and *Royal Oak* at Scapa. Again this very nearly sealed *Repulse's* fate there and then, for the *U-47* entered the Flow on the night of the 13th/ 14th and sank the *Royal Oak* with heavy loss of life. With all attention being paid to aerial attack the base's underwater defences had been neglected and the German submarine made good her escape. It is interesting to note that the U-boat captain, Prien, claimed to have also torpedoed and damaged the *Repulse* in this attack, a claim repeated in several lurid post-war accounts. However the claim was complete nonsense, for although *Repulse* had been photographed there earlier she had in fact sailed before Prien entered the Flow and was in dock at Rosyth at the time, preparing for operations much further afield.

Midshipman Stuart's journal records *Renown's* movements at this time:

> Then on 2 October we suddenly put to sea [at 18.10 and escorted by the destroyers *Bedouin* and *Tartar*] and after firing a 15-inch full calibre practice shoot we steamed westwards out of the Pentland Firth into a westerly gale, bound for Freetown, Sierra Leone. Off the Butt of Lewis we made a rendezvous with the aircraft carrier *Ark Royal,* the flagship of Vice-Admiral Aircraft Carriers. Our route took us out to mid-Atlantic and round to the westward of the Azores. For the next few months we were to be based on Freetown in order to conduct a series of sweeps into the South Atlantic where a German raider was known to be operating.

The Admiralty had responded to the threat of the *Graf Spee* by detaching powerful reinforcements to the South Atlantic, including from the Home Fleet, the *Renown, Ark Royal* and cruisers *Norfolk, Suffolk, Emerald, Enterprise* and *Effingham.* By the end of the month they had formed nine hunting groups of which *Renown* and

Ark Royal, screened by the destroyers *Hardy, Hero, Hereward* and *Hostile,* were designated Force K along with the cruiser *Neptune.* At 04.25 on 11th October the *Renown* and *Ark Royal* were met by the destroyers *Hardy, Hostile* and *Hasty* from Gibraltar, and arrived at Freetown on the morning of the 12th, where they hastily replenished both fuel and stores

On the 15th *Renown, Ark Royal,* the light cruiser *Neptune* and the destroyers *Hardy, Hero* and *Hereward* put to sea at 18.15, leaving Freetown on her first Force K patrol across the Atlantic toward St. Paul's Rocks. After *Renown* had refuelled the destroyers two days later, the Force returned by a more southerly route, sighting the island of Fernando Norowha, north of the eastern point of the Brazilian coastline, returning on the 24th having sighted no enemy vessels. *Neptune* and the destroyers had to attend to boiler clean and fix engine-room defects, and this effectively hamstrung Force 'K' for the next few days, but they sailed again at 20.00 on 28th for a patrol in the South Atlantic. This voyage failed to find any sign of the *Graf Spee* and was also fruitless; beating an empty sea under a blazing sun was more akin to a pleasure cruise than an act of war. The force patrolled as far south as Ascension Island, the destroyers refuelling at St. Helena on the 30th and again from the tanker *Oligarch* on 3rd November. On 30th a reports were received of German merchant ships on the move from both Fernando Po and Lobito, and the destroyers *Hardy* and *Hasty* were sent off to search for the former, the *Pioneer,* while the rest of the force hunted the latter, the short-legged destroyers that remained, *Hero* and *Hostile,* again having to fuel from *Renown* on the 31st. They returned empty-handed again, to Freetown on 6 November, but on the plus side on their return beat they heard that an aircraft from the *Ark Royal had* sighted a German blockade-runner on 5 November. She was the *Uhenfels* (7,603 tons) and smart work by the destroyer *Hereward,* which was sent off hot-footed in pursuit, resulted in her capture before she could be scuttled. *Hereward* brought her in as a prize on the 7th.

The change of climate was much appreciated by her crew after their hectic first month's operations in the stern northern waters off Iceland.

'Life at that time was a succession of dawn and dusk action stations and various drills during the day,' said John Roche.

> Recreation consisted of PT on the fo'c'sle, Tombola, cinema and a dip in the canvas swimming pool on the catapult deck. Everybody on board was hoping for a crack at one of the German pocket battleships and we knew we were more than a match for any of them.

However the tropical conditions had another side to them for those forced to work deep down inside the armour-clad leviathan, as Bill Kennelly pointed out:

> We found ourselves in Freetown, Sierra Leone, totally unprepared for the climate and conditions. The *Renown* had been comparatively cosy as regards warmth, with one exception – a forward boiler-room. It was not unusual to be on watch down there clad in oilskins; it became the custom to wait and listen for the thump as the bows went into a big one, and the Chief and two stokers would huddle in the acoustic phone box and wait for the downpour of icy water. In Freetown and the tropics, such a downpour would have been welcome. As it was, there developed a shortage of ship's mailbags and each

boiler-room equipped itself with canvas air chutes from each of its four turbo-fans in order to make life bearable down below.

We often worked in temperatures above 120°, even 130°. Fuelling ship in Freetown was always a nightmare; after our sorties down to the coast of Brazil and back we often needed 3,000–3,500 tons to fill up, and often at 120 tons an hour, depending on the tanker available. Certain tank fillings which were in the cable passages over the boiler rooms were a real nightmare and could only be manned in short spells by stokers dressed only in underpants and boots. However, we survived.

For the *Renown* these distances were no problem but for the escorting destroyers shortage of fuel oil was a constant headache. The H class destroyers, in common with most pre-war British types of destroyer, and indeed nearly all war-built ships, suffered from very poor radius of action compared with foreign designs and constantly needed topping up from *Renown* in these long cruises. This was an experience in itself for, although fuelling experiments had been practised as long ago as 1917 with battleships and destroyers of the Grand Fleet in Scapa, afloat support and fuelling methods were a neglected art in the Royal Navy between the wars, and methods, and, more important, equipment, were sadly out of date in comparison with the smooth running methods used at that time by the German and American navies.

Bill Kennelly recalls one typical incident:

Life became routine once again with our ten days at sea, fuelling our destroyers as required and we in the DB party became quite expert at supplying them and keeping our bookwork up to date. One incident comes to mind. Things were running to pattern as each came along for its couple of hundred or so tons. Meanwhile the sea was getting up and it came to the next destroyer's turn.

Our commander up on the crane sponson served out a blast at the poor effort put up coming alongside, but eventually the pipeline was connected and our pumps started. Unfortunately the destroyer yawed away beyond limits and the oil pipeline stretched and parted. We were still pumping and she was plastered in fuel oil. We fitted a new section of pipe, and then reconnected and we completed the job, only to hear the destroyer's captain retaliate by broadcasting 'Hands standby to let go oiler!' She then let go with plenty of fist shaking on both sides – and plenty of chuckles.

Another patrol between 14 and 16 November was uneventful. *Renown* had sailed from Freetown with *Ark Royal, Hardy, Hero, Hasty* and *Hostile* at 18.00 to rendezvous with the RFA *Cherryleaf* before commencing a sweep to the south-west. But an Admiralty order that the *Ark* was to be detached and return to Brest with the French battle-cruiser *Strasbourg* as soon as possible, saw this sweep cancelled and the force returned to base. Meantime the *Graf Spee* had found the South Atlantic was getting too hot for her and to throw the hunting groups off the scent she rounded the Cape and operated for a short while in the Indian Ocean, sinking a ship in the Mozambique Channel before doubling back again. News of this sinking naturally drew the hunting groups to that area of the world.

On 18 November Force K was at full strength, *Renown, Ark Royal, Neptune, Hardy, Hero* and *Hostile,* but within a short time the destroyers were detached to patrol the Freetown-Natal route because of their short endurance. The big ships continued on toward Diego Suarez on the north coast of Madagascar to patrol the Mozambique Channel and search for the raider that had sunk the *Africa Shell.* They were too late, for *Graf Spee* had returned into the South Atlantic several days before they arrived but they did manage to inflict further useful damage on the dwindling numbers of German blockade-runners still at large.

Force K was acting as reinforcement to Force H which consisted of the 8-inch cruisers *Shropshire* and *Sussex,* who joined company on 1 December, but it was in fact some excellent work by the British mercantile marine that led to the next success. The British ship *Waimarama* had sighted a suspicious vessel near Ascension Island, and with great presence of mind reported her by radio and shadowed her. She was in fact the German vessel *Adolf Woermann* (8,577 tons) disguised as a Dutch vessel. The *Neptune* was detached from Force K and intercepted her, but could not prevent her crew from scuttling her on 21 November. *Neptune* rescued the 162 crew and passengers and landed them at Freetown. Another victim was soon claimed, when a report of a suspicious ship south of Cape Point was received. The *Sussex* was first on the scene and the German ship, the *Watussi,* duly set herself afire. The crew was taken off by the cruiser and *Renown,* which had come up, finished the job with five minutes fire from 'B' turret, which sent the enemy to the bottom. An eyewitness, Charles Stuart, remembered the affair this way:

> When Force K reached the Cape they did not continue eastward but carried out a patrol between the Cape and Latitude 38°S to 40°S. Weather conditions were unfavourable as the usual westerly winds were experienced there, bringing bad visibility and heavy seas, which prevented *Ark Royal* from flying off aircraft.
>
> After some days of this patrol we turned north again, making for Capetown. The day before we arrived a report came that the German liner *Watussi* of just less than 10,000 tons on encountering coastal reconnaissance planes from the Cape had scuttled and set fire to herself. We approached her and long before she was in sight the thick pall of smoke was plainly visible. Cruisers had picked up the survivors by the time Force K arrived. All that was then left for us to do was sink her, which we did.

The aircraft that spotted *Watussi* (9,552 tons) were from the South African air force and *Sussex* was first on the scene picking up her crew. Bill Kennelly recalls this incident thus:

> We in our wisdom had headed way down into the South Atlantic and had a taste of the 'Roaring Forties'. We woke up one morning to find our sea boats gone and almost their davits with them. One of our companions had intercepted the German liner *Watussi;* she was well alight when we arrived and it was decided to use one of B turrets guns to sink her. Imagine the delight of the engine-room crowd assembled on deck to watch the fun when B gun missed completely at close range, but managed to sink her after a couple of

further shots; her survivors had previously been picked up by *Sussex* and taken on to Capetown.

Force K arrived at Simonstown on the 3 December, the *Renown* being carefully nudged into the harbour and secured alongside the jetty in 'C' and at once commenced refuelling and provisioning again. Leave was granted from 13.00 to midnight to two thirds of the ship's company, and, after the long bleak periods of being stationed at Scapa Flow and Freetown, neither of them famed for their hospitality or amenities, Cape Town was a blessed relief to those lucky enough to get ashore at this time.

Bill Kennelly remembers:

What a pleasure it was to take on fuel in Cape Town, the *Ark* on one billet, *Renown* on another, both fuelling as quickly as possible. Our run ashore depended on when we completed and we finished up in our shore-going No 3s, disconnecting hoses and signing the chits and dashing off along the jetty. We were soon accosted by the local generous families in their cars, offering us a run out to seapoint or home for a meal, but we headed for the local RNR Club and some beer. Returning later on board we heard about all sorts of plans and dates for the morrow, only to find ourselves out in Cape Town Bay resuming our chase of the *Graf Spee*.

'The people of Capetown were truly hospitable and I was lucky to be one of the dozen officers who were being nobly entertained at Wynberg, a short distance from Capetown,' wrote Midshipman Stuart. 'We were driven all round the Cape Peninsula and saw as much as anyone could possibly see in such a limited space of time.'

Meanwhile *Graf Spee* had been busy back in the South Atlantic, and word came in the next morning of her sinking of the Blue Star liner *Doric Star* on the 2nd. She also sank the *Tairoa* and five days later the *Streonshalh*, and the hunters took up the scent again at once. *Renown* and *Ark Royal* sailed at 07.20 on the 12th and headed north once more. While they were still sweeping north on the latitude of Pernambuco, the news of the River Plate battle came through and both ships turned round and headed back southward at 28 knots, making for Rio de Janeiro for a hasty refuelling.

'We sighted the Brazilian coast as dawn broke on 17 December', recorded Charles Stuart and he continued:

The Sugar Loaf or Corcovado at the entrance to the harbour was immediately recognisable and was not as disappointing as such landmarks usually are at first sight. To describe the real beauty of the coast as it was on that morning would needlessly take up space, but Rio fully lives up to the reputation for beauty with which shipping companies and travel posters have endowed it. When we first anchored we were in the middle of the harbour while *Ark Royal* went alongside the wall. At 14.30 we started moving in and without a proper local pilot and using only two small weak tugs we finally berthed astern of *Ark Royal* shortly after 17.00.

The quay was thronged with a very enthusiastic crowd who appeared to be friendly and well disposed towards us. A number of the British community came on board later in the evening.

Bill Kennelly recalls much the same picture:

> Rio was *quite* an experience. There was a verbal exchange on the way in with
> some obvious squareheads; the Harvey Smith V-sign hadn't been invented
> then, but there was a very good naval equivalent. It seems we were moored
> in the 'town centre', surrounded by thousands of cheering and excited locals.
> We in the DB party had to attend to our fuelling from a series of oil barges
> which was slow as each staghorn isolating valve had to be shut before its hose
> could be disconnected and this led to an occasional mishap and spill into the
> harbour.
>
> As there was no shore leave, practically the whole crew lined the rails,
> enjoying the spectacle and beauty of Rio at night. We had a good collection
> of Welsh voices in the crew and it developed into a singsong which was quite
> something. There was a continuous exchange of souvenirs and the canteen
> stall soon emptied of compacts, ship's crests etc. It became quite an open air
> concert, enjoyed by all, when late in the evening, the captain called for atten-
> tion and announced that the *Graf Spee* had sailed from Montevideo; there
> was a sobering hush.
>
> Then, later on, came the tremendous news that the *Graf Spee* had scuttled
> at the mouth of the river. There was round after round of cheering and the
> excitement was great.

In fact *Graf Spee* had taken refuge in Montevideo harbour after a running fight
with the cruisers *Exeter, Ajax* and *Achilles*. Only slightly damaged herself she had
taken casualties and been run ragged. She had, however, heavily damaged the
largest of her opponents, the 8-inch cruiser *Exeter,* which was forced to limp away
to the Falklands to repair. She had also hit the two 6-inch cruisers but they stuck to
her heels and guarded the exit from the Plate until reinforced by another 8-inch
cruiser, the *Cumberland. Graf Spee* still had ample margin of firepower over these
three smaller ships with her six 11-inch main armament and her batteries of 5.9-
inch secondary armament and had she broken for the open sea might well have
made it. However rumours were put about that *Renown* and *Ark Royal* were also
waiting for her, when they were in fact hundreds of miles away. This the German
intelligence service had confirmed but despite this *Graf Spee's* captain still refused
to make a dash for safety and motivated more by the desire to save the lives of his
young crew blew his ship up rather than take the risk. He later shot himself when
the reaction of the world was shown to be contempt for such a gesture rather than
understanding of his motives. Thus the seas were rid of the most daring and
successful of the German raiders. If the Renowns were disappointed not to have
been in on the kill at least they gained consolation that merely from the whispered
presence they so influenced the final outcome of the battle.

With the demise of the *Graf Spee* Force K's work in the far waters was almost
done. *Ark Royal* and *Neptune* sailed from Rio at 17.50 on the 17th and were joined
by the destroyers *Hardy, Hasty, Hereward* and *Hostile* which came hot-foot from
Freetown via Pernambuco to bring the force up to full strength. *Renown* herself
sailed from Rio at 05.05 on the 18th and concentrated with the rest of the force but
there remained nothing to do but to return to Freetown once again, conducting a
search for the prison ship *Altmark* which had the crews of the sunken British ships

aboard as they did so. On the 20th *Hardy* was taken in tow to fuel from astern, and she was followed in turn by the *Hostile* and *Hero*. *Renown* secured at Freetown once more at 09.15 on the 27th and refuelled from the tanker *Cairndale*. They boiler cleaned for the next three days. Since leaving on the 18th they had spent just 36 hours in harbour, 24 at Capetown and 12 in Rio. For the rest of that time *Renown* had steam on her main engines the whole time. She had steamed a total of 15,845 miles in that time.

They boiler-cleaned between 2nd and 6th January, sailing from Freetown at 14.20 on the latter with the destroyers *Hero* and *Hasty* to rendezvous with *Ark Royal, Neptune, Hardy* and *Hostile* from Dakar. The rendezvous was made on the 9th whereupon *Hardy* and *Hostile* were detached to Freetown. They swept south and then west to meet with the cruiser *Ajax*. On the morning of 12th Ascension Island was in view, and three days later they met *Ajax,* who had left Montevideo on 5th and been escorted initially by the heavy cruisers *Dorsetshire* and *Shropshire* before proceeding independently. The *Renown's* group took over and steered toward Freetown once more, being reinforced by the destroyers *Dainty* and *Diamond* on the 19th. Another boiler clean took place between 20th and 23rd before *Renown, Ark Royal, Dainty* and *Diamond* sailed at 18.35 on the 24th.

Charles Stuart reports:

We made one more sweep from Freetown to look for the *Altmark,* then we went down to 10° South to take the *Ajax* up to Freetown, cheering ship as we met her. Then, having brought *Ajax* to Freetown we went to collect *Exeter.*

The damaged *Exeter* had carried out temporary repairs at the Falklands and was now on her way home to make more permanent repairs after the battering she had taken. The German press and radio were claiming that she had been sunk, and to ensure that they did not subsequently do so she was given an escort to mid-way up the Atlantic by the cruisers *Dorsetshire* and *Shropshire,* who, again in turn handed her over to the protection of *Renown, Ark Royal, Dainty* and *Diamond,* who rendezvoused with her on the afternoon of the 20th. After the usual topping up of the destroyers by *Renown* the whole force reached Freetown on the morning of 3rd February. *Renown* was already under orders to join the Home Fleet as quickly as possible following a signal of 21st January and the whole force with *Exeter* duly sailed from Freetown again at 18.00 on 6th February, *Ark Royal* for Portsmouth, *Renown* and *Exeter* for Devonport, after sailing west of the Canary Islands and sending the two destroyers into Dakar to refuel. These were due to be relieved by *Hero* and *Hasty* from Gibraltar but these destroyers were soon diverted on other business. Meanwhile *Ark Royal* left them on the 9th and on 14th fresh destroyers, the *Ardent, Hesperus, Wolfhound* and *Wolverine* were sailed to provide an anti-submarine screen.

'We brought *Exeter* into Freetown,' wrote Charles Stuart, 'where we were able to visit her and inspect the damage done to her at the River Plate. It was of great interest to us and a very heartening and even inspiring lesson.'

'The German radio said then that *Exeter* would never reach home,' recalled Henry Shannon, 'and indeed they made a strong effort to prevent it. On 10 February they worked out the estimated position of *Exeter* and her escorts from radio signals.

Ark Royal had gone on ahead on her own at full speed leaving *Renown* and the two destroyers to continue the final stages of the voyage. The Germans worked out that these ships were due to reach the entrance to the English Channel from the west on the 13th or 14th and they ordered three submarines who had been working in that area to take up interception positions. These vessels, *U-26, U-37* and *U-48,* were unsuccessful for they ran into an easterly gale, which so slowed them down, that they were unable to reach their interception points in time.

By way of contrast Force K was able to take one final swipe at the enemy at the same time. Also on 10 February a concerted attempt was made by six German merchant ships, which had taken refuge in Vigo harbour, to reach home. The Admiralty became aware of this attempt to break the blockade and instructed Commander-in-Chief, Western Approaches to take *Renown, Exeter, Hasty* and *Hero* under his orders to round these ships up. Several destroyers were sailed from Plymouth in support. This operation was code-named Operation VO.

Contact was soon made, and the *Hasty* was detached at full speed to intercept one of these ships, which she captured intact. This was the *Morea* (4,709 tons) and *Hasty* sent a prize crew aboard which took her safely into Falmouth. At the same time as this successful interception was made in 42°N, 15°W on 12 February, other blockade runners were suffering a similar fate, the *Wahehe* being captured by the *Manchester* and destroyer *Kimberley,* the *Rostock* by the French vessel *Elan* and the *Arucas* by the cruiser *York.* Of the remaining two the *Orizaba* was wrecked on the north coast of Norway later and only the *Wangoni* finally got home after an unsuccessful interception by the submarine *Triton.*

To bring this episode to a final satisfactory conclusion *Renown* and *Exeter* both safely arrived at Plymouth on 15 February. *Renown* went straight into dry dock, and seven days' leave were given to each watch as a result. At Devonport *Renown* was the first big ship to enter and dock in the North Slip, for her well-earned refit. Both the First Sea Lord and the C-in-C Western Approaches visited *Renown* on the afternoon of the 15th.

Here another small bonus awaited them for in towing the captured *Uhenfels* back to Freetown earlier they were awarded prize money in the old tradition. Also in the old tradition, this did not amount to very much per man!

'After the war we were paid a few pounds for each member of *Renown's* prize crew', recalled Henry Shannon.

Their stop at Devonport was of the briefest duration for, after leaving harbour and securing to a buoy in Plymouth Sound, at 17.55 *Renown* slipped and proceeded to Greenock, escorted by the destroyers *Acasta, Firedrake* and *Kimberley,* duly arriving without incident the following afternoon.

On 4 March *Renown* rejoined the Home Fleet once more after her long period of South Atlantic voyaging. She lay at Tail 'o the Bank in the Clyde for three days, then, on the 7th, sailed in company with *Rodney, Repulse* and nine destroyers, *Firedrake, Fortune, Foxhound, Hardy, Hostile, Inglefield, Imogen, Kimberley* and *Punjabi,* for Scapa Flow with Admiral Forbes' flag in the former ship, the destroyers *Faulknor* and *Forester* from Scapa Flow augmented the screen off Cape Wrath at 12.30 on the 8th. The *Hood* and *Valiant* were already there, the Flow finally having been made safe for the fleet to return to its true base. However on their arrival at 17.30 on the 8th they found that the Hoxa entrance was closed due to fears that German aircraft had dropped mines earlier that afternoon about one mile 055°

from the north-east end of the Calf of Flotta. It was a welcome they could have done without for it showed just how well aware the enemy was of all their movements at this time.

As a result of this alarm the heavy ships were obliged to remain outside for the night whilst the passage to their anchorage was swept and *Renown* and her companions did not finally enter the Flow until 10.45 on 9 March.

An eventful period in *Renown's* life had closed. An even more exciting period was about to open now that she was again back in the front line.

CHAPTER SIX

Duel off Stromvaer

The hunt for the *Graf Spee* and the first six months of total war had by now knitted the crew of the *Renown* into one family and team, but patrolling the distant southern trade routes was a very different war from the prospect they now faced. With the Home Fleet they were a key unit of Britain's main line of defence and now they had to be confident and able to tackle all that the Germans might throw their way. In the North Sea this would include both surface action against heavy units, in which they would rely on their main armament and the good shooting of the three 15-inch turrets, and also they would sooner or later be subjected to prolonged first-class bombing, in which they depended on their new 4.5-inch batteries. The constant threat from below the water they could do little about themselves; they must rely on the skill and vigilance of their escorting destroyers from the 6th and 8th Flotillas (*Tribal* and F class ships), but they could help themselves by the vigilance of their lookouts. In all these important respects the Renowns, despite their own self-confidence and esteem, still had much to learn and over the next few weeks they were to gain high proficiency in both. This proficiency was soon put to the test but it only came about in the first instance by sheer hard work.

Midshipman Stuart's journal is highly informative on the lessons they now had to absorb after the heady days in the South Atlantic.

> During the week a 15-inch and 4.5-inch sub-calibre shoot was carried out in the Dog Watches. The 4.5-inch shoot was a disappointment due to a certain misunderstanding of the definition of quarters firing. Each group fired separately and after ten salvos the Director would order quarters firing. In some groups this was combined with, and confused with, local control.
>
> A salvo would then be fired and a correction made from the Director, applied in the TS and passed to the guns. The officer of the quarters would simultaneously make his correction and pass it to the guns, which then fired with a double correction. The port forward group was the only one to come out of this shoot with anything resembling credit. Any doubts were later cleared up by the gunnery officer in a review of the shoot.
>
> Since arriving at Scapa we have taken our turn as AA guardship, fortified by the bad example of the *Hood* in letting a German plane circle round the Flow and drop two magnetic mines. The ship is now only too keen to shoot down

anything that comes within range although it may at first sight appear to be British. These last few days have been punctuated by many air raid warnings, none of which have been fulfilled. Over a long period this may lead to a dangerous indifference and it has been thoroughly impressed on all who are in charge of the AA armament that this must be fought all the time. There is also a danger of lookouts becoming indifferent and one must always impress upon them the importance of their job. As the ship has come into more dangerous waters so they have improved.

When the ship left Plymouth most of the lookouts were hostilities only ordinary seamen, some of whom had never been to sea before. They were on watch before we passed the breakwater and had to be taught every small detail of their duty. Discussing the HO's later with Captain of A top, I found that they were becoming useful in that part of the ship. There are some artificers who are now beginning to prove their worth by helping to maintain screen doors and hatches and other such responsibilities in that part of the ship.

Even at anchor in the Flow the *Renown* was not immune from the weather, which could still put on quite a showing even in the early days of spring. Stuart again: 'The week blew itself out in a gale. Two fleet tenders, merchant ships built up to resemble the *Royal Sovereign* and the *Revenge,* dragged their anchors and drifted past the *Renown*. They did not, however, come to any harm.'

These two dummy warships were another innovation of Churchill at the Admiralty and, although they never appeared to have fooled the Germans (except perhaps on one occasion during the *Bismarck* hunt), they showed how his keen and active mind was constantly working. *Renown* was soon to be caught at the sharp end of another one of his pet 'ideas'.

Midshipman Stuart:

On 11 March the Renowns had even more exacting standards to live up to for on that day Vice-Admiral Whitworth transferred his flag from *Hood* which was due for a refit, to the *Renown*. His flag was hoisted aboard her at sunset on the 11th, and it was his intention to use her as his flagship for the two months *Hood* was absent. She badly needed a refit for her speed had dropped noticeably in the preceding few months; by contrast *Renown* had just completed hers. It is worth noting that in the first six months of the war the *Renown* had steamed about 41,500 miles and had spent 124 days at sea against forty-three in harbour or dock. So much for the press and fictionwriters' talk of capital ships spending all their times in harbour aground on their own bottles; such allegations are as stupid as some of their plots.

Young Midshipman Stuart reflected the pride this choice made: '*Renown* with her great mobility and endurance alone is well fitted to be a flagship. In addition to this she has modern fire-control systems, a large and efficient combined HA/LA secondary armament and an advanced W/T organisation.' These were things the old *Hood,* who had *not* been rebuilt, sadly lacked. Alas, she was never to receive them.

The Vice-Admiral soon became part of the *Renown's* team. Young signal boy Herbert recalled the impression he gained of this austere figure with whom he shared *Renown's* bridge:

What I do remember of Admiral Whitworth was that he was rather a strict man and very aloof. For instance when he was in the Admiral's cabin at sea just below the flag deck, he would send his Marine to the flag deck to tell us signal staff to stop making a noise when pacing the deck on lookout, which meant we had to put sea boots on to muffle the noise of our steps.

Whitworth was very much a contrast to Admiral Somerville in this respect as A.N. Herbert also recalls:

I remember Somerville as a very jolly man; he was known onboard as 'Slim' Somerville, very dapper and neat, and he quite accepted that men should carry on with their duties when he passed, whereas Whitworth demanded that they stood to attention, which now looking back seems so futile, especially so as we were inevitably at action stations when he was on the bridge.

A martinet he may have been and lacking Somerville's easy charm, but before many weeks had passed Whitworth was to show that he was a fighter rather than a talker. To join an already established ship's company at this time was not easy. One such newcomer was Ted Smith, and he describes his first days and his duties thus:

I joined *Renown* one dismal March day in 1940 whilst she was lying in Scapa Flow. This was my first RN ship. I was previously a steward in the Merchant Marine with the Union Castle line. My first impression was one of power and pride. At the RN Barracks, Devonport, this ship already had a reputation as a 'happy ship' sailors put great store on such things. Well, *Renown* was really a very happy ship. That was the outcome of a great deal of efficiency on the part of the officers and ship's company. There was really a spirit of teamship aboard this huge vessel. We all were very proud to say, 'I'm in the *Renown*.'

I was steward in the gunroom mess – i.e. the mess for Sub-Lieutenants and midshipmen. Our staff comprised a PO Steward (Truscott), a leading steward and four stewards, plus two ordinary seamen who did the washing up and 'kitchen chores', although in practice we all mucked in. The mess comprised about 35–40 'Subbies' and 'Snotties'. They were a reasonable and cheerful lot – apart from the usual one or two who felt their positions!

In brief our duties entailed cleaning the mess plus all pantry areas and all the catering. The galley in the after gun deck sent the food down in dumb waiters and, as this was situated several compartments away, we had to fetch and carry everything – while stepping over two foot high inlets welded in all the water-tight door frames (to confine flooding in compartments). We worked in watches – port and starboard, half to each. Duty Watch turned to about 5.30 am. We were awakened by the quarterdeck sentry and you turned out of your hammock, lashed it up and stowed it, washed and shaved, and went aft via the quarterdeck flat, down one deck, through the wardroom flat and the day commenced. We really worked hard and at sea there was always watch keepers' work at various times which made for a very tight schedule all day. Also at sea there were always dawn action stations and sunset action stations, which meant more altering of schedules and loss of sleep, especially at dawn. These action stations would last an hour or more depending on the circumstances and no one was excused.

Also at sea odd alarms, e.g. aircraft warning, submarine warning and the like, would suddenly erupt over the Tannoys and everything was left literally where it was and we all made for our action stations at the rush. If the situation allowed, the pipe 'Cooks and Stewards Fall Out' would allow us to return to try and retrieve our own situation in the gunroom. This was no easy task and not all of us necessarily were 'fallen out': it depended on where your action station was and the need for personnel in some of them to remain 'closed up'.

My second action station was the after multiple pom-pom situated on the superstructure immediately above the after 15-inch gun turret and firing over the top of it. At least we were in the open air and could see what was going on. The pom-pom comprised eight guns in a single mounting firing belts of 2 pounder shells, a close-range weapon against torpedo boats, low level aircraft and the like. The rate of fire was high and to keep the loading racks full kept us all working flat out in action and having continually to sweep away empty cartridge cases from under our feet – usually onto the quarterdeck below. This action station became extremely hazardous when the 4.5-inch turrets opened up, the gun muzzles being on a level with us and could swing rapidly round in action causing us to dive to the deck to avoid the blast. When the 15-inch turret fired the gun became untenable and we sheltered on the after gun-deck or in the ready-use magazine, a form of steel hut aft of the after conning tower.

My main action station, however, was the after 4.5-inch barbette as an ammunition supply number in S5 turret serving twin 4.5-inch guns. The shells were about three and a half feet long weighing about 60 lbs, and were delivered to the barbette via mechanical lifts in the flat outside. In action we formed supply lines from the shell hoists to the guns in the barbette, passing from joist to loading trays next to the gun breech in an endless chain, each man carrying a round and depositing his shell in the loading trays as they emptied. The noise was deafening and when air raids were in progress, e.g. then as in the Mediterranean, almost continuously, it was necessary to wear earplugs.

In prolonged periods of Action Stations, during lulls, cooks and stewards were fallen out to prepare food for the ship's company. Usually this comprised inch thick slices of bread with thick slices of corned beef – 'Corned dog sandwiches'.

We in the gunroom prepared and supplied our own gunroom mess personnel and when prepared were required to deliver them wherever our subs and middies were stationed throughout the ship. This was a marathon task and we had it all worked out to a set plan. Some positions we 'delivered' to entailed unenviable climbs – one entailed climbing the ladders to the forward 4.5-inch directors in 'tubs' on top of high towers. All this became more complicated if by chance an air raid occurred *en route*. We still delivered our food parcels and then made it hotfoot back to our own action station.

Their first taste of real 'live' action came soon afterwards, and it happened in the Flow when the long-awaited German aerial blow was delivered against the Home Fleet. Since the return of the Fleet was obviously well-known to the Germans (their daily reconnaissance flights proved that) it was only a matter of time before the *Luftwaffe* paid a return visit to counter the abortive strikes the RAF had made during the winter months. That these British air attacks on anchored warships had proved both futile and costly to the bombers themselves, did not deter the German flyers from trying their luck now that the fleet was back within their range and their two specialised anti-shipping units had been built up to full strength. Accordingly, on 16 March a strong force was sent against Scapa Flow, consisting of sixteen Heinkel He 111 twin-engined bombers of KG 26 and eighteen Junkers Ju 88, twin-engined dive-bombers from KG 30.

In the Flow itself that afternoon all was peaceful as Charles Stuart reported:

On the Saturday afternoon it was fine enough to go sailing; after one false start due to an air raid alarm we were able to go over to Fara and lay a lobster pot for the flag lieutenant, not to mention having a look at some of the local ones!

At eight that evening the alarm to arms, air raid warning red was sounded off, to be followed immediately by a loud crash aft. In the chest flat the noise was loudest and we could tell immediately that the bomb had fallen in the water. Wondering where and when the next one would come was more frightening than the noise of that explosion.

In fact the first warning was received at 19.46 and at 19.52 three aircraft came in at about 7,000 feet and when over the Flow they split up and delivered dive bombing attacks on *Rodney, Renown* and *Norfolk*. Each aircraft dropped two bombs, and, while the attacks on *Rodney* and *Renown* failed, *Norfolk* was hit on the port side of the quarterdeck abaft Y turret. The bomb passed through three decks of the 8-inch cruiser and exploded near Y shell room blowing a hole in the starboard side underwater and starting a fire. X and Y magazines were both flooded as a result. At the same time an attack was made on the old training ship *Iron Duke* that was slightly damaged by three near misses. *Renown* was fortunate only to suffer a single near-miss as the fleet was caught flat-footed.

Midshipman Stuart recorded:

One hand was hurt, but this was from falling down a ladder. The quarterdeck was drenched and a few handfuls of splinters were picked up off that deck.

Norfolk lying in the next door berth was not so lucky and was hit on the quarterdeck. Her midshipmen's chest flat was hit, two midshipmen were killed, two were missing and one very seriously injured. Varied and conflicting accounts of the *Norfolk's* casualties are still being given. Having my action station in an HACP I saw nothing of the raid. As a direct result of the raid all three pompoms are now closed up night and day in harbour.

Bill Kennelly remembers how, when *Norfolk* was hit 'I had to take a party complete with portable pumps to render assistance, but there was little we could do.'

As the exploit of Prien and the loss of *Royal Oak* had shown up the weakness of the Flow's anti-submarine defences, so this raid and the damage to the *Norfolk* proved that its AA defences were still, after six months of war, woefully inadequate. Indeed the Admiralty considered that the fleet stood a better chance out to sea with room to manoeuvre rather than lying at berths and taking whatever the *Luftwaffe* could dish out. On the other hand the *Luftwaffe* pilots claimed to have inflicted much greater damage than they did, claiming that the damage to the old demilitarised *Iron Duke* and the near-misses on *Rodney* and *Renown* were all direct hits, which was not so. Such errors were common on both sides where airmen were concerned of course.

The sharp shock administered was, however, enough to make the Admiralty extremely reluctant to expose the full fleet to such attacks again until a more efficient fighter defence had been scraped up and consequently, when a few days later they got wind of another bombing attack on Scapa, they ordered the fleet to sea. Accordingly, at 14.45 on Tuesday 19 March, the great bulks of the *Rodney, Valiant, Warspite, Renown* and *Repulse,* with a screen of fifteen destroyers, cleared harbour. The weather was thick as they passed through the gate but cleared as they sailed out of the Pentland Firth. The only mishap was that *Renown's* paravanes stuck with their chains ten feet below the waterline when they were being got out. The purpose of the sweep was announced to the crew as a covering operation for contraband interceptions by the Humber Force in the Skagerrak and also to cover for a Norwegian convoy. The whole fleet was to sweep to the north of the Faeroes and Shetlands between the Norwegian coast and Iceland returning to Scapa on the 27th.

Although this sweep would take them well beyond the range of the *Luftwaffe* other hidden dangers were still awaiting them – mines, as the incident with the paravanes indicated, and the ever-lurking U-boats. It was not long before they had ample evidence of the latter menace. The first night at sea found the five great ships, the Home Fleet's greatest strength yet to sail as one body, heading northward to the north-east of Muckle Flugga. Here they were picked up by the *U-44,* which immediately shaped course to carry out an attack. Unfortunately for the submarine's skipper as the battle-cruisers loomed up in his periscope sight, the destroyer *Fortune* was on the screen. Her captain, E.A. Gibbs, was one of the best submarine hunters in the business; the late Admiral Sir Richard Onslow once told this author that he 'used to sleep with the ASDIC headphones on'. Contact was made. Captain Gibbs later described the incident in his book *Two Small Ships.* The sea was calm when they first gained contact off the starboard bow of the battle-cruisers and *Fortune* attacked at once, without waiting to verify her contact, as the two battle-cruisers turned away from the direction of the attack.

The first depth-charges crashed down and erupted in huge geysers of spray and water and then *Fortune* circled and came in again, dropping a second pattern in the same spot. By this time *Renown* and *Repulse* were stern-on in the distance well out of harm's way. *Fortune* raced in for a third attack when a huge air bubble, about thirty feet across, rose to the surface of the still waters and burst. The destroyer's Yeoman of Signals, himself an ex-submariner, had no doubts that it was the end of the U-boat and indeed all contact had faded away after the second attack. It was put down as a 'possible', but after the war it was confirmed that *Fortune* had indeed sunk *U-44* in this brilliant attack.

Apart from this incident the sweep was without major events as Charles Stuart's journal recalled:

We have sighted the coast of Norway once. We have also passed some neutral ships which were not investigated by us. The sweep took us within sight of the coast of Iceland where we experienced snow and hail, the temperature remaining about 30°F while we were in that latitude. After sighting Iceland the fleet turned south again.

On Tuesday the 26th the battle-cruisers did a night practice with full calibre 15-inch and 4.5-inch at destroyers. The destroyers went on ahead, turned round and searchlights were used with a certain amount of success, especially on our port side. This was the first time the ship had fired starshell and the results obtained seemed better than those obtained in *Repulse*. The interest in this shoot rather eclipses the fact that we had carried a successful 15-inch throw-off shoot earlier in the day.

While at sea we oiled the destroyers *Fortune* and *Inglefield*. On the way south the destroyers dropped depth charges on two contacts, apparently without any results. On the day that we arrived back at Scapa we were due to carry out an HA practice shoot. The shoot was not carried out owing to bad weather. And so we arrived back in Scapa with a blizzard as a welcome and yellow air raid warnings to keep us from making life too comfortable.

The ship was visited by Major Clement Attlee, the leader of the Labour Party who was later to be appointed Deputy Prime Minister, on the 30 March.

Stuart reports that on 2 April the *Luftwaffe* tried again:

At 20.30 'air-raid warning yellow' was piped, although this was not preceded by 'for exercise'. The guns had just reported closed up, but not lined up, when air raid warning red was sounded off, followed by the noise of pom-poms opening fire. The raid was carried out by eight or ten planes, which failed to do any damage. They were immediately engaged by heavy fire, which, if not unduly accurate owing to a certain lack of preparedness, proved a strong deterrent. It is now fairly certain that two aircraft failed to return.

The raiders came in from all directions and when faced with heavy pom-pom and machine gun fire they were not disposed to push home resolute dive-bombing attacks. This must be partially due to the shallowness of their dive, which may be explained by German reports that in crossing the North Sea they had been iced up. If these reports were conceivably accurate the pilots might not be sure of pulling quickly out of a steep dive. We have often seen our own Skuas carry out better dives on smoke floats. Their vertical dives under any conditions would appear to promise greater success.

That week was described as, 'typical for Scapa', with alternate gales and fine weather. Another great gale was in the offing on Friday 5 April when *Renown* again put to sea under lowering skies. This time however the elements were to be matched in their full fury by the enemy. The 'Phoney War' came to an end abruptly as the battle-cruiser sailed majestically and proudly from the Flow accompanied by a gaggle of destroyers and turned her bows towards the Norwegian coastline. Both Operation Wilfred and Operation Weser Exercise were being put in motion at the same time, and from Britain and Germany the great fleets were converging on neutral Norway for the first great clash of arms at sea and the opening of the campaign in the West.

Winston Churchill had long raged at the continued use of Norwegian territorial waters by German shipping, especially the vital iron-ore traffic from the Swedish mines via Narvik. The procession of German ships laden with this vital cargo proceeding through the Inner Leads, with complete immunity from any British blockade, infuriated him. In addition Norway was apt to be very one-sided in its interpretation of neutrality, as the *Altmark* affair had shown. Being more frightened of Germany than the two weak-kneed democracies, she was inclined to be more than a little careless in enforcing her neutrality laws in favour of the former, while squealing indignantly at any real, or imaginary, violation by the latter.

The desire to stop this flow of traffic had long been a thorn in the First Lord's flesh, but when the Government finally decided to send military aid to the Finns, fighting against a Soviet invasion, by way of force-marching through Norway and Sweden he saw the chance of coupling this act with his own scheme of mining the Leads and thus forcing the German ships out into the arms of the Royal Navy. Both ideas suffered changes when the Finns capitulated but a landing force was embarking on British ships in readiness and the minelaying operation itself was given the go-ahead.

On the German side Hitler had long nursed fears that the Allies might do just this and deprive him of his iron ore. This fear was played on by Admiral Raeder who wanted the use of the long Norwegian coastline to enable his navy to break the stranglehold of the British blockade; he was able to produce a Nazi sympathiser in the shape of Quisling, who claimed he had a large backing in Norway and would favour German occupation. Thus strong forces were embarked in German ports to make a lightning descent on the main Norwegian ports and seize control of that country before the British could react. Thus both operations were set in train. As *Renown* toiled northward in heavy weather that early April day, the German battle-cruisers *Gneisenau* and *Scharnhorst,* with the 8-inch cruiser *Admiral Hipper* and ten destroyers, were heading on a converging course. Both were bound for Narvik, the Germans to land troops from the destroyers and seize the port and hold it, the British to lay mines in the approaches to Vestifiord. A clash was inevitable.

The part of Operation Wilfred that concerns us here was for a force of four minelaying destroyers, *Esk, Icarus, Impulsive* and *Ivanhoe,* to lay a minefield across the southern face of Vestifiord between the Lofoten Islands and the mainland. They were escorted by the destroyers *Hardy, Havock, Hotspur* and *Hunter* of the 2nd Flotilla, which, after the field was in position, were to patrol their edges warning neutral shipping. To cover this mission, Operation WV, and another, simulated, minelaying operation further south, Vice-Admiral Whitworth sailed in *Renown* with a destroyer screen, *Hero, Hyperion, Glowworm* and *Greyhound.* Of these the *Hero* and *Hyperion* were to simulate laying mines off Bud in position 62° 54' N, 6° 55' E (Force 'WB') while another group comprising the minelayer *Teviot Bank* and destroyers *Inglefield, Ilex, Imogen* and *Isis* were to lay mines off Stadtlandet in position 62° 12'N, 15° 10'E. (Force 'WS'). The operation had been originally planned for 5 April but was postponed for political reasons to the 8th.

Since the four heaviest units of the Royal Norwegian Navy were reported to be at Narvik it was decided to cover the minelayers with *Renown* and the two Gs, while the 6-inch cruiser *Birmingham* and destroyer *Fearless,* already in the area on a sweep against German fishing vessels off the Lofotens, were also to join Whitworth's flag (Operation DV).

As we have seen, *Renown* sailed from Scapa on the evening of the 5th, with her screen temporarily augmented by the *Hyperion* and *Hero* for the crossing.

'The weather was very thick', recorded Midshipman Stuart, 'and the sea fairly high. During the first night three out of four of our escort of four destroyers were lost, returning to our immediate vicinity in the early morning.' But one did not.

In the worsening weather the *Glowworm* struggling to regain contact on the 6th caught up for a time, but then had a man washed overboard. At 06.45 she received permission to conduct a search for him and put about, her slender hull rolling viciously in the rising storm. She was soon lost to sight from *Renown* and no friendly eye ever saw her again.

She failed to find her missing crew member and completely lost contact with *Renown* in the very heavy weather. In the absence of any operational orders she therefore set course back to Scapa Flow on her own. On the evening of the 6th the Commander-in-Chief, learning of the movements of *Glowworm* and concerned at *Renown's* escort being reduced to one when the two minelayers left, ordered *Glowworm* to proceed north to position 67° N., 10° E., in which position *Renown* would pass, but on the 8th she reported herself in action with two German destroyers and, later, in contact with an unknown enemy ship. Meanwhile, as the lonely *Glowworm* cast about amidst the vile weather, Wilfred was proceeding in modified form. *Hyperion* and *Hero* were ordered back for oiling and, with her depleted screen, *Renown* continued her passage with the intention of meeting the *Birmingham*, *Fearless* and *Hostile* off Vestifiord on the evening of 7 April.

On this day the first signals were received indicating that German warships were at sea and an Admiralty message (A.T.1259) gave the clearest possible indication of military action against Norway and Denmark by German forces. The main body of the Home Fleet, which had remained at Scapa, was brought to one hour's notice. Following another message at 17.10 all units at Scapa were ordered to raise steam and the ships sailed at 20.15 on the 7th. Meantime *Renown* was already approaching the Norwegian coast in support of the minelayers in Vestfiord and *Birmingham* was on her way to join her. Force WS was recalled and the simulated minelaying operation was cancelled.

Renown arrived off Vestfiord in the evening of the 7th but she found no sign of *Birmingham* and her two destroyers. The 20th flotilla had joined up however with their destroyers of the 2nd flotilla, and these were detached according to plan and laid their mines between 04.30 and 05.30 on the 8th. Whilst they did so, the *Renown* with the only destroyer remaining on her screen, the *Greyhound*, patrolled in the area 30 miles to the west of Vestifiord and 100 miles from the minefield.

At about 08.30 that morning *Renown* received the signal from *Glowworm* of her contact with German forces. The position of *Glowworm* (65° 04'N, 6° 04'E) was 140 miles away to the southward of *Renown* and she with *Greyhound* immediately turned south and steered to intercept the German force at the best speed possible. *Renown* continued on this southerly course at 20 knots for the first hour but had to ease down later to avoid weather damage.

There was nothing they could do to aid the gallant little *Glowworm*. Her Captain had sighted first one, then a second destroyer, and had accepted the odds, even though the two German ships were larger and heavily outgunned his own ship. Both turned away, the difficult weather conditions and their poor sea keeping qualities, enhanced by the cargo of seasick troops, nullifying the advantage of their superior firepower. *Glowworm* followed them to see what lay beyond so he could report to his commander the exact composition of the German force. Too late, in the murk and wild pitching seas he realised he was up against a ship ten times his size, the 14,500-ton 8-inch cruiser *Admiral Hipper*. It was impossible to outrun her in the seas then raging, and knowing he was doomed the gallant Lieutenant Commander G. B. Roope, determined to sell his ship dearly, and firing torpedoes and all remaining guns, he rammed his mighty adversary tearing away a whole section of her side armour forward, before his little ship capsized, shot through and through. Her sacrifice was not in vain for the damage to the *Hipper* forced her to put into Trondheim, while the ten destroyers pressed on to Narvik alone. The two German battle-cruisers *Gneisenau* and *Scharnhorst* meanwhile had not become involved in this fight and gave distant cover to the edge of Vestifiord before breaking off to take up their patrolling positions further north.

The Admiralty naturally feared a break-out operation by these big ships into the Atlantic and made their dispositions accordingly. At 10.45 on the 8th the Admiralty ordered the eight destroyers of the Vestifiord mining force to join *Renown* and *Greyhound,* an intervention on the part of the Admiralty (where Churchill was constantly making 'suggestions') that, as Admiral Forbes pointed out later, resulted in the entrance to Vestifiord being left unguarded. This was a disaster of enormous consequences, for the ten laden German destroyers, instead of meeting the eight British ships in full fighting trim at sea, where they could have sunk them all and their troops, instead found empty water and continued up to Narvik unhindered to surprise the Norwegians, sink their warships by deceit and treacherous dealings under a white flag and there to land their soldiers. Thus the First and Second Battles of Narvik had to be fought at a disadvantage for the British which resulted in needless losses, while the German troops, though few in number, defied attempts at eviction by numerically larger Allied forces for weeks, until in fact it was too late.

All this did not immediately affect *Renown* however and, at 11.14, Vice-Admiral Whitworth received a further message which indicated that the preliminary message of German movements might well be true and that the ships involved would be at sea and moving northwards. Admiral Whitworth, presuming that *Glowworm* had in fact been engaged with a force *en route* to Narvik, decided that if he allowed the German force a speed of 25 knots, he could reach the line of advance by 13.30 and he shaped course accordingly for the point of interception. In the visibility which was rapidly reducing to two or three miles he began to realise that, with only a solitary destroyer in company and no air reconnaissance, his chances of intercepting were greatly reduced, and, with this in mind, he decided at 13.30 to alter course north-eastwards to rendezvous with the eight destroyers from Vestifiord. This concentration was duly effected at 17.15 some 20 miles west by south of the Stromvaer Light.

Before then, at 15.16 *Rodney*'s signal room had taken in another message from the Admiralty for Admiral Forbes, timed at 14.00, to the effect that a German battle-cruiser, two cruisers and two destroyers had been sighted by an aircraft in position 64° 12' N, 6° 25' E steering west. In actual fact it was the *Hipper* with four destroyers waiting their time to enter Trondheim in conjunction with the other assaults, and had been wrongly reported and identified by the aircraft. This red herring led to further complications.

It was realised that if true this force could have four objectives:

(1) It could return to base at once.
(2) It could be making for Icelandic waters.
(3) It could proceed to Murmansk where it might refuel from a tanker (remember that Germany and Soviet Russia were firm allies at this time; Russia did not change sides until more than a year later).
(4) It could be the force destined for Narvik either as an invasion force or as cover to an invasion force.

As the Home Fleet had various forces now at sea to the south of this reported position Admiral Whitworth conceived a plan, which would cover the position if the German ships moved northwards. This plan provided for a line-ahead patrol by the nine destroyers to the westward of the Stromvaer Light with *Renown* in a position some 50 miles to the northward. At dawn it was intended to form an extended screen and sweep southwards.

Then at 19.15 a message was taken aboard *Renown* from the Admiralty direct, (A.T. 1950/8) which was marked 'Most Immediate'. It directed Admiral Whitworth to '. . . concentrate on preventing any German force proceeding to Narvik . . .', an apparent reversal of their earlier instruction. By this time a full gale was blowing from the NNW and Whitworth saw that the weather situation was such that he had to keep his forces concentrated if he was to maintain his ships in a condition of sea-going and fighting efficiency. *Renown's* great bulk was heaving and shouldering her through the gale, but conditions aboard the frail destroyers were indescribable and it could hardly be expected that they could fire their open mountings or torpedo tubes in such conditions, when to stand up at all was a feat that took a man's whole strength and concentration.

Whitworth therefore ordered his squadron to alter course to 280° and this was done at 21.00. An hour later, at midnight, he again turned his whole force 180° in succession, but the destroyers found themselves completely unmanageable in the seaway and so course had to be altered more to the northward.

Earlier the C-in-C had detached the *Repulse* from the fleet with the 6-inch cruiser *Penelope* and destroyers *Bedouin*, *Eskimo*, *Kimberley* and *Punjabi* to go to *Glowworm's* aid. This was later countermanded and they were instructed to reinforce Whitworth's force while Forbes himself turned south with *Rodney*, *Valiant*, the 6-inch cruiser *Sheffield* and the remaining destroyers. At 22.00 the *Renown* and her destroyers were in position 67° 9' N, 10° 10' E on a course of 310° but reduced to a speed of eight knots owing to a very heavy sea and a north-westerly force 10 gale.

From midnight onwards the weather improved and after spending the night to the west of the Lofoten Islands, the *Renown* and her accompanying destroyers regrouped; a course was set to the south-east at 02.30 on 9 April.

Frequent snow squalls made visibility variable but at about 03.25 dawn twilight (the sun 6° below the horizon) improved the situation.

At 03.37 when steering a course 130° at 12 knots, *Renown* sighted a darkened ship coming out of a snow squall with apparently another ship behind her. This sighting was in position approximately 67° 20' N, 9° 40' E, some fifty miles west of Stromvaer Light. When first seen the newcomers were identified as a *Scharnhorst* class battlecruiser accompanied by a *Hipper* class 8-inch cruiser. The enemy ships lay broad on the port bow about ten miles distant, steering to the north-west on a course opposite to that of the British ships.

They were in fact the sister ships *Gneisenau* and *Scharnhorst*, 31,800 tonners each carrying a main armament of nine 11-inch guns and a secondary armament of twelve 5.9-inch guns plus fourteen 14.1-inch guns and having a top speed of 32 knots. The combined broadsides of the two forces were therefore heavily in favour of the Germans thus:

	British	German
15-inch guns:	6	-
11-inch guns:	-	18
5.9-inch guns:	-	24
4.5-inch guns:	20	-
4.1-inch guns:	-	28

The British destroyers never got into the action, but at first surprise, and the advantage of what light there was, lay with *Renown*.

Gneisenau, the leading German ship, had in fact spotted *Renown* a little earlier but was not sure of her identity; *Scharnhorst* astern made the first positive identification of *Renown*. Vice-Admiral Lutjens, in command of the German force, however, had no intention of pressing his gun advantage and his only concern throughout the action was to put as much sea between his two ships and the old *Renown* as he possibly could.

Renown maintained her course for ten minutes and then altered course to 080° and increased speed to 15 knots and, soon after, to twenty knots. At 03.59 she hauled right round to 305° so that she was roughly parallel to the enemy, with her A arcs just open. At 04.05 when she was just abaft the beam of the leading German ship, *Renown* opened fire at a range of 18,600 yards.

At 04.11 the *Gneisenau* returned the fire. She had not fired earlier having still failed positively to identify the British ships as enemy between 03.50 and 04.00. *Scharnhorst* in fact did not sight the *Renown* until she actually opened fire. Both the German ships concentrated their fire at *Renown* for the next ten minutes or so, while *Renown* for her part concentrated her main armament on *Gneisenau* and her 4.5-inch batteries on *Scharnhorst*, for all the good they could have done against her thickly armoured hide. The destroyers also opened fire with their 4.7-inch guns although at the sort of range at which the engagement was being conducted these weapons can hardly have been effective other than in impressing the enemy with their determination to fight.

On *Renown's* bridge, young signal boy Herbert recalled that little could be seen of the enemy other than their gun flashes. 'The visibility was very poor and everything was confusing at the offset; it was thought that we were engaging the *Hipper* in the beginning, and as we could only see the outline of the ships when they fired their salvos, this is understandable.'

Fighting the guns in such conditions was no sinecure either. John Shattock, RM, recalls his experiences during the battle thus:

I was in B turret shell room which was the lowest chamber of the turret; above are the magazines containing the cordite charges and above these the 15-inch Gunhouse. In the shell room the huge 15-inch shells were stowed in big bins and by the means of an overall hydraulic system and very large 'grabs' we had to hoist out the shells from these bins and transport them to the 'trunk' of the turret which contained the hoist lift up to the gun house.

As you can imagine in the terrible weather, the ship was rolling and pitching and we were being thrown about. It was hard work controlling the shells on the grab, which was suspended by wires from the track in the deck head. In the meantime during the chase the ship was ploughing into very high seas, and consequently the turret was shipping quite a lot every time the breeches of the guns were opened. I believe that A turret being lower, got more of this than we did.

In addition to this the stench of cordite blowing down the hoist was uncomfortable in the extreme.

In conventional ships X turret was the Marine turret but in the three-mounting *Renown* they usually manned B or Y.

Further down in the great ship as she raced through the gale in pursuit were Bill Kennelly and his 'DB' party. Of course they did not see anything but felt the guns roaring through the ship and the smashing effect of the great seas as *Renown* tore along.

We were closed up and nattering quietly when the Intercom crackled and – 'This is the Captain speaking. Two unidentified warships have been sighted and we are closing'. Next came: 'We are about to open fire and ship will increase to full speed.' The weather of course was, as usual, lousy, very heavy seas and snow squalls. We left our destroyer escorts far behind as they couldn't cope with the seas and in every sense it was all ours.

Renown was hit twice without serious damage. A.V. Herbert recalls:

The most vivid memory of that morning is as they fired the first few salvos one of the 11-inch shells went clean through our foremast around which of course the *Renown's* flag deck and bridge were built. That mast remained standing through all the squally weather, and was eventually I think, cut and the piece containing the hole made by the shell placed in the museum at HMS *Drake*, barracks at Plymouth.

Henry Shannon remembers:

They had two remarkable hits on us, one 11-inch shell passed through *Renown* just above the water line aft and went out through the other side without bursting. One compartment was flooded through this hit and one engine room rating was trapped in the compartment underneath. Damage control was of a high standard and the compartment was watertight. He was rescued later after the action when the holes were blocked and the upper compartment pumped out.

The second hit went through our foremast right in line with the 15-inch and 4.5-inch spotting tops, they sure knew what they were aiming for. That shell carried away the main wireless aerial so we were out of touch with the Admiralty for a while, but it was repaired during the action by the wireless officer; he was decorated for this deed later, and well deserved it. We didn't have a single casualty on *Renown* but our own fire from the forward 15-inch guns shook the rivets so much off our starboard bulge forward that 30 feet of it stuck out at the angle of 90° and this caused a terrible, second, bow wave. Our forward messdeck was flooded but the damage control party again pumped it out and erected a false bulkhead, which did the job for a time.

Bill Kennelly was busily employed as a result of this damage.

> One shell drilled a hole in our mainmast, the second clipped the funnel, while
> the third penetrated close aft of Y magazine, into and out through the bottom
> of the Admiral's wine store. Never have I seen so many volunteers to help the
> DB party pump out the compartment, all arriving with their suck-sacks, tool-
> bags and what have you and all subsequently gliding away forrard with their
> loot! I don't know how the Admiral managed for wine but we all did very well
> thank you, our DB section looked more like an off-licence. We returned to
> Rosyth later amidst a lot of bull, all good for morale, but it would appear that
> the sea had damaged us more than the enemy, umpteen feet of our bulges had
> torn off on both sides, and resembled giant scoops.

Captain A.W. Gray was just about the oldest-established member of *Renown's* crew
at that time, having stood by her since September 1937 as commander in charge of
the engineering department, and he was indeed her only officer during her first year
of reconstruction, until July 1938 when other specialist officers were appointed. He
had supervised the installation of her new machinery and tended it with care and
affection ever since. Now those engines, his pride and joy, were working flat out
driving the great ship through the heavy seas in full pursuit of the flying enemy. If
any doubts were felt about the performance of the old veteran with her new heart,
this action dispelled them. Indeed it was not her engines that caused her to ease up,
but the effect of her speed on her firing – as Captain Gray later explained:

Renown had to maintain a maximum speed of 24 knots to avoid the two foremost
turrets being submerged by the high seas; it was found that when she had worked up
to steam at 28 knots it was impossible in those conditions for the turrets to fire.

> The major hit *Renown* received aft passed through the gunroom bathroom star-
> board side and out of the port side above the waterline without bursting. This
> was fortunate as it was above the steering compartment and rudder head.

But if *Renown* took slight punishment, she was more than equally dishing it out as
well. Despite the conditions the two forward turrets performed magnificently. At
04.17 the *Gneisenau* received a hit on her foretop at a range of 14,600 yards and this
destroyed the main fire control equipment and temporarily disabled her main armament. At 04.18, with no means of usefully using her main armament, the German
battle-cruiser, using her secondary armament, turned to a new course of 030° with
the obvious intention of breaking off the action. To cover her consort, the
Scharnhorst crossed the stern of the *Gneisenau* and made smoke.

Renown then turned northwards and concentrated all her fire on *Scharnhorst*. For
an hour and a half until 06.00, there ensued a chase to windward. Weather conditions were deteriorating with a heavy swell and great seas due to the rising velocity
of the wind, which shifted from north-north-west to north-north-east.

The destroyer screen soon found that conditions were so bad that they could not
keep up with the *Renown* and gradually they fell back. The *Renown* continued to
engage the *Scharnhorst* but no hits were observed or recorded. Both German ships
continued to fire at the British battle-cruiser – the *Gneisenau* used her after turret and
the *Scharnhorst* yawed from time to time to fire a full broadside.

At 04.34 the *Gneisenau* suffered a further hit being struck on A turret near to the left hood of the rangefinder. The watertight hood was wrecked and flooding of the turret put it out of action. She was hit for the third time shortly afterwards on the after anti-aircraft gun on the port side of the platform but suffered only minor damage as a result.

Just before 05.00 the two German ships vanished into a rain squall. Early on in the engagement, the *Renown* had increased to full speed but after the turn north-wards, she had to reduce speed to 23 knots and then to 20 knots; at that speed *Renown* barely held the range. This, as we have seen, was in order to keep her guns firing forward; the Germans firing astern were not so affected of course and could hold their higher speed, thus gradually increasing the range.

When the German ships disappeared from sight, the *Renown* turned on to an east-erly course and again increased speed to 25 knots; but at about 05.20 when the weather cleared and the German ships were again in sight, they had further increased the range. The *Renown* turned once again to bring the enemy fine on her bows and opened fire once again. No results were observed and both sides persistently altered course to avoid the fall of shot.

Further squalls of sleet and rain obscured the target and although *Renown* achieved a speed of 29 knots for a few minutes she could not gain on the German ships and they were last observed at about 06.15 at which time they were well out of range of *Renown's* main armament.

Renown maintained her northerly course until about 08.00 and she then turned westward so that she would be in a position to intercept the German ships again should they alter course and attempt to break back to the south and home. No further contact resulted however, and we now know that Lutjens sped at top speed away to the north and then turned due west to the south of Jan Mayen island at noon next day, before making a hesitant foray south-east of the Faeroes on the 11th, awaiting bad weather in which to make his dash for safety. The Home Fleet cast north for him close in to the Norwegian coast but as they searched north-east Lutjens, concealed by poor visibility, slipped past to the west during the night of the 11th/12th and made good his escape.

Meanwhile, soon after 09.00 on the morning of the engagement, Admiral Whitworth received a further message from the Admiralty to the C-in-C (A.T.0820/9), which amongst other things directed that steps must be taken to watch Narvik; accordingly, Whitworth decided to concentrate his force off Vestifiord again. He ordered *Repulse* to rendezvous with *Renown* at 13.00 in position 67° N, 10° E, some 60 miles to the south of his position when making his signal, and he also directed the destroyers he had left behind (of the 2nd flotilla under Captain Warburton-Lee) to join him at 1800 in 67° N, 30° E. But in the event the 2nd Flotilla signalled that they had news of some German destroyers at Narvik, and Warburton-Lee signalled 'intend attacking at dawn', with which the Admiralty concurred (A.T.1240/9) thus countermanding Whitworth's instructions.

Around 14.00 *Renown* was joined by her sister *Repulse*, with *Penelope* and their destroyer screen; with a view to improving the power of attack of the destroyer force in Narvik, Whitworth disposed his force:

(1) The *Penelope* to patrol a line running south from Stromvaer Light some fifty miles outside the minefield and about 150 miles from Narvik.

(2) The two battle-cruisers to cruise north and south on a line about 30 miles further west in company with the destroyers *Bedouin, Eskimo, Kimberley* and *Punjabi.*

The *Penelope* was given leave to go in if required, as were the destroyers; the risk of thereby depriving the heavy ships of their anti-submarine screen was accepted.

Post-war historians question the decision to give Warburton-Lee his head to attack with only five destroyers at the First Battle of Narvik, and at the time Vice-Admiral Whitworth obviously had some misgivings as to the adequacy of that number of destroyers being able to tackle the German ships. (There were six German destroyers *reported* at Narvik; in actual fact the Germans had ten, all larger than Warburton-Lee's five, and, in addition, two U-boats were stationed there). However Whitworth reasoned that the Admiralty knew what they were doing when they issued their instructions. They knew the force available to Captain Warburton-Lee and they had given him ample discretion and so Whitworth came to the conclusion that if he attempted, as the man on the spot, to step in at this late hour with suggestions for increasing the number of ships to be involved at Narvik, this could cause not only delay which was undesirable, but also confusion. He therefore decided to leave things as they stood.

After the initial attack on German warships and merchant ships in Narvik, a signal was received from Warburton-Lee at about 06.00 on the 10th, which suggested that his destroyers were being chased by a cruiser and three destroyers. Whitworth therefore sent in the *Penelope* and his four screening destroyers with instructions to support the retirement of the 2nd Flotilla and to counter-attack the German ships as necessary. Warburton-Lee had attacked Narvik harbour, sinking several merchant ships and two of the German destroyers; his ships had also damaged two others but when further enemy units appeared on his flanks he was heavily outgunned. The *Hardy,* his flotilla leader, was badly damaged and ran aground, and the *Hunter* was also lost. On their way out of this trap they also sank the German ammunition ship *Rauenfels.* Both *Hardy* and *Hunter* sank at about 06.30 on the 10th taking with them their Captain (D) who was awarded a posthumous Victoria Cross.

At 11.16 on the 10th the orders to *Penelope* were modified and elaborated to give a clear directive to the effect that the purpose of the movement of the *Penelope* and the four destroyers was to establish a destroyer line to prevent reinforcements from reaching Narvik. Later still at 15.11, following receipt of a signal from the Commander-in-Chief, the orders to *Penelope* were to prevent the escape of German ships from Narvik either by way of Vestifiord or the alternative Tjelsundet.

Following this exchange of signals and a subsequent exchange between Captain Yates of *Penelope* and the Admiralty, the *Renown* and *Repulse* continued to patrol off the Lofoten Islands stretching some 80 miles westward of Stromvaer Light. An Admiralty report of a possible German rendezvous in 67° N between 4° 30'E and 6° E sent the two battle-cruisers further west to northward of this position during the night of 11 and 12 April. At 07.30 the two battle-cruisers joined with the main body of the Home Fleet which had moved north from the Trondheim area, in position 67° N, 6° E. After the meeting the combined force steered northward for the area of Lofoten.

All these signals and counter-signals did not improve the situation. Indeed at one stage Admiral Whitworth was forced to protest to the Admiralty that they had now given him three different objectives to carry out at once: to stop the enemy ships escaping, to prevent their being reinforced and to attack them. All this time *Renown* was hampered also by the tearing open of her bulges by the heavy weather encountered earlier. Midshipman Stuart recorded events subsequent to this:

> Before the action [with *Scharnhorst* and *Gneisenau*], the fore plating of the port bulge had come loose when speed was increased in heavy seas: this plating, instead of flapping, broke off. This, coupled with strained plates caused a lot of flooding forward.

By the afternoon of the 12th a number of important ships were detached from the Home Fleet and the C-in-C was limited to *Rodney* (flag), *Warspite*, *Renown* and the carrier *Furious* with a screen of six destroyers. Twelve other destroyers were working in the southern approaches to Narvik.

In the evening they were detached with *Furious* and three destroyers to launch an attack by her aircraft against the enemy ships at Narvik. This air strike went in as planned but met with no success; one aircraft failed to return and the survivors landed on at 20.30. Meanwhile the Admiralty had ordered the C-in-C to attempt Narvik again by sea. *Renown* could not go due to her weather damage, so on the night of the 12th/13th Vice-Admiral Whitworth shifted his flag to the *Warspite* after *Renown* and *Furious* had rejoined the main fleet, transferring in the battleship's cutter. During the 13th *Warspite* and nine destroyers attacked the remaining German destroyers at Narvik, sinking them all plus one of the U-boats. While the battle was in process the *Rodney*, *Renown* and *Furious* with five destroyers, cruised outside the Lofoten Islands some 30 miles offshore.

After the successful completion of this attack the Home Fleet, including all the four heavy ships and the carrier, departed for Scapa Flow in the evening of 15 April; in the forenoon of the 16th they heard that the 8-inch cruiser *Suffolk* had taken heavy bomb damage off Stavanger, and was limping home with her quarterdeck awash. *Renown* and *Repulse* were both sent to her assistance, joining up on the 16th and steaming at full speed to find her.

'After some time *Renown* overhauled *Repulse* in spite of the fact that she had been thirteen days at sea and was leaking fore and aft, while *Repulse* had just left Scapa that morning', wrote Charles Stuart proudly.

At 16.25 on the 17th we sighted *Suffolk* and escorted her home via the route between Fair Isle and Sumburgh Head, where *Repulse* left us to continue her journey to the north. At that time we were joined by the Polish destroyers *Blyscawika* and *Grom*.

Stuart reported:

> We arrived back in Scapa early next morning and proceeded to discharge empty cordite cases after which we started to ammunition ship, hoping that the ship would soon be sent to dock for repairs.

While at the flow there was time to count the cost. *Renown* had only one casualty from her duel with the two German ships; a young leading seaman by the name of noble manning the .5 machine-guns was hit by a pinhead of shrapnel, which entered his brain and paralysed him on one side. This grim quirk of fate spoilt an otherwise clean sheet.

But apart from this tragedy there was humour also, as Tom Oliver relates:

The Commander was quite proud of his piece of the *Renown's* hull which had been pierced by shell fire and duly had it mounted on a teak stand made by the shipwrights and, complete with brass plate, displayed it on the half-deck. As was the custom the wardroom had a formal dinner party on some nights in harbour – which were few – and let their hair down. The wine bar was never open at sea. This particular night, after the Commander had left the wardroom and retired, full of pink gins, his brother officers got to work. The plate, complete with hole, was placed horizontally outside the Commander's cabin, making a seat-like contrivance as only Naval ingenuity could make it. This, plus a chain dangling from overhead and a couple of reams of 4-inch x 4-inch toilet paper, brown, for the use of, completed the piece of classical naval sculpture. When the Commander was called in the morning at 'Scrub Decks', suffering from alcoholic remorse, he just about blew his top without the use of Andrew's effervescence!

Meanwhile a direct attack on Trondheim was being considered and the preliminary plans called for the use of the carrier *Glorious* with the *Renown* and *Valiant* as heavy escorts and anti-aircraft fire support vessels but in the event this plan was scrapped late on the 19th. Despite this *Valiant* sailed from Scapa to Rosyth to ship special projectiles for shore bombardment and *Renown* sailed with her. But the decision had been made for *Renown* to dock and have repaired the damaged bulges instead as recounted by Tom Oliver:

At 16.25 we weighed and proceeded from Scapa, bound for Rosyth with *Valiant* in company. Early that next morning we passed under the Forth Bridge, leaving *Valiant* lying below. We anchored off Rosyth and de-ammunitioned ship in readiness for docking. We were delayed in docking by a day by heavy wind and while we were lying in the stream three French destroyers lay near us. They were *L'Indomptable*, *Le Malin* and *Le Triomphant*. When we docked the midshipmen proceeded on twenty days' leave during which Germany invaded the Low Countries.

Thus did momentous events occur while *Renown* lay in dock and the face of Western Europe and the face of the war changed almost overnight for the worse. Her bulges were taken in hand and reset, but it was still a case of grafting new material to an old hull and they never proved satisfactory in heavy weather. Little other modification took place at this time. She had already been fitted with degaussing equipment on her return from the South Atlantic to combat the menace of the magnetic mine, as Bill Cain recalled:

It was obvious that one of the reasons we went into Devonport dockyard on our return from the *Graf Spee* hunt was to have degaussing gear fitted. Apparently we had lost a lot of ships through the German magnetic mine and our answer was to fit a cable inside the hull both sides and when charged with electricity they would render the magnetic mines useless. The dockyard wasted no time and soon got cracking. It looked as if we would be in dock for about two weeks and we got a week's leave each watch. This dock had just been widened and we were the first ship to use it after widening. After I came back from leave I found I was transferred to the dynamo section. *Renown* had several steam turbine generators in their own compartments and our job was to keep an eye on the gauges, check oil locks, temperature of bearings and keep the place clean. I found these compartments very cramped after being used to the bigger engine rooms. Also I was on my own being visited by a senior rating once a watch. We were however in telephone communication with the main engine rooms.

For the Rosyth refit *Renown* remained under repair until the end of May, and at the beginning of June she was earmarked with *Repulse* to cover the evacuation of troops from Norway.

We rejoined the ship on the 15th [wrote Midshipman Stuart], and left the dock on 19 May with a gunroom nearly forty strong. We had ammunitioned ship when a sudden alarm in the North Sea got us ready for sea. We moved below the bridge but did not go further.

On the 21st we went out to do DG [de-gaussing against magnetic mines] cali-bration trials and continued to do so until 23 May, when we proceeded to Scapa where we have lain ever since, having tried once to do a sub-calibre shoot. However we were prevented by fog from carrying it out.

The Home Fleet at that time comprised the *Rodney* (flag), *Valiant, Resolution, Repulse, Renown* and the 8-inch cruiser *Shropshire*. The carriers *Ark Royal, Glorious* and *Furious* paid 'fleeting visits', the *York* spent some time in the Flow and then went south and the *Newcastle* also called in. For the *Renown's* midshipmen including Midshipman Stuart however it was work: 'Training classes are hard at work and a landing party has been organised. So far one company has been formed and it is being trained and equipped.'

The amenities of Scapa Flow were sparse for the crew of the *Renown* at this stage of the war, as all testify. Bill Cain remembers that:

Scapa Flow never did have much of a recreational centre but they did have a canteen and cinema at Lyness. Because the Navy was expanding and because Scapa was going to be further developed as a bigger base it was decided that Lyness would be reserved for small ships and that a new canteen would be built on the island of Flotta for the larger ships. The question was who was going to build it? Contractors were doing more important jobs elsewhere so it was decided that the Navy should build it themselves. Every large ship sent a working party every day they were in harbour. All large ships carried ship-wrights who could do carpentry and welding. I cannot remember where the material came from but it did appear. You can imagine the conditions they worked under; today could be their last day because tomorrow they could sail for anywhere. Anyway by the time we finally left Scapa the foundations were well and truly laid.

As usual then the ships had to rely on themselves for the brief periods of relaxation.

'In the meantime the schoolteacher had started evening classes so I joined', said Bill Cain.

All large ships carried a schoolteacher but funnily enough they were called instructors! While we were at sea for long periods there was plenty to do. First of all you had your job to do and then just before dawn we went to action stations. Now and then the Captain would exercise actions and simulate an incident. After being on watch one had to try and catch up on some sleep depending on what time of the day it was. Also we had domestic chores to do in the mess and after that you had to keep clean by having a shower and washing your clothes. No baths or washing machines in those days.

Spare time activities were introduced during the dog watches, 4 to 6 and 6 to 8 pm, such as PT. In warm climes the Marine band would be sited atop of A turret and the PTI would lead us in a few forms of PT for about half an hour. Also the band would play for us now and again, serious and light music. In addition Tombola (bingo) would be played twice a week, also films would be shown in the hangar. When the *Renown* was reconstructed she was fitted with a hangar for seaplanes but it was hardly ever used as such however, it came in handy for film shows, Tombola sessions, lectures and the like.

The stewards had their own routine as Ted Smith remembers:

In non-action conditions life was very busy but ran to a well-defined and organised system. Six of us 'ran' the gunroom – one petty officer, one leading hand and four stewards and two seamen. We worked in watches as did the whole ship but with certain exceptions to suit our particular job. Cleanliness was supreme and we even polished the inside of our gash cans, even at sea. Sunday mornings was Captain's Inspection, which allowed no leeway, even if there was a war on!! We even polished the steel deck of our pantry with wire wool and we took a fierce pride in trying to outdo the staffs of the wardroom and warrant officers' messes in having a more spick and span pantry than they!

The cooks' and stewards' mess was situated amidships below the main deck, quite a way up and down ladders to get to our working areas. The mess was about 25–30 feet long and 12 feet wide, totally enclosed so we lived always in electric light. Space was very cramped and apart from sleeping spaces in hammocks the messroom seats and tables were also bed-spaces. I eventually collared a sleeping space between two huge fan motors in a 'flat' (alleyway) outside the mess where I could sling my hammock and considered it first class since I enjoyed the warmth from the motors – the noise one just became used to.

Shore leave whilst I was in *Renown* was mainly at Scapa Flow and Gibraltar. At Scapa Flow we were taken to the Lyness Fleet Canteen and on production of beer tickets and money, got pints of beer – so-called. There was quite a trade in beer tickets on board. Two were issued to each man going ashore and not all going ashore drank their beer and so they made a bit flogging their tickets to more thirsty members. The Lyness Canteen was an enormous hut and along one side were rows of huge barrels of beer, and I believe we could get several hundreds of sailors queuing up for beer at one time. It was quite a sight.

The trials that followed her refit in the Forth were initialised on 19 May when *Renown* oiled and ammunitioned ship, weighing anchor next morning and proceeding down under the Forth Railway Bridge where she anchored for the night. Next afternoon she conducted her trials over the DG range, escorted by the destroyers *Ashanti* and *Highlander,* returning to Rosyth that evening. Next day *Renown* conducted her further DG trials, passing the Inchkeith Gate under escort of *Ashanti, Bulldog* and *Highlander*. On completion she passed Oxcars Gate and anchored off Rosyth once more. A third run was made on the 23rd when she was pronounced fit for service and they sailed to Scapa Flow arriving that evening.

This routine was abruptly broken on 5 June when the fleet auxiliary *Prunella* sent a sighting report of two unknown vessels in position 64° 38' N, 00° 04' E, some 200 miles off the Faeroes. They were reported to be steaming at 20 knots towards the Iceland-Faeroes passage. At 17.30 therefore *Renown* was ordered to raise steam with all despatch and soon after, with the flag of Vice-Admiral Whitworth again flying aloft, she left Scapa and headed westward at 23 knots with *Repulse,* the 8-inch cruiser *Sussex,* the 6-inch cruiser *Newcastle* and the destroyers *Forester, Foxhound, Kelvin, Maori* and *Zulu.*

A later report was received from the *Prunella* that the vessels she had sighted had two masts and one funnel and were probably merchant ships and then there was silence. The *Renown* and her companions pounded north using the *Sussex's* Walrus to scout ahead but nothing at all was found. On the 7th the *Forester* picked up a raft but found no survivors. Meanwhile another scare manifested itself. The Commander of the Royal Marine detachment based at Seidesfiord, Iceland, reported that he had been informed that an enemy landing had taken place and at once *Renown* and her group swung round at full speed to reach that area. Aboard hurried preparations were made to send ashore their improvised landing parties to reinforce the garrison. On the 7th they arrived off the reported invasion area and the *Maori* was sent in to investigate.

She returned soon after reporting that all was clear and the Walrus from *Sussex* made a similar report. It was not until later that it was learned that the local mayor in Iceland, presumably having Nazi sympathies, used the opportunity to spread the rumour of the false landing. Whether he was so briefed by Germany to draw off the Home Fleet at this crucial time is not clear, but seems likely, for on 4 June, the *Scharnhorst, Gneisenau, Admiral Hipper* and four destroyers sailed from Kiel on the first leg of their foray to the north of Norway that was to end in their destruction of the carrier *Glorious* and her attendant destroyers *Acasta* and *Ardent* after a brave fight in which *Scharnhorst* was hit by a torpedo.

Meanwhile grave fears were being expressed at the lack of heavy ships at Scapa Flow, and the Admiralty decided that there should never be less than two heavy ships ready to deal with an invasion in the south of England. Accordingly the C-in-C signalled that *Renown* should return from Iceland forthwith and during the first watch the battle-cruiser turned south and headed at full speed for Scapa, escorted by *Kelvin* and *Zulu*. Ted Smith remembers:

The weather was unusually calm for the North Atlantic and a very thick fog came down, making us reduce speed. Only a solitary Finnish merchantman, the *Regulus,* was sighted in this fog.

Renown arrived back at Scapa at 06.00 on the 9th, and at 09.30 the hands went to Sunday divisions. Almost immediately afterwards a signal was received from the C-in-C to raise steam again, and hastily casting off from the oiler which had come alongside *Renown* weighed and proceeded to sea with *Rodney* and a screen of six destroyers at 12.00. The two German ships had sunk the troopship *Orama* (19,840 tons), [who was a sitting duck proceeding independently from Scapa to Narvik in ballast; eighteen of her crew of 297 and 2 gunners were killed]; but had spared the hospital ship *Atlantis*. The latter had complied with the terms of the Geneva Convention and kept wireless silence. Not until 09.00 on the 9th did she fall in with the *Valiant* and inform her of what had happened.

As other vital convoys were in the area it was feared a major disaster was about to take place but luckily the German admiral broke off his sortie because of *Scharnhorst's* torpedo hit and, while the rest of his force sped back to Germany, *Scharnhorst* put into Trondheim for temporary repairs.

Meanwhile *Renown* and *Rodney* headed northwards at best possible speed until the evening of the 10th. In the forenoon they met the *Ark Royal* with the destroyers *Ashanti, Highlander and Mashona,* and shortly afterwards were picked up by a shadowing floatplane.

'She shadowed us for some time, while we occasionally warmed her tail with single long-range shots. We were joined by a Sunderland flying boat and *Ark Royal* flew off Skuas. We remained at Air Raid Warning Red for some time until the C-in-C deemed the danger to be over', recorded Midshipman Stuart. This activity resulted in a signal that, '*Ark Royal* aircraft protecting a troop convoy on Sunday managed to prevent it from being bombed and shot down one Heinkel 111 and damaged others.'

The floatplane was shot up by the Skuas, and another signal, this time from the C-in-C, gave the position as follows:

> Three enemy cruisers and four destroyers are reported to be in Trondheim. I have no idea where enemy battle-cruisers or pocket battleships are unless included in the above. I intend convoying the considerable number of merchant ships and trawlers making their way back from Narvik and Trondheim, most of which should be slightly to the westward of us now. (1035/ 11th)

The next day *Renown* sighted some ships and the C-in-C signalled:

The party we have just sighted should be the northernmost of our children except for the *Walker* and her Norwegian convoy. We are proceeding to the eastward to try and give Skuas a chance of attacking German warships in Trondheim, flying off at midnight. (09.59/12th)

The gallant dive-bomber attack by the Skuas next day met with heavy fighter opposition and many were lost; one hit was made on *Scharnhorst*, but this did little damage as the bomb failed to detonate. Shortly after the surviving aircraft had landed back aboard *Ark* a thick fog descended and one of the screening destroyers, *Electra,* was badly damaged in a collision with the *Antelope*. Mourning the loss of the

Glorious, Ardent, Acasta and half the young dive-bomber crews, and nursing the crippled destroyers back home; it was a very subdued *Renown* that finally anchored back at Scapa Flow at 17.00 on 15 June.

After such high promise, the Norwegian campaign had ended in total aerial and military defeat and with two naval disasters. No compensation had been wrested from the enemy and, with France tottering on the edge of defeat in the south, the whole picture of the war looked very bleak indeed.

CHAPTER SEVEN

Force H

In those hectic days, as the Germans overran Europe and the Italian jackal came snapping in at their heels to collect any titbits that might be left over from France's defection and surrender, the events described involving the *Renown* off Norway in the final hours of our retreat from that part of the world became overshadowed. At home the evacuation of Dunkirk followed by the rest of the Channel Ports brought the threat of invasion ever closer. A great deal of bickering went on between the C-in-C, Admiral Sir Charles Forbes, and the War Cabinet about the disposition of his heavy ships, of which *Renown* was one, but Forbes successfully fought attempts to move them further south, maintaining that their best place was at Scapa until the threat of invasion became a reality, which, of course, it never did.

In the Mediterranean Admiral Andrew Cunningham, with the main Mediterranean Fleet based at Alexandria, Egypt, at once took the offensive and soon showed up the 'paper-powerful' Italian fleet for the sham it was. At the Battle of Calabria in July, the *Warspite*, last seen at Narvik, chased two Italian battleships up their own coastline and in several smaller actions the enemy were whipped back to port. In the western basin, a special squadron was formed based on Gibraltar under Admiral Sir James Somerville, to deal with the Vichy French fleet lest it come under Axis control as seemed very likely. Among the ships forming this squadron, Force 'H' as it was termed, were the capital ships *Hood, Valiant, Resolution*, three light cruisers, and destroyers of the 8th flotilla, along with the *Ark Royal*, all of which had but shortly before been operating with *Renown* off Norway.

At Mers-el-Kebir the Vichy fleet was crippled in an indecisive action; with the modern battle-cruiser *Strasbourg* escaping unharmed to Toulon, while other ships were seized or agreed to be demilitarised. At home the opening stages of what was to be subsequently termed the Battle of Britain were beginning, with heavy dive-bombing attacks on Channel convoys, which caused severe losses. At Scapa, the Home Fleet, deprived of many of its ships by transfers to the Mediterranean and the Humber, stood watch over the North Sea, ready to move south but always with an eye cocked towards the breakout of German heavy units.

For the men of the *Renown* this period of waiting and watching meant long periods of boredom at Scapa and brief sorties in response to alarms. For the members of her crew life went on as before with routine duties, exercises and limited recreation, as their memories reflect. Bill Kennelly recalls:

My only memories of this period are of walks, or tramps, around the paths and heather of Flotta, rare drinks in the canteen with the many old ships and very enjoyable concert parties, one of which featured Gracie Fields. She did not prove very popular when she announced her next song as 'Coming in on a Wing and a Prayer' featuring our rivals – the 'Brylcream Boys'. The RAF was not exactly popular at this stage of the war after Norway and Europe! Gracie had her way, saying we could like it or lump it! Those concerts were really something; Jack, you know, has his very own brand of humour.

John Roche recalls:

I was made ordinary seaman, and then qualified as a seaman torpedoman and moved into the torpedomen's mess, which was always the smartest mess deck with a marvellous crowd of messmates. My job changed from quarterdeck part of ship to electrical maintenance of the 4.5-inch guns, which was a very interesting job, and we prided ourselves that we never had an electrical misfire on one of our guns.

On the Sunday following their return from the Trondheim raid, the *Renown* lay at anchor in the Flow. Divisions were held in the forenoon and there was a Fleet sailing race in the Flow in the afternoon. *Renown* took her turn as AA guard and lookout on the Tuesday and the next day, 19th, she sailed and, escorted by the destroyers *Maori*, *Mashona* and *Tartar*, proceeded to the west coast of Hoy in order to carry out a 15-inch and 4.5-inch full calibre shoot in the Pentland Firth. These shoots had as their basis a plan to give defence against MTB attacks, and whether it was possible to spot for line and range simultaneously. This was with an anti-invasion role in mind in which case high-speed E-boats would almost certainly be encountered. The big guns fired four rounds each and then the range was closed to 4,000 yards and the secondary armament carried out a low-angle shoot.

AA firings were carried out against a target towed by a Hawker Henley plane, a sister aircraft to the famous Hurricane, which had originally been designed as a high-speed dive bomber for the RAF but they had spurned the idea in the 1930s leaving the proving of that type of attack to the Fleet Air Arm and the German Stukas. With a top speed of 240 mph the Henley provided much more realistic target practice than the usual plodding old aircraft like Swordfish and Walrus normally used in that duty. *Renown*'s results were recorded as 'fair' in this instance! They passed the Hoxa Gate at 13.50 to anchor.

On returning to the Flow there was a sudden alarm that had *Renown* abruptly turning round and racing out again up the east coast of the Orkneys in search of a force reported by the RAF as eight enemy destroyers and two transports off Burgh Head, with three further escorts off Deerness. This 'invasion fleet' turned out to be a solitary destroyer, the *Zulu*, and three British minesweepers, '. . . all friendly . . .', and was due to a garbled signal transmission, but it showed what tenterhooks everyone was on at this time. *Renown* and her destroyers were recalled at 15.00 and re-entered Scapa at 16.07, finally anchoring at 17.02.

Meanwhile, across at Trondheim, the *Scharnhorst* was sufficiently patched up to make her dash for home. On the way she was spotted by the submarine *Clyde* who attacked her and reported that she had scored a hit. Here was a chance to finish off the cripple. And on 21st the battle-cruisers were despatched to finish her off. Soon *Renown* was steaming hard at 24 knots, increasing later to 27 knots, toward the last reported position of the enemy in company with *Repulse* and a destroyer screen comprising *Diana, Forester, Escort, Inglefield* and *Zulu*.

Aircraft of Coastal Command reported *Scharnhorst* steaming south-east at twenty knots escorted by six destroyers. As they neared the point of interception at around 22.00 *Repulse* prepared to fly off her aircraft but before she could do so the squadron was attacked by three Heinkel 111s who approached at a height of 4,000 feet. There was a delay in engaging them due to an attempt to challenge them and the German bombers were left free to drop two salvos of six to eight bombs on *Repulse,* all of which fortunately missed. They then passed close over the stern of *Renown* in a perfect position to make a good bombing run, but probably had no weapons left for they made off under heavy flak fire unscathed.

Shortly after being bombed the force reversed course and headed back for Scapa; *Scharnhorst* was obviously well clear of her reported position and the danger of further bombing was not justified. That aircraft were not the only hazard was revealed when *Repulse* narrowly missed a floating mine, which she did not see until almost too late. Only an emergency turn saved her, the mine being pushed away by her bow wave; shortly afterwards *Renown* passed between two others on the surface. It was decided to stream paravanes and *Repulse* caused some delay by losing her starboard one. The squadron reached Scapa on the forenoon without further incident.

On 23 June came the announcement that the French Government had thrown in the towel; the reaction in the Fleet was that they had 'pulled a fast one on us.' But there was no despair; quite the opposite, the matelots' opinion of the French as a fighting nation placed them on par with the Italians. On the 27th *Renown* carried out a reduced charge 15-inch and 4.5-inch shoot in company with *Repulse,* the ships firing a concentration in alternate groups by sectors of a clock. Satisfactory results were obtained but it was noted that the *Repulse* '. . . is unable to concentrate with us as is the *Valiant*.' The *Valiant* of course had been modernised like *Renown,* not so the old *Repulse*.

Next day HF/DF trials were carried out in the Flow and an HA shoot was carried out at anchor, which was not satisfactory owing to the 'wooding' of some guns forward. Meanwhile great events were in train, which were soon to transform *Renown's* brief period of relative inactivity, but at the Flow life proceeded quietly. On the day that Force H pounded the Vichy ships at Mers-el-Kebir *Renown* was carrying out yet another sub-calibre shoot designed to exercise directors taking over whilst in action and in breakdowns. She also carried out a rare evolution, firing two of her port side torpedoes. During the afternoon further AA shoots were carried out at a Swordfish towed target. Prior to the shoot S2 4.5-inch gun fired off a round by accident while the gun was in the lining up position at 30 degrees elevation. The shell landed in Kirkwall Bay but was fortunately set to safe. On return to the Flow they found that the battleships *Nelson* and *Barham* had rejoined the fleet after earlier damage. And so it continued with shoots and bombardment practices, the starboard tubes were fired; the weather remained thick and rainy. Ships came and went, the 8-inch cruisers *Sussex* and *Shropshire* on 15 July, the latter still resplendent in her pre-war Mediterranean white. The *Furious* joined the flag of BC1 the same day and Captain Kirk, USN, the American Naval Attaché in London spent a few days aboard *Renown,* joining a growing list of distinguished visitors, Churchill had been aboard when she was in the Clyde earlier, and Clement Attlee had paid a brief visit at Scapa also. Constant patrols were made; on the 16th the *Nelson* called with the cruisers *Devonshire, Shropshire, Sussex, Glasgow* and *Southampton* but this patrol was marred by tragedy when *Glasgow* rammed and sank her escorting destroyer *Imogen* in thick weather a few days later.

On the 18th a lighter came alongside and took away the sheet anchor from *Renown*, other heavy ships similarly gave up one anchor '. . . in order to prevent their loss in action and to reduce weight.' Quite what substantial difference one anchor would make is not quite clear. By far and away the greatest weight saver had been her new engines and machinery, as we have noted, but as the war progressed there was a natural tendency to embark more and more equipment and the men to operate it, so any saving that could be found would be welcomed. The new engines not only saved valuable weight and space however, they also made life much easier for *Renown*'s 'black gang' – as Captain Gray points out:

> The rearrangement of the machinery spaces giving independent units was entirely successful and I would add that during the first two years at sea from the South Atlantic to the Arctic, Mediterranean to North Atlantic, in spite of the unpleasant conditions of heat and humidity, and the considerable period at sea, which necessitated being below deck for the majority of the engineering personnel, there was no tendency for the men to lose interest, fatigue was comparatively rare and their morale was exceedingly high.

These summer days at Scapa could be boring ones. Little else disturbed their 'idleness' at this time. The Admiral inspected the messdecks on the 20th, the 8-inch cruiser *Australia* arrived to supplement the growing strength in that class of vessel at Scapa the same day and another new addition, on the 25th, was the *Bonaventure* of the new *Dido* class of anti-aircraft cruisers, which had just completed her working-up period by escorting a Halifax convoy. She was without her X 5.25-inch turret, which showed just how shortages were affecting our new warships, even at this desperate stage of the war, a legacy from the 1930s.

Renown carried out further HA shoots on the 26th and showed her steady improvement by bringing down the sleeve target; and the *Naiad* arrived to join her sister *Bonaventure*, flying the flag of Admiral Commanding 15th C.S. At 16.30 next day *Renown* received the order to raise steam with all despatch and, at 19.04, she sailed from Scapa with *Repulse*, and the cruisers *Devonshire, Australia, Sheffield* and *York* screened by the destroyers *Punjabi, Mashona, Ashanti, Tartar, Firedrake, Fortune, Fury* and *Arrow*. They set course to the east at 27 knots. The reason was a report that *Gneisenau* was at sea off Trondheim.

The force, under the overall command of CS1 aboard *Devonshire*, was instructed to proceed through the Pentland Skerries at 20.00 at 24 knots and the destroyers *Maori* and *Zulu* were instructed to reinforce them early on the 28th.

They steamed throughout the night and next day patrolled off Norway, with a screen of Blenheims overhead from time to time. *Sheffield* boasted the RDF device (radar), which showed its worth by reporting three enemy bombers approaching but no attack developed. It proved another false alarm and the squadron returned to the Flow on the 29th at 07.30 after detaching *Devonshire* to escort a convoy. Here they found their old friend from the River Plate *Ajax*, freshly refitted at Chatham and also carrying radar.

Further HA firings took place against a target towed by a Blackburn Roc and a sub-calibre shoot was conducted with Y turret. On 2 September the last day of the first year of war was celebrated by a German attack on Scapa; some twelve bombers were overhead, but their attack was frustrated by thick fog. Further south the destroyer *Somali* was attacked in the Pentland Firth. Meanwhile the indefatigable source of future movements, the lower deck 'buzz', was rife throughout the ship. *Renown* would not stay cooped up in Scapa, the three-striped veterans nodded sagely and sucked their teeth; there was too much action down south, by which they meant the Mediterranean, for a top-class fighting unit like the *Tiddley Renown* to swing round a buoy. The younger crew members listened in respect, and indeed, so rife did this tale of a transfer become that Captain Simeon took the unusual step of addressing the ship's company about it. He stated that the 'buzz' season had started. Well, so had the raider season, and the reason *Renown* was being fully stored and ammunitioned was that she would be able to sail in pursuit of such a raider should one slip out into the South Atlantic. Far from scotching the rumour of an 'up the Straits' transfer the speech confirmed it for many, Charles Stuart recorded that, 'It is to be regretted that the gunroom remained sceptical!'

And so they might. Nothing could fox the lower deck and in the early part of the week storing and ammunitioning were continued to an unprecedented extent. By the time ammunitioning had been completed the *Renown* had taken aboard 12,000 HE 4.5-inch and 2,000 4.5 SAP shell; in fact she was so overstocked that shells were stowed in the bomb rooms and firework rooms. Fifty-one 15-inch shells were also embarked at this time, and on Thursday twenty spare 4.5-inch gun barrels. Final confirmation came on the 8th when six officers arrived on board who had transfers to ships already in the Mediterranean and the paymaster director visited ships in the Fleet. In fact the Admiralty had long made its plans for *Renown*. Admiralty Message 1700/25/7/40 gave the proposed composition of forces to operate under the overall command of the Commander-in-Chief, Mediterranean at this date as:

(a) Mediterranean Fleet
Warspite, Valiant, Malaya and *Ramillies* where the latter was to be relieved by *Barham, Illustrious, Eagle, Kent, York, Gloucester, Liverpool, Orion, Neptune, Sydney, Calcutta* and *Coventry* with existing destroyer force

(b) Force H
Renown, Ark Royal, Sheffield, Resolution and *Enterprise* with existing destroyer forces.

Admiralty Message 1950/25/7/40 provided: that on completion of Operation Hats the following movements were to take place:

(a)   *Hood* to replace *Renown* as Flagship of Battle Cruiser Squadron with the flags of Vice-Admiral BCS and Senior Officer, Force H to be exchanged on arrival of *Hood* at Scapa Flow.

(b)   *Valiant* to dock and embark reserve ammunition, high angle guns and other stores for Malta and Middle East.

(c)   *Arethusa* to be taken in hand for repairs preparatory to joining Home Fleet.

(d)   *Argus* to embark Hurricane aircraft for repetition of Operation *Hurry* (flying-off for Malta's defences).

(e)   All destroyers at Gibraltar except the 13th Flotilla (a Local Defence
Flotilla under Captain (D) De Winton under Admiral North, Flag Officer,
North Atlantic at Gibraltar, but free to work and supplement Force H's
screen as desired), to return to United Kingdom.

On completion of (b) and (d) above the following ships were to sail together
to Gibraltar: *Renown, Illustrious, Valiant, Argus, York, Sheffield, Calcutta* and
destroyers as designated in (e) above.

At 05.54 on 10 August the *Hood* passed Hoxa Boom and entered Scapa Flow at
about 05.94 when she then anchored. Vice-Admiral Somerville, the senior officer of
Force H, left the *Hood* at 09.30 to travel to London and his flag was hauled down
at 18.00. And so the 'buzz' was triumphantly vindicated once more!

The 10th and 11th were marked at Scapa by a howling gale, despite the fact that
it was high summer, and preparations for sailing continued unabated. On the afternoon of the 13th Vice-Admiral Sir James Somerville first stepped aboard his new
flagship after flying back from London, and later he paid a visit to the C-in-C aboard
Nelson. At 10.54 the Admiralty signalled that *Renown* was to proceed to sea toward
Iceland. 'At 16.40 we weighed and proceeded to an "unknown" destination,'
recorded Charles Stuart. She headed west screened by four destroyers *Bedouin,
Mashona, Punjabi* and *Tartar* through the submarine zone.

Before she had gone too far on her voyage south, however, and before she could
join up with the other ships, another alarm abruptly changed her plans. Another
invasion scare from Iceland came on the 14th and *Renown* was instructed to change
course and remain in the vicinity. Her screening destroyers had left her at 10.12 the
same day and she was on her own. To further heighten the tension an unknown ship
steering west was reported and investigated but it turned out merely to be a Swedish
merchantman, that was located at 21.10. Next day they also came across the AMC
Dunnotar Castle and, at 22.10, the battleship *Malaya* escorting a convoy of forty-
two ships.

Renown continued her lone vigil on the same beats, but orders had already been
received (at 0102/ 16th) to resume her voyage south to Gibraltar; the Iceland affair
had been another false alarm. The weather grew steadily warmer as they voyaged on.
At 15.10 they sighted the *Ark Royal* and destroyers *Encounter, Gallant, Greyhound,
Hotspur* and *Wrestler* of the 13th Flotilla, which had sailed from Gibraltar to meet
them, along with the cruiser *Enterprise*. That night a mock destroyer attack was
practised but next day the real war took over again.

At 02.15 on the 19th a shore broadcast was received stating that the SS *Rowallan
Castle* was being shelled by a raider. The *Enterprise* had earlier been detached to
investigate a suspicious ship and the destroyers were low on fuel and ordered to return
to Gibraltar and replenish. *Renown* and *Ark Royal* turned east and steamed at 26
knots to the AMC's aid, and at 07.02 the next morning *Ark* flew off a Swordfish to
find her. She found instead another AMC, the *Circassia,* which shamefacedly
admitted that the 'raider' was herself who had put a shot across *Rowallan Castle's*
bows, as she would not stop. Another false alarm.

At 12.30 therefore the two big ships altered course and made for Gibraltar being
met at 10.55 on the 20th by the destroyers of the 13th Destroyer Flotilla again and
the whole force arrived finally at Gibraltar 19.15 making fast to the South Mole.

They arrived to a hot reception, for that night Italian aircraft made two attacks on shipping and installations on Gibraltar. Radar reported their approach at 23.30 and again at 00.30 that night. *Renown* took the opportunity to demonstrate her many HA drills had not been in vain and made a fitting debut to her new station, as Charles Stuart describes:

> One plane made a wide circle from the south and came over the harbour from the north. The searchlights picked it up just before it passed over the harbour when it was on our port quarter. The plane then let go its bombs. Looking through the binoculars on the ADO sight it was possible to see the bombs being released, a very striking sight. The plane was being fired at as it went out to sea until, off Europa Point, a salvo from *Renown's* starboard battery burst very close. His tail was blown right off and then his port wing and he slowly spiralled down to the sea, held by the searchlights for some time, while the shore batteries fired some vindictive parting shots.

The second raider later cut his engines and glided over the harbour, and the search-lights failed to find him. His bombs hit the top of the Rock and started a brush fire near an ammunition dump, but it was controlled. Strangely enough Gibraltar town itself was not blacked out during these attacks, although the warships in harbour were darkened. The war had not yet really touched the Rock, but it was soon to do so. One wing of the bomber that *Renown* had brought down was later recovered and it was identified as a Savoia-Marchetti 82 bomber.

And so *Renown* joined Force H, a force soon to become synonymous with her name and that of her companions, *Ark Royal* and *Sheffield*. Although other ships joined the Force frequently for different operations it was on these three vessels, plus their escorting destroyers of the 8th (E and F class) and 13th (G, H D and VW classes) that the main burden of holding the Western Basin of the Mediterranean Sea was to fall for the next twelve months. They were soon to become a legendary group under the inspiring leadership of Admiral 'Slim' Somerville, himself a great character and well-loved by his team.

There were not to be many dull periods during *Renown's* time with Force H. Feasibility studies were being made of a dawn attack on Cagliari base in Sardinia as well as a follow-up to Operation Hurry with further Hurricanes for Malta and the passing through the Mediterranean of the reinforcements already mentioned for Admiral Cunningham. The staff conferences occupied Somerville's time on 21 and 22 August and he also visited the AA central control on shore to discuss defence against further air attacks.

While the Vice-Admiral discussed the immediate plans the ships of Force H did not lie idle. On the 25th *Ark Royal* sailed to carry out much needed flying practice at 07.30 with *Enterprise, Gallant, Griffin* and *Hotspur*, and after the Vice-Admiral had re-embarked, *Renown* followed her out at 20.30 that night escorted by destroyers *Encounter, Greyhound, Velox* and *Vidette*, also of the reconstituted 13th Flotilla. The F.O.H. in *Renown* rendezvoused with the Mediterranean Fleet reinforcements on the 27th and *Valiant, Illustrious, York, Calcutta* and *Coventry* arrived at Gibraltar at dawn on 29 August with *Sheffield, Faulknor, Foresight, Forester, Firedrake, Fury, Fortune* and *Greyhound* to join Force H.

The pressing need for fighter aircraft at Malta had only been partially relieved by Hurry and taking advantage of the passing through of the reinforcements to

Cunningham the supplementary operation codenamed Hats was put into effect, into which a series of sub-operations and missions were incorporated. The outlined intention of the C-in-C for Hats was signalled to the Admiralty at 1757/28/7/40 and provided for:

(a)   Force A: *Argus* with Hurricanes and her escort.
(b)   Force B: *Renown, Ark Royal* and escorts.
(c)   Force F: Ships earmarked to reinforce Mediterranean Fleet.
(d)   Force I: Mediterranean Fleet units.

The original intention was that on the third day of the operation *Argus* would fly out her Hurricanes and then immediately retire to Gibraltar. Meanwhile the *Renown* and *Ark Royal* were to make a detour towards the Balearic Islands with a view to getting into position for an air attack on Genoa.

Vice-Admiral Somerville would have none of this however and offered a revised plan by signal 2111/30/7/40 to the C-in-C which was that:

(1)   Force A should be abolished and instead *Ark Royal* should carry six to nine Hurricane aircraft on the flight deck.
(2)   That *Renown* and *Ark Royal* together with the ships earmarked for reinforcement of Mediterranean Fleet should sail from Gibraltar together and the aircraft should be flown off on the third day in position 7°20'E.
(3)   That Force B should then make:
   (a)   a diversion to distract the attentions of enemy aircraft from ships of Force F as they proceeded eastwards or, better,
   (b)   to stay with Force F until dark on the third day and then bomb the airfield at Cagliari.

Admiral Cunningham broadly accepted these amendments by a signal timed at 10.07/1/8/40 and indicated that operational instructions would be made out accordingly.

It was agreed that four destroyers should be transferred to Gibraltar to assist in the escorting of the reinforcing units as they passed through the Sicilian Channel. The four ships chosen were *Mohawk, Nubian, Hero* and *Hostile*, but unfortunately the *Hostile* struck a mine and sank off Cape Bon and the *Nubian* suffered two complete failures of forced lubrication of the main engines and had to return to Malta for repairs. *Mohawk* and *Hero* also returned with survivors from *Hostile*. The *Janus* took the place of *Hostile* and the four ships, now designated Force A, finally arrived at Gibraltar on 29 August.

The possibility of mounting pre-emptive air strikes on the main Italian airbase at Cagliari had been discussed at a staff conference held on 22 August and two such attacks were planned for the operation, Smash, to be carried out on 1 September, and Grab to be conducted the following night by Swordfish from *Ark Royal*. As a further diversion, in the hope of convincing the Italians that they were to penetrate the Gulf of Genoa, two destroyers of the 13th Flotilla, *Velox* and *Wishart*, were to carry out Operation Squawk by sailing to the north of the Balearic islands and there to broadcast fake wireless signals. All was now ready.

Naturally the Spanish were inquisitive as to what was the purpose of this large gathering of warships and, on 21 August, General Gandi, the Military Governor of Algeciras, paid a visit aboard the destroyer *Almirante Valdez* to the Governor of Gibraltar. He was met by a salute of nineteen guns, but clearly the Italians were left in no doubts that something large was brewing: During that same afternoon Somerville addressed the ship's company and later *Renown's* bows were turned round to face the north.

At 08.45 on the 30th the ships from Gibraltar sailed together with the reinforcements for the Eastern Mediterranean and Operation Hats was underway. Only the battleship *Resolution* and a few light units remained at the Rock and the harbour looked strangely empty within a very short time. Once out to sea the whole force split into two groups as planned:

Force B: *Renown, Ark Royal, Sheffield* with destroyers *Faulknor, Firedrake, Foresight, Fortune, Forester* and *Fury* (8th DF) and *Gallant, Greyhound, Griffin, Encounter, Hotspur, Velox* and *Wishart* (13th DF).

Force F: *Valiant, Illustrious, Calcutta, Coventry,* with destroyers *Janus, Mohawk, Nubian* and *Hero.*

The *Encounter* was an addition to the group.

The first scare was a submarine contact reported by *Fortune* at 10.23 but the contact was later identified as 'probably a whale'. Somerville had some confidence in his air defence as besides the two carriers and their fighters, early warning would be given by the modern radar sets mounted in three of the ships, *Illustrious, Valiant* and *Coventry,* as well as his own aboard *Sheffield.* At 21.50, after an uneventful progression, the two old destroyers were duly detached and carried out Operation Squawk that night. Although Somerville's biographer dismissed their value later, reports of the operation at the time stated that lack of opposition was due in part to their work.

In truth it turned out to be a quiet cruise in and out of *Mare Nostrum* that lacked any opposition whatsoever. The only sign of the Italians were brief visits by reconnaissance aircraft, as Midshipman Stuart recorded:

In the afternoon two Savoia 79 bombers hove in sight, circled round and went away again. The ship was in second degree of HA readiness and a fighter escort was later sent up. Two more shadowers came out and although we did not see them they were shot down by a patrol of Skuas. A tall column of smoke from one could be seen far away on the starboard bow.

And so, although the *Renown's* gunners awaited 'the ordeal with not a little relish', nothing further disturbed them during the operation. Nor did the Italian Navy make an appearance, either atop or below the waves, and thus *Renown* was denied the chance that Somerville described as an opportunity to 'have a go at the ice-creamers.'

Ark's aircraft carried out their two raids; nine Swordfish, armed with four 250-lb bombs and eight 25-lb incendiary bombs each, attacked at 06.00 on 1 September the airfields of Cagliari and Elmas being met with some flak, including 'Flaming Onion' projectiles that so lit up the area that they were able to bomb with some precision , a barracks, aircraft on the ground and some buildings were hit and four hangars were destroyed. Another submarine alarm the same day led to an attack, without result, by *Greyhound* and *Hotspur* some 11 miles off the port quarter of the fleet; at 22.00, the ships of Force B parted company with those of Force F and, after a relatively uneventful passage, rendezvoused with Admiral Cunningham's ships as arranged. Meanwhile Force F proceeded northward for a quarter of an hour, then altered course to the westward and- increased speed to 24 knots to reach a suitable position for the second air strike to be launched.

This in fact was done on the 2nd, nine Swordfish each armed as before attacking the same objectives but heavy cloud lying at 500 feet prevented better execution of this raid. After this peaceful foray into Mussolini's backyard the whole force returned to Gibraltar at 11.00 on 3 September, the first anniversary of the war, to find there the battleship *Barham* that was a welcome sight for she brought mail from home for the Renowns. Although a minor operation, Hats was a very successful one and set the stage for a great many repeat performances for the Renowns and their companions in the months that followed. Not all were to be so easy however.

Back at the Rock events were fully in training for the Dakar operation, Operation Menace. A large proportion of Somerville's strength was taken away from him at this time to help in this abortive coup by the Free French against a staunchly pro-Vichy target, but *Renown* was not part of that force and remained at the Rock. Meanwhile the *Gallant, Greyhound, Griffin* and *Hotspur* had accompanied Force B through to Malta to augment their escort and also to meet the destroyer *Garland* from Alexandria, which was to transfer home to be handed over to Poland. She had helped escort a convoy through from the east to Malta, which had been heavily bombed and *Garland* had been near-missed and forced to stop for a while in one of these attacks. *Griffin* took her in tow for a time until she again raised steam and all five of these destroyers arrived safely back at Gibraltar at 20.20 on the 5th.

Renown therefore lay alongside the dockyard wall at peace until 9 September with little activity to disturb her. Captain De Winton's 13th Flotilla, not at full strength, were the only other warships in port, although they were conducting routine anti-submarine patrols during this period. Aboard *Renown* itself life continued to a new routine.

On Friday a new AA defence routine was started, [wrote Midshipman Stuart] 'All HA personnel now sleep at their action stations, with a midshipman ADO on watch on the bridge. Should an alarm be given, he is responsible for rousing the ship's company and closing up the HA armament.

Opportunity was also found for the *Renowns* to relax a little. 'A number of gunroom officers were shown round the anti-aircraft defences of the Rock, being transported in a very dirty army lorry. This was not in any way due to lack of consideration on the part of the Army as this unit had left the flower of its transport on the beach at Dunkirk.' The method of fire control was stated to be '. . . primitive compared with that on board ship.' The new 40-mm Bofors however drew more appreciation; it was something sadly lacking in the Royal Navy at the time and was wistfully described as being 'particularly effective against dive-bombers.

They also visited St Michael's Cave and were taken to the summit of the Rock and shown the patch of scorched earth where the bombs had fallen.

Ted Smith recalls:

> Shore leave at Gibraltar meant going down Main Street; nine out of ten establishments were pubs, many with 'girlie bands' who conned you for drinks. They must have made a fortune in the course of the war. We could also buy many things not obtainable in England – notably silk stockings and other delights for our folks at home, and we used to store them in our lockers and post them home when we had enough money.
>
> The local port was cheap and we used to buy pint glasses of port and lemon for 6d [2½ pence]!!

Bill Kennelly remembered the strong ties the Renowns established with the Rock at this time.

> We had one very happy relationship at Gibraltar. The engine-room chief and POs had found their way to the sergeants' mess in the barracks occupied by a Canadian mining and engineering section busily occupied in carving out new underground hospitals etc. We all became good drinking companions and we were quite moved to learn at a later date that it became their custom to close the bar when *Renown* went to sea and only open it on our return, on the principle that 'we boys' couldn't enjoy a pint while at sea so neither would they. We returned the compliment in a small way by saving a tot of rum into a common bottle or two, and whenever any of them came onboard they usually went out on their ear. They were a great crowd.

Mr V. Holmes recalled some rather different memories for the *Renown's* ship's company, as at home the Blitz was commencing and many had their families in Plymouth, which was to suffer very badly later on.

> I recall the times when the mail came aboard for us, as it was the early part of the war and quite a lot of the chaps were getting news of their wife and family being bombed out of their homes. Many of the chaps put in requests for a home posting or leave as a result, but as you can guess these were all turned down as it was impossible to let them go at this critical stage and the important place Force H held at that time. But there was also good news from time to time, which cheered us all up quite a lot.
>
> I did learn one thing in *Renown* and that was to put my faith and trust in God. We had church 'compulsory' to attend, but I cannot remember trying to dodge attending at all.
>
> We also had quite a lot of happy times to take our minds off things in harbour at Gibraltar. On Saturdays when 'in' we had a ship's programme called 'In *Renown* Tonight' run by our Commander. This consisted of a broadcast in best BBC style to the ship's company, which was very humorous. Any chap who looked interesting was called to have a talk with the Commander in his cabin and talked about his job in Civvy Street when we began to get large numbers of conscripts; this gave an insight to the way the 'other half' lived and worked.

Some of the interviews were hilarious.

Among our other pastimes were arts and crafts shows, exhibitions and fishing matches; there was a thriving Ludo league with teams from all parts of the ship and in the evenings we had record requests and plays were broadcast throughout the ship over the speaker system. One thing I always enjoyed was the traditional pastime of the sailor, listening to the yarns and tales of the 'old sailors', the long-service men who had been all over the globe with a tale from each place, the 'Story Tellers' as we called them.

Stores Chief Petty Officer Charles ('Shiner') Wright recalls a host of famous *Renown* 'characters' that enlivened the lower deck during the war:

Characters? We had a legion of them; take for instance Torso the AB from Chatham Division who could lift a 140-lb bag of flour like a pennyworth of peanuts. He was later killed on active service after he left *Renown*. What a loss!

Then there was Tom Tealeaf, who thieved everything from everybody in order to keep his superior well supplied and equipped. I can remember him going into action singing 'Little old Lady, passed for Chief . . .'.

'Flash Harry', the HO rating. Spotlessly clean, a self-admitted East-End crook. What did Burns say, 'There is so much good in the worst of us'.

We were like a family in *Renown,* and like a family we always solved our differences. What a spirit the old ship radiated.

These peaceful interludes were few and far between in Force H but very precious to the men because of that. On this occasion their quiet period was burst into abruptly on 11 September when a signal to raise steam was accompanied by a great flurry and many comings and goings by the Admiral and his staff. At 16.30 that afternoon the great battle-cruisers sailed at high speed from the Rock escorted by the destroyers *Griffin, Velox* and *Vidette,* three others, still hastily refuelling *Hotspur, Encounter* and *Wishart* were due to join them as soon as possible.

This marked the beginning of the panic that was later to earn the title 'The Dudley North Affair' the vibrations of which continued long after the war was over, but for the bulk of the *Renowns* it was just another flap, cause unknown.

Our story is the story of *Renown* and her crew at war and so we will not do more than briefly sketch out the details of this unhappy affair, but as *Renown* was the principal ship involved some description of the events and those involved in it is necessary in order to understand why this nearly resulted in her first major action in the Mediterranean.

The points that need stressing on this unfortunate incident are that Admiral Sir Dudley North, Flag Officer Commanding North Atlantic at Gibraltar did not have Admiral Sir James Somerville and his Force H under *direct* command: the latter force, of which only *Renown* was present at the time, was a detached command and the Admiralty had often signalled operational orders direct to Somerville without consulting North every time. The destroyers of the 13th Flotilla, of which six were available at this time, *were* directly under North's command, although they were frequently seconded to Somerville to supplement his always slender destroyer strength. The second point is that the passage of a French squadron through the Straits of Gibraltar was communicated *in advance* by the French to their naval attaché in Madrid who, as ordered, passed the information to his British opposite number and he sent an 'Immediate' priority signal to London accordingly.

Due to an oversight in London this was not dealt with right away. When therefore the destroyer *Hotspur* sighted the Vichy squadron, which consisted of the three 6-inch cruisers *Georges Leygues, Gloire* and *Montcalm* and the three destroyers *L'Audacieux, Le Fantasque* and *Le Malin,* and duly signalled this fact and that she was tailing them, it was left to the initiative of both North and Somerville to do what they considered necessary about this situation. North's instruction had been that only in the event of war with France would inferior Vichy forces be stopped by his ships and ordered into British controlled ports; that situation had not yet come to pass despite Mers-el-Kebir. Furthermore in a further signal the Admiralty notified him that if French warships tried to force the passage of the Straits, then the Government 'reserved the right' to deal with them. North, assuming that the Admiralty knew more about the passage of the French squadron, or at least as much, than he, and receiving no instruction to the contrary, assumed that their passage was not to be disputed and all the French ships met as they passed through the Straits was the signal 'Bon Voyage'.

Somerville was of a like mind; on receipt of the *Hotspur's* signal at 05.10 on the 11th the *Renown* and the destroyer, *Vidette,* were brought to one hour's notice for full steam. Meanwhile North ordered aircraft into the air to track the French squadron and ensure that they did not turn north for the French Biscay ports. They did not; they were *en route* to Libreville in the Gabon, with the permission of the Axis, under the strict condition that they resisted any British interference with force. This did not prove necessary.

No further instructions having been received from London Somerville, after consultations with North, reverted his ships to normal two hours' notice to steam at noon on the 11th. The French ships were by this time well clear through the Straits. North had meanwhile signalled to Commander H.F.H. Layman of *Hotspur,* who had increased speed after her sighting to keep in touch, to cease shadowing and take no further action, and he duly informed the Admiralty of what he had done.

However in London the first that the First Sea Lord, Pound, knew of this passage was later that same morning when *Hotspur's* signal was handed to him. With the Dakar operation underway it seemed obvious, to him, that Vichy reinforcements were *en route* there and must be stopped, and indeed this is the (totally false) interpretation of their voyage that Churchill persisted in relating to the Commons later, and incorporating in his post-war memoirs. Although it was far too late for Somerville to do anything about it by this time Pound immediately alerted the Admiralty and they despatched a signal at 12.39 ordering *Renown* and all available destroyers to raise steam for full speed and followed this up after deliberations with a signal to Somerville ordering him to sea at once and to stop the French squadron going to Dakar if southbound, or the Biscay ports if northbound; if their destination was Casablanca no action need be taken, but if either of the first alternatives minimum force was to be used.

As the two other destroyers were still being fuelled Force H had to wait until 16.30 as we have seen before sailing, leaving the remaining destroyers to catch up. The French ships were reported at 16.00 to have entered Casablanca and in accordance with Admiralty instructions; Somerville established a patrol to intercept them if they should attempt to resume their voyage southwards towards Dakar. A patrol was therefore set up between Cape Blanco (N) and Agadir, but the effectiveness of this was marred by the need to keep his few destroyers close to *Renown* to guard her against submarine attack, and by the fact that inshore Casablanca harbour was shrouded in mist.

At 03.00 on the 12th the *Vidette* in fact sighted one of the large four funnelled French destroyers, and, on challenging her four times and receiving no reply, she opened fire. The French destroyer then retired at high speed behind a smoke screen, according to Charles Stuart's journal for the 13th:

> At 04.00 three darkened vessels were observed to pass down our starboard side in line ahead steaming at about 25 knots. As they were thought to be French destroyers of the *Fantasque* class we again went to action stations for the second night in succession and remained closed up until dawn. That day reconnaissance aircraft from Gibraltar reported that only the battleship *Jean Bart* remained in Casablanca.

In fact the French squadron had refuelled and sailed around 03.00 on the 12th for Dakar, where they duly arrived. The fact that French destroyers were sighted by *Renown* at 04.00 on the 13th but not engaged is an interesting one, which receives no mention in many of the major works that cover this affair. Shortage of fuel for his seven ships forced Somerville to return to Gibraltar at 01.00 where they all *(Renown, Hotspur, Griffin, Encounter, Wishart, Velox* and *Vidette)* arrived later that day*.

Whether in fact the arrival of the three Vichy destroyers and the cruisers stiffened the resistance or will to fight of the Dakar garrison is debatable; it *was* probably a morale-booster if not decisive. The Menace operation was probably foredoomed anyway and was badly organised.

The subsequent allegation that North was sacked as a scapegoat for the Dakar fiasco had been found not proven by the major historians and really is outside the scope of this book; but certainly the failure of North to take more positive steps (as the Admiralty saw it), despite the confused chain of command, the ambiguous nature of his instructions and the lack of decisive rulings, was one major nail in his coffin and he was removed.

Nor did Admiral Somerville improve his relationship vis-à-vis the Admiralty or the Premier with his unselfish defence of North and willingness to accept the blame, if there was any, for the passage of the French squadron. Somerville was in no doubt that had it come to a fight he would have been at a grave disadvantage and might well have been defeated and in this he had the general support of most historians. At first sight it might seem strange that the *Renown* with six 15-inch guns and twenty 4.5-inch guns, heavy armour and with a screen of three, albeit mixed, destroyers should be outfought by three light cruisers and three destroyers. It must be remembered in making a balance that all the French ships, though lacking armour protection, were much faster than most of the British ships, the French destroyers being credited with 40 knots plus. *Hotspur, Griffin* and *Encounter* were faster than the three French 6-inch cruisers but only mounted four single 4.7-inch guns and

---

* The incidents *are* mentioned in Mordal, Jacques: *La Bataille de Dakar* (Ozanne, 1957). But see my book *Action Imminent* (William Kimber, London, 1980), for the full details.

torpedo tubes against the French destroyers' much larger batteries of 5.4-inch guns and nine torpedo tubes; in fact the French destroyers were almost in the light cruiser class themselves. Nor would there have been any lack of fighting quality; many of the Vichy seamen would have welcomed the opportunity to avenge Mers-el-Kebir even if they went down fighting. *Renown's* 15-inch guns might have decided the issue if the Vichy ships could have been kept at arm's length, but if not then the issue would have been a close one.

Perhaps then it is just as well that it did not come to the test. The crippling, or even possible loss, through torpedo attack, of the *Renown* at this juncture of the war would have been a terrible blow, especially as the *Resolution* was damaged by torpedo off Dakar soon after.

Perhaps the last word should be left to someone who was there at the time; the late Captain F.S. De Winton, commanding the 13th Flotilla, was with North and Somerville at this period. He told me that:

> I think Somerville has been largely misquoted when the impression is given that he took a gloomy view of his chances with a rather limited destroyer screen. The situation of a possible confrontation in the Strait of Gibraltar had been much considered by Admirals North and Somerville and it was rightly felt that any such scramble in such a confined space was neither seamanlike nor desirable.
>
> Knowing Admiral Somerville quite well I am quite sure he would never have refused an engagement; we always agreed that someone might get hurt and if a fight was needed then it should be well out to sea.

Having arrived back at Gibraltar from this fruitless pursuit late on the 14th there followed a quick refuelling but little rest. The *Renown* was turned bows-on to the entrance, alongside the mole, in her usual berth and remained at two hours' notice to steam. At 01.30 hands were called and they prepared to sail once more, slipping at 03.40 in order to conduct a further patrol off Casablanca with the *Vidette* and *Wrestler* as escort.

Captain F.S. De Winton, RN, wrote:

> During the forenoon of the 17 September the *Vidette* reported she had a sick man aboard and arrangements were made to transfer him to *Renown* for urgent treatment. There followed a neat piece of seamanship. 'The manoeuvre was carried out very smoothly in only six minutes in spite of the fact that there was sufficient swell on to make it slightly uncomfortable for *Vidette*.

The two old destroyers were relieved on patrol the next day by *Firedrake* and *Gallant*. As always on these patrols, opportunity was taken to conduct the standard exercises, *Renown* fired smoke bursts to give the destroyers AA practice and next day she carried out a full-calibre throw-off shoot at the *Gallant*. The 15s marred a good practice when there were failures and mistakes in the TS, the range not being found until the ammunition had been expended. During the bright moonlit night that followed both destroyers enlivened the hours by depth charging several possible submarine contacts.

Meanwhile Somerville had been asking just why he was stooging about off West Africa and, when told by the Admiralty that the Menace Operation was underway and that the *Renown* was to prevent further French ships from reinforcing those already at Dakar he made the point that this could be better done by being at instant readiness at Gibraltar than roaming the wide seas open to U-boat attack. At 07.15 on the 19th *Renown* nosed in through Gibraltar breakwater once more.

Three quiet days passed thus while the Dakar operation dragged on to its humiliating close and failure, and then Vichy 'honour' again touched raw was avenged by heavy and prolonged air attacks on Gibraltar. These retaliations were not unexpected of course. From 01.00 on the 24th *Renown* had her HA armament closed up at action stations in readiness. At 12.30 a 'Levanter' was blowing giving broken cloud cover between 10 and 12,000 feet above the harbour, and taking advantage of this the Vichy Glenn Martin bombers commenced their attacks in wave after wave bombing through the cloud, thus presenting little or no targets for the guns to get their teeth into. The attacks lasted until 14.45 during which time the French bombers made twenty attacks dropping 150 heavy bombs; twelve fell in the harbour dockyard and twenty in the harbour itself, fifty-five ashore and seventy-five in the Bay, but hardly any physical damage was done. Nonetheless it was far from pleasant being a stationary target, and *Renown* was near missed by two of these heavy bombs. Midshipman Stuart recorded his impressions:

> The most striking is when a stick of bombs starts to fall out in the bay and advances majestically towards the ship. As it approaches the whistle of the falling bombs becomes louder and the feeling that the next one is destined for you and only you becomes more and more insistent. A cloud of dust and debris is thrown up from somewhere aft the catapult deck and you wonder if we have been hit. All this time the 4.5s are firing in barrage broadside. The heat and smoke and noise would, in cold blood, be overpowering, but in a raid they pass almost unnoticed save for their reassuring influence.
>
> The sound of a plane diving out of the sun was another, which made us wonder whether or not it would be *Renown's* turn next. A few minutes before the all-clear was sounded we started to prepare for sea and we were under way at 15.30. We turned eastward, sped on our way by loud cheers from the soldiers on the jetty.

David Divine later recalled how *Renown* went through the breakwater with all her light guns blazing, an unforgettable sight. Gaining sea room in which to fight back *Renown* steamed up the Spanish coast until nightfall when she turned westward to pass through the Straits. As dusk fell reports came in that the Vichy warships were also on the move and sure enough the *Wishart* and *Wrestler* were attacked by the destroyers *Épée*, *Fleuret*, *Fougeux* and *Frondeur* from Casablanca but they drove them off eastward. *Renown* did not make contact, although they remained closed up at their action stations from 20.30 to 01.30 at the end of a very long day.

Renown remained on patrol in the Atlantic until the 28th and while they were away further severe air attacks took place by the French. The only warship in harbour, the destroyer, *Firedrake,* shot down one attacker, while the only casualty was the trawler *Stella Sirius* bombed and sunk next door to *Renown's* normal berth alongside the mole. As further entertainment a signal was received that six Italian submarines were going to attempt to force the Straits that night. *Renown's* escorting destroyers *Encounter* and *Griffin* had been relieved by *Firedrake* and *Wrestler* and, when at 10.00 on the morning of the 28th a lookout aboard *Renown* sighted a submarine on the surface, these two ships carried out a series of attacks which produced a pool of oil but no defined 'kill' as such.

Renown arrived back at the Rock at 18.30, refuelled, remained at HA readiness throughout the night and sailed again soon after 07.15 next morning. Their quarry this time was the Vichy battleship *Richelieu* that, it was thought by the Admiralty, might be at sea trying to regain a French Biscay port after her damage at Dakar earlier. Two large French destroyers were sighted soon afterwards; they increased speed at once but *Renown* and her screen made no attempt to interfere with them and they vanished to the westward. During the forenoon Somerville broadcast to the ship's company, giving them a summary of the situation as he saw it and of *Renown's* important place in it.

Despite the strain he was undergoing at these fruitless patrols and missions against the Vichy, which he hated, Somerville managed to show flashes of his famous humour from time to time. During the 29th the over-eager destroyers of the screen several times mistook the planet Venus that was clearly overhead, for an aircraft and 'invited us to open fire on her'. After the third such report Somerville made a caustic signal to them referring to, '. . . spots before the eyes or Film Stars'.

It became clear that *Richelieu* had not in fact sailed, but a new alarm kept *Renown* at sea. A report was received that two German troop transports had been sighted in the south-east corner of the Bay of Biscay, it was thought that an invasion of the Azores might be afoot. The *Renown* and her four destroyers were therefore diverted to patrol in the vicinity of these islands and the destroyers were sent in two at a time to patrol off the potential landing beaches. During the afternoon of the 1 October each destroyer in turn closed *Renown's* quarterdeck and had these sealed orders passed over to her. That night the Azores were in sight on *Renown's* starboard beam and she increased speed to 24 knots and started a heavy zigzag until nightfall to forestall any U-boats that might be in covering positions.

Next day *Hotspur* and *Firedrake* were refuelled then went back on patrol and this patient marking-time continued until the 3rd when all the ships rejoined and course was set back to Gibraltar where they arrived on the 6th at 08.15. This arrival marked a total of 15,000 miles steamed by *Renown* since 13 August, all of it fruitless. Such heavy spates of sea-time again showed up the defects of her bulges and it was found at Gibraltar that forward plating on the starboard side had again sprung and once more repairs were necessary. This occupied them throughout the 8th and 9th. *Renown* was given an 8-degree list to port and the bulge was patched up with cement. On the 10th they embarked some 1,000 rounds of 4.5-inch HE to replace that shot off during the Vichy air raids. Then the manoeuvring valve was found faulty and the ship went to twelve hours' notice to steam while it was stripped down.

They were off again on the 11th, sailing at 05.15 for further patrols in the same areas. One of the destroyers was detached on the 12th to search for survivors from a Yugoslav merchant ship, which had been torpedoed in trying to run the blockade. She was located and her captain, being pro-Nazi, was 'looked after carefully'. Events on this patrol included meeting a troop convoy of two liners escorted by the *Greyhound*, which suddenly appeared out of thick mist. On the 14th they sighted the Vichy destroyer *Fleuret* exchanging only signals not shells; they arrived back at Gibraltar at 10.30 to find their old companion *Sheffield* was back. Next day the troop convoy arrived followed by the battleship *Barham,* the 8-inch cruiser *Australia,* and most of the missing 8th Destroyer Flotilla destroyers back from Dakar. The battle-ship went straight into dock on the 16th for repairs. Aboard *Renown* the crew were mustered and addressed by Sir Samuel Hoare. He was followed by Somerville who made a short speech. On the 23rd the hospital ship *Somersetshire* arrived bringing welcome and long overdue mail, and another addition at this time was Lieutenant Commander A.D. Clark, US Navy, who joined *Renown* as a naval observer.

As well as inflicting further weather damage on her hull these long periods of Atlantic patrolling had showed another defect, not in *Renown* herself but in the Royal Navy generally. This was the limited endurance of the ships themselves. *Renown* herself had been much improved of course during her great rebuilding but even the most modern destroyers in the fleet only had a range of about two-thirds of those joining the American or Japanese navies at this period. The need for a constant screen against submarines could not be ignored, save in the direst emergencies, and there-fore the whole fleet was tied to the endurance of the flotilla craft.

The Germans and Americans, and to some extent the Japanese, had overcome this problem by the effective development of a highly efficient fleet fuelling and store 'train'. Large, fast tankers put to sea, effected a rendezvous and topped the ships up enabling them to stay out for weeks at a time whereas the average British squadron was in trouble after three days. It was a point noticed by Churchill of course; the *Scharnhorst* and *Gneisenau* and the pocket battleships roamed the high seas at will without a single friendly base to fall back on outside Europe, while the hunting British ships constantly had to withdraw and top up. Fuelling of destroyers from the larger ships had been practised for many years. Experiments had been conducted at Scapa Flow in 1917 and we have recounted Captain De Winton's experiences between the wars with his ships and *Renown;* but the equipment of the Fleet Auxiliary tankers did not lend itself for prolonged operations on the German scale until specialty built, manned and equipped craft joined the fleet, but these always remained very few and far between.

The RFA *Orangeleaf* for example had been sent out unescorted from Gibraltar to top up *Renown* on her last sortie but was not used; further experiments in order to find the best way she could be utilised were conducted while *Renown* was berthed alongside the Gibraltar mole at this time, with the tanker (or oiler in naval parlance) made fast ahead of her.

Nor was her fuelling from the base itself always a marked success as Bill Kennelly recalls:

Fuelling in Gib. was another of those slow endurance tests. Once started it was a case of phoning through to the Rock and they would then put on the booster pumps. The essential thing was to phone the base in plenty of time so they could stop the booster pumps and restart the gravity. Most times a local Gibraltarian performed the task but on one occasion we had to provide one of our leading stokers. Somehow or other he fell down on the job; we were at the topping-up stage on the last few tanks and easing down on the filling valves and thinking we had got the message through. Disaster struck. The large copper pipes from shore to ship burst and its open end was swinging in an arc of 180° rapidly changing *Renown's* upper works, funnels, bridge and decks into an overall brown colour while our famous leading stoker was on the jetty helpless with laughter instead of shutting down the valve! It takes all sorts no doubt!

During the forenoon of 30 October the men on *Renown* were shaken by a myste-rious explosion, which took place just outside the southern boom. Speculation was rife as to its cause. All anti-submarine precautions were taken including the despatch of the duty destroyer and armed picket boats but nothing came to light. Midshipman Stuart recorded:

> No theories as to the cause of the explosion have yet been officially advanced, but either a submarine may have fired torpedoes at the boom or a long delay-action bomb may have blown up. The unofficial theory of the one-man torpedo is also rife.

This latter guess was the correct one. The Italians had used similar methods during World War I and had sunk an Austrian battleship. It was to be expected that they would try their hands again and in fact between 27 and 30 October the Italian submarine *Scire* had launched three of their *Maiali* human torpedoes against Gibraltar harbour but none of them were successful this time. They were to return however and later scored some outstanding successes there, as we will see; they later badly damaged two battleships at Alexandria towards the end of 1941 despite their methods being by then well known.

Another brief sortie took place on 31 October when *Renown* sailed at 08.15 in company with *Barham,* and a destroyer screen, *Faulknor, Forester, Fortune, Firedrake, Gallant, Greyhound* and *Griffin,* to patrol along the west coast of Morocco after reports of suspicious movements by the Vichy were received. Four French destroyers were reported coming through the Straits *en route* to Dakar or Casablanca and they were tracked south from Cape Spartel but were not intercepted.

A submarine contact came at sunset and attacks were made without result and in the late afternoon at 17.00 *Renown* carried out a 15-inch full calibre shoot on the *Barham,* which was then returned. In the darkness a night encounter exercise was practised from 20.00 onward, the screening destroyers making two torpedo runs and the heavy ships replying with starshell. By 10.30 on 1 November the squadron was back at Gibraltar once more.

They had five days without incident save a submarine alarm and then, in the after-noon of the 5th, the Captain spoke to the ship's company. He stressed that secrecy about service matters had to be observed strictly when ashore. 'A secret leaking out in Gibraltar would be known in Rome two hours later', he told them. It was not hard to guess that something big was in the wind and this the Captain confirmed telling the crew that ships would be arriving within the next few days and no theories or rumours about their future operations were to be discussed.

But the next alarm was an unexpected one for, early next day following the receipt of reports of an attack by the pocket battleship *Admiral Scheer* on Convoy HX 84, gallantly defended to the last by the AMC *Jervis Bay,* the Admiralty ordered Admiral Somerville to transfer his flag to the *Ark Royal* for the impending Mediterranean operation and despatch *Renown* into the Atlantic to cover the homeward-bound convoys in the Gibraltar area. *Scheer* had been reported by CS 15 at 17.15 in mid-Atlantic and *Renown's* job was to cover three northbound convoys through the danger zone.

They slipped at 04.00/6th and headed north. At 08.40 they sighted *Ark Royal* with the cruisers *Berwick* and *Glasgow* with a convoy heading south; included in the merchantmen was the French liner *Pasteur* and the destroyers *Duncan, Foxhound* and *Isis*. Soon after this two smoke candles were let off by the submarine *Utmost*, which surfaced rather inopportunely in the middle of this assembly. One of *Renown's* screen, *Encounter,* naturally took her for a U-boat and turned at full speed to ram, discovered her mistake, and, when she actually touched, her engines were going astern. Despite this the collision was a bad one; both *Encounter* and *Utmost* had to be docked. The destroyer was far more heavily damaged; indeed she could not be repaired at Gibraltar, because only Malta had the necessary facilities.

Meanwhile *Renown* carried on with the duties assigned to her and spent the 8th and 9th meeting the convoys which were about a hundred miles apart, two plodding up from Freetown and one from the West Indies. This slow shepherding was of no liking to the crew of the *Renown* who were used to more rapid motion about their business, as Bill Kennelly has special memories of:

> This proved to be one of the most uncomfortable trips. Imagine conditions in the engine room and boiler rooms having to ghost along in the middle of a convoy doing a maximum speed of 8 knots. We had one boiler in each unit shut down but at the ready, in order to be able to increase the forced draught and keep a higher oil fuel pressure on the boiler in use. In the tropics at these speeds we practically melted. Here the practice of dawn and dusk action stations proved a boon as then we connected up all boilers and did a long fast run around the convoy and cooled the ship down.

On the 10th shortly after church a report was received of an enemy ship 200 miles away and *Renown* at once turned to chase and quickly worked up to 26 knots. She passed through the convoy at high speed but 10 minutes later the report was cancelled and they returned to their charges. At 16.00 *Renown* left the convoys and returned to Gibraltar, arriving there in the afternoon of the 12th to find *Ark, Sheffield* and the 8th Flotilla which had themselves just returned from the Mediterranean after Operation Coat. This had been the passing through to Admiral Cunningham of the *Barham, Berwick, Glasgow* and destroyers *Gallant, Griffin* and *Greyhound* as reinforcements and *Ark* had had another go at Elmas airfield with her aircraft in Operation Crack.

The next in the series of operations that Force H was to undertake was Operation White, the object of which was to pass further reinforcements of Hurricane fighters into Malta from the deck of the ancient carrier *Argus*. These twelve aircraft were to be flownoff in two flights each being guided by a Skua from the Fleet. *Argus* actually arrived at Gibraltar, escorted by the 6-inch cruiser *Despatch*, on 14 November and these ships together with Force H, *Renown, Ark Royal, Sheffield, Faulknor, Fortune, Forester, Firedrake, Foxhound, Duncan* and *Wishart*, sailed next morning at 04.00 to carry out the operation, the old *Argus* restricting the speed of the fleet by 20 knots.

Tragedy resulted, for Operation White was not a success. Although the flying-off position had been calculated to enable the Hurricanes to make their landfall without difficulty, strong headwinds made nonsense of the plans and of the first flight two had to ditch about 30 miles from Malta when they ran out of fuel, having flown off *Argus* at 06.15 on the 17th. Of the second flight, which was flown off at 07.15 the same day, none reached their destination. It was a cruel blow and a bad error of judgement not to allow some greater margin for pilots inexperienced to long overwater flights. The force returned to Gibraltar in sombre mood on the 19th.

They were not given long to brood on this failure however for the third of the operations planned now had to be prepared. During the earlier passage of the *Barham* and her consorts Cunningham had launched a torpedo bomber attack against Taranto and had severely damaged three of the Italian battleships there. But three others remained and for the next operation, Collar, Somerville had to plan on the possible intervention of these ships plus the numerous cruiser squadrons and destroyer flotillas that the enemy had on hand, together with his vast submarine fleet and the enormous numbers of high altitude and torpedo bombers which the *Regia Aeronautica* could, in theory, deploy against him. Luckily, at this stage of the war, the Italians had no worthwhile dive-bombers and the German Stukas, although under orders to move to the Mediterranean, had not yet arrived. Nonetheless it was a daunting prospect that faced *Renown* and her crew towards the end of November.

But another of her greatest achievements lay ahead of her in the central basin of *Mare Nostrum*.

CHAPTER EIGHT

Battle off Spartivento

R*enown* arrived in Algeciras Bay in the small hours of 19 November intending to anchor there, oil and go straight out into the Atlantic but instead she proceeded into the harbour and secured alongside the mole ahead of the battle-ship *Royal Sovereign* which had recently arrived from Alexandria via Durban and the Cape and Freetown, having spent five weeks in dry-dock.

As the recent spate of submarine alarms had shown, the Italians were eager to get at the big ships at Gibraltar. On the 20th extra precautions were taken to protect the two capital ships alongside the south mole. Two buoys were connected by torpedo nets and a store ship was moored between two other buoys as further anti-torpedo protection. The only activity was by a Vichy reconnaissance aircraft which flew over the Rock and, according to Midshipman Stuart, was fired on 'heavily but ineffectively by the ships and the shore batteries.' The steady build-up of forces for Operation Collar continued however. On the 22nd the *Manchester,* flying the flag of Vice-Admiral Holland (CS 18), *Southampton* and the liner *Franconia* arrived. They were reported to be full of troops and were completely isolated. This was to prevent any word reaching the enemy, but rumour was rife enough. Next day the cruiser *Despatch* arrived with a Vichy merchant ship for examination and the destroyers *Jaguar* and *Kelvin* arrived escorting four Canadian-built corvettes, which were to join Cunningham's command under cover of the main operation.

The night before *Renown* suffered a casualty when a stoker, presumably drunk, fell overboard and was drowned. Only his cap and identity card were discovered. One of the hazards of Main Street nightlife was apparently drugged drinks; it was quite common in some of the less reputable bars, which were 'off-limits'.

On the morning of 24th Somerville held a conference aboard with the senior officers of the assembled warships for the final seal on the complicated planning for Collar which was the most complex set of operations yet put in hand from the Western Mediterranean. Somerville's task had been made no easier by the continued prodding signals from London. For example after a gruelling voyage back from Operation White against a westerly gale many of his too few destroyers badly needed a brief rest after a period of non-stop running in time to be ready for the major operation. During Coat *Faulknor,* along with two of her flotilla, *Fortune* and *Fury* equipped for fast minesweeping had gone through to Malta with the *Barham's* force, returning next day. Since then they had taken part in White and various patrols, and now, before Collar they were to be sent out to intercept a group of Vichy merchant ships expected to pass through the Straits on the 20th. Somerville protested, but in vain. Nor was Somerville inclined to under-estimate the Italian battle fleet in the forthcoming operation, calculating that they could if they wished still concentrate three battleships, up to seven 8-inch cruisers and lesser vessels to bar his passage, despite the knock they had received at Taranto.

Somerville therefore requested that *Royal Sovereign* be added to his strength as she was refitting at the Rock, and to this request the Admiralty agreed. It was unfortunate that, in the event, she could not be got ready on time so once more *Renown* remained the only capital ship with Force H until the rendezvous with the *Ramillies* and her force, which was coming westward from the eastern basin, could be effected. The Italians had the opportunity therefore of meeting and destroying two separate weaker British squadrons and of gobbling up the vital convoy if they acted with flair.

Let us now examine in detail the operation as it was to affect Force H. The plans also involved a whole series of movements by Admiral Cunningham's main Mediterranean fleet in the eastern basin but these do not concern our story. Collar evolved around the passage of military and Royal Air Force stores and vital personnel to Malta, which were embarked in the 6-inch cruisers *Manchester* and *Southampton*, which were then to join Cunningham's flag with the four corvettes. Altogether some 1,400 RAF and military personnel were embarked. Three large and fast (16 knot) transports were carrying vital stores, equipment and motor transport for the Middle East; these were the *Clan Forbes*, *Clan Fraser* and *New Zealand Star* which also had about half the personnel for Malta embarked. The destroyer *Hotspur* was to accompany these ships for a refit at Malta dockyard. She was in a damaged condition and had been temporarily repaired to make the journey, but had no Asdic equipment and was of limited value as an escort. The four corvettes, *Gloxinia*, *Hyacinth*, *Peony* and *Salvia* were fitted with anti-magnetic mine sweeps (L.L. sweeps) and thus Force H would not have to detach their minesweeping destroyers through the Sicilian Narrows to perform this task this time as they did during Operation Coat. Somerville's main strength was again designated Force B for this operation and consisted of *Renown* and *Ark Royal*, cruisers *Despatch* and *Sheffield* and destroyers *Faulknor*, *Firedrake*, *Forester*, *Fury* and *Encounter* (8th DF), *Duncan* and *Wishart* (13th DF) and *Kelvin* and *Jaguar* (specially attached).

These two forces were to proceed through the western basin and were to be met at approximately noon on the 27th by Force D from the Eastern Mediterranean. This comprised the battleship *Ramillies*, the 8-inch cruiser *Berwick* and the 6-inch cruiser *Newcastle*, all of which were en route for home waters via Gibraltar, and the anti-aircraft cruiser *Coventry* and destroyers *Defender*, *Greyhound*, *Griffin* and *Hereward* which were to take over the escort of the two cruisers, four corvettes and the three merchant ships through the Sicilian narrows until met by Cunningham's main fleet for the rest of their passage east. The whole force would be concentrated as cover for the dangerous period between noon and dusk on the 27th as Far East as the Skerki Bank, when Somerville and his additions would turn back, leaving the convoy to penetrate the narrows under cover of nightfall.

This was the basic plan but various factors involving the ships required some modifications. For example the merchant ships had a maximum speed of 16 knots, but the new corvettes were painfully slow, 14 knots being reported as the best they were capable of except in fair weather. The *Manchester* and *Southampton* were splendid ships but with 700 non-naval personnel aboard were somewhat cluttered for a major fleet action. The *Ark Royal* had a tremendous reputation and élan but was still equipped only with low-performance Fulmar fighters and obsolete Swordfish biplanes for her main striking force. In addition an unduly high percentage of her pilots and observers were at this time inexperienced and the efficiency of her torpedo striking force, her major asset, was reported as being low due to lack of opportunity for exercise in the busy weeks just past. The destroyers of Force H were, as related, in need of some refitting but were in reasonable fighting order, save *Hotspur,* but overall only these vessels and *Renown, Ark Royal* and *Sheffield* had worked together before as a fighting squadron.

Of Force D the *Ramillies* of course was painfully slow and had not been modernised in the 1930s at all. Her main armament of eight 15-inch guns was powerful enough if she could get in range, but had not been increased in elevation and could thus be out-ranged by the Italian ships; this is one reason why she was being sent to the North Atlantic station as Cunningham had complained earlier after Calabria. The two cruisers both had defects, which is why they were on their way home. The *Berwick* had had some of her rows of turbine blades removed and the higher water temperature of the Mediterranean had affected her vacuum; she was therefore not capable of speeds higher than 27 knots. The *Newcastle* was also unreliable as her boilers had developed defects.

Admiral Holland indeed objected to the allocation of his two cruisers as part of the main escort on the grounds that:

Extreme importance was attached to the safe and timely arrival of the RAF personnel at Alexandria. The best way to ensure this was for the cruisers to proceed independently and rely upon their high speed and mobility for the achievement of their object. With so many additional men aboard, the ships were not in a fit condition to fight. If obliged to engage, casualties amongst the RAF personnel might be heavy and the object of this part of the operation compromised.

Although agreeing that these two ships would not be in a satisfactory state to fight an action Somerville held that the success of the overall objective, including the merchant ships and corvettes' safe arrival, was more likely to be achieved if a concentrated show of force could deter the Italians. Cunningham's opinion was that the importance of the personnel was greater than that of the convoy but the Admiralty overrode this and insisted that if Italian forces were in sight action taken by these cruisers must be the same as if the personnel were not embarked; the destruction of the enemy fleet was the chief and main concern always.

We shall see how all these possibilities became realities and how Somerville coped with them.

At 06.00 on 25 November *Renown* began to prepare for sea and the whole force sailed east at 16 knots. Alas for all the hopes of achieving surprise, their departure was almost at once communicated to the Italian Naval Command *(Supermarina)* in Rome and preparations were at once put in hand to dispute their passage. On that same day *Ramillies'* force was sighted and duly reported by an Italian civilian aircraft off Malta and this final confirmation led to the following reaction by the Italians.

Two submarine patrols were established. The first to the south of Sardinia consisting of the *Alagi, Aradam, Axum* and *Diaspro,* the second off Malta with the *Dessie* and *Tembien.* A division of torpedo boats was also sent to lay in wait in the narrows, four ships of the 10th Flotilla, *Alcione, Sagittario, Sirio* and *Vega* sailing from Trapani. These latter did in fact make a torpedo attack on Force D on the night of the 26th/27th without effect.

From Naples: Admiral Campioni Battleships: *Giulio Cesare* and *Vittorio Veneto.* Destroyers: *Alpino, Bersagliere, Fuciliere, Granatiere* (13th DF), *Dardo, Freccia Saetta* (7th DF)

From Naples: Admiral Iachino

8-inch Cruisers: *Fiume, Gorizia* and *Pola.*

Destroyers: *Alfieri, Carducci, Gioberti, Oriani* (9th DF).

From Messina: Admiral Sansonetti 8-inch cruisers: *Bolzano, Trento, Trieste.* Destroyers: *Ascari, Carabinieri* and *Lanciere* (12th DF).

A comparison of the two forces available for an actual battle, providing of course that the two British squadrons could join forces in time, therefore came out as follows:

Type	British	Italian
Capital Ships:	2	2
Aircraft Carrier:	1	
8-inch Cruisers:	1	6
6-inch Cruisers:	5	–
Destroyers:	13	14

In fact the odds were more in the Italians' favour than this for of the thirteen British destroyers two had to screen *Ark Royal,* and two more the convoy, reducing the total available to fight to nine. To offset *Ark Royal's* dozen Swordfish the *Regia Aeronautica* could provide more than 200 modern bombers heavily escorted by modern fighters, all of which outclassed the British Fulmar.

On the 25th Somerville's ships and the convoy headed east undisturbed by the Italian submarine line, the three merchant ships passing straight through on the night of 25/26 November being joined by the four corvettes early next morning. *Renown* sailed at 08.00 with Forces B and F. On the 26th there were two items of interest. Firstly the corvettes could not maintain the speed of the convoy and had to be detached to proceed independently. Secondly the day was marred with a series of flying mishaps by *Ark Royal.* A Fulmar stalled on take-off and went into the sea with loss of both crew; two Skuas crashed while landing-on, not a happy omen. Nor was Somerville better served by the RAF and no indication was received from reconnaissance of any Italian movements prior to the first sighting by *Ark's* own aircraft on the morning of the 27th, which thus came as a complete surprise.

Sunrise on the 27th was at 08.24 and at that time the composition of Somerville's squadron was as follows:

About 120 miles to the south-west of the southernmost tips of Sardinia, Cape Spartivento, lay the convoy itself, the three merchant ships steering east at 16 knots in position 37° 37'N, 06° 54'E, escorted by the *Manchester, Southampton, Despatch* and the destroyers, *Jaguar, Kelvin, Duncan, Encounter, Wishart* and *Hotspur*. The four corvettes were some 10 miles to the south and rear of the convoy having fallen steadily behind during the night.

The main strength, Force B, was maintaining a position of cover some 10 to 20 miles ahead and to the north-east, in position 37° 48' N, 07°, 27' E, steering 083° at 16 knots, with *Renown, Ark Royal, Sheffield* and destroyers *Faulknor, Firedrake, Forester* and *Fury*.

Aboard *Renown* at this time the engineering staff had been nursing her engines with some care. In view of the statement made by Arthur Divine in his book* that she 'ran a bearing in the last stage of the chase and could not make her normal speed', it is of historical importance that Captain Gray shows that this in fact was not so and that the defect had nothing to do with her being unable to chase the Italian force before they ran behind their minefields. According to his official report the following is the true story**.

> After two days at sea, on 27 November, the temperature of the Aft HP pinion bearing on the starboard inner shaft was reported at 11.40 to have increased to 170, the average temperature of the other pinion bearings being 114, which is normal for high speeds. Five minutes later the temperature had dropped to 165 and the bearing oil pressure was increased from the usual 12 lbs to 18 lbs. The ship had worked up to 270 revs from 198 revs in 52 minutes and at 11.17 commenced easing down to 216 revs.
>
> At 11.35 orders were received to work up to 260 revs, the engines at that time were running at 220 revs, and then increased to 240 revs, with the intention of working up to 260 revs as ordered. *On receipt of the information* concerning the temperature of the Aft HP bearing (i.e at 11.40) and observing that the ship was about to go into action against the enemy, it was considered essential to keep the starboard inner engine in use if practicable. With this end in view this shaft was run at 240 revs, and the starboard outer increased to 276 revs, the port shafts being run at 260 revs. The temperature of the bearing continued to fluctuate between 153 and 160 at this speed. At 1,245 revs ordered were 278 but the starboard inner shaft was kept at 240, observing it was essential to keep the ship in action at the highest possible speed.

Captain Gray adds that: 'I believe the continued zig-zagging on course at sea and interaction of the propellers may have had some effect on the inner shaft.'

There was also the worry that her long-standing bulge problems might show up again. During her docking on 25 September, after escorting Convoy WS6 as related, several examinations were made of this long-standing defect and reports submitted. Further limited patching was carried out as time and labour permitted, but a full-scale inspection and detailed repair programme could not be conducted at this stage as the ship was in constant demand operationally. Some necessary work had been done then, but there was always the chance that high speed and prolonged periods

---

* A.D. Divine, *Destroyers' War*, (John Murray, 1942).
** Report, *Main Pinion Bearing-Defect*, dated 2 December 1940.

of main-gun firing would undo this work in short order. They had also taken advantage of this docking to carry out extensive repairs to brickwork defects on the boilers and to some steam joints, which was just as well as it turned out.

To revert to the preliminary movements of the battle. At 08.00 *Ark* flew off the first of her air searches; seven Swordfish were despatched to cover the sector west of Sardinia and between Sardinia and Africa.

Not only were they to be on the lookout for any Italian movements but to make contact with Force D, which should be well through the narrows and on its way to the planned midday meeting point. A fighter patrol and an anti-submarine patrol was also flown off at this time, and the former in fact intercepted a Cant Z506 aircraft north-west of Bone at 00.30 and shot it down. Meanwhile news of the attempted attack on Force D and its sighting by aircraft the previous day was received so the presence of that group would appear to be well known to the enemy, but as yet no word had come in of any Italian fleet movements so optimism was high.

Somerville held on eastward until 09.00 towards the expected rendezvous to keep himself well placed between any enemy and the convoy; as no report came in from his Swordfish he changed course south-west to close the convoy in order to provide AA protection in anticipation of bombing attacks from Sardinian airfields. The convoy was sighted twenty minutes later and *Renown* and her consorts placed themselves south of it up-sun but at 09.56 the first indications that the enemy fleet was in fact out, came by a visual signal from *Ark Royal.* The Swordfish had sighted a force at 08.52, closed and sent out an alarm report at 09.06 for four cruisers and six destroyers, but this was not picked up by *Renown.*

The position was not clear at this time; *Ark's* signal, '5 CR 5DR 325–8–255' might have referred to Force D. *Sheffield* and one of the destroyers had been sent to join the convoy's escort and the whole force was unprepared for such unexpected news of the enemy after the previous total silence since leaving Gibraltar. *Ark* was asked to confirm that it was indeed an *enemy* sighting report, while steam for full speed aboard *Renown* was rung down and Captain (D) in *Faulknor* was instructed to detach two destroyers to screen the carrier and leave two with the convoy and then concentrate.

At 10.15 a sighting amplification timed at 09.32 was picked up from the Swordfish reporting two battleships and seven destroyers some ten miles north-east of the original reported enemy and *Ark* confirmed that this former concentration was of six cruisers and eight destroyers. At once *Renown* came about and worked up to 28 knots and steered 075° to join Force D as quickly as possible.

Somerville made his fighting dispositions now that his worst fears had been realised. His two squadrons were still separated and the enemy was just over the horizon with a superior force. He acted quickly. The *Ark Royal,* screened by the *Jaguar* and *Kelvin,* was instructed to prepare a torpedo bomber striking force and act independently under cover of the battle fleet. The convoy was instructed to continue towards Malta but to adopt a south-easterly course away from the probable field of battle and hug the French North African coastline. The cruiser *Despatch* and destroyers *Duncan, Wishart* and *Hotspur* were assigned to its defence, and *Ramillies* was ordered to detach *Coventry* to supplement these units.

Ramillies was also given *Renown's* course and sped to effect a concentration with her four destroyers and CS18 was instructed to take up position in the van with *Manchester, Southampton* and *Sheffield,* together with the five destroyers of the 8th

Flotilla, some 5 miles ahead of *Renown*. At 10.32 Somerville signalled Malta reporting the position of the two Italian battleships, and 8 minutes later a Sunderland of the RAF closed *Renown* and gave the welcome news that Force D was 34 miles away at 070°, which meant that a concentration was possible before the enemy hove into sight. This aircraft was asked to shadow and report the composition of the enemy bearing 025°, 50 miles. In the meantime *Renown* reduced speed to 24 knots to keep between the convoy and the enemy, and the conflicting sighting reports were studied and plotted. The general picture that emerged from the various sightings that had come in was that there were either one, two or three enemy battleships at sea, together with five or six cruisers and that further cruisers might also be about. As Admiral Somerville wrote in his report:

> But, whatever the composition of the enemy force, it was clear to me that in order to achieve my object – the safe and timely arrival of the convoy at its destination – it was essential to show a bold front and attack the enemy as soon as possible.

Meanwhile further sighting reports continued to come in to *Renown's* bridge and from them it was clear that the Italians were scurrying about with their usual confused reactions on being aware British capital ships were over the horizon. The enemy who had originally been reported as steering to the westward were now reported as altering course to the eastward at 11.15.

An observer who witnessed this alteration of course reported that the eastern group of cruisers appeared to be thrown into a state of confusion. The leading ship turned 180° whilst the two following ships turned only 90°. Collisions appeared to have been narrowly averted and at one time all three ships appeared to be stopped with their bows nearly touching each other [ran the report].

It appeared highly unlikely that the Italians were any more eager to engage in direct combat now than before, and they seemed to wish only to sort themselves out and head for home as quickly as they possibly could. Somerville held on and at 11.28 the ships of Force D were sighted bearing 073° at 24 miles; soon afterwards *Ark Royal* got away her first torpedo bomber strike at the reluctant enemy. As the action was obviously going to develop into a stern chase after faster ships with no inclination to 'mix it', the *Ramillies* was ordered to cut the corner so as not to lose ground while the *Berwick* and *Newcastle* were to join CS 18's ships as one squadron ahead of the heavy ships. *Renown's* speed was increased to 28 knots at 11.34 and six minutes later course was altered to 050° to close the enemy ships.

At this point the three 6-inch cruisers were in single line ahead about 5 miles fine of the port bow of *Renown*, with *Berwick* and *Newcastle* on their way to join them from the eastward. Two miles astern of the cruisers *Faulknor* was collecting the scattered destroyers, some of which had to steam hard from their screening positions with the convoy and the four ships from the east were also joining him, being eventually placed 3 miles, 270°, from Captain (D)'s flotilla leader. Ten miles fine of *Renown's* starboard bow the *Ramillies* was making a fine show, as she turned into a parallel course, while far astern the *Ark* was dropping behind and she turned into the wind to fly off and land on her aircraft.

Let us now examine the Italian movements that had led to the panic at 11.15. Admiral Campioni was leading the operation from the bridge of the brand-new battleship *Vittorio Veneto,* a 35,000 tonner armed with nine 15-inch guns and with a speed of over 30 knots. In company was the old *Giulio Cesare,* of the same vintage as *Ramillies* but about 8 knots faster due to a modernisation pre-war. Her ten 12.6-inch guns were smaller than *Ramillies'* main armament, but more numerous and had a better range. The two main units were therefore roughly equally matched overall.

Campioni had made his rendezvous with the various cruiser squadrons well before having crossed the Tyrrhenian Sea during the afternoon and evening of the 26th and at dawn had been some 30 miles east-south-east of Cape Spartivento heading west at 16 knots. The two Italian battleships with their screen of seven destroyers were preceded by the two heavy cruiser squadrons and their destroyers, being some 11 miles in the van 5 miles apart.

Campioni had already been acquainted with Force D's movements from the torpedo boat attacks of the night before and had correctly concluded that the two British forces were to rendezvous, but he had the power to effect a battle before they did so if he moved fast enough. Unfortunately for him although he had a mass of friendly high-performance aircraft to back him up from shore airfields, he was very badly served by the *Regia Aeronautica,* as so often before, and no amplifying recon-naissance reports reached him on the two British groups until 10.15 when a seaplane from one of his own cruisers, *Bolzano,* sighted *Renown* and reported one battleship *(sic)* two cruisers and four destroyers 135 miles south-west of Cape Spartivento.

This initial sighting report was amplified by another scout plane from the cruiser *Gorizia* at 11.44, which failed to report that *Ramillies* and her consorts had joined up. Here, he thought, was his chance to wipe out a part of the British fleet before it could meet the ships of Force D and he altered course to attack. It was this sudden change of course that had led to some considerable confusion among his cruiser force, but this was eventually straightened out and the Italians held on towards the *Renown* until just before noon. Then Campioni got cold feet.

A shore-based reconnaissance aircraft reported at this time that the British forces had not only joined up but were in fact 20 miles closer to him than at first thought. He came to the conclusion that discretion was the better part of valour and that in his opinion his force was outnumbered now 'numerically and qualitatively'. Quite how he justified such an assumption is unclear, despite MacIntyre's interpretation of events* in which *Ark Royal* was held to be the vital 'trump card', for Campioni had all along known of her presence.

Whatever the logic behind his reasoning its conclusions were quickly evident, - '. . . I decided not to become involved in a battle.' The Italian fleet came about 180° and headed north-east at full speed for home. The question then arose as to whether *Ark Royal's* aircraft could so damage the enemy battleships that *Renown* and her consorts could close them sufficiently to put them under.

Back on *Renown's* bridge Somerville was forming his battle plan in the light of further reports. The issue was clouded by an incomplete message from the Sunderland, which reported back at 11.54 that six cruisers and eight destroyers were bearing 330°, 30 miles from *Renown* and that *no* battleships were seen. Neither the course nor speed of this squadron were given by the flying boat which then sheered off. If their position was correct then a group of the enemy was much further west

---

* Captain Donald MacIntyre, *Fighting Admiral, (op cit).*

than those previously sighted and were in a good position to move in astern of *Renown* and catch the *Ark Royal* unescorted. As no further report on this squadron came in Somerville decided partially to accept this risk and hope that *Ark's* own aircraft would spot them in time should this eventuality arise. Nonetheless the fate of the *Glorious* a few months earlier was a grim reminder of the vulnerability of aircraft carriers on their own (she too only had two escorting destroyers when caught by the two German heavy ships, it will be recalled) and this had the effect of somewhat restricting *Renown's* movements, for Somerville altered course more to the north in order not to get too far to the eastward thus lessening his chances of getting between the flying enemy and their bases.

Nor did this restriction *Ark's* vulnerability imposed have its compensations in the results of her air striking forces, for two torpedo bomber attacks by Swordfish and one dive-bomber attack by Skuas during the afternoon all resulted in no hits of any kind despite claims at the time to have hit a battleship, two 8-inch cruisers and destroyers. The battle therefore resulted in a long-range duel at high speed in which the chances of scoring a lucky hit were meagre.

At noon however the situation still seemed promising to Somerville, and he wrote:

(i)   We had effected our concentration of which the enemy appeared to be unaware, since no shadowers had been sighted or reported by RDF, and his speed had been reported as between 14 and 18 knots, which suggested he was awaiting the reports of reconnaissance.

(ii)   The sun was immediately astern and if remaining unclouded would give us the advantage of light.

(iii)   There seemed every possibility of a synchronised surface and T/B attack if the nearest position of the enemy was correct, and providing he did not retire at once at high speed.

He later gave his priorities as follows during the ensuing chase:

(i)   To drive off the enemy from any position from which he could attack the convoy.

(ii)   To accept some risk to the convoy providing there was a reasonable prospect of sinking one or more of the enemy battleships.

This latter consideration is worthy of note in view of subsequent developments in Whitehall.

To effect this latter choice the enemy had to be slowed down to 20 knots or less *(Ramillies'* best speed) and the two British capital ships would have to attack together (because of *Renown's* light armour and *Ramillies'* short range) to support one another. Nor, with the hot shaft condition and her bottom being dirty, without a proper dockyard cleaning, could *Renown* match the enemy's speed; 27 knots was the best she could attain according to the report.

Nonetheless to reach the safety of their minefields and protection of their home airfields the Italian ships had to cross Somerville's line of advance and at 12.07 there were reports of puffs of smoke being observed on the horizon bearing 006° and the *Berwick,* the leading cruiser in the van, sighted masts and ships between the bearings of 345° and 006°. At this time the British cruisers had almost concentrated to form a line of bearing 075°–255°, in sequence from west to east, *Sheffield, Southampton, Newcastle, Manchester* all of the same class of twelve 6-inch gunned ships, with *Berwick* with her eight 8-inch guns being an extension to the east and slightly ahead, the only cruiser capable of matching the range of the six Italian heavy cruisers. *Newcastle* in fact never did quite achieve her correct position on the line due to the restriction on her speed by her boiler troubles. At 11.58 *Berwick* was also forced to drop out, reporting her best speed at 27 knots. As she turned back CS 18 ordered her to rejoin his force, but she had lost so much ground that this proved impossible and she took station on the starboard bow of *Manchester* and steadily fell behind during the chase.

The nine destroyers meanwhile formed up to a position 5 miles 040° from *Renown* so that they would be available to counter attack any Italian destroyers moving against the British heavy ships with torpedo attacks.

The journal of Charles Stuart recalls this moment well:

By now the horizon ahead was smudged with a number of large clouds of thick black smoke and white masts could be seen. At 12.20 the range of the leading *Zara* class cruiser was estimated to be 34,000 yards. At 1223 FOH signalled to C-in-C Med, 'Am engaging enemy' and at 12.24 *Renown* opened fire at the leading enemy cruiser. After seven minutes firing, during which eight two-gun salvos were fired, the enemy ship was lost behind smoke. The target was crossed at a mean range of 26,500 yards.

The target ship for *Renown's* opening salvos was the right-hand ship of the western group of two that could be made out and in fact six salvos were forced before it retired behind the massive smoke screens being laid by the Italians. Just before fire was opened at this ship *Renown* sighted two ships, who were not making smoke, at extreme visibility, bearing 020°. These were at first thought to be the Italian battleships but they later turned out to be more cruisers of the Eastern group.

Ramillies had worked up to 20.7 knots, a magnificent achievement, as she had only been good for 21 knots when first built a quarter of a century earlier. She got off two salvos at maximum elevation to test the range but thereafter *Renown* steadily forged ahead of her.

When the *Zara* had vanished into the murk *Renown* altered course to switch her fire to the Eastern group of ships and to bring the western group broader on her bow and at 12.31 two salvos were fired at the second in line, or centre ship of the western group. Course was then altered further to starboard to open the main A arcs so that all three turrets could engage these targets which then bore 356°.

At 12.35 *Renown's* 15-inch salvos again crashed out against the leading ship at a mean range of 30,000 yards, eight three-gun salvos being fired.

In A turret gunner Pittendreigh was finding it hot work.

My recollections of the atmosphere in A turret are mainly ones of noise, cordite fumes and the heat. The power to operate the turret and all the machinery involved from shell room to Gunhouse being hydraulic (the mixture was oil and water), after a time the pipes became quite warm, especially in the working chambers immediately below the Gunhouse; it was just like very efficient central-heating. When we eventually came up from the working chamber afterward we could have rung the sweat from our boiler suits and anti-flash gear.

At full speed the three-gun salvos created a shock and sensation even deep down in the engine rooms as Bill Cain remembers: 'I was down below during the action and the sensation of having those 15-inch guns firing was terrific. One had the sensation of standing still for a second, then leaping forward again after the concussion.'

It was equally as shattering elsewhere below decks as Ted Smith recalls: '15-inch gunfire created its problems. The ship literally shook in such conditions and dust rose and loose cork (anti-drip condensation) dropped from the deck-heads in great showers.'

If the Renowns were finding the pace rather warm then so was Campioni. He cracked on extra speed, and, with his ships firing full astern and pouring out volumes of smoke lit out for home waters. The return fire from his 8-inch cruisers was at first accurate and *Berwick* took two direct hits which put her after turrets out of action but she kept in line. In return the British cruisers scored a hit on the destroyer *Lanciere* that had to be towed out of the action. Both *Newcastle* and *Faulknor* reported a hit by a heavy shell on one Italian cruiser and this was duly confirmed post-war as correct. *Renown's* salvos were accurate enough quickly to effect a marked falling off in accuracy from the enemy as the range opened after she hit *Fiume*.

The first torpedo-bomber attack went in against the Italian battleships at this time and flak burst could be seen peppering the sky, but no slowing down in the enemy's rate of retirement could be observed and it was obvious the aircraft had failed. *Renown* had by this time lost sight of her original cruiser targets and was seeking fresh prey. Two large ships suddenly appeared out of the smoke cloud left by the fleeing enemy and they were observed to be steering sedately to the west. *Renown's* three great turrets swung round and were trained on this new target but before the firing key could be depressed they were identified as three-funnelled French liners. Quite what the Vichy captains thought they were doing in the midst of a naval battle, remains a mystery: with more than sixty warships blazing away at each other and planes diving and attacking one would have thought that they would have exercised some basic prudence. But no, upholding a firm and defiant neutral stance, they steamed on between the two fleets oblivious to their danger.

They steamed slowly and steadily 'between the two Fleets', recalled Midshipman Stuart, 'narrowly avoiding being sunk by both sides. Some of our destroyers did, in fact, take a pot shot at them. Then a French Glenn Martin carrying the High Commissioner of Syria to take up his appointment was shot down by a Fulmar.'

As Renown was no longer engaged and it appeared possible that action with both Italian battleships might result from the overoptimistic reports of the Swordfish crews, Somerville decided, in confirmation of his original battle-plan, to concentrate on *Ramillies* and act in conjunction with her; he began to turn back. As this turn was commenced however, the eastern group of cruisers was observed to present a possible target, and as the plot on *Renown's* bridge indicated that both enemy battleships had not in fact slowed down but were still speeding away north-east, course was steadied on 070° to engage these new targets.

This was delayed by the need to execute a swing to starboard to avoid a reported submarine, and then course was altered by 045° to close the position of the two enemy battleships, which CS 18 had just reported on that bearing.

At 13.11 *Renown's* great guns spoke again, firing two ranging salvos at those ships, thought to be battleships, but later found to be the easterly group of heavy cruisers. Both salvos fell well short however and the range continued to open rapidly. The enemy battleships did in fact loose off some departing shots from the rear turrets against the British cruisers, which fell near *Berwick* and *Manchester*. Somerville signalled Holland, 'Is there any chance of catching cruisers?' to which CS 18 replied, 'No', estimating that the Italians had an excess of three knots over the fastest British ships. The British ships were now rapidly approaching the Italian coast. Submarine alarms had been reported, and there were fears the enemy was leading them over a submarine ambush and into unplotted minefields. These factors, along with the likelihood of prolonged and heavy air attacks off Cagliari led Somerville to weigh up the alternatives of continuing a losing chase or turning back.

The only factors in favour of going on were the remote possibility of a reduction in the speed of the enemy's retreat by some unforeseen eventuality or that he might change his mind and turn back to offer battle. Neither was very likely; indeed battle was the last thing the Italian commander had on his mind at this moment. It is interesting to notice that in a subsequent post-war account of this battle Campioni is said to have broken off the battle at *this* point! * In fact of course, as he himself admitted, he made his decision well before *Renown* even had him in sight and never changed his viewpoint at any time during his pell-mell flight.

Points considered by Somerville in favour of abandoning the hunt at this stage were listed by him as follows:

(i)   There was no sign that any of the enemy ships and especially his battleships had suffered damage, nor was there reasonable prospect of inflicting damage by gunfire in view of their superior speed. Unless the speed of the enemy battleships was reduced very materially he could enter Cagliari before I could bring him to action with *Renown* and *Ramillies*.

(ii) I was being led towards the enemy air and submarine base at Cagliari and this might well prove a trap. His appearance in this area appeared to be premeditated since it was unlikely that this was occasioned solely by the information he had received the previous night of Force D's presence in the Narrows.

(iii) The extrication of one of my ships damaged by air or submarine attack from my present position would certainly require the whole of my force and must involve leaving the convoy uncovered and insufficiently escorted during the passage of the Narrows.

(iv) The enemy main units had been driven off sufficiently far to ensure they could no longer interfere with the passage of the convoy.

(v)   A second T/B attack could not take place until 1530 to 1600 by which time the convoy would be entirely uncovered and the enemy fleet could be under the cover of the A/A batteries and fighters at Cagliari. I entertained little hope that the attack would prove effective as I knew that the second flight was even less experienced than the first.

---

*J. Rohwer and G. Hummelchen, *Chronology of the War at Sea, 7939–7945*, Vol 1. (Ian Allan, 1972). British edition edited by A.J. Watts.

I had no assurance that the cruisers reported to the North-west might not be working round towards the convoy and *Ark Royal*. It was necessary for contact to be made with the convoy before dark to ensure the cruisers and destroyers required for escort through the Narrows should be properly formed up. It was also necessary to provide the fullest possible scale defence against T/B and light surface forces attack at dusk. To effect this a retirement between 13.00 and 14.00 was necessary.

All these points were well made and after reviewing them Somerville had no doubt in his mind that the correct course was to break off the chase and return to join the convoy and this was done. Although a report was received afterwards, at 13.35, of a damaged enemy cruiser 30 miles away, within 10 miles of the enemy coast, he did not despatch a cruiser force to hunt for her, *Manchester* and *Southampton* because of their cargo, *Sheffield's* radar was needed against expected air attacks and both *Berwick* and *Newcastle* had defects. Instead *Ark Royal* was instructed to mount a strike, but the target (not a cruiser at all but the damaged destroyer) escaped further damage.

Meanwhile *Manchester* and *Southampton* were sent to rejoin the convoy and after the carrier strike, the main force followed them eastward. Thus ended the main phase of the battle, which reflected most creditably on the British force, which had accepted battle even if it lacked the legs to enforce a decision. From *Renown's* viewpoint the knowledge that the latest Italian battleship had run away from her in the same manner as the two German heavyweights earlier in the year, raised morale to a new peak.

'Our gunnery, though criticised, was creditable when the extreme ranges at which we were firing are considered', wrote Midshipman Stuart, while Admiral Somerville made the following personal observation in his report to their Lordships:

> It was a pleasure to observe the enthusiasm with which the ship's company of *Renown* closed up at their action stations on hearing that enemy forces were in the vicinity and their subsequent disappointment when it was clear that the enemy did not intend to stand and fight was obvious.

The *Regia Aeronautica* now strove to remedy the situation as expected. At 14.07 while steaming east at 19 knots to rejoin the convoy radar reports indicated that enemy bomber formations were on their way and the line was staggered. From *Renown* bomb splashes on the horizon were seen as the Fulmars made their interceptions and some more cautious Italians quickly jettisoned their cargoes. Another formation got through and ten SM 79 three-engined aircraft were soon spotted approaching the fleet in a steady V-formation. A Blue Turn was immediately made, all ships turning together to bring maximum firepower to bear on these aircraft, but despite the barrage this formation held its course steadily and straight before releasing. The volume of defensive fire, although not accurate, was sufficient to deter them from pressing right in to the heavy ships and the majority of the bombs fell near the destroyers out on the screen.

At 16.30 further attacks came in at a great height beyond the range of the ship's guns. They were carried out by two formations of five aircraft each and, as the *Ark Royal* was operating apart from the main force, they naturally chose her as their target. The bombing was very accurate indeed, and one attack caused the carrier to vanish completely behind a wall of spray from near misses, but she survived intact and unharmed. The steadiness of these bombers in the face of both flak and fighters was commented upon, as was their accuracy, but unfortunately for the Italians altitude bombing always proved the most useless method of hitting moving ships at sea, despite the wholly misplaced faith in such methods by airmen of all nations, and once again their courage went unrewarded.

These were the last air attacks and the convoy was sighted at 17.00, and the operation continued as planned without further interference from the enemy; *Renown* arrived back at Gibraltar on the 29th to a rousing welcome. Force H responded accordingly.

'At a given signal all the ships in the advanced force consisting of *Renown, Berwick* and *Sheffield* made smoke and the resulting spectacle was fine to see', recorded Charles Stuart. 'We all flew our largest ensigns, the band played "Run Rabbit, Run" as we entered harbour and we were, to our gratified surprise, cheered by an envious *Royal Sovereign* and the destroyers.'

A more sour note was struck by Churchill and the Admiralty, which however distasteful, should be recorded. Although they had only two signalled reports, made while he was still at sea, from Somerville on which to judge his actions and reasons Churchill pressured Alexander and Pound into setting up an immediate Board of Enquiry headed by Admiral of the Fleet, the Earl of Cork and Orrery. News that he had already started on his way to Gibraltar before Somerville had even reached port was received and this 'procedure without precedent' gave Somerville some indication of the feeling against him in Whitehall. Indeed it went much further than he realised for we now know that the findings of even this hastily assembled Board had already been pre-judged in London, Churchill suggesting that Admiral Harwood, then ACAS (Foreign), should take over Somerville's command.

Not surprisingly this high-handed attitude and the total unfairness of it made a sour impression in the fleet. Admiral Cunningham has recorded his feelings on the matter in his memoirs; he had enough similar treatment to know just who was at the back of it. 'I don't believe he [Pound] is at the bottom of it but he allows himself to be talked into these things, by W.C. and others', he was to write.

The Board duly sat for three days from 3 to 5 December and, on the 4th, announced their findings, which were:

(a) That the original orders for the operation by Admiral Somerville were clear and concise.
(b) That the action was conducted in a correct and spirited manner conducive to the safety of the convoy and its timely arrival at its destination in the face of a superior enemy.
(c) That the decision to abandon the chase at 13.10 although slightly early was the correct one.

Somerville was therefore completely vindicated, although the Admiralty accepted these findings with a certain grudging reluctance, stating they felt he had been over-influenced by his anxiety for the security of the convoy and that he should have continued his pursuit until it was clear beyond all doubt that no Italian ships could have been brought to book. 'No opportunity must be allowed to pass of attaining what is in fact the ultimate object of the Royal Navy – the destruction of the enemy's forces whenever and wherever encountered', they informed him coldly.

Although Churchill's pressure to have the Admiral relieved of his command was squashed it left a nasty taste all round. Force H was naturally most upset at this slur on their leader, which they also took as a slight on themselves.

This affair however, far from breaking the morale of Force H, had the happy result of closing ranks and Slim's popularity with his men, if anything, increased. How the average sailor aboard *Renown* felt about his commander, his force and his ship was reflected later in the words of Bill Cain: 'I shall never forget the man in charge of Force H, Sir James Somerville, he was the right man for the job.'

CHAPTER NINE

The Genoa Gala

W hile these events of high drama were taking place the *Renown* was preparing herself for her next operation. Attention had to be given to her engines before she again took on the Italian fleet, as Captain Gray recalls:

When we arrived back at Gibraltar the ship's staff themselves removed the troublesome bearing and, after some adjustment in machinery, fitted the spare. The dockyard re-metalled the defective bearing and machined it. The ship's staff then removed the remaining fifteen bearings one by one, the dockyard assisting as necessary. During this whole time the ship was at six hours' notice to steam and the whole operation took four to five days. The engineering department was duly congratulated by Admiral Somerville for a 'very smart piece of work'. We had no further trouble with these bearings while I was in the ship. I left her in August 1941.

Opportunity was also taken during this self-refit to embark eighty-two rounds of 15-inch APC and 164 rounds of J charge cordite ammunition, together with 800 rounds of 4.5-inch HE. While they lay thus employed, various movements took place; the *Royal Sovereign* sailed for home on 1 December escorted by *Newcastle, Jaguar* and *Kelvin,* and the cruisers *Despatch* and *Sheffield* both sailed in the days that followed on patrol work. On the 6th the *Manchester* arrived back from Malta safely. *Ramillies* left harbour for a 15-inch shoot the same day. As usual though this rest period was only a prelude for further activity. On the Axis side of the fence too a reorganisation was taking place that was to bring new problems to the British command of the Mediterranean.

Although the German plans to capture Gibraltar with the agreement of Spain – Operation Felix – finally fell through at this time, thus ensuring the safety of Force H's base and its continued operations, other problems were being set in train. On 9 December a general reorganisation of the Italian fleet took place with Campioni being replaced by Admiral Iachino. Next day agreement was reached for the *Luftwaffe* to station the 150 Stuka dive-bombers of *Fliegerkorps* X on airfields in Sicily and Southern Italy, and their task, as laid out by Hitler himself, was to close the Narrows to the Royal Navy.

However until these deadly dive-bombers actually arrived the Royal Navy continued, in the words of one German historian, 'to do as it pleased' in the Mediterranean. With the crippling of three of six Italian battleships at Taranto and the concentration of the others on the Western Coast, Admiral Cunningham felt strong enough to transfer another of his older battleships west, and arrangements were made to pass the *Malaya* through the 'Narrows' to Gibraltar. At home the success of Operation Collar had led to the demand to mount an even more adventurous operation, that of running a large convoy through to the Eastern Mediterranean once more, together with more reinforcements for Cunningham. Planning of all these moves got underway at once, but before they could be implemented a fresh alarm was raised about the safety of the Azores; on the 14th Force H once again put to sea to establish a defence patrol in that area. The whole force sailed at 10.40, forming up in the Straits and heading westward; *Renown, Ark Royal* screened by *Faulknor, Duncan, Fury, Forester, Encounter and Isis.*

Their patrol took place in heavy weather as far as just north of the Azores before they returned to Gibraltar on the 19th. Apart from investigating a few suspicious neutral merchantmen about their lawful affairs and the usual shoots and exercise the whole patrol was incident free. They entered Gibraltar, fuelled and were off again to the east at 1716 on the 20th to carry out Operation Hide. *Renown, Ark Royal, Sheffield, Faulknor, Fortune, Firedrake, Forester, Foxhound* and *Fury,* the Force H regulars, sailed with the objective of meeting *Malaya* from the Eastern Basin, and bringing home the *Clan Forbes* and *Clan Fraser* from Malta. These ships, known as Force F, were escorted through the Narrows by five Mediterranean Fleet destroyers. The ships of the 13th Flotilla from Gibraltar were sent out ahead to carry out Operation Seek. These destroyers, *Duncan, Encounter, Isis* and *Jaguar,* were to patrol the Skerki Channel while Force F passed through, then to take over the escort from Cunningham's flotilla. Force H was to rendezvous off Galita Island.

The whole operation passed off well, save for the fact that one of the Mediterranean Fleet destroyers struck a mine off Cape Bon on the 22nd. This ship, the *Hyperion,* could probably have been towed to safety by the *Ilex* had time allowed, but was ordered to be sunk instead. She was the only casualty received; attacks by three Italian submarines. *Bandiera, Dessie* and *Serpente* on Force F earlier had failed. All ships returned to the Rock on the 24th.

The prospects of a peaceful Christmas alongside the mole seemed good for the *Renown.* The Christmas tree was hoisted atop the mainmast and the messes prepared to celebrate. *Renown's* band struck up a selection of Christmas carols and Sir James visited each mess in turn, exchanged wisecracks with the men, and commented on the decorations they had improvised. While this was in progress a signal came in that was far from festive.

The German heavy cruiser *Admiral Hipper* had left Kiel, had passed through the Denmark Strait undetected on 7 December and was loose on the Atlantic trade routes. On 22 December she flew off her aircraft to search for Force H, which had been reported off the Azores earlier, but at this time they were deep in the Mediterranean and no contact was made. Refuelling from waiting tankers on the 23rd, the 8-inch cruiser then made her move and on Christmas Eve found a glittering prize, the southbound troop convoy WSSA, sixteen heavily laden ships which had sailed from the UK on the 18th. She held them on her radar screen and early on Christmas morning fired torpedoes into the convoy none of which hit a target. She then decided to hold off until dawn.

At 06.38 on the 25th the *Admiral Hipper* moved in for the kill some 700 miles off Cape Finisterre. Her target was indeed a Christmas feast for in the convoy were not only the valuable merchant ships, including the five fast transports that were destined to pass through the Mediterranean, but two old aircraft carriers, the *Furious* and *Argus,* their decks laden with fighters for the same destination. Captain Meisel had the chance to wreak untold havoc to the British war effort. Unfortunately for him he had no sooner started his attack, scoring hits on the transport *Empire Trooper,* when he found that three British cruisers were included in the escort, the light cruiser *Bonaventure* for Gibraltar and the *Berwick* and *Dunedin* for the UK. This put a different aspect on the matter. The two 8-inch cruisers had a brisk exchange of salvos; the *Berwick* suffered the worse being hit twice, but the German had had enough and broke off the attack, heading for Brest. As soon as the first signal of the attack came in Force H hastily abandoned its celebrations and headed out to sea in the face of a rising storm.

At 10.38 *Renown, Ark Royal* and *Sheffield,* screened by *Faulknor, Foxhound, Fortune, Firedrake, Duncan, Hero, Hereward* and *Wishart,* cleared the Rock and set course to the west; they were given a sympathetic 'chuck-up' by *Fury* and other ships who stayed behind as they left. *Renown's* crew answered with a burst of cheering that left little doubt that the *Hipper* had better beware.

The convoy had meantime scattered in foul weather, the *Hipper* had vanished, sinking a lone merchant ship on her way, and for four days there was a confused situation in the Bay of Biscay. *Renown* and her consorts, battered by the heavy seas, strove to locate the enemy ship and also to gather the precious merchant ships together again under their protection before the storm abated and the U-boats moved in. *Hipper* meanwhile slightly damaged from shell hits and with her unreliable machinery playing up, entered Brest on 27 December.

In the huge swells the starboard bulge of *Renown* again gave way, peeling back over a length of 30 feet; rivets again sprang and the hull began panting. Her speed had to be restricted to 20 knots. After some of the *Ark's* aircraft had flown close by the flagship this state of affairs drew the following exchange of signals:

Ark Royal from FOH:

Your boys appear to exhibit a morbid curiosity about the hole in Father's pants. I hope there is nothing sticking out?

FOH from *Ark Royal:*

Your 11.30. I hope they would be too polite to say so.

But *Renown* was clearly in no fit state to fight a major battle and when she finally returned to Gibraltar on 30 December she went straight into dry-dock for repairs, which further delayed the major convoy operation.

Bill Kennelly remembers that: 'I believe we were the first big ship into the new dock at Gib and we promptly soiled it with the fuel oil draining from out of bulges which in turn had leaked from the outer oil-fuel tanks.'

While these repairs were being carried out planning went ahead to pass the convoy through to Malta, in the operation codenamed Excess. Since early in December the Admiralty had expressed the intention of running another fast convoy through the Mediterranean with ships for both Malta and Piraeus (AT1615/6/12). It was planned to run twenty ships from the UK – sixteen were to go by the Cape route (WSSA) and five were to go by Gibraltar and on through the Med. Of these five, four, *Clan Cumming, Clan MacDonald, Empire Song* and *Northern Prince* were destined for Greece and one, *Essex,* was to go to Malta.

Force H as designated for this operation comprised: *Renown* (Flag), *Malaya, Ark Royal, Sheffield, Faulknor, Firedrake, Fortune, Forester, Foxhound* and *Fury* (8th DF) with *Duncan* (13th DF).

To supplement Force H were two forces:

From the Mediterranean Fleet – Force B: *Gloucester* and *Southampton* with the destroyer *Ilex.*

Reinforcements for the Mediterranean Fleet – Force F: *Bonaventure* with destroyers *Hasty, Hero, Hereward* and *Jaguar.*

The combined forces were to take the convoy right through to the Sicilian Narrows, and then Forces B and F were to take it through the Narrows and then for the combined forces of B and F together with Cunningham's main fleet units, to take it from there onward.

However, as always, there were some modifications at the last minute, chief of which was the fact that a few days before the convoy was due to sail from Gibraltar one of its ships, *Northern Prince,* dragged her moorings in a gale and drove ashore. She took no further part in the operation.

Special elaborate plans were set in train in attempts to fool the enemy in collaboration with Admiral North's new successor as FO North Atlantic, Vice-Admiral Edward-Collins, who had arrived on New Year's Day. The four remaining merchant ships of the convoy sailed shortly after dark on the 6th escorted by *Bonaventure* and the rest of Force F, and steered to the west to deceive onlookers by heading into the Atlantic. After a while they reversed course and passed eastward through the Straits passing Europa Point after moonset and before daylight of the 7th. Force H sailed from Gibraltar at 08.00 and rendezvoused with *Bonaventure;* it was planned that this force would overtake the convoy on the night of the 7th/8th but keep some distance to the north and east of it to screen it against air attacks.

The first days passed uneventfully and at dawn on the 9th *Malaya* and *Bonaventure* were sent to join the convoy to provide heavy AA protection; Force H proceeded ahead and, at 05.00, flew off five Swordfish to Malta where they were to operate. At 09.18 air patrols made a sighting report, which turned out to be the ships of Force B, and they joined an hour later. Meanwhile the Italian reconnaissance aircraft had not been idle, the first locating Force B at 09.00 being joined by a second at 10.00 which *Ark's* aircraft failed to destroy.

However it was not until after 13.00 that the first incoming air raid was located. *Ark's* Fulmars were scrambled away but failed to make contact with the enemy aircraft who therefore only had the fleet's gunfire to contend with. All forces were by this time in loose company and the barrage was quite a large one. The four merchant ships were steaming in two columns in line ahead, the columns being led by *Malaya* and *Gloucester,* with *Southampton* and *Bonaventure* similarly placed astern of each. Seven destroyers formed an ahead screen while *Renown, Ark Royal* and *Sheffield* with a screen of the remaining destroyers, were in close support on the port quarter of convoy. All ships were zigzagging at a speed of 14 knots.

The ten Italian aircraft, SM79s, were first detected by *Sheffield's* radar at a range of 43 miles, fine of the starboard bow. Twenty-six minutes later the attack commenced, at 13.46, and all ships opened fire. Midshipman Stuart sets the scene for us once more:

> The Italian aircraft flew over from the southward at a height of about 8,000 feet. Nearly all the bombs were dropped on the south side of the fleet, the *Malaya* attracting most of the enemy's attention for reasons which we were to learn later. The barrage was ferocious and had the effect of keeping the Italians up at a good height. It was claimed later that one plane was brought down by anti-aircraft fire. *Renown* fired heavily, and in my opinion, rather too fast as her fire became ragged by the time the bombers were right overhead.

The fighter defences being impotent while the enemy was in the barrage, the effectiveness of the fleet's fire was all-important. The captain of the *Bonaventure* thought later that most of the shells fired burst well below the aircraft, but Admiral Renouf in the *Gloucester* thought that the barrage from *Renown* and her consorts, bursting over the convoy, diverted most of the aircraft. In effect both were partly right.

Aboard *Renown* the bark, bark, bark of her twenty 4.5s was deafening. 'Conditions in the living spaces, pantries etc after a heavy air raid and sustained gunfire, left a trail of disarranged gear and, despite expert packing, dislodged and broken crockery,' recalled Ted Smith.

Although many of the bombs dropped fell near to *Malaya* and *Gloucester* no hits were obtained; altitude bombing had again failed. In addition to one aircraft probably shot down by the fleet's gunfire, *Ark's* Fulmars redeemed themselves by pouncing on the enemy aircraft as they turned away and shot down two of them. Their crews were picked up by *Forester* and *Foxhound*.

One of the rescued Italian airmen paid due tribute to the fleet's gunfire, and his testimony was recorded by Charles Stuart:

> His plane had been one of a group of two, which came over some distance to the right of the main formation. Before the attack commenced the port engine had given trouble. The major in command of the flight ordered him to keep out to the right and detached another plane to back him up.
>
> This pilot said that the barrage had been good and kept them up to what was a fairly normal high level for bombing. The attack was directed mainly against the merchant ships and the *Malaya*. The *Malaya* attracted great attention as the Italians were under the impression that she was a new *King George V* type battleship.

This says little for *Regia Aeronautica's* ship recognition, since *Malaya* was single-funnelled with four turrets, and the new ships two funnelled with three turrets, as well as much larger!

Although further air attacks were expected they did not in fact materialise and so this solitary effort was the sole Italian contribution in stopping Operation Excess. At dusk on 9 January therefore, Force H parted company in a position some 30 miles westward of the Narrows and the convoy continued under the protection of the ships of Forces B and F. Somerville's ships returned to Gibraltar on 11 January.

If *Renown* and her consorts had an easy passage, once the convoy reached the Narrows it was a vastly different story. Here it suffered attacks by all manner of weapons; from the submarines *Bandiera* and *Santarosa,* which were ineffective; the torpedo boats *Circe* and *Vega,* the latter being blown to shreds by the *Bonaventure* and finished off by the *Hereward;* and mines, which crippled the destroyer *Gallant,* which had to be towed into Malta by the *Mohawk.* Next day the Stuka dive-bombers took over, hitting *Illustrious* six times and crippling her, and next day damaging *Gloucester* and sinking *Southampton.* Clearly with the arrival of the Ju 87 in the central Mediterranean convoys to Malta were no longer to be walkovers.

Admiral Somerville was putting his mind to a completely different form of offensive however. With the safe passage of Excess Force H was presented with a brief opportunity to carry out an attack without having the complications of a convoy under its wing. It was reported that one of the Italian battleships torpedoed at Taranto was repairing damage at Genoa dockyard. It was thought to be one of the new ships, *Littorio,* but it was in fact the older vessel *Caio Duilio* which was in drydock just north of the Molo Ciano. In addition to her there were ample worthwhile targets in the dockyard area for Somerville's heavy guns to engage. *Renown's* commissioned gunner, Mr Stillitoe, studied detailed maps of the area and from them constructed a detailed relief model aboard the battle-cruiser, which was studied intently in the days that followed.

Meanwhile Captain C.E.B. Simeon of *Renown* had been promoted to Rear-Admiral in the New Year list and his replacement arrived at Gibraltar and assumed command on 23 January. This was Captain R.R. McGrigor and his arrival as flag captain was a great asset, for he and 'Slim' Somerville got on perfectly together. 'Wee Mac' as he was known was a very popular choice with the men as well.

Bill Cain recalls that: 'He was a small chap and had to stand on a stool on the bridge to see what was going on', but he was right for the job. Somerville soon commented that, 'Mac's a real acquisition.'

The danger that Force H was in was not minimised; they would in fact be entering a natural trap with the main bases of Genoa, Spezia and numerous Italian airfields all around them. Close by lay the Vichy Fleet, sullen and hostile, at Toulon, from which no help, but probably considerable resentment, could be expected if sighted. Corsica and Sardinia would lie on their eastern flanks and a neutral, but hardly unbiased, Spain to their western flank. Nonetheless the risks were found acceptable.

In fact the risks were greater than they realised for, although the German Stukas were based too far south to intervene, the Italian Fleet had concentrated in the north under Iachino and had found some enthusiasm at last. Based at Spezia only 40 miles from Genoa the Italians had a force of three battleships, three 8-inch cruisers and destroyers in an ideal position to trap Force H deep in hostile waters. The need for extra security was therefore stressed.

On 22 January the destroyer *Foresight* arrived to join the 8th DF from the UK and with her she brought maps and plans of the Tirso Dam in Sardinia, for this was to be a combined operation as follows:

(a)   Operation *Picket* in which the *Ark Royal* was to mount an air striking
       force of torpedo bombers against Tirso Dam to get the Italians on the
       wrong foot.

(b)   Operation *Result*, the bombardment of Genoa by the heavy ships of Force
       H, *Renown*, *Malaya* and *Sheffield*, while *Ark Royal's* planes bombed
       Leghorn and laid mines off the port of Spezia itself to seal in the Italian
       fleet.

The operations were put into effect on 31 January, the fleet sailing at 1215 in three
groups:

Group I   – *Renown, Malaya, Ark Royal* and *Sheffield.*
Group II   – *Foxhound, Fearless, Firedrake, Foresight, Fury* and *Jersey.*
Group III   – *Duncan, Encounter, Isis* and *Jupiter.*

At 19.30 on 31 January, Group II was detached to proceed at economical speed to
rendezvous with the main force north of the Balearic Islands during the forenoon of
2 February.

At 09.10 the *Renown, Ark Royal* and *Sheffield*, screened by *Duncan* and Isis,
increased speed and altered course to be in position to fly off the aircraft from the
carrier against Tirso Dam. This attack position was about 60 miles west of Cape
Mannua, Sardinia, and the target itself some 22 miles further inland.

Meanwhile the *Malaya*, escorted by *Encounter* and *Jupiter*, was detached to
proceed at economical speed, to rendezvous with the main force in position 40° 55'N,
6° 30'E some 240 miles from Genoa, at 09.00 on 2 February.

During the night of 1/2 February *Renown* and her consorts steamed at high speed
eastward towards the flying-off position but a freshening north-east wind compelled
some changes in the plan inasmuch as a decision had to be made that the flying
position after the attack would have to be the same as the flying-off position – this
meant the rendezvous with the other two forces had to be altered by some 60 miles.

At 05.55 on the 2nd the striking force of eight old 'Stringbags' armed with torpedoes was duly flown off *Ark Royal*, and at the same time two other Swordfish were
prepared to be flown off at 07.30 to contact *Malaya* and to direct her to the revised
point of rendezvous at 10.00 so that wireless silence need not be broken.

Alas, the air strike was a failure. Weather conditions were very bad and severe
icing conditions, rain and hail were met by the fragile old aircraft, which caused their
formation to break up and lose cohesion. Attacks were made independently by four
aircraft but they were met by fully alerted AA defences, which shot down one
Swordfish and put the others off their aim. Of the torpedoes actually released in the
lake none reached the dam at all. The surviving aircraft landed aboard *Ark Royal* at
09.05. At about 10.30 on the 2nd *Renown* met *Malaya* and shaped course for
Operation Result to be carried out as planned.

A full north-easterly gale now set in and the big ships were soon shipping it green
as they plunged on into the teeth of it. Aboard the escorting destroyers conditions
were ghastly and soon they were reporting weather damage. Speed was reduced to
15 knots with no easing of the situation. It was clear that the mission would have
to be abandoned. Force H held on until they met the destroyers of Force II north of

Majorca at 18.30 and then reversed course with a rising sea behind them, arriving back at Gibraltar on the 4th.

Despite this disappointment Somerville was determined to carry out his planned operation as he felt sure his movements had not been revealed to the enemy. However there were several reports of breaches of security while the ships were back at the Rock, as Bill Kennelly remembers:

> Next day lower deck was cleared; everyone was set ashore onto the jetty and we all received a terrific dressing down from Wee Mac about security. It appears that one of our sailors had spotted a chum in the local cinema and shouted across in his greetings that we had set out to bombard Genoa but had been frustrated by the weather. The message we got that day, in very forceful language, was that he, the Admiral, would have no hesitation in having such a man shot rather than jeopardise the lives of all concerned.

There seems little doubt that word did reach the Italians for they were ready and waiting at sea, if not at the target itself, when the operation was restarted. Elaborate deceptions were incorporated in the revised plan, code-named Operation Grog, but not all of these could be carried out.

Orders were issued to the force that a sweep was to be conducted against Vichy shipping in the Western Mediterranean in a similar manner to earlier such operations. Special boarding parties were assembled from the battleship *Resolution* repairing at Gibraltar, and sent aboard the destroyers. A destroyer force was to make a feint towards Sardinia on the day before the bombardment was to take place and broadcast radio signals to give the impression that the whole of Force H was concentrated to the west of that island. The RAF at Malta was asked to help by mounting bombing raids against Cagliari or Alghero and then to retire from the area as if they were returning planes from *Ark Royal*. However due to non-availability of planes at Malta this could not be complied with.

The real operational orders were sent aboard the destroyers in sealed packages only to be opened at sea, and when the fleet did finally sail, at dawn on 6 February in three groups, they steamed westward to give the impression that they were to form escort to a homeward bound convoy which was in fact assembling in the Straits at that time. All these ruses failed to convince Iachino, however, who knew of *Renown's* departure almost at once.

After heading west in conjunction with Convoy HG53 Group 1 and Group 2 reversed course and passed through the Straits at night. Group 3 carried out an anti-submarine hunt in the Straits. (The only difference in the compositions of the forces was that *Encounter* and *Firedrake* switched groups.) They all rendezvoused inside the Mediterranean on the 8th, remaining there until 19.00 when course was set to 070° and speed increased to 21 knots. That evening at 19.00, *Firedrake* and *Jersey* were detached to implement the W/T part of the plan while the rest of the force cracked on northward towards the Gulf. Shortly before midnight lights on the French Riviera coast were sighted and at 23.40 course was altered to 070°. During the run up the Gulf a fairly strong wind had been blowing but it had died down by midnight when the *Renown* went to action stations. A bright moon was shining.

Meanwhile the radio signals had led Iachino to believe that another Malta convoy might be on its way. He had sailed from Spezia at 19.00 on the 8th with the battleships *Vittoria Veneto*, *Andrea Doria* and *Giulio Cesare* and eight destroyers, and made rendezvous at 08.00 next morning 40 miles west of the Bonifacio Strait between Corsica and Sardinia with the 8-inch cruisers *Bolzano*, *Trento* and *Trieste* and two further destroyers from Messina. This powerful force passed within 40 miles of Force H on its outward leg without either side realising it.

Meanwhile in the early hours of the 9th Force H had made its final approach in complete silence, the *Ark Royal* being detached at 04.00 to carry out her part of the operation, screened by *Duncan*, *Isis* and *Encounter*. Due to a brilliant piece of work by the Fleet navigator, Commander Martin Evans, the *Renown* and consorts made precise landfall soon after moonset; at 06.30 the two heavy ships and the *Sheffield* were manoeuvring into position to the eastward and then turned westward to commence their bombardment run. The coastline was covered in a low haze through which the hills behind the port stood out as markers. The sea was perfectly calm and empty of enemy shipping, the sky was equally bare of the *Regia Aeronautica*. Ashore there was dead silence.

This strange quiet was broken by the arrival of an aircraft from *Ark Royal* to spot for *Renown*, while *Malaya* and *Sheffield* catapulted their own planes for their shoots. Somerville himself described the scene that Sunday morning as the last seconds ticked away:

Not a sign from shore, not a ship except our own on the sea. We steamed up to the beginning of the run – about 10 miles off Genoa – and then crash went the broadsides . . . The first salvos fell almost exactly where we wanted them and *then* I felt content. the curtain was up, and the tragedy was on.

The log book of the destroyer *Fury* spells out the next period in stark simplicity:

0635:	Flaming onions sighted 090° (These were Italian flares).
0715:	Battleships opened fire.
0720:	Aircraft in sight 125°.
0730:	Destroyers on the engaged side stand by to make a smoke screen. Some shots have fallen astern of *Malaya*.
0740:	Make smoke.
0750:	*Renown* and other bombarding ships ceased fire. *Renown* to *Ark Royal*: 'Bombardment completed.'

Shiner Wright was one of the very few who managed to get an eyeful of the bombardment from 'up top', albeit briefly:

What a delightful place this was in peacetime when I was in *Resolution*. How different in war. I remember being on *Renown's* boat deck watching the destruction of the wharves and the Ansaldo works, when a voice behind me said, 'What are you doing up here?' My reply was to the effect, 'I was in Genoa in peacetime, Sir, and made many friends.' The Commander's reply left me in no doubts, 'Get below. This is war!'

In that period of time Force H pumped some 300 tons of shell into Genoa, *Renown* fired 125 rounds of 15-inch, *Malaya* added another 145 rounds, while *Sheffield* contributed 782 rounds of 6-inch and *Renown* 400 rounds of 4.5-inch. Four freighters in the harbour and a training ship were hit and badly damaged, eighteen others were damaged to a lesser extent by near misses and shell splinters. Italian broadcasts afterwards admitted hits were obtained on the barracks and in the new fitting-out yards. It was estimated that shells fired in the sixteenth salvo from the *Malaya* fell in the near vicinity of the battleship *Caio Duilio* but she escaped lasting damage. One of the salvos from *Sheffield* hit the tanker *Santa Andrea* which was waiting for a pilot before entering harbour. She was damaged on the port quarter but was later towed into harbour.

The Gibraltar *Daily Despatch* recorded that:

> The bombardment of Genoa was in many ways *Renown*'s greatest day. That dawn approach, that perfect navigation, were matched and bettered by some of the best gunnery that this war has seen. Genoa's battered waterfront, Ansaldo's ruined works bore witness to the mightiness of that grey ship slipping along the horizon in the dawn.

The Italian press screamed a different story, of how most of the shells landed in the city, causing severe damage and this of course is the theme taken up post-war by many so called 'objective books'; but in truth most of the blow fell on legitimate targets. There were bound to be casualties from 'overs' in such a bombardment of course, this was unavoidable but the total number of dead, 144, was far less than that suffered almost nightly at this time in Axis air attacks on London, as Somerville himself pointed out.

> For half an hour we blazed away, and I had to think of Valletta, London, Bristol etc., to harden my heart. But I was watching the map and the reports of the aircraft and I do believe practically all our salvos fell on works, warehouses, shipping, docks etc. Still it's no use pretending that some innocent people were not killed. War is lousy.

There were also moments of humour too. The old *Malaya* had been blazing away with a vigour that defied her age. She had originally been a present to Britain by the Federated Malay States and in battle was entitled to fly the Malayan Jack as well as the White Ensign. This somewhat resembled a well-known shipping line's flag, which drew the signal from *Renown*'s bridge, as she became wreathed in smoke and flame:

> You look like an enraged P and O!

Bill Kennelly recalls another incident:

> An enemy aircraft was shot down in the forenoon and another in the afternoon. Very soon after firing at the two aircraft we sighted a French southbound convoy consisting of seven ships and soon after that we sighted a floating mine on our starboard bow. In the afternoon the sky, which had been blue and clear, suddenly became cloudy and overcast.

Somerville signalled to his ships:

I congratulate all concerned on a first class shoot under extremely difficult conditions and especially those responsible for the initial practice and training.

To an anxious Admiralty he signalled before the fleet returned to harbour on the 11th:

It must have been a rude awakening for those ashore as it was a very heavy bombardment while it lasted. One comical incident according to those on deck was the arrival out of the fog and during the bombardment, of a small Italian tanker, who, on spotting our warships promptly took to their boats and rowed like hell. Can't say that I blame them.

As the ships came about at the end of their runs the first belated signs of opposition appeared, a few shots from shore batteries plonking well clear of *Malaya*, and this was followed by a solitary aircraft which released two bombs 11 miles away from the destroyer screen before scuttling back inland. At 07.45 the fleet altered course to 180° and at 21 knots made an undisturbed withdrawal. *Ark Royal*'s force rejoined the flag at 09.00 and the whole fleet continued on its course towards Corsica until 10.30 when it was changed to 244°. Midshipman Stuart recorded:

Ever since the bombardment had begun we expected to be bombed ceaselessly by enormous waves of Italian bombers, not to mention German dive-bombers. We saw no enemy aircraft until 11.40 when the fleet let fly at two enemy planes which suddenly appeared overhead. Their presence seems to have been a mistake on their part, for they dropped three bombs very wide of the fleet and made off at high speed.

Thereafter we were not troubled by the enemy. One shadower was shot down in the forenoon and another in the afternoon. Very soon after firing at the two aircraft we sighted a French south-bound convoy consisting of seven ships and soon after that we sighted a floating mine on our starboard bow. In the afternoon the sky, which had been blue and clear, suddenly became overcast.

Somerville signalled to the Admiralty in London on the 11th:

Bombardment completed. From all accounts Genoa is in a bloody fine mess.

This later brought the following response from Churchill:

I congratulate you on the success of the enterprise against Genoa, which I am very glad to see you proposed yourself.

What of the Italian Fleet all this time? Reports of the bombardment did not finally reach Iachino until 09.50 and, on receipt of this signal, he at once turned northward to intercept Force H. Complete lack of reliable reports from the few aircraft that had made contact with the British force did not help. At 12.35 he sent off one of his own scouting planes and he changed course north-west. Had he held this course a fleet action might have resulted, but false reports from the scouting aircraft led him to the same French convoy that Force H had passed earlier. At one stage the leading Italian cruisers were ranging on the masts sighted at a range of 35,000 yards before they realised their error. Not until the survivors from one of the aircraft shot down by a Fleet Air Arm Fulmar earlier had been rescued by a destroyer late on the 9th did they realise that Somerville had given them the slip. The closest the two forces had come had been at 14.30 that afternoon when they were within 30 miles of each other. However, the great emphasis placed on Force H's 'lucky escape' must be questioned. Had it come to an action *Renown* and *Malaya,* with *Ark Royal* and a full screen, and no convoy to worry them, might well have dished out more than they got, as they did on less favourable occasions. Perhaps then it was just as well for Iachino that he failed to find Somerville that February day.

The effects of the bombardment itself, were admittedly mainly ones of morale. The aggressive movements of Iachino's fleet, which had for once genuinely sought action, were not generally known to the Italian people; the damage done to Genoa, and the audacious way it was carried out, was. On the British side much useful mileage was got from it by the delighted Premier but post-war feeling has varied. Captain Roskill wrote in the Official History in 1954 how Force H had '. . . inflicted much damage on enemy shore installations.' In 1977, however, he had changed his mind and was to record* that the bombardment was 'not very effective'.

Nonetheless Force H entered Gibraltar on 11 February to a great welcome, being cheered by the mass of shipping there and with the garrison bands at full blast on the jetty. *Renown* flew her largest ensign and her newest admiral's flag in response but if they felt that her efforts were to be duly rewarded with a period of idleness for her crew, then *Renown* and her ship's company were soon disillusioned. The Western Mediterranean might be quiet but out in the Atlantic new crisis reports came over the wavebands. The pocket battleship *Admiral Scheer* was at large on the convoy routes; then the *Admiral Hipper* sortied once more from Brest and fell like a ravaging wolf upon a convoy of unescorted merchantmen. Worse still, the battle-cruisers *Gneisenau* and *Scharnhorst, Renown's* old opponents, had broken out also, sailing from Kiel on 22 January and were still undetected a month later having sunk five ships and cruised for 11,000 miles.

Convoy HG53 meanwhile was grievously mauled by other enemies. On 9 February she had been attacked by *U-37*, which had torpedoed and sunk two ships. The submarine then surfaced and homed German aircraft onto the convoy and in heavy attacks they had bombed and sunk five more vessels. Next day *U-37* returned and sank another and signalled *Admiral Hipper* to close and finish off the survivors. This she started to do but on the way the heavy cruiser ran into the unescorted Convoy SLS64 and quickly sank seven of its ships and damaged another. With all hell breaking loose in the Atlantic *Renown* could afford no respite. A telegram from the Admiralty dated 12.40/12/2/41 ordered Somerville to sea with Force I to the aid of HG53 and shortly after 16.00 *Renown, Ark Royal, Sheffield* with five destroyers sailed into the teeth of a rising gale. Bill Kennelly recalls:

* *Churchill and the Admirals,* Oxford University Press, 1977.

This was a mystery trip as far as most of us were concerned We had a sudden shout to proceed to sea in a hurry, westwards and into a heavy gale. On deck, seamen were busy preparing a large timber raft, with flagpole, provisions which included a barrel of rum. We surmised that a ship, or ships, had been sunk off Portugal and we were looking for any survivors. We didn't see any wreckage or bodies however in that weather.

Charles Stuart wrote:

Our sudden and hurried departure was due to an attack on a convoy. The weather was quite heavy on the northward trip and *Ark Royal* was unable to fly-off aircraft. Before we met the convoy, acting on information that a ship had been torpedoed not far away from us, we prepared a large raft filled with supplies of food, drink and warm clothing, a boat's compass and other aids and comforts. This raft was to be dropped near any boats we might encounter for we could not stop to pick up survivors in the middle of a dangerous submarine area.

A further Admiralty telegram (20.14/12/2/41) changed the plans and in the event only *Sheffield* went to help HG53 while *Renown* and *Ark Royal* were diverted to take over the escort of Convoy WS6 from the *Rodney* on the 16th in a position some 1,300 miles north-west of Gibraltar. This was done. As Midshipman Stuart wrote:

With *Ark Royal* we went north-west, hampered by strong winds and a heavy head sea. At times we had to reduce to 12 knots. This prevented us from being in our rendezvous at the appointed time. Finally, on the morning of the 17th, in or near the position 51° N, 30° W, we met the convoy, thirty ships strong, escorted by the *Birmingham*. This convoy was carrying what must have amounted to 150,000 troops plus equipment. Although we were not told, it was assumed that they were bound for the Far East.

On the 18th we turned south with the convoy. By day we stayed in the middle of the convoy with *Birmingham* astern and *Ark Royal* for the most part as a separate unit. At night we went on ahead at 18 knots and steering an increased zigzag to keep close to the convoy whose speed was 8 knots.

By the 21st they had escorted the convoy down to a position 30° N, 31' W and at 10.00 met the *Malaya* handing the ships over to her care and returning to Gibraltar 1,200 miles to the north-east. On the long journey back they received a report that *Hipper* was out again. After her earlier slaughter she had run low on ammunition and fuel and had gone back to Brest, but this latest report proved to be a false alarm for she was still there. *Renown* therefore continued towards the Rock arriving there on the 25th. Immediately on arrival she went straight into dock where she remained until 2 March.

This time her bulges were given a more permanent going over, as the Report of Proceedings dated 25 February 1941 shows. She was docked down to the 25 foot draught mark for repairs to both port and starboard bulges and to the forepeak. On inspection some 111 rivets were found to be loose in compartment lower-decks to maindeck 1–10 and ten frames were cracked.

Repairs were carried out to the bulges, loose rivets renewed and the frames repaired temporarily by strapping: advantage was taken of this period in dock to carry out extensive repairs to brickwork defects and to steam joints.

During her time in the dock the Governor of Algeciras arrived at Gibraltar aboard a German-built E-boat to lunch with the Admiral. 'It must have been his first square meal for months. After inspecting the ship he departed bearing a large and ornate loaf of bread in the shape of a wheatsheaf', recorded Charles Stuart. 'His staff were also presented with an assortment of breakfast rolls. I imagine that no gift could be more welcome.'

Renown was undocked at 11.00 on 2 March and later that day carried out a series of exercises in the Mediterranean, which lasted for two days. Torpedo-Bomber barrages were tried out, dive-bombing attacks by *Ark*'s Skuas tested the 4.5s and the destroyers made night attacks to keep all the armament in trim. They returned to Gibraltar on the 7th.

During this period of enforced idleness Somerville had been eager to mount a further offensive operation in support of Cunningham to help take some of the pressure from his hard-pressed ships in the Eastern Mediterranean. However the Admiralty advised FOH that it was not desirable for him to enter into any new commitments in the Mediterranean because Force H would be required to cover the Atlantic trade routes at this critical time. *Scharnhorst* and *Gneisenau* were still at large although they had not had much success to date.

Having refuelled at sea on 25 February the two German battle-cruisers moved south to pounce on the convoys from Sierra Leone, secure in their intelligence that the Home Fleet had returned to Scapa Flow and that Force H was in harbour at Gibraltar. However the timings of these convoys had been altered by the Admiralty. When the German Admiral learnt this he took his two ships further south than ever before hoping to catch two SL convoys off the Canary Islands. On 8 March he did indeed sight one, SL67, and made his approach. Unfortunately for him this convoy was escorted *by Malaya* and two of Force H's destroyers, which had been working out of Freetown for just such an eventuality.

On sighting the German battle cruisers *Malaya*, *Faulknor* and *Forester* moved out to offer battle whereupon the two German ships turned tail. *Malaya* was too slow to chase them, and anyhow her duty lay with her convoy. Her sighting reports however sent *Renown* hurrying to sea at 21.00 on that same day after a recall had been sounded throughout the town. *Renown* sailed with only one man adrift out of over 1,200 and set course to meet SL67 and *Malaya*.

Rendezvous was made at midday on the 10th and there followed another slow crawl northward with the convoy that lasted for nine tedious days. Not until the 19th were they rid of this boring task and free to go on the offensive once more. Meanwhile the two German battle-cruisers had been having better luck. They came across a number of independently routed tankers from Convoy OB294 capturing six of them. Three were then sunk and prize crews put aboard the others, which were told to make a run for France. Meanwhile the *Admiral Hipper* sailed from Brest and returned safely to Kiel without detection; for a time she was also thought to be operating against convoys and a desperate situation prevailed in the central Atlantic area.

On 16 March the German ships sank further ships, ten being despatched by their 11-inch guns before they were suddenly surprised by the British *Rodney* whereupon they made off at high speed. *Rodney* was escorting Convoy HX114 and at once signalled a sighting report as the two German ships made off for Brest. The Admiralty at once set in train wide-ranging movements to try and head them off. *Renown* and *Ark Royal,* released from their convoy far to the east, immediately swung around and increased speed to cut across the Bay of Biscay after refuelling at Gibraltar.

On the 20th patrolling aircraft from the *Ark* sighted all three of the German prizes and *Renown* soon intercepted two of them, the *Bianca* and the *San Casimiro;* both of which then immediately scuttled when *Renown* came into view.

Bill Cain was a member of the hastily assembled boarding party, which had been mustered in the hope of saving the ships.

> The Germans, unfortunately, had the habit of scuttling their ships and had done so much of it in two wars that they were very proficient at it. The boarding parties were trained in what to do; the engine room section makes its way down to the boiler and engine rooms and shuts off the sea cocks if they have not been damaged. To scuttle a ship one method is to open the sea cocks wide and snap the wheels off with a hammer. It is then impossible to close them so the sea rushes in until she sinks. Another method, though not commonly used by the Germans, is explosive charges with which a hole is blown in the ship's bottom.

In both cases the Germans were too fast for them and there was no hope of reclaiming the two tankers but rescue of the British prisoners and of the German prize crew took place. A total of forty-six British merchant seamen were rescued along with their erst-while captors, many of which came from the *Scharnhorst,* but they had managed to set off the scuttling charges in good time. From the German seaman under interrogation the Renowns were able at last to learn at first-hand why the two German ships had fled in their last encounter off Narvik, as Captain Gray recalls: 'On interrogation the sailors from *Scharnhorst* replied that the Germans imagined that the other two battle-cruisers, *Hood* and *Repulse,* would obviously be in company with us and they did not appreciate *Renown* was by herself.'

It was while the transfer of these men from the sinking ships was underway that a Fulmar from *Ark Royal* appeared overhead with her radio out of action and began flashing an urgent message to *Renown.* At 18.30 Admiral Somerville reported to the Admiralty that this aircraft had sighted the two German battle cruisers at 17.30Z in 46° 50'N, 21° 25'W and that they were steering 000° at twenty knots. *Renown* was at this time about 120 miles to the south-east of this sighting position but had only 45% fuel remaining. The destroyers had meantime been sent back but Somerville pressed on in the forlorn hope of closing the gap, which after the 45-minute delay had now increased considerably.

Hopes of another search plane establishing contact were poor for it was nearly dusk but another Fulmar was sent out to try without success. Force H pressed on through the night with poor visibility and rapidly draining oil tanks and with no destroyer escort into the Bay. Dawn on the 21st brought further bitter disappointment. The Admiralty had sailed three destroyers of the 5th Flotilla from Mountbatten's command, based at Plymouth, to provide Somerville with a screen, but with the coming of daylight thick fog descended on the area of operations nullifying any hopes of a re-establishment of contact by *Ark*'s aircraft. The Admiralty therefore signalled for Force H to return to Gibraltar and replenish and they arrived back there on the 24th, having been at sea for fifty days out of the preceding fifty-six.

The *Scharnhorst* and *Gneisenau* meanwhile reached the sanctuary of Brest on the 22nd, although their presence was not finally confirmed by air reconnaissance until six days later. Meanwhile after a quick refuelling Force H had again sailed back to the Bay and established a patrol there until the air reports of the 28th enabled them to once more return to Gibraltar. Their second chance to have a crack at their old enemies had gone forever.

Meanwhile far to the east the island of Malta was undergoing her first great ordeal by fire and being subjected to almost non-stop air attack by German and Italian squadrons. Her reserves of fighter aircraft were rapidly melting away and further flying-off operations to replenish her air defences were planned at this time. The first of these, Operation Winch, took place between 2 and 4 April; *Renown*, *Sheffield* and five destroyers, *Faulknor*, *Fearless*, *Foresight*, *Fortune* and *Fury* escorted the *Ark Royal*, *which* had embarked twelve Hurricanes from the *Argus* at Gibraltar. These were flown off some 400 nautical miles from Malta led by three Skuas and arrived safely.

On completion of this Club Run, as such sorties had become known, ('The Club' of course being Force H itself and its longer serving members) further complications with the Vichy fleet loomed up to add to their worries. Apart from several interceptions of French convoys from time to time off the Straits by destroyer patrols from Gibraltar, backed up by a cruiser when warranted, the Admiralty continued to express concern at the further concentration of the main units of the Vichy Navy which were now recovering from Mers-el-Kebir.

Early in April reports were received that the French battle-cruiser *Dunkerque* was preparing to leave Oran for Toulon and Admiral Somerville was instructed to prevent this. In view of his commitments elsewhere the only thing he could do was to arrange for a submarine ambush, and this plan, Operation Principal, was set in train by sailing the *Olympus* and *Otus* to patrol off Oran. Second thoughts were in evidence, however, when it was realised that should either of these submarines successfully attack a Vichy ship it would almost certainly lead to further Vichy air raids on Gibraltar in reprisal, as it had before. Malta's plight was desperate; another aircraft ferry run was planned and in preparation for this the *Ark Royal* was even now transferring aircraft from the *Furious* at the Rock (Operation Fender).

Thus if Principal took place it would be necessary, in view of the vulnerability of the Gibraltar defences, to clear all ships from the dockyard and to carry out the transfer of the Hurricanes to *Ark* at sea, by no means a simple task for RAF pilots, without training, to do. On 5 April, therefore, much to Somerville's relief, Principal was cancelled. As an alternative diplomatic pressure was applied through the United States, with the eventual result that *Dunkerque* remained at Mers-el-Kebir for the time being. It was just as well, for Somerville had more than enough to cope with.

To maintain a 'close blockade' on the two German battle-cruisers at Brest the Admiralty had arranged that part of the Home Fleet and Force H should take turns in establishing a powerful force in the Bay and between 8 and 16 April it was the turn of Somerville's command. *Renown*, *Ark Royal*, *Sheffield*, *Faulknor*, *Fearless*, *Foresight* and *Fury* therefore sailed to comply, being reinforced for this operation by the cruiser *Fiji* and destroyer *Highlander*, both of which were at Gibraltar and available.

As Captain MacIntyre recorded in *Fighting Admiral*:

It was round this time that a piece of cross-talk between some of *Renown's* sailors and a visiting boat's crew from a ship of the Home Fleet had come to the Admiral's ears and pleased him mightily.

'Had any leave lately, mate?' asked one of the *Renown's* men. 'Yes. Forty-two days, chum,' came the reply. 'You get your . . . . . . names in the papers. We get leave. We prefer it!'

CHAPTER TEN

Hunting the *Bismarck*

Again *Renown* was on the move, this time into the Mediterranean again after only a brief period of rest. The object of this sortie was a double one, the flying-off of further Hurricane reinforcements to Malta (Operation Dunlop) and the passing through to the island of the 5th Flotilla to operate as a surface striking force against Axis supply lines to Libya. Also taking passage through to the Eastern basin was the light cruiser *Dido* to join Admiral Cunningham, along with the fast minelayer *Abdiel*. Their movements were codenamed Operation Salient.

Renown, Ark Royal, Sheffield and *Fiji, Faulknor, Fearless, Foresight, Fortune* and *Fury* again provided the covering force for *Dido, Abdiel, Kelly, Kashmir, Kipling, Kelvin, Jackal* and *Jersey*. Poor weather delayed the flying-off of the twenty Hurricanes, led by three Fulmars, until 27 April, but there was no opposition from the enemy to their passage, and *Renown* was back at the Rock on the 28th.

Meanwhile events in the Eastern Mediterranean had taken a turn for the worse. Hitler had decided to bale out his struggling Axis partner in the Balkans and powerful German forces were thrusting through Yugoslavia and Greece. The victorious British army which had been chasing the Italians across North Africa had had much of its strength taken from it and transported to Greece in a belated and forlorn effort to stem this tide. Thus weakened it was forced to fall back with the onslaught of Rommel's Afrika Korps and Egypt was threatened again. In view of the dire straits of the Eighth Army the Premier decided to rush a fast convoy through the Mediterranean with tanks and other transport despite the cautionary advice from his Naval advisers on the strength of the Axis dive- and torpedo bomber units guarding the middle of that sea. The decision having been taken further detailed planning took place which incorporated the passing through of yet more warship reinforcements for Admiral Cunningham at Alexandria.

The Renowns took it all in their stride; considering the tempo of their life at this time it is remarkable how high their morale remained.

It must be remembered too that life aboard one of His Majesty's ships of war was no sinecure at the best of times. Stoker Holmes provides just one small example:

A small point maybe, but what really amazed me in the *Renown* at this time, with her very large crew over and above her normal complement, was how the basic routine of hygiene was kept up. We all managed to keep ourselves clean despite the problems and this took some doing. Water was rationed when at sea, but even so we had no hard times over it. All our washing and shaving was done from a bucket; in fact most sailors had their own bucket for these jobs.

They continued to find humour in the midst of such conditions, as Bill Kennelly records:

A certain Stoker Petty Officer, was known as 'Von' for his habit of stirring up the mess by praising the German effort and continued victories. He particularly upset one petty officer, Giles. Now Giles was a devout Roman Catholic and did his little bit extra by taking responsibility for the washing for the Roman Catholic Chaplain's vestments etc. He did this in the bathrooms and left them to drain over the shower rails. The PO, coming off the last Dog Watch a little irritable, came bursting into the mess one day enquiring 'Who the Hell is wearing nightshirts in this ship?' which was *not* well received!

Overall though *Renown* had a happy and harmonious atmosphere at this trying period, as he also relates:

We were fortunate in that there was a keen and happy spirit throughout the ship, not like some I have served on. I can recall only one or two officers who caused resentment. The most irritating thing was the censorship of our mail; my wife once returned a letter to me that I had sent to her that had been so mutilated that what was left didn't make any sense at all. I hadn't written anything of importance, except perhaps to allay her fears that Lord Haw-Haw's reports about *Renown* returning to port 'on fire from stem-to-stern' were just so much nonsense, but at least she could guess we were O.K.

Their limited entertainments and day to day routine upheld them to some extent as Bill Cain says:

By now I had made all the rugs I was ever likely to need so I took up wood-working classes during the evenings when off duty. I made quite a few things out of scrap wood, and I still have them.

I had also been promoted to acting leading stoker, which meant more money and responsibility. It also meant that I would be leaving *Renown* at the first suitable opportunity to take the leading stokers' course at Devonport. A leading rate in the Navy is equivalent to a corporal in the Army and you are usually put in charge of a mess. Even when off-duty you are still responsible for that mess except when ashore. We were told when we first joined up that we were paid for twenty-four hours daily and seven days a week. How true that turned out to be! No extra money for overtime although sometimes a kind officer would let you have half a day off or 'make and mend' as we called them in lieu of extra duties. When closed up at action stations for long periods as we were in *Renown* at this time such rest periods went by the board, but we survived.

Planning for convoy operation Tiger was nearing fruition. The forces involved consisted of the fast transports *Clan Chattan, Clan Lamont, Clan Campbell, Empire*

Song and *New Zealand Star* all of which were capable of 14 knots. *Renown, Ark Royal, Sheffield* and three destroyers were to cover these vessels laden with vital war materials. This group was known as Force B.

The reinforcements for Cunningham's fleet were the battleship *Queen Elizabeth*, not long having completed a major rebuilding similar to *Renown's* and mounting a first-class AA armament as a result, and the light cruisers *Fiji* and *Naiad*. They were to be escorted by six of Force H's destroyers, three of which were to act as high-speed minesweepers as before for the night passage of the Narrows.

In the event unexpected reinforcements for the fighting through of this convoy arrived at Gibraltar from Malta. The cruiser *Gloucester* had been sent by Cunningham to work with the 5th Flotilla in its sweeps against Axis shipping but at 07.09 on 2 May, one of the flotilla, *Jersey*, struck a mine and sank in the entrance to Grand Harbour in such a way that *Gloucester, Kashmir* and *Kipling* were prevented from entering until her wreck could be moved. They were therefore ordered to Gibraltar and underwent heavy air attacks on the way, during which the cruiser was damaged by a bomb. She carried out temporary repairs at Gibraltar and both she and her two destroyers were able to join in Operation Tiger as Force D.

The basic plan was the normal one: all three warships forces should accompany the convoy up to the Sicilian Narrows and up to that point the operation should be conducted by FOH in *Renown*. On reaching the narrows on Day Four the convoy would be met by the cruisers *Phoebe, Calcutta, Carlisle* and *Coventry*, all of which mounted powerful AA armaments, for passage and then covered by the main Mediterranean Fleet for the rest of their voyage.

As usual in order to try and gain some time, various deceptions were carried out. The convoy itself was met out in the Atlantic by the *Queen Elizabeth* and four destroyers, who escorted them through the Straits at night. Force H also sailed on the 5th, out into the Atlantic and then reversed course. However the enemy were not deceived for the ships had to pass, as usual, through the mass of Spanish ships of the fishing fleet that infested the Straits, some of which no doubt were equipped with wireless transmitters and caught little tunny in their nets. In all events the sailing of Force H was duly broadcast on German radio next morning.

At 06.30 on the 6th *Renown, Ark Royal, Sheffield, Fiji,* and destroyers *Kashmir, Kipling* and *Wrestler* increased speed to 24 knots and by midnight of the 6th/7th were in a covering position some 150 miles ENE of the convoy. During the 7th they were joined by *Queen Elizabeth* and *Gloucester* but no movements were made by the Italian battleships, and, despite crystal clear weather, the convoy itself remained undetected throughout the 7th.

The main opposition would therefore rest with the Axis aircraft and Somerville had to some extent foreseen this. At Gibraltar, before the operation commenced, had arrived the *Repulse* escorted by the destroyers *Harvester, Havelock* and *Hesperus*. The Admiralty had placed these ships at his disposal but Somerville, although accepting the destroyers, had declined to include *Repulse* on the grounds that her lack of armour decks and her poor AA armament would make her too vulnerable.

In anticipation of heavy air attacks being mounted on the 8th the whole force combined after *Ark Royal's* scouting planes had reported no sign of enemy surface vessels for a radius of 140 miles to the north-east. The *Renown, Ark Royal* and *Queen Elizabeth* were then placed on the convoy's starboard side, giving the carrier room to fly on and off her standing patrol of twelve Fulmars, while giving her the protection of the capital ships' AA firepower. The cruisers *Sheffield, Gloucester, Fiji* and *Naiad* were similarly placed ahead and astern of the two columns of merchant ships while the destroyers of the escort, *Faulknor, Fearless, Foresight, Forester, Fortune, Foxhound* and *Fury* (8th DF), *Kashmir* and *Kipling* (5th DF), *Harvester, Havelock, Hesperus* (temporary attachment), fanned out to form a powerful defensive anti-aircraft and anti-submarine screen for all these vessels. All was now set and the enemy were not long in obliging.

By midday the largely overcast sky had begun to clear and at 11.15 an enemy aircraft report was intercepted which showed that the whole force had been under aerial surveillance since 08.00 that morning. The first attacks commenced at 13.45 and was by eight three-engined SM 79 torpedo-bombers, which approached the fleet from the starboard bow at low level. The destroyers out on that side of the screen engaged them with long-range fire and destroyed one bomber; the others kept outside the screen and deployed towards the line of three big ships, and were met by a furious barrage, which destroyed two more. The remaining five aircraft pressed in and released their missiles. The *Renown* was violently swung round to 'comb' those aimed at her.

All the torpedoes were avoided save one, which seemed almost certain to hit *Renown*. By a miracle it reached the end of its run within yards of its target and sank slowly as the battle-cruiser raced past. It was a lucky escape and seemingly a good omen.

The loss of three of the attackers was marred by the destruction of one of the defending Fulmars, which was shot down by the Italian CR 42 biplane fighter escorts. There followed a long lull and the next attacks did not develop until 16.30 when five SM79s delivered a high-level attack which landed mainly close to the destroyers of the outer screen. This method was also employed by the third wave, of just three SM79s, at 18.00, and again no hits were made. Although the *Ark's* fighters failed to intercept they did destroy one of the shadowers during the afternoon.

Meanwhile the convoy had plodded on steadily eastward untouched, nearer to safety, nearer to covering night, but also nearer the bases of the Stuka dive-bombers. By this time *Ark Royal* only had seven operational fighters left and when, at 17.10, a large formation of aircraft was picked up on the radar screens boring in from Sicily, every available machine was sent out to intercept them. In fact there were two squadrons of Ju 87s, of twelve and sixteen machines each, escorted by six twin-engined Me 110 long-range fighters. They could have proved decisive but for the great gallantry of the seven Fulmars which hurled themselves at this mass of aircraft and so distracted the German pilots that they took cover in the cloud formations, and lost all cohesion, which is essential for dive-bombing. They were forced to abort the mission without even sighting the convoy. It was a great achievement by *Ark's* planes.

The Skerki Channel was reached at 20.15, and, according to the prearranged plan, the ships of Force B turned back westwards leaving the convoy under the protection of the cruisers and destroyers with the minesweeping destroyers from Somerville's command, leading the way. Just as *Renown* was making her turn with *Ark Royal* and *Sheffield,* with only four destroyers to protect her and those not yet in position, a skilful attack was delivered in the half light by three Italian torpedo bombers who pushed in to close range before dropping. Only remarkable ship-handling by Wee Mac saved *Renown* at that instant; two torpedoes passed close alongside to port and the third to starboard. It was enough to save *Renown* but it did not prevent her receiving her first serious casualties of the war, and these were made more tragic in that they were self-inflicted.

As the three Italian bombers swept close by the ship all the guns of the close-range armament were hammering away with their sights locked onto their targets as they spewed out a hail of high explosives. Naturally at such short ranges the four-point-fives were at low depression and as they tracked round disaster struck. Bill Cain describes the accident:

> Our 4.5s were firing at the torpedo bombers with their barrels pretty well depressed. For some unknown reason P3 gun fired into the back of P2 and blew the crew and guns to smithereens. Theoretically this should not have happened because when a gun is trained on a dangerous bearing it cuts out and breaks the firing circuit and so automatically prevents the guns from being fired. This did not happen and when we got back to Gibraltar they erected angle iron around the outside to prevent this type of ghastly accident happening again. It is ironic to think that this should happen to ourselves, the only casualties of war we suffered.

Bill Kennelly adds a grim postscript to this incident: 'Our party had the unenviable task of fighting the resulting fire and clearing up the mess afterwards. My Stoker PO, Charlie Hunt, certainly deserved a medal that day, but as is often the case, he didn't get one.'

Five men were killed outright in the pulverised turret and another five very badly wounded of whom one later died. An officer and twenty-one ratings were wounded, most of them very young men. It was a bad end to what had, up to then, been an unqualified victory. As only a minor compensation two of the bombers were hit by the ship's gunfire but were not observed to crash.

Renown and the rest of Force B proceeded slowly west during the night with the intention of waiting north of Algiers for the return of the 8th Flotilla. During the night the convoy ran into a thick minefield and, despite the efforts of the destroyers, two of the merchant ships, *New Zealand Star* and *Empire Song*, struck, the latter sinking. She was the only casualty however. The six destroyers refuelled at Malta and then started on the return journey that evening at high speed. Unfortunately one of them, *Foresight*, developed engine defects, which reduced her speed to 12 knots. *Faulknor* with Captain (D) embarked, decided to keep his flotilla together for mutual protection, but despite valiant efforts the fault could not be made good and *Foresight* had to return to Malta. The delay left the remaining five ships deep in hostile waters with dawn approaching and not surprisingly they were subjected to heavy and prolonged air attacks at dawn, and on through the day, during which the *Fortune* was so shaken by near misses that her speed also was reduced.

Further attacks followed and, on learning of their predicament Somerville turned *Renown* and the rest of his force back to provide them with cover, a gesture greatly appreciated by the destroyer crews; the whole force arrived back at Gibraltar without further mishap on 12 May. In all the arrival of the four merchantmen resulted in the landing of 238 tanks and forty-three Hurricanes to the hard pressed Middle East forces in a fraction of the time the round-the-Cape voyage would have entailed. But the operation had been hazardous, and the full strength of the enemy had not been employed against it. If it had the outcome might have been less happy.

The next series of operations planned for *Renown* and her companions was the further reinforcing of Malta's fighter defences. A series of Club Runs was planned under the overall designation Operation Jaguar. These flying-off runs were to be conducted in three phases, Operations Splice, Rocket and Tracer. The first got underway on 19 May with the *Ark Royal* and *Furious* with the Hurricanes, and *Renown, Sheffield* and six destroyers as escorts. In all forty-eight Hurricanes were flown from the two carriers from a position south of Sardinia, with the loss of only one and a guiding Fulmar. Force H was back at Gibraltar on the 22nd ready for the next stage, but there was to be a dramatic interruption to their schedule.

They had two days in harbour on this occasion for much needed relaxation. But in the meantime momentous events were brewing up in the North Atlantic. The Germans had set in train Operation *Rheinubung*, the despatch of the battleship *Bismarck* and the 8-inch cruiser *Prinz Eugen* to carry out a raid against the convoy routes and then join their two battle cruiser consorts at Brest to form a raiding force of tremendous potential and power.

Once the German ships had been confirmed at sea the Admiralty set in train widespread movements to bring her to bay, but these mainly concerned the Home Fleet. Two squadrons were despatched to bring *Bismarck* to battle, the *Hood* and *Prince of Wales* and the *King George V, Victorious* and *Repulse*. It was not expected that the German squadron would get past these forces but should they evade them both then the Admiralty naturally took all precautions to protect the most vital convoys then at sea. At that time there were eleven convoys at sea in the North Atlantic of which six were homeward and five outward bound. One of the most important of these was a troop convoy, WS 8B, which had sailed from the Clyde on 22 May with an escort of two cruisers and eight destroyers.

At 05.00 on 24 May, the Admiralty ordered Force H to its protection and at 01.50 the *Renown* was once more plunging out to sea in company with *Ark Royal, Sheffield* and six destroyers, *Faulknor, Foresight, Forester, Foxhound, Fury* and *Hesperus*. Then came the shocking news of the destruction of the *Hood*, the damage to the *Prince of Wales* and, later, the loss of contact with the enemy squadron. This changed the whole picture. The Admiralty retained direct control over Force H and, although Somerville himself thought that the German ships would make for Brest, the possibility of their doubling back to Germany had to be allowed for. There was also the chance that they would head for the deep mid-Atlantic water and refuel from waiting tankers before making their next move and to cover this eventuality the Admiralty instructed Somerville to steer north-west. At 10.00 on the 24th however these orders were modified and Force H swung round to a more northerly course to cover the French Atlantic ports.

Throughout the 25th the ships of Force H had punched, rolled and slammed their way through a north-westerly gale and the weather continued to worsen. Not surprisingly the destroyers were finding it difficult to maintain station, even though speed was reduced again and again. Three destroyers had not had time to top up at Gibraltar and they were soon reporting themselves low. Refuelling in the storm was obviously out of the question and so *Foresight, Foxhound* and *Fury* had to be sent back at midday. The remaining three clung on tenaciously in the raging waters but by nightfall Force H was down to 20 knots and still finding it heavy going.

By dawn on the 26th they had reached the latitude of Brest but the three destroyers left were also running low on fuel. Somerville had no choice but to send them back also and accept the risk of submarine danger. He instructed Captain (D), De Salis, to alter course to the east, and, when 150 miles from *Renown's* estimated position, to signal to the Admiralty Somerville's position at 07.30 and to ask Plymouth for the results of air searches to the north of him. This they did but Plymouth had no sighting reports to pass to *Renown*.

Renown had by this time been forced to reduce speed still further, to 17 knots, but at least they were between the enemy and Brest. But still no word of their where-abouts had come through although by now the majority opinion was that Brest was their target. At 07.16 *Ark Royal* managed to fly off two Swordfish to conduct a search but they returned at 09.30 having sighted nothing.

An hour later, at 10.30, came the turning point in the chase when a Catalina aircraft of 15 Group, Coastal Command, sighted the *Bismarck* in 49° 30'N, 21. 55'W. This put her about 690 miles from Brest and well to the westward of the *Renown*. The 10.30 aircraft sighting report was received in both *Renown* and *King George V* about a quarter of an hour later and within the hour *Ark Royal's* shadowing Swordfish were firmly in contact with the German giant.

The C-in-C Home Fleet, in *King George V,* was by this time some 130 miles to the north of the *Bismarck* and unless she could be slowed down, there was little chance of the Home Fleet units catching her before she made the French coast. All now rested on Force H whose ships were ideally positioned to catch the enemy. Somerville was therefore given the nice problem of how to go about it. Obviously it would be helpful if *Ark Royal* could score enough torpedo hits to slow down the German battleship for *Renown* to engage her, and should this be possible his staff set to work on the best way this could be done. The old *Renown* with her slender armour was obviously no match for the brand-new German leviathan in a straight slugging match; nonetheless she might well have no choice but to take her on.

Accordingly he signalled the Admiralty to that effect but they ordered Somerville that *Renown* was not to become engaged with the *Bismarck* unless that ship was already being heavily engaged by the *King George V* and *Rodney,* the two real heavy-weights on the scene. Afterwards it was commonly expressed that the crew of the *Renown,* '.., could not understand this and were firmly convinced that their Admiral had held back the battle-tried *Renown* to allow the *King George V* and *Rodney,* who had never experienced action, to be blooded.' The fact that a cartoon to that effect later became a bestseller aboard probably gave rise to this fiction. Those that were there were much more realistic and far less naive than post-war historians have credited them, as Bill Kennelly confirms:

> Our efforts re the *Bismarck* are now history. All we actually did was escort *Ark Royal* and *Sheffield* and wallow in the dirty weather. Things could have been so very different though. There was doubt as to whether *Ark's* planes would be able to get airborne, owing to the heavy seas and the rise and fall of her bows. We, on *Renown,* were all closed up at action stations. Over the intercom came the following: 'This is the Captain speaking – I have signalled Admiralty, requesting permission to engage *Bismarck* – That is all'. Thinking in our minds of what that ship had just done to the *Hood,* that was plenty! It was a very subdued D/C party that sat around. About an hour later, or so it seemed like, the intercom crackled again. 'This is the Captain speaking – In reply to my signal, Admiralty has sent the following reply. 'On no account is *Renown* to

engage the *Bismarck* unless already engaged'. It's just as well the Jerries couldn't hear the cheers throughout the ship at that announcement; we felt we'd probably lived to fight again by that decision.

John Roche however was more of an optimist:

We were looking forward to having a go when we were told to stand off and wait for the *Rodney* and *King George V* to arrive. At that time we had the best captain and admiral combination of all with Wee McGrigor and Slim Somerville and *Renown* was a really happy ship.

Admiral Somerville therefore took up a position within 50 miles ready to launch a torpedo attack with the *Ark Royal's* Swordfish and at 13.16 the cruiser *Sheffield* was detached to the southward to shadow the *Bismarck* but unfortunately the signal to her was not repeated to the *Ark Royal,* and later this omission could have had dire results for the cruiser. The Swordfish flown-off from the carrier mistook the *Sheffield* for the enemy, despite the fact that she had been their constant companion for many months and bore no superficial resemblance to the *Bismarck* whatsoever. Fortunately she had the good sense to hold her fire and concentrated on avoiding the torpedoes. In a second attack the vital hit was scored which so disabled the German ship that she could be brought to battle and the Home Fleet duly despatched her next day with gunfire and torpedoes.

Meanwhile *Renown* and *Ark Royal* moved to the southward so that they should not inconvenience the movements and actions of the C-in-C. Following the sinking of the *Bismarck, Sheffield* rejoined and they set course back to Gibraltar. On their way, and still without a destroyer screen they were sighted by the German submarine, *U-556.* Her commander later claimed that he had both ships in his sights in a perfect attacking position but that he had no torpedoes left. Whether this was in fact so (he originally claimed that it was the *King George V),* no attack was made and the next day they rendezvoused with the 8th Flotilla up from the Rock and returned there in company on the 29th to another rousing reception.

When we got back to Gibraltar, [wrote Bill Cain] a few days later, a pipe band from the Black Watch came out to meet us in a launch and escorted us back into harbour. It was good to be appreciated even though our help was indirect. Unfortunately we could not celebrate in the usual style because the Rock was short of beer, but there was a small supply of onion beer made in Spain, which tasted like jungle juice. If you did not like that you could have a port and lemon, which was a pleasant drink.

Bill Kennelly remembers that:

On entering Gib harbour on our return from the *Bismarck* hunt we were treated to a welcome by the army-bands and all the usual badinage. One soldier indulged his wit by shouting across to us – 'Does it take all the Bloody Navy to sink the *Bismarck*?' The reply from our side probably sank him too – 'No, only half. The other half is evacuating you bastards from Crete!'

Following the conclusion of the *Bismarck* hunt the prestige of the Club was at its height. Those ships entitled to join that exclusive happy band whose mythical tie was described as having for its motif 'raspberries on a field of Mediterranean grey', were now world-famous. The famous trio of *Renown, Ark Royal* and *Sheffield* were known world-over and shared their special relationship with the hard-worked destroyers of the 'F' class of the 8th Flotilla under the inspired leadership of James Somerville. Unfortunately such a bond could not be sustained forever in time of war. The ships of Force H had been run ragged in the preceding eight months and soon some could not go on without a major refit. Gradually the composition of the Club began to change, both through replacements, the *Hermione* taking over from the *Sheffield,* the *Nelson* from the *Renown* and the 'L' class destroyers from the 'F's and through losses, like the *Ark Royal* and the *Fearless* later on that year. Considering the waters in which they had been operating losses were remarkably small and the first casualty the Club suffered did not occur until August.

In the case of *Renown* just what this meant in terms of mileage is best illustrated by Captain Gray:

> From September 1939 until *Renown* returned to Rosyth in August 1941 for a refit, the ship had steamed 135,347 miles and she had steam on her main engines for 454 days. The number of days spent at sea in that period was 381. The greatest monthly distance was 10,237 miles covered in December 1939 and at one period *Renown* was at sea for thirty-seven out of thirty-nine days when searching for *Graf Spee.*

Such facts should finally quash the popular image, fostered by post-war writers of imaginative fiction, that the capital ships of the Royal Navy, rarely, if ever, left their moorings. Indeed as Captain Gray writes: 'From the foregoing I imagine one could justifiably claim that *Renown* was the most important warship in the Royal Navy for the first two years of the war.'

And she continued to be so.

CHAPTER ELEVEN

'Twixt Biscay and Malta

With the immediate threat of the *Bismarck* removed from the Atlantic, and with the heavy losses being suffered by the Royal Navy during the evacuation of Crete, Malta again loomed foremost in the plans of Force H in the summer of 1941. After a brief respite Somerville could now turn his attentions to completing the flying-off operations already interrupted and thus the first sortie that *Renown* engaged in this new phase was Operation Rocket. Again both the *Ark Royal* and *Furious* were employed to convey and fly-off a total of thirty-five Hurricanes to the island, which were this time led there by a Blenheim from Gibraltar. *Renown, Sheffield* and six destroyers provided their escort. The operation, carried out between 5 and 6 June, with the Hurricanes flying-off on the 6th, was again successful and met no opposition from the enemy.

Furious then returned to the UK to embark still more Hurricanes and, while awaiting her return, *Renown* put to sea again with *Ark Royal, Hermione, Faulknor, Fearless, Forester, Foresight* and *Foxhound* to conduct a sweep in the Bay of Biscay as part of a general round-up of German supply ships following the *Bismarck* sortie. Force H sailed from Gibraltar on 16 June and swept the area without success for several days. Their destroyers were sent in to the Rock to refuel on the 18th and on their way located and destroyed the submarine *U-138*. Further patrolling by *Renown* and the rest of Somerville's command again went unrewarded and the whole force returned to Gibraltar on the 21st. Next day an air search located the German supply ship *Alstertor* and the 8th Flotilla was despatched to intercept her, which it did on the 23rd off Cape Finisterre. Seventy-eight British prisoners were rescued in this neat sweep.

Between the 13th and 15th *Renown* was again deployed in the Mediterranean providing cover to the *Ark Royal* and *Victorious* and six destroyers, which carried out Operation Tracer, flying off forty-seven Hurricanes to Malta, forty-three of which arrived safely.

These Club Runs continued to be Force H's main commitment throughout this month. *Furious* duly returned to Gibraltar with a fresh consignment of fighters and on 26 June, after some of these had been transferred to *Ark Royal*, she sailed to carry out Phase 1 of Operation Railway escorted by *Renown, Hermione* and six destroyers. This sortie encountered very bad weather, the Mediterranean in June not being all the travel brochures claim of it; despite this *Ark* got away twenty-two

Hurricanes, all of which reached their destination. The force returned to Gibraltar on the 28th and sailed again next day to carry out Phase 2 of this taking with them the *Furious* herself and a screen of seven destroyers. This part of the operation was only a limited success however, for although twenty-six Hurricanes were launched from *Ark Royal* the *Furious* only managed to get nine away safely before a deck accident stopped all further operations aboard her. The whole force returned on 1 July with the remaining eight Hurricanes still aboard.

This continuous shuttle service sufficed to keep Malta's air defences going during the most critical time, and with the switching of the bulk of the *Luftwaffe* units to the Russian Front early in June the situation from that point of view eased considerably. However the supply problem still remained acute and to bring succour to the population and garrison as soon as possible the Admiralty decided to mount a very large convoy operation from the west, to be codenamed Operation Substance.

On 30 June a signal was received from the Admiralty advising Somerville that *Renown* would be relieved by the *Repulse* so that the former could return home for a long-awaited refit. On 1 July it was advised that it was hoped that *Repulse* would be available for this relief around the end of the month. Somerville was convinced that the *Repulse*, which had not been modernised in any way, was totally unsuited for any operation, which involved facing modern heavy ships or bombers and duly informed Their Lordships of his feelings on the matter. The upshot was that, on 16 July, when *Renown* was ordered home to refit on the 16 July, on completion of Substance, she was to be relieved instead by the battleship *Nelson*.

Because, as always, this operation involved considerable subsidiary operations the planning of Substance was a long and complicated affair. It was thought that the non-intervention by the Italian fleet earlier could no longer be counted on for they had at least three and possibly four battleships available for action in addition to powerful cruiser and destroyer forces, a mass of submarines and E-boats as well as the still considerable strength of the *Regia Aeronautica* upon which to call. The departure of the bulk of the Stuka dive-bombers was obviously a relief as there were no modern carriers available to reinforce Force H. The *Illustrious* and *Formidable* had both been badly damaged by the Ju 87s and were repairing in America, while the only other ship, *Victorious,* was needed by the Home Fleet to keep watch over the powerful Brest squadron; the *Scharnhorst* and *Gneisenau* had now been joined by *Prinz Eugen,* while the *Tirpitz* was thought to be approaching operational readiness in the Baltic.

However if Somerville's force could not receive extra air cover the Admiralty made arrangements to strengthen his surface units considerably and the battleship *Nelson,* cruisers *Edinburgh, Manchester* and *Arethusa,* the fast minelayer *Manxman* and destroyers *Lightning, Cossack, Maori, Sikh, Nestor, Farndale, Avonvale* and *Eridge* were despatched to help. *Duncan* and *Encounter* of the 13th Destroyer Flotilla were also added to the screen.

During June the many phases of the plan's requirements were brought together and arranged within the basic framework. The convoy itself consisted of six fast store ships, *City of Pretoria* (8,000 tons). *Deucalion* (7,500 tons), *Durham* (13,000 tons), *Port Chalmers* (8,500 tons), *Melbourne Star* (11,000) and *Sydney Star* (12,500 tons) and one naval personnel ship, *Leinster* (4,302 tons), as a troopship with 1,000 soldiers for the Malta Garrison aboard. Altogether some 5,000 troops were to be carried to the island in the ships and the escorting cruisers of the close escort, Force X. This comprised the cruisers *Edinburgh, Manchester* and *Arethusa,* the minelayer *Manxman* and the destroyers *Cossack, Maori, Sikh, Nestor, Farndale, Avonvale* and *Eridge.* The *Encounter,* also part of Force X, was to act as screening ship to the fleet oiler *Brown Ranger* which was to accompany them for part of the journey and top up the destroyers so that they had full bunkers in which to make the final dash through the Narrows and back to the west again after offloading the troops from the cruisers.

Force H itself, which was to provide the heavy cover as usual, then comprised *Renown, Nelson, Ark Royal* and *Hermione* screened by the destroyers *Faulknor, Fury, Forester, Lightning* and *Duncan.* Somerville as usual was in overall command with Vice-Admiral Syfret in command of Force X. His flagship arrived at Gibraltar early to help coordinate the intricate planning details with Somerville's staff but the transports and most of the other ships of war that joined Force H for the operation came from England direct with the *Nelson.*

The normal elaborate deception ruses were of course carried out and as many ships as possible were sailed directly through the Straits on the night of 20/21 July without entering harbour. But the short-range Hunt class destroyers had to refuel there and some of the other ships had to embark passengers from among the troops. Those ships that had to enter harbour were to leave the convoy in two groups in time to arrive on the 19th and 20th respectively. The passengers were to move to their new ships after dark on those two days. The oiler *Brown Ranger* with her escorting destroyer was to leave Gibraltar on the night of the 20th/21st to join the convoy next morning.

Force H itself was to sail last, leaving harbour in time to clear the Straits before dawn on the 21st.

Supplementary to this movement the *Ark Royal* was to fly off further Swordfish torpedo bombers to Malta, and seven empty store ships already lying in Valletta harbour were to sail for Gibraltar in convoy and return under cover of the returning Force X and Force H. The latter was positioned in a 'waiting' area north of their route to prevent any Italian fleet from intervening at a late stage.

It was on the occasion of this convoy that Somerville, under no illusions as to the dangers involved should the enemy stir themselves at last, issued his famous call to the warships of his force, that later became the hallmark of the Malta convoys: 'The Convoy Must Go Through!'

The initial stages of the operation boded ill for the success of this convoy however, for on the crucial night of sailing a thick fog descended over the Straits and Gibraltar itself. Fortunately the main convoy negotiated the Straits without mishap and on schedule escorted by *Nelson, Edinburgh, Manxman* and five destroyers. Inside the harbour the troops were transferred from the liner *Pasteur* to the *Manchester* and *Arethusa,* and, after some delay, they sailed with three destroyers, as did the oiler and her escort, but the *Leinster* ran herself aground while turning out of Gibraltar bay, and she and her cargo of troops had to be left behind.

The *Renown* overtook the convoy at midday on the 21st and, having adjusted the destroyer screens with a view to economy of fuel, Force H moved off to its usual covering position ahead and to the northward of the convoy; both groups were given further anti-submarine escort for a time by Sunderlands from Gibraltar.

On the 22nd the day passed uneventfully. The ten destroyers of Force X took it in turns to refuel from the *Brown Ranger* as planned, a ten hour operation, on completion of which she went back to Gibraltar. But what of the Italian counter-moves?

In truth there were few. The enemy had been completely outfoxed once again. Although it was known early on the 21st that Force H had put to sea the reconnaissance aircraft that sighted *Renown's* group early the next day did not press its search any further southward and thus the convoy itself was not reported to Rome at all that day. *Supermarina* therefore assumed that Force H was merely conducting yet another aircraft ferrying run and the Italian Fleet remained steadfastly in harbour and made no move at all to intervene.

Only two submarines therefore remained to dispute their passage at this time, *Alagi* and *Diaspro*, and the latter indeed made contact with Force H north of Bougie and made a torpedo attack on the *Renown* just before midnight. Although Lieutenant Commander Dotta was undetected in his approach and was able to make a perfect attack, *Renown* was saved again, this time by a timely warning from the destroyer *Nestor* which enabled Wee Mac again to swing his ship round in time to avoid being hit.

It was not therefore until early on the morning of 23 July that further shadowing aircraft were able to report back the full extent of the British operation and thereafter the ether was full of their excited gabbling. It was decided in Rome that there was nothing the Italian Fleet could do at this late stage but heavy air attacks were hurriedly fixed up and further submarine patrols were sailed, the *Bandiera, Dessie, Manara* and *Settimo* all taking up interception positions between Pantelleria and Malta along the edge of the Narrows that evening, while several E-boats were sailed later that day to take up watch in the same area for a night attack on the convoy. The bulk of the attack, however, once again rested with the enemy aircraft, and as before Somerville now closed the convoy to provide the strongest possible defence against this eventuality.

The sea was calm, the sky was clear and only a light breeze was blowing from the north-east when *Renown* and the other big ships joined the convoy again at 08.00 that morning. The fleet was deployed in cruising disposition number 16, the ships zig-zagging on a mean course of 090° and the speed of advance was 13.5 knots. With the destroyers fanned out in a wide screen, the cruisers and minelayer of Force X stationed ahead of the columns of merchant ships and astern as before and with Force H itself, 'formed as a flexible port column of the convoy with the object of providing anti-aircraft protection whilst still remaining free to manoeuvre for flying,' the fleet was now ready.

At last learning from their previous failures that independent attacks produced little or no result, the Italian airmen in the first wave, which was picked up by *Hermione's* radar and broke over the fleet at 09.45, took great pains at achieving close co-ordination in a well-planned synchronised attack. Although the *Ark Royal* managed to deploy no less than eleven Fulmar fighters against this incoming force, which consisted of nine high-level bombers and six or seven torpedo bombers, all SM79s, the Fleet Air Arm got the worst of the encounter which took place about 20 miles from the convoy.

Although the fighters managed to destroy two of the enemy bombers they lost three of their own number in doing so and failed to deter the Italians from pressing their attack to its conclusion.

The surviving high-level aircraft worked their way calmly across the head of the destroyer screen and proceeded to drop their bombs from an altitude of 10,000 feet. The convoy was wheeled and the bombs fell harmlessly among the leading ships. But although they scored no hits they did achieve their main objective by breaking up the defensive formation and drawing the fighters, for the torpedo bombers were able to press in from ahead out of the sun without hindrance, taking the ships by surprise at low level and picking their targets before becoming heavily engaged.

These torpedo bombers were professionals. Splitting into two groups of two or three aircraft each they attacked the convoy from both sides with devastating effect. Two baulked at penetrating the destroyers' barrage, which was by now developing considerably, and chose the *Fearless* out ahead as their target, dropping their torpedoes at ranges of 1,500 and 800 yards from a height of 70 feet. The destroyer avoided the first torpedo but was hit by the second, which, after coming to the surface and appearing to pass harmlessly down the ship's port side, suddenly porpoised 30 feet away and turned into the ship's side. It struck aft setting her oil tanks ablaze, jamming her rudder. As a tow was out of the question she was sunk by the *Forester* who embarked survivors.

The other group penetrated into the convoy lines and the *Manchester* narrowly avoided two torpedoes by a sharp alteration of course. As she turned to resume her station a third aircraft dropped its torpedo between two of the transports, and although *Manchester* immediately reversed her helm the torpedo hit her causing considerable damage and killed thirty-eight of her crew. As a result of this attack she could only use one of her four engines, which gave her a speed of 8 knots. Somerville ordered her back to Gibraltar with the *Avonvale* as escort. She was eventually able to work up to 12 knots, and, although subjected to another torpedo bomber attack that evening, about 100 miles to the westward the ship's guns kept the three bombers at safe distance and she reached Gibraltar.

This skilled and daring attack had been met by long-range controlled fire against the high-level bombers and barrage with both long-range and close-range guns against the torpedo bombers; the ships destroyed three of them and the *Renown* added her quota of fire to the total.

Half an hour after this first engagement at 10.10 five more bombers tried to attack the convoy, crossing this time from north to south. Five fighters from *Ark Royal,* though unable to reach within 1,000 feet of the enemy, forced them to drop their bombs at a great height and mostly outside the screening ships. Again, at about 16.45, five torpedo bombers led by a seaplane, came in from the northward but three Fulmars caught them nearly 20 miles away, shot down two and drove off the rest.

Soon after this the fleet arrived off the entrance to the Skerki Channel and there Somerville sent the *Hermione* to take *Manchester's* place with Force X and the destroyers took their proper stations with the 8th DF ships *Foxhound, Firedrake,* fitted with their special gear, acting as leading minesweepers. *Renown, Nelson* and *Ark Royal* turned back to the waiting position at 17.13.

The night passed uneventfully for *Renown* and her consorts but Force X and the convoy soon ran into further opposition. Beaufighters from Malta were supposed to take over the fighter cover until nightfall but proved completely ineffective and made no interceptions; but torpedo bombers again struck the convoy at 19.00, and both *Edinburgh* and *Hermione* were near-missed. They were again unable to prevent an accurate high-level bombing run by a further formation at 19.45, during which the *Firedrake*, going slowly and steadily with her minesweeps out made an easy target. She was near-missed by a heavy bomb close amidships. Fortunately she was taken in tow by the *Eridge*, and after a long tow managed to reach Gibraltar.

The convoy however had still not been touched and steamed steadily through the Narrows during the night. At the narrowest point of the channel around 02.50 on the 24th they were attacked by numerous E-boats but the escorting destroyers drove them off, damaging several; the E-boats' only success was to put one torpedo into the *Sydney Star*, which was not mortal. Her troops were transferred to the *Nestor* and she followed the rest of the convoy safely into Malta.

Despite further attacks by Ju 87 dive bombers (one of which was destroyed by *Hermione*) and high level SM 79 bombers, no further casualties were taken on the morning of the 24th and the *Edinburgh*, *Arethusa* and *Manxman* went on ahead, disembarked their troops and sailed again the same evening. The five destroyers followed them later, leaving one behind to repair defects, and overtook the cruisers of Force X on the morning of the 25th. Meanwhile the six empty supply ships and the naval auxiliary *Breconshire* had sailed for the west earlier that day and got through without loss.

In the meantime *Renown* and her force, after parting company with the convoy on the evening of the 23rd, steamed northward at 18 knots until the afternoon of the 24th, going as far as 38° 30'N. Here Somerville turned back to cover the movements of all the various scattered forces, the empty merchantmen, the damaged *Manchester* with *Avonvale*, the damaged *Firedrake* in tow of *Eridge* and the ships of Force X, all of which were open to heavy air attacks now that the enemy was fully alerted.

In position 37° 42' N., 7° 17' E at 01.00 on the 25th the *Ark Royal* flew off the six Swordfish destined to join Malta's striking force; soon after rendezvous was made with the cruisers and destroyers of Force X under Syfret, and the combined force turned back toward Gibraltar once more. Fighter patrols from the carrier were soon busy and quickly shot down one shadower, losing another of their number in the process, but others soon took its place. At 11.00 a strong formation of high-level bombers was reported approaching from the north with a second group of torpedo bombers coming in from the east. *Ark* had four Fulmars in the air and flew off six more to engage. In the resulting air fight the Fleet Air Arm again performed wonders, shooting down three of the high level bombers at a cost of two Fulmars, and forcing the remainder to jettison their bombs some 15 miles from the fleet.

Although no fighter intercepted the torpedo bombers they were tracked on the ship's radar screens and a barrage was prepared, but in the event these aircraft aborted their mission while still some miles from the ships.

There remained nothing further to do but return to base, although a bombing attack against the returning merchant ships did result in a torpedo hit on the *Hoegh Hood* (9,351 tons) on the 25th, but she reached port, under escort of the main force. *En route* for home Somerville overtook the little *Firedrake* struggling along in tow of *Eridge* with a large hole in her hull. He lined the decks of *Renown*, *Ark Royal* and *Nelson* and cheered ship as they passed her.

Back at Gibraltar the damaged destroyer provided the scene for a classic tale about Slim. He had the habit of donning nondescript clothing and sculling about on his own round the harbour. Doing this soon after the *Renown's* return to Gibraltar, he came across the damaged *Firedrake* and rowed right through the hole in her hull into her boiler room. Here he met the indignant gaze of one of her stokers, who, resentful at this intrusion into his domain by a scruffy 'civilian', promptly told him in no mean language to, '. . . off art of it!', which piece of advice the Flag Officer, Force H promptly and without a word, complied with!

Renown was back in her berth on 27 July but the operation was still not concluded. Apart from the stranded soldiers from *Leinster,* fifty officers and 864 other ranks, there were another forty-two officers and 850 other ranks who had returned to Gibraltar in the damaged ships. It was obviously essential that they join their comrades at Malta without further undue delay and Somerville therefore arranged a rush operation to do this, codenamed Operation Style.

The cruiser *Hermione,* and *Arethusa,* the fast minelayer *Manxman* and two destroyers therefore embarked the seventy officers and 1,676 men most needed, along with 130 tons of urgently required stores and set sail for Malta once more on 30 July. *Renown, Nelson, Ark Royal* and five destroyers sailed to provide heavy cover. Somerville had arranged a diversionary operation for 1 August to draw the attention of the Italian Fleet away from the Narrows during the passage of Force X.

All went well and at 02.00 the destroyer *Maori* bombarded Porto Conte in Sardinia while her sister ship, *Cossack,* demonstrated off Alghero where aircraft from *Ark Royal* attacked the nearby airfield the same day.

The Italians were not taken in by all this however, for the Sardinian authorities were informed by the Minister of Marine that the two destroyers were possibly part of an escort force for a convoy passing south-west of the island. They therefore did not anticipate a large-scale landing despite a charade laid on by Somerville at Gibraltar to that effect, but they did not completely rule out a quick raid by a small landing party. All fixed and mobile defences were therefore placed on the alert in the Upper Tyrrhenian Sea, Sardinia and Sicily. They were not, however, 'completely Botched, Beggared and Bewildered', as Somerville later claimed in a signal to the Admiralty. However the operation by Force X was successfully carried out, the cruisers going straight through to Malta and arriving there at 09.00 on 2 August; they left again at 16.00 the same day for Gibraltar once more after a quick disembarkation. *Renown* and the main body of Force H showed themselves near the Balearic Islands and then met Force X; the whole group returned safely on the 4th. The only incident on the whole journey was the ramming and sinking of the Italian submarine *Tembien* by the cruiser *Hermione* early on the 2nd to the east of Pantelleria.

This marked *Renown's* last appearance for many months in the Mediterranean Sea she had come to know so very well and dominate. It was increasingly plain that the enormous distances she had covered since the outbreak of the war, the prolonged steaming at high speeds in bad weather and the continuing problems with her bulges, which could only be satisfactorily rectified in a major home port, necessitated her return to the UK. Somerville therefore hauled down his flag from *Renown's* masthead and, with the arrival of the battleship *Nelson* at Gibraltar, transferred to that ship. A unique year in *Renown's* long life was thus terminated, although both the Mediterranean and Somerville were to see her again before the war finished.

Renown sailed from The Rock in the very early hours of 7 August, slipping at 01.35 and leaving harbour in company with the *Pasteur* and escorted by the destroyers *Cossack, Maori, Sikh* and *Lightning. En route* this force was ordered to adjust their course in order to meet the President of Portugal at sea aboard the old gunboat *Carvalho Araujo*, escorted by the destroyers *Dao* and *Lima*. This was done and at 18.35 on the 9th, the two groups meeting in 37°42'N, 18°53'W. *Renown* fired a salute of twenty-one guns with the 4.5s as a mark of respect for Britain's oldest ally.

Late on the evening of the 12th *Renown* was met by the destroyers *Eclipse, Impulsive* and *Inglefield* from Scapa and *Pasteur* parted company, while *Renown* continued northabout, passing beneath the Forth Rail Bridge at 10.13 on 14th. With the warm waters of the southern oceans already a fading memory, *Renown* nosed her great bows into Rosyth dockyard once more. De-ammunition commenced immediately, being completed by the 16th and two days later started a long major refit that was to last until the end of October.

As well as a general overhaul of all the overworked machinery, engines, boilers and auxiliary equipment, opportunity was naturally taken to modify her armament. Six single 20-mm Oerlikon cannon were thus added to supplement her close-range AA armament, two atop 'B' turret, two others abreast her bridge at the front of the 4.5-inch batteries, and two more port and starboard in gun pits abreast the fore funnel. Opportunity was also taken to overhaul the 'fail-safe' mechanism of the secondary armament to prevent a repetition of the earlier accident.

The other major improvements taken during this refit were the installation of modern radar sets so that she no longer had to rely on other vessels in this respect. Several kinds of sets were now in production and the latest marks were installed aboard *Renown* at this time. A type 273 was fitted on the foremast. This was a surface warning set, a 10 cm waveband being employed with a 50-kw output. A type 281 set was installed, with the transmitting office at the after end of the signal deck and the receiving office at the after end of the signal deck and the receiving office on the after superstructure, with aerials at the mastheads. This was capable of providing both air and surface-warning; aircraft could be detected up to 120 miles away at height of up to 25,000 feet, while surface vessels could be located at ranges of up to 12 miles. Two type 282 sets were put in with their aerials on the bridge pom-pom directors and a combined receiving/transmitting office aft the No. 2 bridge-platform. This set was designed specifically to work the close-range armament and its range of only 4 miles was sufficient to cover the extreme limits of the pom-poms, 1,800 yards. Three type 283 sets were also installed. These were to facilitate barrage blind-firing by the close-range weapons. In order to accommodate the three new barrage directors the after pom-pom director was removed from the ship, as were the 9 ft range-finders on the lower bridge. A transmitting/receiving office was fitted on No. 1 bridge-platform and a single office aft. Type 284 radar was fitted with an office on the signal platform and the aerials on the main director-control tower structure. This set, the 284, was designed for use with the main armament only and could be utilised in conjunction with the three 15-inch turrets at ranges up to 18,000 yards (about 10 miles). It was a successful set but main battle ranges of course took place at double this distance so its usefulness was limited. Finally two type 285 sets were installed, with a double office on the signal platform and aerials on the HACS. The purpose of this set was to control long-range AA fire, and it had an effective range of 8 miles.

All this extra radar equipment meant that *Renown* was one of the best-equipped ships in the fleet at this time in this vital arm, but it also meant a large increase in her complement as specialised officers and ratings had to be accommodated to man these arrays as well as her additional close-range weapons. These continued to be added to over the next year as they became available until a further ten 20mm Oerlikons were shipped. To compensate for this the largely ineffective 0.5-inch multiple machine-guns were removed from the ship during 1942.

Another item of electrical equipment to be embarked during the Rosyth refit was a FM2 type medium-frequency direction-finder, with its office located on the No. 2 bridge platform and the aerial fitted on a projection at the front of the bridge structure. Provision had always existed to carry two Walrus amphibian aircraft aboard but this was not done until after this refit and then only for a short period. The allocation of so much space was really wasted as the development of the carrier made it obsolete and the stowage amidships of these fragile craft with their high-inflammable fuel in a highly vulnerable position was also looked upon with considerable distaste in the fleet. *Renown* embarked her aircraft therefore for only a year or so.

Extra Carley rafts were also shipped at this time, but with the increase in her complement they were still insufficient had the worst have happened. There was however a limit to the number of boats and rafts, which could be accommodated on any ship, even one the size of *Renown*. She was also given a highly colourful facelift, changing her rather rust-speckled light grey colour scheme for the new Admiralty Disruptive Camouflage scheme, promulgated by the Camouflage Section as the first official design for capital ships. It employed a pattern of varying irregular areas over the whole hull and superstructure, including the turrets, of paints of varying tones and shades designed to break up the outline of the vessel when seen from a distance. Greys, and blacks with dark green predominated, the patterns being different on each side of the vessel. In theory this made the ship hard to spot, but with the development of radar it is doubtful whether this had much real effect on capital ships other than to confuse their escorting destroyers in the grim wastes of the North Atlantic and Arctic!

With these changes to the ship, of course, came changes to her personnel. From the outbreak of the war *Renown* had been fortunate, and her efficiency reflected this, in that her crew were mainly long-service regulars with only a small dilution taking place during her service with Force H. By the beginning of the third year of war however it was inevitable that with the great expansion of the fleet these veterans were on call to man the more modern ships of the fleet, and this, coupled with normal promotions and changes, led to the breaking up of the 'old team'. Fortunately the *Renown* managed to retain her old spirit, for the greater proportion of her 'new' officers and men proved to be of an equally high calibre, although of course there were some exceptions. For example, on 23 August it was reported that some malcontents had smashed up the ventilation fans as an act of suspected sabotage.

And so in the autumn of 1941 men left *Renown,* and others joined her for the first time, aware of her remarkable war record to date and equally proud to serve in her.

Some, of course, had already gone, like Midshipman Stuart, whose log has proved so informative, freshly promoted. Others, like Captain Gray who had watched her new engines being assembled, had nursed them during their infancy and kept them going over all the thousand upon thousand of mile without proper refit, moved on to new appointments.

One of these was Stoker Cain:

> I went on leave a few days after our arrival at Rosyth and, after returning, remained with the ship only until 5 November, when as expected I left for Devonport and my course. So ended a commission on a ship that I was proud to have served in. Looking back I am glad to have sailed in the last of the battle-cruisers. It was an honour to have served in her.

Another new arrival at this time, Seaman Anderson, gives a picture of the routine duties he and his mates from Devonport soon settled down to in their new home.

Many of her regulars continued to do so of course, an enormous number of men that had joined her in August 1939, continued to serve in the *Renown* for another commission, some even remaining with her until the war was over. One of those who remained at this time was Bill Kennelly:

> I have hazy memories of docking in Rosyth and lively evenings ashore at the Queen's in Inverkeithing, or a run to the cinema in Dunfermline. Also the rare opportunity for leave. As my home was Ireland I usually had to travel down to Holyhead from Rosyth, or via Burnshaird, Glasgow to Belfast. Travelling conditions were poor at best and we sometimes didn't get back on board in time, owing to ferries not running due to the weather etc. One occasion after such a delay we were billeted in the old *Caroline* at Belfast and arrived only to find *Renown* had sailed. We were berthed in *Killarney III* and later issued with travel warrants to Portsmouth. Being senior rating in command, I had to shepherd my flock and my first and worst obstacle was the Scottish lady ticket collector at Edinburgh station. Nothing would convince her that we 'Civvies' hadn't acquired naval travel-warrants illegally. In the end a Naval shore patrol sorted out this virago and we were able to get on with the war.

Others joined the *Renown*, such as Engineering Officer John Stuart. He recalls one of the most secret modifications carried out aboard the ship during this refit:

> After *Hood* was sunk the Admiralty issued orders for the *Renown* to be modified so that 167 valveless penetrations of the main deck (the armour deck) would have heavy duty valves installed. These penetrations were principally for ventilation ducting and the added valves would be closed in action in the belief that flash from an enemy shell might have penetrated the magazine and caused the explosion that broke up the *Hood*. This modification was carried out with classification Top Secret. Equally secret was the order that *Renown* should not engage a German battleship of the *Tirpitz* class on her own.
>
> When a man joins a ship he is given a division, that is the part of the ship where he will work and report for duty; in my case it was the fo'c'sle. This always had to be kept clean, painted etc. Each division had its divisional officer and various petty officers and leading hands to administer and carry out the various duties required. In addition you were assigned a duty watch (port, starboard, red, white or blue); in Renown's case it was three watches,

...own as first completed in 1916. (*Vice-Admiral B.C.B. Brooke*)

...own passing through the Suez Canal, 1921. (*W.F.J. Waller*)

Renown passing through the Panama Canal locks, 1927. (*Peter C. Smith*)

mage to *Renown's* bow after collision with
od 1935. (*L.P. Stirk*)

Physical drill on the fo'c'sle of *Renown* in the
South Atlantic, 1939. (*A.V. Herbert*)

e ship's mascot (Right). Flagship of Force H (Below). (*W. Cain*)

Renown in action at the Battle of Spartivento, November 1940. (*John M. Roche*)

'Slim' Somerville stirring the
Christmas pudding.
(*H. Shannon*)

'That was Force H – that was'
(*W. Cain*)

arding party aboard *Renown* during interception of prize tankers. (*E.J. Smith*)

e *Bianca* afire and sinking. (*E.J. Smith*)

e German prize crew from the *Scharnhorst* (*W. Cain*)

An amphibian alighting alongside *Renown*.
(*V. Holmes*)

A Fairey Fulmar fighter over *Renown*.
(*John M. Roche*)

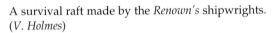

A survival raft made by the *Renown's* shipwrights.
(*V. Holmes*)

e starboard forrard 4.5-inch gun battery. (*E.J. Smith*)

After the *Bismarck* chase, May 1941. (*W. Cain*)

'Take it easy youse guys – I gotta build these boys a Reppytation'. (*W. Cain*)

Renown in the Mediterranean in 1941. (*W. Cain*)

Covering Arctic Convoys, 1942. (*H. Shannon*)

Renown at Hvalfiord, Iceland, May 1942. (*Maurice Balaam*)

ctic Seascape. (*W. Pittendreigh*)

The North African landings, November 1942. *Renown* firing a salvo, the battleship *Nelson* is astern. (*J.T.Y. Dobie*)

Operation Sextant – the morning after the hurricane, 27/28 August, 1943. (*Maurice Balaam*)

amage control exercise. (*P. Elain*)

amage control centre (*P. Elain*)

Leaving Greenock, September 1943. Quarterdeck Men and Royal Marines fallen-in for leaving harbour. (*Maurice Balaam*)

Renown in Trincomalee harbour, 1944. (*Maurice Balaam*)

...atching oiling at sea in Indian Ocean, 1944. ...mewhat 'informal' attire for the C-in-C, Captain ...ll and Captain Searle. (*Maurice Balaam*)

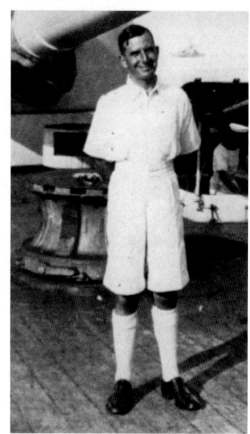

The Padre aboard *Renown* at Trincomalee. (*Maurice Balaam*)

...*nown* oiling the destroyer *Napier*, 1944. (*G. Kennon*)

The German Naval delegation aboard *Renown* for the formal surrender conference, May 1945. (*Maurice Balaam*)

Delegates attending at the surrender of the German Navy, May 1945. (*Maurice Balaam*)

e President of the United States, Harry S. Truman, aboard *Renown* in Plymouth Sound.
t. Cdr. E. Walker)

M. King George VI boarding *Renown*, 2 August 1945. (*Lt. Cdr. E. Walker*)

H.M. King George VI and Truman aboard *Renown*. (*Tom Oliver*)

Renown in Plymouth Sound, September 1945. (*Maurice Balaam*)

red, white and blue. Also you were given your action stations; for me this was as a member of S1 4.5-inch gun's crew. More specifically I was a 'loading number' and my job was to lift the rear end of the shell and my mate would lift the fore end and we would place it into the loading tray and push the tray over to behind the breach. The shell would then automatically push into the breach ready for firing. The rapidity of firing would depend on the directors' crew who fired the gun from their position. In other words all the crew did was load and prepare the gun for firing. Gun drills were carried out at frequent intervals for obvious reasons to become more efficient. At sea the watch would remain at their gun until relieved by the following watch.

The refit was conducted initially in No. 2 Dock at Rosyth from 8 September, the completion date of the work being advised as 30 October. The C-in-C Home Fleet requested Admiralty approval for Vice-Admiral commanding 2nd Battle Squadron to hoist his flag in *Renown*, which was approved the next day *Renown* was undocked on 24 October, but it was advised that a further 48 hours was required to complete all the work satisfactorily, but this date was not achieved either and her sailing was postponed until 14 November. Even so, it was not until 21st that *Renown* finally sailed for Scapa Flow escorted by the destroyers *Arrow*, *Vimiera* and *Wallace*.

And so, the *Renown*, freshly re-equipped, brought up to date, her fighting efficiency much improved, her reputation formidable, sailed to join the Home Fleet under the command of Sir John Tovey at their old stamping ground of Scapa Flow.

It could have been very different indeed. Hard-pressed in the Mediterranean, where *Renown's* faithful companion of many years, *Ark Royal* had finally been sunk by a solitary U-boat torpedo, and at full stretch in the North Atlantic, the Royal Navy was girding itself for the opening of yet another front as the storm clouds gathered in the Pacific. Plans were afoot to despatch a powerful fleet to Singapore to deter the Japanese and a clash of opinions resulted between Churchill and the Admiralty about what form that fleet should take.

Much discussion took place between August and October while *Renown* lay at Rosyth out of action. The Premier wanted to send a fast squadron out East, including one of the latest battleships. The First Sea Lord, more realistically, wished to build up a more powerful force further back as he realised two battleships would hardly deter the Japanese ten. To complicate matters further the losses in capital ships during the final months of 1941 reduced the Navy's strength in that field considerably. Indeed Cunningham's battle line was eliminated; *Barham* had been torpedoed and sunk and *Queen Elizabeth* and *Valiant* both damaged. Of the remaining ships *Warspite*, *Rodney* and *Resolution* were refitting in America at this time, *Renown* and *Royal Sovereign* at home, *Ramillies* and *Revenge* were escorting convoys in North Atlantic, *Nelson* was being replaced at Gibraltar by *Malaya* after being torpedoed during a Malta convoy, leaving only the *King George V* and *Prince of Wales* with the Home Fleet guarding against *Tirpitz* and the other German heavy ships.

Sir Dudley Pound wished to send out the four old 'R' class battleships to the Indian Ocean in December and follow them up in March 1942 with the *Nelson*, *Rodney* and *Renown*, which were to be based at Ceylon. Churchill would not hear of this and so *Prince of Wales* was taken from Tovey and sent to Singapore to join the weakest of the British heavy ships there, *Repulse.* In fact this weakness was realised, for on 22 September a signal had been received ordering the *Renown* to relieve the *Repulse* on the East Indies Station around January 1942, but this was rescinded on 27 October when the Admiralty advised that on completion of the refit *Renown* was to come under orders of the Home Fleet instead. Who knows what the outcome would have been had the fates decreed otherwise. The resulting tragedy off Malaya is well-known, but, with the loss of the *Prince of Wales,* the addition to the Home Fleet's strength of the modernised *Renown* was very welcome that bleak December of 1941.

A new page in the battle-cruiser's life was about to open and now she was the sole representative of her type on the Navy's strength. She was the fastest capital ship in the fleet and was to remain so until the end of her days. 'Last of the Battle-Cruisers' became her unofficial title, but to her crew, and those who had seen her move, she had a different nickname, a very apt one, to them *Renown* was simply the 'Largest Destroyer in the Fleet'

CHAPTER TWELVE

Across Northern Seas

U nder the command of Captain C.S. Daniel, who was soon after to be promoted to the rank of Commodore, and sailing at last from Rosyth dock-yard, *Renown*, after completing her delayed working-up trials during November 1941, finally arrived at Scapa Flow on 09.00 on 22 November, to join the Home Fleet and here the flag of Vice-Admiral A.T.B. Curteis, second-in-command Home Fleet, was raised at her masthead.

The C-in-C, Admiral Tovey, had quite a complicated task on his hands as 1941 gave way to 1942. He only had two capital ships other than *Renown* under his command, his flagship, *King George V* and the older *Rodney*. Of these only the former was of modern construction and fit to stand up to the *Tirpitz*. *Renown* was of course faster, but less powerfully armed and protected; *Rodney* was the exact opposite, having strong armour and nine 16-inch guns but a speed of not much over twenty knots. How he was to deploy three ships of such differing capabilities against the enemy, was just one problem facing Tovey at this time. A second modern ship, *Duke of York,* had completed and was due to take the place of the *Prince of Wales,* but at this time she had not yet fully worked up and had taken Churchill across to America whilst so doing.

In lesser vessels there were four heavy and six light cruisers in his command but only eighteen destroyers. Not all of these ships could be relied upon to join the main fleet as constant demands were made upon them from other sources, not least of which were the Russian convoys which were growing in size and complexity and being faced with a steady increase in opposition from both U-boats and aircraft along their long flanks from enemy-held Norway. Destroyers from the Home Fleet's screen were more and more called upon to reinforce the convoys' escorts as this opposition grew, leaving few to perform in that role to the heavy ships, which were also required to sortie to provide heavy cover. Usually a cruiser squadron was detached for the same purpose as well.

The biggest potential threat to these vulnerable convoys was however the heavy ships of the German Navy and these were *Renown's* main opponents in her new theatre of operations. At this period the Germans had the brand-new battleship *Tirpitz* ready for sea, along with the pocket battleship *Admiral Scheer,* the 8-inch cruiser *Admiral Hipper,* four light cruisers and twenty big modern destroyers.

Another powerful squadron, consisting of the *Gneisenau, Scharnhorst* and *Prinz*

Eugen with six destroyers, lay still at Brest, and was reported almost ready for sea. The situation was therefore a bad one for the truncated Home Fleet, for if the enemy chose to do so he could sail both these powerful forces into the North Atlantic at the same time in a gigantic pincer movement and Tovey only had the forces at his disposal to match one of them.

In order to maintain a constant watch on the vital artery linking these two fleets, the Denmark Strait, Tovey had to maintain a constant cruiser patrol in that area, despite appalling weather conditions, and to back these ships up he was forced to split his few remaining heavy ships between Scapa and Hvalfiord, that bleak and inhospitable anchorage at Iceland. It was on this duty that *Renown* first found herself detached during the Christmas and New Year period and a bleak and dreary 'holiday' venue it turned out to be, for her and her three destroyers The flag of VA2 was transferred to the depot ship *Dunluce Castle* and, at 15.17 on the 20 December, *Renown*, escorted by the destroyers *Forester, Montrose and Worcester*, sailed to rendezvous with the battleship *Rodney* whom she was relieving at Hvalfiord, escorted by the destroyers *Verity, Walker* and *Witherington*. The two big ships exchanged escorts and *Renown* arrived at Hvalfiord at 12.45 on 22nd. The destroyers were themselves relieved on 2 January by *Marne, Offa* and *Onslow*.

We had endless days of boredom in Hvalfiord [stated Bill Kennelly], interspersed with escorting convoys on the North Cape run. There was little excitement as such, just the constant strain mainly caused by dirty weather. We did, however, have one lively event in January, a 128 mile-an-hour blizzard which caused *Renown* to drag 200 yards up the fiord, in spite of both anchors down and having slow steam ahead. In the morning it was chaos with a reported twenty ships aground and one collier high and dry not far from us.

We celebrated at least one Christmas Day in Hvalfiord and, in spite of the cold, a few of us had a run ashore to the 'Canteen'. Maybe it was the atmosphere or rarity of the air itself, but three cans of beer apiece was ample. I can still see Joe Pugh spinning a yarn to a pal in one of the local Liberty Boats, one foot on the gunnels and one on the pier, with the boat slowly drifting off and Joe ending up in the icy water. He surfaced with his piper sending up steam signals and to a great chuck-up from the rest of us. Such was our entertainment.

I personally got some good out of our long spells in Hvalfiord; I made a model of the *Cutty Sark* and a dolls' house for my growing family. We sometimes took a walk up the track along the Fiord and on one occasion met a couple of the locals who jeered and cheered the loss of the *Hood* and *Repulse*. Nice people. There was a daily rota for a trip to Reykjavik in one of the destroyers, but I was never fortunate enough to get my name on.

John Stuart remembers the January blizzard also:

When the storm blew up all the ships had to raise steam with the utmost despatch. So great was the wind that, with two anchors down and with speed for fifteen knots, the ship was just able to prevent dragging her anchors! Some gusts were 180 miles per hour. The American heavy cruiser *Wichita*, with the Yankee Admiral aboard went aground and the flag had to be transferred to her sister ship the *Tuscaloosa* – much to the annoyance of the latter's crew by the way. We made up a song in *Renown* about this, each stanza ending with the line, 'Producers of the Hottest steam this side of the USS *Wichita*!'

A.B. Anderson has similar memories of Iceland:

When in the harbour there you could go ashore; I believe we were allowed two hours shore leave. There was nothing there, only a solitary Nissen hut with Canadian bottled beer to drink. Some of the lads would have a skinful occasionally to break the monotony, but, by and large, it was not worth stepping off the ship for.

On 9 January *Renown* was ordered to rendezvous with the heavy cruiser *Kent* from Scapa, bring VA2 north and carry out exercises, but the weather was so bad that this was cancelled

Meantime Hitler had ordered his heavy ships to concentrate in Norway, ever-fearful that the British had ideas of making landings there. To carry out the first part of this concentration the battleship *Tirpitz* was sent from the Baltic to Wilhelmshaven and sailed with an escort of four destroyers on the night of 14/15 January 1942. This was carried out with great success and not until the 17th did Admiral Tovey get word that the *Tirpitz* might be at sea. By then it was far too late to intercept her for she had actually reached Trondheim the day before.

Renown was placed at readiness to sail and this state of alarm was maintained until the 23rd when finally aerial reconnaissance confirmed that the German battleship was still at anchor in Aasfiord and not sortieing into the Atlantic Ocean as her sister had done. The reason for her enforced idleness was that her destroyer screen had to reverse course back to Germany in order to help with stage two of the German plan, the break-out through the English Channel of the Brest Squadron. This duly took place, also with complete success save for mine damage, between 12 and 14 February.

Meanwhile, on 3 February, *Renown* had sailed with *Rodney* and the carrier *Victorious*, and the two capital ships conducted a 15-inch 'throw-off' shoot. After embarking 523 tons of oil from the *War Bharata*, *Renown* sailed for further exercises on 12 February, escorted by the destroyers *Icarus*, *Inglefield* and *Marne*, during which she carried out full power trials, 4.5-inch and pom-pom firings, a 15-inch full-calibre shoot with *Rodney* again and this was followed by a night exercise.

By this time *Renown* had been joined at Hvalfiord by the *King George V* and the *Rodney* had been detached to cover another large troop convoy to the south. It was with these two heavy ships, the carrier *Victorious* and light forces, that Tovey sailed on 19 February following reports that *Tirpitz* had been sighted underway from Aasfiord. *Renown* and her consorts therefore steamed hard in the direction of Tromso in order to intercept her before she could break north. While they were still so engaged further enemy movements were signalled to Tovey. The pocket battleship *Admiral Scheer* and the 8-inch cruiser *Prinz Eugen* had been sighted steaming north through the southern North Sea with an escort of three destroyers. Plainly the long-feared concentration of the enemy battle fleet was taking shape more rapidly than the Admiralty had feared.

At once the Home Fleet turned south to counter this new threat and the carrier was sent on ahead to launch a torpedo striking force. However the heavy seas and frequent snow showers made progress slow and *Victorious* was unable to launch her aircraft. Both German ships therefore joined the *Tirpitz* at Trondheim, but fortu-nately the *Prinz Eugen* had been torpedoed and damaged by a British submarine and was in no condition to fight.

Nonetheless the two German big ships now presented a formidable threat to the Russian convoys for they lay within easy striking range and, with the passing of winter and the approach of spring, the Germans would have numerous chances of swooping down on them with the two battleships, overwhelming their close escorts and the covering cruisers and doing great execution among the merchant ships before the Home Fleet could intervene.

It was clear, as Admiral Tovey appreciated, that the full strength of the Home Fleet must now be given to each convoy during the dangerous stretch between Jan Mayen and Bear Islands. In order to accomplish this with the forces at his disposal it was therefore arranged that the next pair of convoys, PQ 12 outward and QP 8 of sixteen and fifteen ships respectively sailing from Iceland and the Kola Inlet, should leave simultaneously.

These were the first Arctic convoys to be afforded the protection of the Home Fleet and it was fortunate that at this time the *Duke of York* joined Tovey's flag. He could now mount a strong enough fleet to engage the German squadron with some confidence, although it was doubted, on past form, whether the German Admiral would accept battle unless he was trapped. The passage of the two convoys in fact nearly led to just such a situation, for on 6 March *Tirpitz* did sail with three destroyers to attack them, not realising that the Home Fleet was already at sea in anticipation.

The *Tirpitz* was in fact sighted by a patrolling submarine as she left her lair and sailed northward at 18.00; at this time *Renown* was in company with *Duke of York*, the cruiser *Kenya* and destroyers *Faulknor*, *Fury*, *Eclipse*, *Echo*, *Eskimo* and *Punjabi*, south-east of Jan Mayen island heading north-east astern of PQ 12. Further south and closer to Norway Admiral Tovey was on a parallel course with *King George V*, *Victorious*, heavy cruiser *Berwick* and destroyers *Intrepid*, *Icarus*, *Ashanti*, *Bedouin*, *Lookout* and *Onslow*.

At 10.30 these two groups concentrated and they patrolled astride the cross-over point between the two convoys during the rest of the afternoon and night. It was not until midnight on the 6th/7th that the submarine's sighting report arrived on Tovey's bridge. The Home Fleet continued northward during the hours of darkness, and at 08.00 next morning increased steam for full speed. The weather meanwhile continued to be atrocious, and, although the *Victorious* was told to make ready a torpedo-bomber striking force and to conduct air searches to the south of the convoys, no flying was possible. The limitations of the aircraft carrier therefore prevented any contact being made with the *Tirpitz* which meanwhile, blissfully unaware of how close she was to the three British heavy ships, continued north in search of the convoy.

The Germans were no more successful in finding their prey than were *Renown* and her companions, although at noon on the 7th the *Tirpitz*, the Home Fleet and the convoys were all within 90 miles of one another. Never again did *Renown* come so close to taking part in a major fleet action again as she did at that time. It was a great disappointment.

By midnight the *Tirpitz* was far to the north and heading for Altenfiord and the North Cape. She had detached her destroyers, who, although they sank a Russian straggler, did not locate either convoy. Tovey meanwhile had turned to the south in the opposite direction of his quarry. His destroyers were becoming low on fuel and half were sent to refuel while the other six were detached at 04.00 on the 8th to conduct a sweep along the German ships' probable line of return.

The big ships were now deep in hostile waters without a screen, but Tovey hung on. The weather had moderated sufficiently to enable a possible air strike again off the Lofoten islands that *Renown* knew so well two years before, but after four hours of fruitless patrolling Tovey concluded that *Tirpitz* had already slipped past him and steered back out to sea at 04.00 to rendezvous with returning destroyers. At 06.40 following an evaluation from the Admiralty, the Home Fleet turned back to the west towards the Lofotens, but at 08.00 one of *Victorious* search planes located the *Tirpitz* herself steaming hard about 200 miles west of *Renown*. Unfortunately an attack by twelve Albacores failed completely with the loss of two machines and by the same evening *Tirpitz* was safely in Narvik.

The *Luftwaffe* was equally ineffective in air strikes against the fleet on its return to Scapa, although an attack at 15.45 on the 9th by three Junkers Ju 88s came awfully close, as Henry Shannon witnessed from *Renown*:

I remember it was twilight, *Victorious* was in company and she had still got some of her aircraft aloft which were due to land back on before darkness. She nearly had her chips for a plane was seen approaching from astern as if to land on her flight deck. Fortunately it was spotted just in time as a Ju 88. His bombs exploded just astern of her and he made his escape. If he had released over her flight deck I'd say she would have been very badly damaged with a lot of casualties. No one would have survived long in the water in that region, that's for sure. The gun turrets in the *Renown* were like freezers; the messdecks had the steam pipes running through them and were fairly warm but we could not use them being at first-degree readiness while at sea.

Somewhat disconsolate, *Renown* arrived back at Scapa Flow on the 13th. After their narrow escape the Germans were even more wary of using the big ships and the task of bringing *Tirpitz* to book became even more difficult for the ships and men of Tovey's command. *Renown* now alternated between Scapa and Hvalfiord, and although the former was slightly more amenable for her crew, there was not a lot to choose between them during the rest periods between numerous Arctic patrols covering PQ convoys, as Seaman Anderson remembers:

Scapa wasn't very much better. There was a beer canteen and a cinema there and leave was for longer periods. On the other hand at Scapa there were far more ships and the canteen was always full. It was difficult to get a glass because of this and prior to stop-tap times the men would stockpile pints of beer which soon went flat, and they would continued to drink the stuff until it was time to return to their ships. Sometimes it could be very entertaining with the old piano going and a sing-song. But beer also had an adverse affect at times, with tempers raised and rows breaking out.

The *Renown* was a big ship and the mess areas were very crowded. A mess consisted of a long table (whitewood) and narrow stools to seat some twenty men, within a yard would be another table and so on. On the table you had your food, wrote your letters, played games, in other words that little spot was yours. The hammock billets were similarly placed above the tables and when all the men had slung their hammocks there were only inches between them.

At sea on the long patrols in dirty weather conditions were worse of course.

> In port we always had a night's rest in our hammocks, but at sea it was much different. If you were on watch you would get your head down anywhere, on narrow mess stools or tables, tops of lockers, anywhere, with a gas mask or a life belt for a pillow with a coat over you, and when you went on watch someone else would take your position.
>
> Dusk and dawn action stations were a regular feature when we were in Northern waters, so that the ship was completely ready for action if we were faced with the enemy coming out of the darkness. Sometimes dawn action stations could be a perishing nuisance, particularly if you had gone off watch at 4 a.m. and dawn action stations piped again soon after going off watch.
>
> Our food was cooked in the galley on the upper deck and two men were detailed in turn each day to get the food, distribute it out on plates, and be responsible for washing up the dishes afterwards.
>
> They would have to draw potatoes and peel them and take them to the galley for cooking. There were four meals a day, breakfast, dinner, tea and supper. A recreation space was used to play Tombola, cards and other games. This space was also used for divisions on wet days.

Between 10 and 22 March *Renown* lay at Scapa and the VA's Flag moved to *King George V*. It was at this time that the happy inspiration of 'Warship Week' was originated. The idea served two purposes, it helped raise funds for the war effort through stimulating the purchase of Defence Bonds, National War Bonds and Savings Certificates and, after a set sum had been raised by an area, they were allowed to 'adopt' a warship; this gave the civilians some insight as to how the service was contributing to the war and gave them and the crews of their adopted ships a lasting feeling of 'belonging'. Visits were arranged and comforts sent to the ship, which helped alleviate life aboard a little. It also gave the crews on their lonely vigils the slight comfort that someone at home knew what they were doing, and in the Navy this was important, for the newspapers, as always, tended to concentrate on the war on land or 1,000-bomber raids, both of which were ready copy as they happened. Most of the Navy's work however was conducted far from the glare of publicity, only the major disasters proving 'newsworthy'; this had the effect of making the sailors feel they were forgotten, even though if *they* failed the whole nation went under in starvation and such a possibility was far more serious than the capture of a desert town or the pulverisation of a German city and its civilian inhabitants.

Leicester was the city chosen for *Renown* and during their 'Warship Week', which was held between 28 February and 7 March 1942, the target set was £30,000. Captain Daniel wrote to the Lord Mayor, Miss Councillor Elizabeth R. Frisby, MBE, JP at that time, expressing their honour at being so chosen and including a list of fourteen crew-members, seamen, stokers, telegraphist and marines, who were then serving aboard his ship. The city was presented with a replica of the ship's badge for exhibiting in the Town Hall and in return the City Authorities presented a commemorative plaque designed by the Leicester College of Art and Crafts.

Meanwhile the war approached its grimmest stage. In Russia the German armies were commencing their great advance towards the Volga, the Crimea and the Caucasus, and the Soviet armies again bled and fell back; in the Pacific, Singapore and Hong Kong had fallen to be followed in rapid succession by the Philippines and the Dutch East Indies, Burma was crumbling and in the Indian Ocean Admiral Somerville almost had his fleet annihilated by the powerful Japanese squadron that swept into the area sinking the carrier *Hermes,* cruisers *Dorsetshire* and *Cornwall* and inflicting heavy damage on British bases in Ceylon. In the Western Desert campaigns in North Africa Rommel was about to launch his assault that would culminate in the fall of Tobruk and the withdrawal of the Eighth Army beyond the Egyptian frontier, while a renewed blitz on Malta exceeded in ferocity anything yet seen in intensity and effectiveness.

It was however the situation in the Arctic that first concerned *Renown* and she was off into those grim waters again at the end of March providing cover for Convoys PQ 13 and QP 9 in company with *Duke of York,* the *Victorious,* the cruiser *Nigeria* and screening destroyers *Ashanti, Eskimo, Faulknor, Ledbury, Middleton, Onslow, Punjabi* and *Wheatland.* The Germans had meanwhile further reinforced their heavy squadron at Trondheim with the heavy cruiser *Admiral Hipper.* She arrived safely at Trondheim on 21 March, at the same time as the two convoys left Reykjavik and Murmansk and the threat further increased. Accordingly, Vice-Admiral Curteis sailed from Scapa next day, patrolling to the north-east of Iceland in appalling weather. All the ships were struck by a ferocious gale producing some of the worst conditions aboard *Renown* she had known. The convoy was scattered, and in the aftermath the Germans sailed three destroyers which were beaten off by the cruiser *Trinidad* and destroyers *Eclipse* and *Fury,* which sank one of them. However the cruiser damaged herself and the convoy lost a quarter of its ships to the destroyers and U-boats, one U-boat being destroyed in compensation. Fortunately the German big ships remained in harbour and *Renown's* only opponent was the vicious northern weather. She returned to Scapa on the 28th.

On their return to base Captain C. S. Daniel hoisted his Broad Pendant as Commodore Commanding Force 'W' in *Renown* at 08.20 and she sailed for Greenock escorted by the anti-aircraft cruiser *Charybdis* and destroyers *Inglefield* and *Echo.* This force passed Cape Wrath at 12.15 and *Renown* arrived at C2 berth at 07.38 on the 13th. Here she found the American aircraft carrier *Wasp* busily embarking Spitfires and they learned some details of a new ferry operation, which had been planned at the highest level to bring some slight relief to Malta whose fighter defences had taken an almighty pounding the previous weeks and were at a very low ebb. Thanks to intervention by Churchill himself the Americans had generously put the carrier at the disposal of the British in this period of dire emergency. The old *Argus* could not fly out Spitfires for her flight deck was too short, and the *Eagle,* which had conducted many such runs during the first months of 1942, had temporarily been laid up for repairs to her ancient engines, while the *Victorious* had been built with lifts too small to accommodate fixed-wing Spitfires. Roosevelt's response had been immediate and early in April *Wasp* had arrived in the Clyde and between the 12th and 14th fifty-two Spitfires of Nos 601 and 603 Squadrons had been embarked with their pilots. At first light on the latter date she sailed to carry out Operation Callendar.

The whole force, under the command of Commodore Daniel with his flag in *Renown,* with the British destroyers *Echo, Inglefield, Ithuriel* and *Partridge* and the

US destroyers *Lang* and *Madison* as their screen, weighed anchor at 06.50 on 14th and passed the gate. They steered south throughout 15 to 19 April out into the Atlantic in a wide sweep towards the Straits of Gibraltar. Not surprisingly U-boat alarms were frequent, and one such led to a demonstration by *Renown* that proved that she still had the legs over much newer ships despite her age. John Stuart describes the incident, and its aftermath:

> On one occasion a submarine warning went up in mid-Atlantic and the ships were ordered to disperse with utmost dispatch. *Renown* was almost over the horizon and *Wasp* was left well behind. An enquiry was set up and it was determined that *Renown* had exceeded the rate of increase in power and the maximum power authorised by the Admiralty. The practice was ordered to be stopped. However examination of boilers and turbines did not reveal any damage attributed to the practice – a tribute to Fairfields of Govan. However one exception on the use of excess power was made when Churchill and his party went through the Mediterranean to the Yalta conference; when passing Pantelleria *Renown* developed 160,000 hp for a speed of 32 knots, when 'Authorised' power was 120,000 hp!

On the 17th the screen was exchanged to enable the destroyers to refuel, their place temporary being taken by the destroyers *Antelope, Vidette, Westcott, Wishart* and *Wrestler* from Gibraltar.

Off Gibraltar the escort was reinforced by the cruisers *Cairo* and *Charybdis* on the 19th and *Renown* once more cut the sunlit seas of the Western Mediterranean, a welcome change from the Arctic wastes to which they had become familiar. Five more destroyers had come out from Gibraltar to supplement their screen but although four Italian submarines lay in ambush only the *Velella* was able to attack and she unsuccessfully. The enemy air force made no appearance although the *Wasp's* Wildcats flew constant patrols over the squadron. The weather was good, the sea calm and, at 05.18 on the 20th in position 37° 30'N, 03° 20'E., some 50 miles north of Algiers, the first Spitfires began to fly off the carrier's wooden decks for Malta. In all forty-seven were launched successfully and of these all but one reached Malta according to plan. *Renown* and her consorts thereupon reversed course. On 20th the destroyer screen was again exchanged and on 21st the *Wasp* embarked No. 812 Squadron from Gibraltar for passage back to the UK, before being detached while *Renown* herself entered the harbour, where she entered No. 1 Dock. She was due to refit prior to joining the Eastern Fleet on completion.

Despite the ease of the purely naval side of this operation, and the smooth way in which this first major piece of co-operation had been conducted afloat, Operation Callendar was *not* a success. This was due to the RAF embarkation authorities who carried out a very careless job. Ninety per cent of the Spitfires' long-range fuel tanks were found to be defective, leaking their highly potent fuel all over the American carriers' decks, ninety-five per cent of the aircraft's guns were unsynchronised and dirty, incapable of being fired in fact, and seventy per cent of their radios were inoperative. All these defects had to be made good at sea by the US Navy leaving them with a bad impression on their Ally. Although the Spitfires arrived in good condition Malta had been ill-prepared to receive them despite their desperate need and the majority of them were destroyed within hours of their arrival by enemy bombing and within three days they had all gone.

It says much for the Americans that after this they allowed the *Wasp* to conduct yet a second ferry run almost immediately. On 30 April therefore the American carrier proceeded up the Clyde again to the King George V dock and commenced embarking a second consignment of sixty-five Spitfires. Exactly the same faults were found in this second batch as with the first; again the RAF were at fault. After twelve such specimens had been loaded the *Wasp* refused to take any more until something was done but again it finally rested with the Americans to remedy British negligence. With the planes embarked *Wasp* again sailed for Gibraltar to conduct Operation Bowery, sailing from Scapa Flow on 3 May. Meanwhile the *Eagle* had finished her repairs and had also embarked further Spitfires at Gibraltar and, on the night of 7/8 May *Renown* sailed from The Rock with her, escorted by the *Charybdis,* the US destroyers *Sterret* and *Lang,* and British destroyers *Echo, Intrepid, Ithuriel, Partridge* and *Vidette,* along with the old 'four stackers' *Georgetown* and *Salisbury.*

Again they met no opposition whatsoever during their approach and on 9 May the *Wasp* flew off forty-seven Spitfires and the *Eagle* seventeen for Malta. One other was lost during launching but those that got to the island found a better reception had been prepared and were able to refuel and get back in the air to engage enemy bombers within a short time of arrival without prohibitive losses. Operation Bowery was therefore much more of a success. Bill Kennelly remembers this trip as a pleasing interlude from northern operations:

> The main problem on our arrival at the flying-off point was the Med climate, beautiful and sunny and no wind as a rule, and all ships would have to run at full speed in order to get sufficient airlift for the planes to get off the flight decks. Sadly, on a few occasions, the Spitfire didn't quite make it, and ended up in the sea with the carrier ploughing over it, intent on getting the next one away. On a couple of occasions we had a Yank carrier in company. She didn't need to fly the Stars and Stripes to denote her origin, we could hear her, everything was one continuous squawk over her loudspeakers.

With Operation Bowery completed, the *Renown* arrived back at Scapa Flow at 08.25 on 15th, oiling from the *Celerol* before sailing again with the destroyers *Echo, Matchless* and *Somali* to bleak Hvalfiord once more. It was back to the Arctic for the *Renown* after her brief excursion to sunnier climes, the move East now being abandoned for the time being.

The addition of so many extra short-range weapons necessitated another reorganisation aboard *Renown,* which took some time to sort out as Tom Oliver recollects:

> It was found that at air raid warnings it took longer than it should to man the anti-aircraft guns. So once again a change was called for. The forrard end of the starboard 4.5-inch battery was made into a messdeck and the starboard hangar was divided into two tiers, the upper tier being converted to a messdeck, the lower to ablutions. The messdecks thus created were used by the short-range weapons crews and this increased efficiency enormously. The Marine barracks was the after messdeck so they were already near their action station, which at this time was Y turret, the after turret on the quarterdeck.

During operations in such bleak conditions, the welfare of the ship's crew needed to be tended even more carefully than usual. Tom Oliver was in the forefront of this facet of *Renown's* life and he gives us an insight into how it operated.

> The welfare of the ship's company was an important factor with regard to the family life of the ship and her efficiency. We had an excellent padre to whom the men could go to without embarrassment. There were also the usual service channels to seek compassion. The two methods sometimes clashed but it worked.
>
> It was an unwritten law that when information was received that a man's family had a crisis or bereavement through bomb action etc, that the Commander had to be told immediately. The man was then taken by me to the Commander's cabin. The usual routine was 'medical comfort' first from the bottom drawer of the Commander's desk, then a gradual talk-in to the truth. When possible the man was given compassionate leave right away and money was conjured up from a special fund.
>
> Of course there were cases that came up that required the Service be placed first. For instance the man who requested compassionate leave for 'My wife is stagnant, Sir!' The Commander used to say invariably that this was a completely normal human function and nothing could be improved by the man's presence. Then there were men who said their wives were very ill or that their wives were being seduced by the lodger etc. In cases like these it was usual to send a telegram to the local police to enquire if the presence of the man was necessary. Usually it was not.

Among those settling in aboard *Renown* at this time was her new Walrus pilot, Peter Allbeury. Although a newcomer to the ship he was no stranger to *Renown* for he had flown the *Sheffield's* Walrus during her Force H days. When that ship had been mined and heavily damaged off Iceland, a victim of our own minefields in those waters, she was sent to carry out extensive repairs at Newcastle. Peter remembers:

> We therefore found ourselves out of a job and before long ended up aboard *Renown,* which seemed enormous to us after *Sheffield*. *Renown* was carrying two Walrus amphibians at this time and both were of the old tin type, later marks being constructed of wood. We were well looked after, being given a cabin each and we used to explore the rest of the ship, even entering the 'Grand Casbah', as the Admiral's quarters and state rooms preserved from the round-the-world cruises of the twenties, were irreverently christened.
>
> At this time, with both hangars in use, the Walrus perched on their catapults brimful of aviation spirit and a potential fire hazard in action, we were not exactly approved of by some of the salt-water officers, but with regard to life aboard we found the wardroom a very happy place with RN, RNR and RNVR officers intermixed. Captain Daniel I liked. He was the most senior captain on the Navy List at the time; he was later made Commodore, and this eased our work when we took our turns as OOW for there was no need to look through the lists of ships to check on seniority, *Renown* was it, hands down, every time.
>
> The bulk of the aviation fuel was kept deep down in the ship in special tanks almost by the keel out of harm's way and used to have to be pumped up for

refuelling. Whenever the hangar was required for cinema services one of the aircraft, resting on bogies, would be unceremoniously wheeled out to make room. At sea all our launches were catapult but in harbour we were lowered over the side and took off from the water. Our main missions, while with *Renown,* were anti-submarine patrols, a little reconnaissance and lots of target-spotting during main armament shoots. Our main employment came later, with the North African landings in late 1942, early 1943. We had been flown off the ship on a mission, and on our return found she was heavily engaged with enemy air attack. We were shooed off and landed at an airfield near Algiers. Eventually quite a few of such Walrus orphans congregated here and we formed the 'Special Walrus Squadron', which continued to operate ashore, apart from our ships, for three months. We eventually rejoined *Renown* at Gibraltar but soon after that all aircraft were removed during a refit.

I always remember, during our days in the Arctic, the dog owned by our gunnery lieutenant, Smalley. It was a small Shetland-type sheepdog who lived in a wooden box tucked under the catapult. He seemed totally adapted to life aboard ship. During firings of the main armament the blast and shock would sometimes knock him from one side of the ship to the other, but he seemed impervious to gunfire and got up unharmed. His one great fear was going ashore; he hated to venture from the safety of his adopted home.

When the aircraft later departed the starboard hangar was converted into a messdeck for the short-range weapons crews and a bathroom, as recounted, while the port hangar was fully converted into a permanent cinema, complete with sloping deck. 'It was a horrid place really', recalls Tom Oliver, 'and London smog had nothing at all on the smoke from the "fragrant weed" that choked it.'

Peter Elvin recalls that when he had first joined the ship, in April 1941, as an acting lieutenant (E) he was the youngest officer in the ship. Over the next eighteen months he moved through all departments, engine and bearing room, boiler rooms, outside machinery, domestic machinery, boats and was finally appointed as *Renown's* first full-time Damage Control Officer.

One of his duties was Catapult Engineer Officer for the short time one was embarked and in operation:

This gear, a D111 H, carried the two Walrus amphibians which we didn't like using because of the problem of slowing down to pick them up – we had to create a slick so that the plane was steady enough to hook the crane wire onto – a very hazardous procedure!

It was a very confusing catapult to operate (it was fired by a cordite charge) because there were two breeches and to launch to starboard you had to remember to order the port breech to be loaded! There were many calculations to be made to get the exact amount of cordite to load. Fortunately that wasn't my responsibility but the gunner's! The launching procedure had to be seen and heard (if you could above the noise of the engine) to be believed!

Peter Elvin gives an interesting insight to his job as Damage Control Officer in a ship as vast as *Renown:*

I was appointed full-time Damage Control Officer at the time when the Admiralty were getting somewhat alarmed at the way ships were being unnecessarily lost – *Ark Royal* was a classic example where, had the Damage Control Officer had proper authority to take counter measures by flooding the ship could have been kept upright and saved.

I was given full authority to take any immediate post-damage counter-measures I thought necessary, including counter-flooding. By that stage of the war, late '42, we knew a lot about the effects of torpedoes from submarines and I used a tool called a 'damage triangle' which enabled one to predict the effects of a torpedo hit anywhere in the ship.

I was very concerned about the decrease in stability in *Renown* as a result of two major refits; during them a lot of extra top weight was added in the form of guns, control gear, radar etc. We used to keep very careful records of weights added and removed during refits and very seriously my sums showed a decrease in Metacentric height to 4.3 feet. An average for a battleship was about 7 feet. Later, at Trincomalee, where one could get a very still day and no sea movement in the anchorage, I carried out an 'inclining experiment'. The result of this (which Naval Architects maintain can't be done at anchor with a fully manned ship – or that's what they said at that time), was most impressive and came out within 2-inches of our theoretical calculated figure!

I was always an enthusiast for realistic exercises and the damage control exercises we held in *Renown* became quite famous. I could (and did) heel the ship to 14 degrees using the rapid floor bulges and a bit of cross pumping of liquids. I could heel the ship to 10 degrees in a few minutes – quite a frightening situation but excellent for training people when coupled with certified smoke from 'exercise fires', light failures etc. At one exercise in Scapa we sailed into the anchorage with a list of 10° on the ship – panic everywhere and frantic signals from the Commander-in-Chief, 'Are you all right?' This type of exercise revealed a whole range of equipment, which failed when the ship was at an angle far less than the designed failure angle! – including the 15-inch gun training hydraulic engines!! You can imagine some very rude signals were sent to the Admiralty when we discovered these things.

I realised that the naval system for identifying one's whereabouts in a big ship and finding the appropriate valves, hatches etc, was utterly hopeless for the large numbers of hostility-only personnel carried by the mid-war years. I therefore set about designing and implementing in *Renown* a simple and logical system of identification and marking, which ultimately formed the basis of the RN's present standard system.

It was around this time that they received a letter from Admiral Somerville in reply to their sending him a photograph of *Renown* so he would not forget his old flagship in his new command. The reply was typical of the man:

I really am most grateful to you, the officers and ship's company of *Renown* for the excellent photograph of my former flagship. I had such stirring times, and I was so happy in her that I shall always look on *Renown* as my home from home. I must confess that when she went home to refit I quite expected to have her back again in Force H but things have turned out differently for all of us.

However a kind fate may bring *Renown* my way again and if it does there is no ship in the Navy that will receive a warmer welcome from me. Please convey my grateful and sincere thanks to all concerned for this memento which I shall always treasure. Good luck to you all from your old shipmate, James F. Somerville.

In his predictions the Admiral spoke truer than he could have realised. After nine days at Scapa, between 14 and 23 May *Renown* sailed again for Hvalfiord on the 24th with the destroyer *Ledbury*, *Somali* and *Wilton* to resume her stint of watchfulness there, arriving on the 26th. Here they remained for the allotted spell throughout July, without incident, returning to Scapa on 27th escorted by the destroyers *Inglefield*, *Intrepid* and *Offa*. But this was their last stint of unrewarded waiting at Iceland and after another dreary month *Renown* sailed again for Scapa Flow arriving on the 27 July escorted by *Inglefield*, *Intrepid* and *Offa*.

For the rest of July and early August they swung round the buoy in the Flow with the rest of the Home Fleet in idleness and then, on 26 August, she left for the Clyde escorted by the destroyers *Farndale*, *Partridge* and *Puckeridge* to give extended leave and carry out minor repairs. She arrived at Greenock on the 27 August and remained there a month before returning to Scapa on 25 September, escorted by destroyers *Obdurate*, *Porcupine* and *Rotherham*. By now the buzz was round the ship that they were off to warmer climes after their long year in the bleak Arctic wastes, but nothing happened save for usual 'Scapa routine' of waiting, exercises and more waiting for an enemy who refused to bestir himself. Great events were portending however and the Flow was gradually filling with heavy ships and other vessels undergoing vigorous training programmes. Plainly something was in the wind. During this time *Renown* continued to add to her list of distinguished visitors. The young King Peter of Yugoslavia inspected the ship in September, and in October Admiral Fraser conducted Stafford Cripps round the *Renown* during his visit to the fleet.

In order to ensure that the heavy ships were in top condition to meet the enemy in the near future the *Renown* and *Duke of York* were sailed from Scapa Flow on 15 October, escorted by destroyers *Escapade*, *Faulknor*, *Marne* and *Middleton*, and arrived at Rosyth dockyard once more on the 16th for a quick docking. After this inspection *Renown* was undocked again on the 19th and sailed once more for the Flow with destroyers *Forester*, *Onslow* and *Tartar*. On her arrival there on the 20th she and *Duke of York* were assigned to Force H for a special mission. After long years on the defensive the Allies were about to take their first great stride forward toward ultimate victory. On 30 October *Renown* sailed to cover the landings in French North Africa.

CHAPTER THIRTEEN

Churchill's Racehorse

The Allied invasion of French North Africa had been decided upon by the Combined Chiefs of Staff on 25 July 1942 and the highly complex planning got under way in London almost at once. Admiral Sir Andrew Cunningham was appointed as Allied Naval Commander Expeditionary Force, and the whole series of landings that were to put British and American troops ashore in Morocco and Algeria were to be covered against intervention from either the Italian or Vichy French main fleets, by Force H which was to be powerfully reinforced by the heavy units of the Home Fleet. Plans were approved by the Chiefs of Staff in September and the orders were issued on 8 October. The main landings were to take place at Casablanca, Oran and Algiers and it was to cover the two latter inside the Mediterranean that the bulk of the Royal Navy's contribution was concentrated. Although the assaults on Algiers and Oran involved troops of both British and American armies, under the overall control of General Eisenhower, the decision was taken to adopt a common markings system of a white star inside a circle as a political move hopefully to present the whole affair as an American show and thus dampen Vichy resistance. This ruse failed in its objective but it did cause widespread comment aboard *Renown* who felt that the predominantly British fleet and landing ships' part were played down in favour of their Allies. The final date for the landings was fixed for 8 November.

By the end of October all the great convoys and escorting forces were at sea in the Western Atlantic heading for the Straits of Gibraltar. *Renown* actually sailed from Scapa Flow on 30 October in company with the *Duke of York* and *Nelson,* the cruiser *Argonaut* and seven destroyers *Ashanti, Eskimo, Martin, Meteor, Milne, Quiberon* and *Tartar.* They next rendezvoused off the northern coast of Ireland with the carriers *Victorious* and *Formidable* and destroyers *Pathfinder, Partridge, Quality* and *Quentin* that had sailed from the Clyde. The combined force then sailed south in a wide sweep passing east of the Azores during the 3rd and approached the Straits at nightfall on the 5th. *Renown* refuelled in Gibraltar Bay during the night of the 6th/7th leaving before first light with the ships that were to constitute Force H for the operation, *Duke of York, Nelson, Renown, Formidable, Victorious, Furious,* cruisers *Argonaut, Bermuda* and *Scylla* and seventeen destroyers, all under the command of Admiral Syfret. During the daylight hours of the 7th they made their final preparations, as Norman Hopwood relates: 'As I recall the first pipe of the day prior to the operation was, "Aircraft handling party to muster and camouflage aircraft with American markings", which surprised me as the RN seemed to be very well represented. I can only imagine it was a political move to pacify the French.'

Certainly the Walrus carried by *Renown* was marked up but whether any Vichy gunners would have been fooled by such a paint job on such a distinctive aircraft is doubtful in the extreme. Anyway, with the two fleet carriers in company, there was little work for *Renown's* spotter. *Nelson, Furious, Bermuda* and three destroyers were then detached to assist the landing forces.

Their original orders were for Force H to cover the Eastern and Central Task Forces and their respective follow-up convoys against seaborne attacks by Vichy-French and/or Italian surface fleets. Force H was instructed not to proceed east of 4°30'E, except to engage the enemy. Unless strong enemy forces were at sea, then *Rodney* with the destroyers *Beagle, Boreas* and *Bulldog*, was to join the Central Task Force off Oran. Force H was to refuel from Force R, the oilers *Brown Ranger* and *Dingledale*.

During the night before the landings *Renown* and her companions patrolled to the north and west of Algiers without any disturbance and while the landings went ahead successfully they continued to stand watch. Despite their hopes of a more eventful return to their old stamping ground neither the Italian nor the Vichy fleets budged, although local resistance ashore and from the local warships was at first fierce. However this was soon crushed by the covering forces without Force H having to intervene, and *Renown* was denied the opportunity of the cruiser *Aurora*, which finished off three Vichy destroyers in a neat single-handed action, or *Rodney* which carried out several satisfactory bombardments of the Oran forts. The only major Axis reaction against the huge fleets of ships and escorts was by U-boat and torpedo-bomber attack during the days that followed during which they had some slight successes, while the destroyer *Panther* was damaged by a bomb and had to be sent back to Gibraltar.

German He 111 and Ju 88 torpedo bombers made a determined attack on Force H late on the 8th but these aircraft were driven off without achieving anything, despite having evaded the fighter patrols in the dusk. Much of the credit for repelling this nasty attack was due to the alertness of *Renown's* gunners, as John Stuart recalls:

> One evening at sea off the coast of Algiers the ship's crew had just fallen out on completion of dusk action stations. The gun crews had packed up. Suddenly a Heinkel torpedo bomber appeared very low on the starboard quarter. Lieutenant Maurice Balaam in charge of the nearest battery saw the plane and ordered the crews to fire at the aircraft in emergency. This they did and exploded the two torpedo warheads as they were launched at very close range, and the plane was shot to pieces. Thus a very well pressed home attack by the German pilot was frustrated.

The Axis submarines were more determined however and several destroyers on *Renown's* screen were hit and sunk at this time. On the 10th the big destroyer *Martin* was sunk by the *U-431*, which launched torpedoes against Force H northeast of Algiers. Three torpedoes hit the unlucky little ship which went down instantly with only sixty-three survivors and were rescued by the *Quentin*. 'One moment *Martin* was there, the next she had vanished,' remembers one of *Renown's* gunners. Two days later her sister ship *Marne* had her stern blown off in the same waters.

On 15 November Force H returned to Gibraltar to replenish and *Duke of York* and *Victorious* immediately left for home, leaving *Renown* to operate with *Nelson, Rodney, Formidable* and *Furious* working alternately from the Rock itself, and Mers-el-Kebir, now that it had been finally occupied by the Allies, and here they remained until early February.

On 24 November, *Renown* sailed from Gibraltar with *Nelson, Formidable* and *Furious* escorted by the destroyers *Eskimo, Lookout, Meteor, Milne, Partridge, Pathfinder, Penn, Porcupine, Puckeridge* and *Tartar*, and arrived at Mers-el-Kebir the following afternoon. Force H sailed again next day and cruised in the vicinity of the Balearic Islands to cover the invasion forces from any move south by the Vichy fleet based at Toulon, which was known to contain many bitter die-hards eager for a fight against their former allies. No movement south being detected Force H returned to Mers-el-Kebir on the 30th.

On 4 December 1942, *Renown*, with *Nelson, Formidable, Furious, Charybdis* and the destroyers *Antelope, Lookout, Meteor, Milne, Partridge, Pathfinder, Penn, Porcupine, Puckeridge, Quality* and *Quiberon* sailed at 10.45 and arrived at Gibraltar on the 6th, where they remained for the rest of the month.

Apart from the stray air attack and the ever-present menace of the twenty or so German submarines in the area life was reasonably attractive at this time. On 12th for instance, *Renown* embarked six officers and eighty ratings who were survivors from the destroyer *Blean* torpedoed the previous day. These men were discharged to the *Llangibby Castle* next day. On another occasion, early on 28th, another accident occurred when the accidental firing of three live rounds from *Renown's* after pom-pom caused casualties aboard the destroyers *Erne* and *Velox* who were moored astern of her.

Renown remained at Gibraltar between 1 and 30 January. The First Sea Lord visited the ship and addressed the ship's company on New Year's Day.

We had one welcome occasion in Gib when a bunch of landing craft arrived in, brand new from the USA and ballasted down with Carnation Milk, thousands of crates of the stuff, [recalls Bill Kennelly]. Being billeted alongside *Renown* we had the job of helping to offload the cargo, across us, to the jetty. Dozens of those crates never found their way to the shore and many a middle watch found that cocoa tasted so much better with Carnation, instead of Pusser's tinned milk, during the months that followed.

We were also based at Mers-el-Kebir but no shore leave was given because of the bitterness that still remained from 1940 when we sank most of their fleet there. While here we saw the minelayer *Manxman* stagger in with an enormous list. She had stopped a torpedo while doing 25 knots but had survived. Just another reminder of how lucky we had been on *Renown* to date.

Norman Hopwood remembers another incident that took place at Mers-el-Kebir during this time:

I remember we took oil aboard at one of these North African ports. It was highly polluted or had been diluted with water. I was in charge of one of the engine rooms one middle watch when flickering lights and a drop in steam pressure established that we were on one of these suspect tanks. As we were in units, as normal in wartime, the hands of both myself and my leading stoker were well skinned opening the cross-connecting valves necessary to restore steam to run the engine, particularly as we were running at high speed at the time.

Meanwhile although the Italian fleet failed to move, French resistance had been fanatical at first and several small ships had been lost. However after a severe drubbing off the Moroccan coast by the American Task Force and once the troops were firmly ashore, they soon began to see which way the wind was blowing and Admiral Darlan himself hastily changed sides once more and called upon the Vichy Fleet at Toulon to do the same. Unfortunately its commander, Admiral de Laborde, was even more anti-British than Darlan and he scornfully rejected any such ideas. However with the German occupation of the southern half of France on 14 November, this particular dilemma was solved rapidly – for the warships at Toulon scuttled themselves *en masse* rather than join the Allies or be taken over by the Axis. There was therefore little chance of any major surface action developing in the Western Mediterranean although *Renown* was retained in the area for a while longer just in case.

The German submarines scored some considerably successes at this time however; Among the major warship losses were the escort carrier *Avenger,* sunk with heavy loss of life, the depot ship *Hecla* and the AA ship *Tynwald.* Several large liners serving as troopships were also sunk during this period, among them the *Warwick Castle* (20,107 tons), the *Ceramic* and the *Ettrick,* while during a heavy air attack on Bougie three more, *Awatea, Cathay* and *Karanja,* were sunk and the monitor *Roberts* badly damaged, due to lack of fighter defences.

Renown, as always, bore a charmed life despite continued patrols in the danger zone. Just how lucky *Renown* was to escape any damage at this time is shown from the casualty list of her escorts at this period; the destroyer *Porcupine* was cut in half by a torpedo off Gibraltar on 9 December (The sailors immediately dubbed the two halves *Pork* and *Pine!*), the *Blean* was hit and sunk by U-443 west of Oran on the 11th, many of her survivors being picked up by other destroyers and transferred to *Renown's* sick bay for treatment – alas, as we have seen, there were terribly few from the little ship. On 18 December the destroyer *Partridge* went the same way when torpedoed in the same area by *U-565.*

Some compensation was gained in that no less than fourteen German and Italian submarines were sunk in the Mediterranean in this period, along with six Vichy boats that tried to intervene against the landing fleets. *Renown* had no part in any of these sinkings though the Walrus 'Special Squadron' did. The *U-331* was attacked and damaged by Hudson aircraft of No. 500 Squadron, and when she surfaced not far from Force H Albacore torpedo bombers from *Formidable* completed the job by sending her to the bottom with a direct hit. An FAA Walrus was quickly on the scene and managed to rescue a few of the U-boat's survivors.

Renown was, perhaps, involved in another 'sinking' according to John Stuart, who states that:

On another evening *Renown* spotted a submarine beam on the surface ten degrees on the bow, speed of the fleet 18 knots. The *Renown's* officer of the watch ordered a small change in course and before the sub was able to dive deep enough it was cut in two; there were pieces of metal plating off both sides of our bows.

However this author has been unable to find any positive verification or confirmation of this incident in any records he has consulted and it now seems somewhat doubtful whether an enemy submarine was destroyed thus. Nor were there any reports of damage to any Allied submarine at this time. What is certainly true is that shortly after this the *Renown* left Gibraltar for home to carry out a long refit and that she arrived at Scapa Flow towards the end of February 1943 in full fighting trim.

'Later on in dry dock, we could not detect any damage other than missing paint!', recalls John Stuart, adding: 'Of course, the ship had a reinforced bow.'

He also remembers an incident on their arrival back at Scapa, which reflected some considerable credit on her new crew who were now knitting together as a fine team.

On return from the invasion of North Africa *Renown* was at Scapa Flow where the ship's company was catching up on maintenance work. The Commander-in-Chief sent a signal to capital ships in company to proceed to sea for gunnery practice. *Renown* sent a reply requesting exemption on grounds she had the best gunnery record in the fleet. The C-in-C concurred.

The *Renown* along with the carrier *Furious*, had finally left Gibraltar on 31 January, sailing at 05.00 with their destroyer escorts *Antelope, Boreas, Brilliant, Vanoc, Wishart* and *Wivern*. They were joined at sea by the carrier *Illustrious* and destroyers *Calpe* and *Puckeridge*, these latter pair being relieved by the *Panther, Pathfinder* and *Penn* from Casablanca for the journey back to the UK. *Renown's* destination was the Clyde from whence she was then to proceed to Rosyth for another major refit planned to commence on 20 February. This was necessitated by the fact that she was suffering from major boiler defects reported as early as 15 December. *Renown* finally arrived back at Greenock at 17.48 on 4 February and next day weighed and proceeded to Rosyth escorted by the destroyers *Boadicea* and *Lauderdale*, passing under the Forth Bridge and anchoring at 10.30 on the 7th.

The Admiral Superintendent, Rosyth, signalled that *Renown* had been taken in hand on the 22nd with the date of completion being provisionally end of May, although, as usual, this was later extended to the 6 June. In fact, this major overhaul kept her in dockyard hands from 22 February 1943 until 9 June, during which four months most of her crew managed to get a long period of leave. There were also, as usual, many changes in her complement, but Captain W.E. Parry CB, who was appointed in command on 2 January 1943, still remained in command at this time.

The refit this time involved the removal of the Walrus aircraft, seldom employed as we have seen, and all its associated catapult equipment. The space thus left was used to improve the ship's boat stowage and also to site some of the many new additions to her close-range armament. In all *Renown* was fitted with no less than thirteen twin and three single 20-mm Oerlikon cannon, and of course the extra gunners to man them. All this increase in top weight was not at this time compensated for and thus the ship's stability was considerably affected. In her extreme condition, with 4,871 tons of oil fuel aboard and 320 tons of water protection, her displacement tonnage was now estimated to be 37,600 tons, giving her a mean draught of 31 feet 71 inches and an angle of maximum stability of 39°.

Let three of the newcomers who joined *Renown* at this time give their first impressions of the ship. The first was her new Padre, the Very Reverend H.M. Lloyd, DSO, OBE, MA, whose previous ship had been the carrier *Illustrious*. The Padre was a very remarkable man according to all who knew him during *Renown's* final commission and had a great influence on the ship's well-being. How did *Renown* first strike him?

Some ships seem to have a sort of built-in happiness and the *Renown* was a happy ship, she was an extremely efficient ship and we were all proud of her. Incidentally she was beautiful in outline. She was very fast, considering her vintage, and I think she was pretty vulnerable except for this considerable factor of speed, which made her to be considered safe enough to take Churchill on two trips. On joining her in 1943 I was immediately impressed by the friendly spirit right through the ship. A naval chaplain has a tremendous advantage in not carrying any actual rank. At that time we did have a plain uniform with a distinctive cap badge but no other insignia except the dog collar, and in tropical rig, a simple Maltese cross.

My cabin was right forrard in the forecasement flat which was a small flat on the port side including several cabins. I remember that next to mine was the dental surgery and those waiting for treatment provided many pastoral opportunities, even if they also provided a background of conversation interspersed with an incredible repetition of words, which today are acceptable to the BBC if not to all their listeners, but which in those days would have made Lord Reith's hair stand on end!

This cabin was well placed for the chaplain because the ship's company had very easy access to it, in fact across the way from it was the stokers' broadside mess. I always used to feel embarrassed that my circumstances were so much more comfortable than theirs. My cabin was known as 'The Vicarage' and in the usual naval parsons' tradition the whole ship was my parish. I think I knew the names of almost everyone on board, although once I was stumped, but the seaman had obligingly left his cap on a chair where I could see his name inscribed on the lining, so I took a chance and called him 'Jones'. He looked mystified and I later discovered he had borrowed the cap from someone else!

The very fine chapel was right aft and was not used as access required the opening of two watertight doors which were normally required to be closed, also the vibration at sea would have been very great. It was a peacetime chapel and I had a small chapel in a very convenient space; this was a very vital centre for a faithful group of regular worshippers of a variety of traditions, which anticipated the ecumenical movement! This core of committed Christians was a tremendous help to me in the real essence of my work as a chaplain, which meant sustained prayer and care for the whole ship, and as you well know in wartime there were many men burdened with great anxieties and grief's. The parson's work is always hidden, it is not for him to talk abroad of the many things that his parishioners share with him and his rewards are also hidden in knowing that perhaps he has been able to do more than he imagined. All this is, of course, extremely true in the close-knit life of a great ship in time of war. The arrival of the mail in some foreign port brings a flow of visitors to the padre's cabin and gives him much to think about and do. The regular daily services in the little chapel were the spiritual source of inspiration for the great

Sunday evening gatherings when all available members of the ship's company gathered on the forecastle for Padre's Hour.

Incidentally when I joined the ship Sunday Service was still compulsory. On my second Sunday I asked for it to be voluntary and the Captain and Commander agreed. The first service was naturally packed out with volunteers expressing their approval of the decision; this soon settled down to a fair-sized regular congregation and the great advantage was that one had quite a different spirit in the service, which became a real expression of worship. The Padre's Hour being entirely voluntary in all respects gained enormously from the new approach, for such it was at the time, to the morning service.

Another newcomer was Peter Churchill:

I was a brand-new lieutenant (E), straight from Keyham, when I joined her up in Rosyth, and I shall always remember the thrill of the vibration of the polished steel floor-plates of the controlling engine-room under my feet for the very first time, as 120,000 horse-power moved that beautiful ship. She was indeed a lovely ship to look at; her lines were quite classical.

A third member of *Renown's* crew at this time who saw her for the first time was a young seaman who wishes to remain anonymous. We will respect his wishes and refer to him simply as 'G'. He tells a fine story and well remembers joining *Renown* that spring:

It was late 1942 when I awaited draft from RN Barracks Devonport, after having completed my initial training as a Quarter Gunner at HMS *Glendower*. I had also, on the advice of a Naval schoolmaster, sat an examination to carry on my craft as a joiner and shipwright and to my delight had sufficient marks to qualify. Already I had visions of the dizzy heights of petty officer and all that it meant. However after a spell of leave over Christmas (the only Christmas leave I was to enjoy for the coming four years) I was told I was to be drafted to sea and would pick up my rank on board ship. This news to me was a great relief. Anyone in RNB Devonport would endorse that, and at last, like many others on the same draft, I could get away from this flea-pit and the incessant air raids that Plymouth was subject to in those days.

So my station card was stamped, the number inside being D58 something or other. As I am inquisitive by nature I asked what ship it was, hoping that I would go into the patrol service where a civvy-street pal had recently gone. But alas no luck, and just before we were due to report for draft I learned I was to join HMS *Renown* in Rosyth Dockyard. The drafting officer did little to cheer me up when he said (as all the superstitious naval characters do), 'Bugger your luck. Everything happens in threes, laddie and she's the third, having lost her two sisters, *Repulse* and *Hood'*. This statement gave me considerable thought about an early watery grave. After travelling all day and well into the night on a special train along with a lot more new scholars for the *Renown* we arrived at Rosyth Dockyard; but I managed to bribe a porter on Carlisle station with some duty-free cigarettes to post my letters to my parents and my girl friend so that at least they knew my whereabouts.

Even though it was dark I can still picture that enormous hulk of steel some 800ft long with a weight of over 32,000 tons. Once aboard we were taken round to different messes and to our individual mess. As I was awaiting regrading to shipwright (who had a snug little mess) I was put on the engine-room messdeck and was very quickly told by the leading hand what was expected of me while I was there.

During her refit we learned our way around and the dark depths of Devonport Barracks soon faded from our memories. Her aircraft were taken off and the hangars converted, one into a signalmen's mess and the other into a cinema, which was to play a major role in all our lives.

For the older members of *Renown's* complement this novelty had long worn off; their lives continued at the pace of the ship and men who had joined as raw young seamen in August 1939 were now battle hardened veterans compared with the new HO ratings who joined them in 1943. John Roche provides a typical illustration of a steady climb during his service aboard *Renown*: 'I was rated AB on 2 March 1941, leading seaman in October 1942 and petty officer in April 1944 and I was a torpedoman and LTO during that period.'

The veterans still carried the ship along as the newcomers shook down and became part of the team. The Master-at-Arms recalls the effect of the new padre on his depart-ment, which was most beneficial:

It was always known that the majority of any ship's company did not like being ushered compulsorily to church. We used to sweep through the ship from forrard to aft on each deck and drive the men like sheep on to the quarterdeck where church service was held. There was a sigh of relief if the 'doors were closed' and there was a full house. The overflow could then repair to their messes and go about their various pastimes, if any.

The Padre, I believe, knew all this and he instituted the Padre's Hour every Sunday evening on the forecastle. An impromptu stage was rigged, flanked on three sides by canvas and bunting. It was all informal, any old dress, or even none in the tropics later. Singing and musical talent was gathered from the ships in company and there were very good renditions of religious and semi-religious songs and music which was interspersed with a hymn or two and ending with a prayer. The Hour was a great success.

On 14 May, Rosyth had advised the C-in-C, Home Fleet, that it was not possible to sail *Renown* on the 9 June, 'having regard to what has to be done after the dock-yard completion date. Assuming that dockyard work permits embarkation of 4.5-inch ammunition, provisions and stores by p.m. 6th, i.e. during the course of the refit and assuming that the basin trial a.m. 7th was satisfactory, the ship would unbasin p.m. 7th and should be ready to sail a.m. 14th.'

In fact the *Renown* was undocked on 19 June and moved out into the stream, ready for sailing for her working-up exercises, at 16.21.

On completion of this refit *Renown's* armament comprised 3 x 2 15-inch, 10 x 2 4.5-inch, 3 x 8 2pdr, 1 x 4 2pdr, 20 x 2 and 24 x 1 20mm guns.

Next day, 20th, the Captain addressed the ship's company, following which, at 12.17, she sailed for Scapa Flow, escorted by the destroyers *Obedient, Onslaught* and *Scorpion*, steaming north through the night and arriving at the anchorage at 09.21 next morning. Here they were to remain, at four hours notice to steam, while the new crew shook itself down and the full range of exercises, sub-calibre -shoots, AA shoots, torpedo firing (for they still retained their above-water tubes at this time) and the like took up most of their time during this period, and there was little rest for anyone, as G recalls:

> Our first trip, north to Scapa Flow, had begun and although all the new boys, including myself, joked and jested when it became dusk and we started to lose sight of land, we were all just more than a little nervous and no doubt already waiting for the bang as a torpedo struck home, so no sleep for us on our first night at sea.
>
> Morning arrived and we tied up to a buoy safely in Scapa Flow. Days seemed like months at Scapa; shore leave restricted to two hours a day in harbour and typical Scapa weather, but we did manage a few games of rugger and soccer. The canteen sold only beer and tickets were issued on board limited to four a man, so if you wanted a skinful you had to barter with cigarettes or rum to gain more tickets, (a bigger racket than Wembley).

At this time the Arctic convoys had been suspended for a time but the Flow was packed full of heavy ships undergoing training for the invasion of Sicily, which was imminent. Among the heavy ships sharing the crowded anchorage with *Renown* at various times in June and July were the *Nelson*, *Rodney*, *Warspite* and *Valiant* which were practising shore bombardments, and the *King George V* and *Howe* of the Home Fleet, which were also detached to the Mediterranean at the end of the month. This left the C-in-C Home Fleet with two modern battleships, *Duke* of *York* and *Anson* and one old one, *Malaya* and one working up, *Renown*. As the latter became more proficient, and the other two modern ships were expected back in due course, the *Malaya* left them during July to pay off into reserve. It was a sad fate for their companion of Genoa, but the *Renown* was more fortunate.

For a short time also two American battleships operated with the Home Fleet, the *Alabama* and *South Dakota*, but in August these fine vessels, which had alternated with Home Fleet battleships between Hvalfiord and Scapa, left for the Pacific war.

In Norway at this time the Germans had built up their surface striking force to include *Tirpitz*, *Scharnhorst* and *Lutzow*, with light cruiser and destroyer support. During the landings in Sicily during July the main strength of the Home Fleet, *Anson*, *Duke* of *York*, *Malaya*, *Alabama*, *South Dakota*, the carrier *Furious*, 1st and 10th cruiser squadrons and three destroyer flotillas carried out an offensive sweep off Norway. Not surprisingly the German heavy ships did not venture out against such a powerful array, nor did they when the operation was repeated at the end of the month with the addition of the carrier *Illustrious*. But *Renown* was still working up at this period and not yet fit to stand her place in line and her only voyages were short ones in and out of the Flow on innumerable exercises. Not until August did her captain feel satisfied enough to tell them that she was now considered an efficient fighting unit.

The highlight of this otherwise dull period of necessary hard work came with the visit to the Home Fleet between 12 and 15 August of His Majesty King George VI. *Renown* was selected to escort the King to sea in *Duke of York*, for exercises with his ships, the first reigning monarch who had ever sailed with his fleet during wartime. It proved a great success: although the weather was poor the King seemed to enjoy being with his men. G remembers that:

> After re-entering harbour King George VI had to inspect our ship's company 'tween decks. He was so wet that much of the facial mascara etc. was running down his face. But we all enjoyed the super concert given on shore afterwards even though the front rows were taken up by the miles of gold braid, and to cap it all some matelots shouted out at the top of his voice during an acrobatic act, when a smart piece of stuff was being swung around a chap's neck by her feet, 'Why don't you bite the B . . . . . . d'. This caused much concern during the following days onboard every ship in the Home Fleet; I don't think they ever caught the culprit but everybody suffered.
>
> We made our own fun; I managed to purchase a small piano accordion, a twelve bass instrument that made a lot more noise than it would suggest, as some notes were badly sprung much to the annoyance of other messes, but it worked. It did not last long – one night a drunk knocked it off my locker and broke the keyboard.
>
> Our complement was now about 1,600 officers and men, which included a Royal Marine Band, and I felt that our crew was predominantly Welsh, so much so that I, as a Northerner, used to sing in our Welsh choir, and after a number of years with the same lads, developed the Welsh dialect unknown to myself.
>
> A great bunch of lads they turned out to be and like all ships we soon sorted out the petty thieves etc, and corrected them in no uncertain way.
>
> My part of the ship was the shipwright's shop, and I was now learning new skills, welding, metal work, and most important, the art of boat building and repair, and I remember well doing a lot of work in the ship's church. We had a first class padre. I can't remember names but he certainly dedicated a lot of time to organising our talents and arranged concerts and the like from other ships. We had a smashing cinema and it always amused me to see all the lads sitting there with their mugs of tea and bread as the film started at 6.30 pm which was supper time, and it was first come first served, so the picture goers had to dine out!
>
> Speaking of the entertainment side of *Renown*, one of our Royal Marines formed a dance band, he himself being the leader of the Dundee Theatre Orchestra in civilian life, and a first class professional he was. So, including cards, Tombola, 'Huckers' and a first class library, we were pretty well catered for socially. By now we were really a smart and efficient ship in most departments and reasonably happy but getting rather cheesed at the thought of the continued cold and rain in Northern Waters.

This Scapa routine was soon to get its first break for at this time the Quadrant conference was taking place between Churchill and Roosevelt; the British party sailing aboard the giant liner *Queen Mary* from the Clyde on 5 August for Halifax, Nova Scotia. During the talks, which centred on the Italian campaign and the proposed invasion of Europe, the First Sea Lord, Admiral Sir Dudley Pound, suffered a stroke and tendered his resignation to the Premier. Meanwhile it had been decided to send the *Renown* to Halifax to bring the whole party home at the conclusion of the talks, and she sailed from Scapa Flow at 12.09 on 24 August, escorted by the destroyers *Matchless* and *Orwell*.

'Then it happened', recalls G, ' "Commander Speaking – We are leaving harbour at such and such a time and also leaving the Home Fleet, destination later". Buzz, buzz, buzz. Everyone knew better than the skipper where we were going – Far East, back to the Mediterranean, Russia – you name it. Only the lads on watch at sea knew that we were heading south and west, the Atlantic and America.'

The outward trip was memorable enough for they ran slap into a full-scale hurricane in mid-Atlantic on 27 August that lasted throughout the night. It was too much for the destroyers, who were detached to St. Johns but *Renown* clawed her way through the eye of the storm. G remembers Operation Sextant well:

After three days' steaming we hit a real mid-Atlantic gale with waves God alone knows how high but certainly making life really miserable. Ship proceeding at about 2–3 knots, or so it seemed, and the gale worsening. Hardened sea dogs were green in colour and, speaking for myself, praying for Almighty God to either calm the storm or take me quickly. 'Commander speaking – escorts have left us because of the storm. Can now tell you we are to make extra large ash trays for our future guest and will be met shortly by units of the Canadian Navy.' So the secret was out, we were to pick up the Prime Minister.

The storm was soon forgotten, apart from the mopping up operations, which included badly flooded heads; it may be of interest to note that the heads were in the fo'c'sle and consisted of two rows of pans with no doors or privacy and you can well imagine that you always had a queue for company waiting for a pan. It was here you threw away all modesty or remained forever constipated!

So great excitement: rumour had it Brooklyn Dockyard in New York and pick up our guest, but the pick-up point later proved to be Halifax, Nova Scotia and here we were soon tied up.

Renown in fact arrived at Halifax, with an escort of three Canadian destroyers, all ex-RN ships incidentally, at 11.02 on 29 August, and here they remained for a fortnight awaiting the arrival of their distinguished guests. Opportunity was taken to give leave. G recalls:

Here we got our first major shock – *no pubs!* Beer and spirits sold by liquor and licence only to be consumed at home. Licences were obtainable, as was the drink, but where could we drink it? Many took to public parks, local cemeteries and toilets – anywhere out of sight – and I'm sorry to relate some were caught and so Anglo-Canadian relations suffered badly. But a few days in Halifax gave us a little break and a chance, I think, to buy up all the silk stockings in the shops. While we lay there the liner *Queen Elizabeth* lay berthed ahead of us and for days on end a never-ending stream of GIs and Canadian servicemen were taken on board over about four or five gangplanks.

Bill Kennelly also remembers his runs ashore in Halifax: 'It gave us the chance to explore and buy a few presents for home, a huge dressed doll for my daughter and real moccasins for my wife with lots of goodies from the shops.'

Winston Churchill and his party, including his wife and daughter, General Ismay,

Brendon Bracken, Lord Moxton and their staffs, came aboard and *Renown* sailed for home at 15.10 on 14 September, escorted by the heavy cruiser *Kent* and the destroyers *Obedient* and *Obdurate*. He has described the voyage in his memoirs and there is another excellent account in the book *The War and General Warden*, but here let us see the journey and life aboard through the eyes of the Renowns.

Peter Churchill of course had a special problem: 'While he was onboard, I was given an official alias, and became Lieutenant Smith, (who, incidentally, ran up a fair wine bill, but I never paid it!)'

> During our subsequent mad dash across the Atlantic [G says] we had on board The Premier, Cabinet Minister, First Sea Lord, Wren Officers, Uncle Tom Cobley and all, and of course, some of the Churchill Family. It was during this trip that Mary Churchill celebrated her twenty-first birthday and the ship-wrights' department played a part in the celebrations by making a wooden cake and the chef decorating it. No doubt she caused a lot of laughs trying to cut it, but, the Navy and the Chef to the rescue – another *real* cake was duly produced and all was well.

Unfortunately after reaching England the First Sea Lord suffered a second, paralysing stroke and he died in hospital on Trafalgar Day 1943.

The Padre's chapel had to be relinquished and was used as the map room for Churchill while he was aboard. John Stuart remembers this and other typical Winston episodes:

> It was during this voyage we found that Mr Churchill had developed a peculiar habit, which was getting up at all times of the night and going to the cinema, so our poor old projectionists were on 24 hours call duty. The *Renown* was not only our longest capital ship but also one of the fastest and made maximum speed on the crossing and when we arrived at Greenock the paintwork was actually burned off her funnels. I think I'm right in saying that this was Dudley Pound's last trip to sea.
>
> Churchill ran the war from the ship. *Renown* officers were allowed to visit the map room and the decision to hold Salerno was made in mid-Atlantic. Churchill used to run bridge parties in the Admirals Quarters and when an officer of the ship had to take his leave Churchill would get up and escort him to the door with the remark, 'Thank you Mr – for coming – come back again.' It did not matter how junior the officer was.
>
> Mary Churchill was among the staff. One day there was a submarine warning and the ship was doing 28 knots and pitching up to 40 feet. This meant that half the quarter deck was awash with over 10 feet of water every 15–20 minutes or so. No one was allowed beyond the forward end of the quarter deck. Mary Churchill was walking with the *Renown's* Instructor-Lieutenant when one of these waves broke over and washed the two of them to the stern of the ship where they were entangled in the guardrails. They hung on and when the pitch changed they ran up to the front of the quarter deck, only to be greeted by the Commander, Conder. Mary told me afterwards that she would sooner have been washed overboard than to put up with the dressing down she received!

The additional passengers caused problems, [says Bill Kennelly] particularly for No. 4 fire-party sleeping in the Wardroom flat. Sailors slept in their 'normal' rig of singlet and pants in hammocks, only to have Wren officers passing under them *en route* to their cabins. No doubt many sailors wished that this could be a permanent feature. One unfortunate incident: Mrs Churchill fell and broke her arm. On one occasion I recall that *Renown* fired a 15-inch gun for the entertainment of the passengers. On the way over we passed a US carrier, the *Ranger* I think, but we were in top gear and left her far behind.

Harry Shannon remembers that:

He never bothered us very much but he had a big staff and his own detective to guard him. He always had his big cigar in his mouth and he used to like to see a film as well but it would always be during the night. Our old seaplane hangar had been converted into a cinema for the ship's company and he used to monopolise it each night.

On 16th *Renown* managed to pick up the heavy cruiser *Norfolk* on her Type 273 radar at a range of 34,000 yards; she joined company at 14.02 with the *Matchless* and *Orwell*. The *Obdurate* lay off for despatches and was sent off to the west with them in company with *Opportune* at 15.00. Next day saw a similar performance when the destroyers *Scourge* and *Scorpion* were detected 280 degrees at a range of 15 miles.

Renown and her precious cargo arrived safely at Greenock at 09.45 on 22 September, and Mr Churchill addressed the ship's company before disembarking, granting 14 days leave to each watch, which proved very popular.

Much of the homeward journey was done through thick fog and at high speed, and the *Renown* was steered by radar, again the destroyer escort was left behind for much of the passage as the old girl flew. When they finally arrived at Greenock they found the *Queen Elizabeth* there. She had left ahead of them but the *Renown* had matched her speed for the crossing. On 21 September they sailed once more to join the Home Fleet at Scapa Flow and that was the last any of them expected to see of the Premier.

Back at Scapa the fleet had continued its long watch but the day *Renown* arrived there, 22 September, an attack by midget submarines had damaged badly the *Tirpitz*, and *Scharnhorst*, although not attacked as planned, was left on her own operationally for when *Lutzow* sailed for home. When the pocket battleship was first reported as having sailed from Altenfiord the usual precautions were taken, lest this be a final attempt at a break-out into the North Atlantic, and *Renown* sailed to carry out a long patrol off Iceland between 22 and 28 September, which some of her crew missed, as G relates:

When we returned to Scapa from leave – a previous arrangement, as we had proceeded on leave from Greenock – we found we had to report back on board the old *Iron Duke,* a floating barracks, the *Renown* having sailed for Iceland. Whilst the *Iron Duke* was no one-star hotel, none of us was worried at missing that trip.

CHURCHHILL'S RACEHORSE
179

Back aboard *Renown* again and the drab Scapa routine, but not for long. On 8 November 1943, at 12.25, they sailed from Scapa Flow with the battleship *Queen Elizabeth* and destroyers *Oribi* and *Urchin*, and set course westabout for their home port of Plymouth where they arrived at 14.10 on the 10th after being met by the destroyer *Rocket* off Bardsey Island. They anchored off the Hoe in dismal weather in readiness to carry out Operation Quadrant. This was the passage of Churchill and his staff once more, this time including the American Ambassador, Mr Winant, the First Sea Lord, Admiral Cunningham and General Ismay, to Gibraltar on their way to attend the Cairo conference with Roosevelt and the Chinese leader Chiang Kai-shek. The party duly aboard, *Renown* sailed again from Plymouth at 1830 on the 12th and set course south for the Rock, escorted by the heavy cruiser *London*, and destroyers *Rocket, Teazer* and *Ulster*. As Commander Donald of the *Ulster* was later to record:

> It was blowing a full westerly gale as we slipped from our buoys at dusk, and joined *Renown* just outside the breakwater. Twenty knots was ordered before we reached Eddystone, and then speed was increased to twenty-seven as we turned our noses into the open Atlantic. It was no fun at all for the destroyers; we were taking it green all the time as we slammed our way into the huge rollers, and my sea cabin was flooded, thanks to some ass who left a voice-pipe cover open.

Renown and her four escorts however kept up the pace and arrived at Gibraltar at 19.07 on the 15th. The plan was to have been for a York aircraft to fly the Premier on to Cairo but the aircraft failed to materialise. Churchill therefore suggested continuing the journey in *Renown* and this was agreed, much to the consternation of the Staff ashore for the destroyers were all fuelling. A panic signal was made for any destroyers available to proceed to sea and carry on with the escort to Algiers, the next port of call for *Renown* where she was to refuel herself. They sailed at 19.30 with the *London*, and destroyers *Grenville, Anthony, Antelope* and *Douglas* at 27 knots.

Roger Hill aboard *Grenville* described his role thus:

> When we had caught her *up*, *Renown* went on to 26 knots and with the heavy seas some of the older destroyers could not keep up with us. We had our asdic dome hoisted, our gunfire would have been useless in such weather conditions – the seas were going right over A and B guns – so we were really there for the look of the thing*.

They arrived at Algiers 12.48 on the 16th and sailed again at 18.51, again taking most of the escorts by surprise, Hill wrote of Bill Churchill of *Inglefield* being pushed away from *Renown*'s bows with no steam on after a crisp word form Admiral Cunningham, and only *Grenville* had been canny enough to keep steam on just in case. *Inglefield* and *Rocket* being left behind. At 19.23, after another high-speed dash, *Renown* arrived at Malta to a terrific welcome on 17 November.

* *Destroyer Captain* (Kimber, 1975)

Norman Hopwood remembers that:

My own particular recollections of this passage were that it was thought that Mr Churchill should be provided with ashtrays of special size and design with cigar-sized flutes. Being the senior ERA and a coppersmith, it fell to my lot to make them there-and-then in copper aboard ship. They disappeared into the wardroom of course never to be seen by me. I would have liked to have been able to keep one as a souvenir but never got the chance.

Harry Shannon recalls the great secrecy under which the Premier first embarked and during the subsequent voyage out:

I was a petty officer by this time, not too long rated for you have to do twelve months in the Blue jacket rig before you got the peak cap, and we had a Commander aboard by the name of Conder – a tough man. He sent for me while at Plymouth. It was getting on for dusk and we had anchored well out in the harbour. He gave me very precise orders, 'You are to go ashore in the launch with the mail party and land the mail on the jetty. It will be taken from your party and you must not allow them to speak to anyone but return to the launch at once and return to the ship', and this we did.

The next thing we heard was that the ship would be sailing very shortly and we were all wondering what next, and then who should arrive on board again but the Old Bulldog and his daughter Sarah. He was not allowed to appear on the upper deck and so a canvas foyer was erected around the old crane-deck in case we might be passed by other ships during the daylight hours who might spot he was aboard. During the voyage we did a 4.5 inch barrage practice and Sarah Churchill went up to the 4.5-inch battery's top director and fired the guns. She must have enjoyed her trip on *Renown* and all this was top secret of course, women never being allowed aboard a man-o-war at sea.

While at Malta Churchill became ill and, while the rest of his staff continued on in the heavy cruiser *London*, *Renown* stayed at Valletta harbour, giving her crew a brief opportunity to view for the first time since the outbreak of war the island they had steamed so many thousands of miles to protect. They finally sailed just before midnight on 19 November, escorted by the *Grenville, Ulster, Rocket* and *Echo*, and, after an uneventful passage through the Eastern Mediterranean, now strangely deserted, arrived at Alexandria at 12.10 on the 21st. Again Winston took the opportunity to address the ship's company, and the *Grenville,* the only destroyer that had managed to keep pace with *Renown* through from Gibraltar, was sent the signal:

The Prime Minister and Chiefs of Staff have been very impressed with your station keeping and seaworthiness.

Which was a nice gesture for Hill was an ex-*Renown* himself, having served aboard her as a Midshipman in 1928–29 under Captain Talbot. Forty-eight hours leave was given to the ship's crew in Alexandria, which the crew spent according to their various natures. Certainly they found that that particular port had long experience in catering for a matelot's every whim, as G recalls:

The sun lovers like myself really enjoying getting baked and hoping to go home brown as berries. We learned a lot of things in Alex, how to deal with foreign currency being only one. The topic of conversation on the lower deck had taken a dramatic change from the Churchill theme to that of the organised brothels ashore. This was something new and for those who it seemed had forgotten their parents' advice, it must have been a dream come true. And for others who had abandoned all advice (including medical) it was a fool's paradise, only to find themselves changing messes to 'Rose Cottage', (the VD Mess) and sacrificing their rum ration. So much for the cosmopolitan metropolis of Alexandria.

Renown sailed again on 23 November at 16.37 and retraced her steps westward through the Mediterranean, a sea strangely empty of enemies, the Vichy fleet had scuttled itself, the Italians had tamely surrendered two months earlier without a struggle. *Renown* called briefly at Algiers on the 26th leaving with the destroyers *Grenville, Isis* and *Ulster* and reached Gibraltar on the 27th, to embark passengers. They weighed again at 22.40 that same day having stayed less than a day at each port, and set course for home escorted by the *Rocket, Tumult* and *Ulster*. They were met by the destroyers *Athabaskan* and *Janus* next day and these were in turn relieved by *Meteor* and *Opportune* from Scapa and then arriving in the stream off Rosyth where she dropped anchor at 12.47 on 2nd December, having steamed a total of 9,381 hours in the five-and-a-half months since she had last left it.

CHAPTER FOURTEEN

Voyage to the Tropics

The object of their new refit, which lasted just over Christmas, was to fit them out for the tropics, for the decision had been taken to reinforce heavily Admiral Somerville's East Indies Fleet in the Indian Ocean in conjunction with long-term planned offensives in that area to recapture Burma and Malaya from the Japanese. At this time Somerville's force was at a very low ebb and hardly adequate to carry out even the basic routine patrolling and convoy protection duties. At the end of 1943 the East Indies Fleet consisted of one old battleship, *Ramillies,* and a solitary escort carrier, *Battler,* one 8-inch cruiser, *Suffolk,* and seven light cruisers, *Ceylon, Danae, Emerald, Hawkins, Frobisher, Newcastle* and *Kenya,* and eleven destroyers. It was planned to add substantially to his strength.

As well as 'tropicalisation' of the ship a few more alterations were made to her armament during the refit. Yet further Oerlikon 20-mm mounts were added to her close-range defence, seven more twin mountings and five singles were positioned about her upperworks, two of them replacing the two 44-inch searchlights on the signal bridge, because the improved performance of her latest marks of radar rendered these latter obsolete and just so-much deadweight. In further alterations the Oerlikons atop B turret were moved elsewhere and in their place was mounted a four-barrelled pom-pom.

A major change was the appointment in command of *Renown* of Captain B.C.B. Brooke who replaced Captain Parry. Captain Brooke had the reputation of being a fighting sailor and had had two ships sunk under him in action so far during the war; the more pessimistic ratings therefore sucked their teeth and speculated gloomily about the 'threes' again. Coming to command the great ship that he had first known as a young midshipman was a unique honour for Brooke.

On Boxing Day 1943, *Renown* was moved from the No. 2 dock at Rosyth into the river once more and there prepared to hoist the Flag of Vice-Admiral Sir Arthur Power, who had been appointed second-in-command of the Eastern Fleet. The Admiral was duly piped aboard, and at 12.16 on the 27th *Renown* sailed for Scapa Flow with the Admiral's flag flying. Here they found the heavy ships that were to form the core of the regenerated fleet waiting to sail, the main units being the modernised battleships *Queen Elizabeth* and *Valiant.* Sailing of the fleet was however delayed, for the weather worsened and soon a full gale was blowing from the south-west. Not until a full twenty-four hours after their original planned hour of departure did the fleet leave Scapa; *Valiant* led the heavy ships out of the Flow in the last of the evening light at 16.54 and was followed by *Queen Elizabeth* and *Renown* with destroyers *Kempenfelt, Tenacious, Termagant and Tuscan,.* The wind from the westward was still strong, and was accompanied by black rain squalls. They found the Pentland Firth in one of its most unpleasant moods, the eddies and tide-rips setting the ships uncertainly. It was not until the squadron cleared the Firth that it could form up satisfactorily. Clearly the northern waters were saying farewell to the familiar hull of *Renown* with the greatest reluctance.

Off the coast of Northern Ireland they were joined by the carriers group which had sailed from the Clyde, with Rear Admiral Clement Moody flying his flag in *Illustrious*, and the small maintenance carrier *Unicorn*, which in lieu of sufficient fleet carriers was to operate initially in the light fleet-carrier role, a job she performed most satisfactorily in the months ahead. The 2nd Battle Squadron's escort of seven destroyers was supplemented by the frigates *Berry, Blackwood* and *Domett* for the initial stages of the voyage south. The force was met by the destroyers *Active, Anthony, Brilliant, Inglefield, Isis* and *Urchin* from Gibraltar when some 230 miles west of The Rock on the 5th.

Although a total of 146 ships was promised to Somerville by the Admiralty during the first half of 1944, with the carrier *Victorious* from the Pacific and cruisers and destroyer flotillas from the Mediterranean, the 2nd Battle Squadron was the core of the new East Indies Fleet and indeed many of the ships promised were delayed during the months ahead. Of the ships in company with *Renown* at the end of December 1943, only the two battleships were of the same class and so the fleet was more in the nature of a Task Force, and an oddly assorted one at that. Admiral Power therefore immediately set to the task of converting this collection of ships into a fighting unit, and during their voyage south to Gibraltar and on through the Mediterranean drill and manoeuvres were almost continuous. The weather was now fair as they steamed south, and they made good progress to Gibraltar where a proportion of the fleet refuelled.

Renown entered the well-known harbour at 21.50 on 5 January; she left again at 04.37 next morning and few knew she had passed by.

They passed on into the Mediterranean to find bright, calm weather and passed at high speed along the coast of North Africa where a great deal of shipping was congregated. In the Eastern Mediterranean the fleet received two reports of enemy aircraft formations searching for them. The still nights were brilliant, with a full moon, but although these enemy formations were tracked to within 20 miles of the ships no contact was made.

They arrived at Port Said on the morning of 12 January and soon entered the Canal. The whole fleet passed through the canal before nightfall and anchored in Suez Bay. For the older *Renowns* there was much interest in getting a close-hand view of the new Italian battleships *Italia* and *Vittorio Veneto* lying forlornly at anchor in the Bitter Lakes. The last time *Renown* had been close to the latter battleship she had been hull-down on the horizon steaming at full speed for harbour at the Battle of Spartivento. Now here she lay in idleness, a brand new, powerful ship, with her sister a fine addition to any fleet, while the three British heavy ships, twenty-five years their senior, passed them by to offer battle to the third Axis partner.

'Our passage through the Suez Canal was frequently interrupted by the carrier *Illustrious* ahead of us', remembers Bill Kennelly, 'sucking the water away and resting on the bottom until refloated, so progress was slow.'

Nonetheless after refuelling the fleet carried out two days' exercises before continuing their journey. After oiling from Toorak they sailed on 16th escorted by the destroyers *Paladin*, *Pathfinder*, *Petard* and *Rocket*.

Captain Brooke had many memories stirred by the voyage through the Mediterranean, as he was later to recall:

> Steaming through the Mediterranean, now a peaceful sea, after having seen it earlier as a holocaust, and indeed, having lost my previous command in it two years earlier, was a most memorable experience. In the earlier days Great Britain had been so nearly defeated in those very waters. The soldiers were rescued from Crete, they were supplied from Alexandria as they advanced and retired along the coast of North Africa. Malta had stood fast under a continuous hail of bombs. The Navy had suffered grievous loss of men and ships. Having been involved in all this provoked memories mainly sad, but some extremely amusing.

The fleet called at Aden on 19 and 20 January, and there was time for a brief run ashore at this forsaken place, as G recalls:

> In Aden we got our first glimpse of a leper colony – not a pretty sight and one you don't easily forget. The monotony was only broken by one of our ship's disc jockeys who had a weird sense of humour and seemed to play George Formby's record of 'It serves you right you shouldn't have joined' on each and every occasion when things were going wrong, i.e. no hot meals, bathrooms blocked, shore leave cancelled, etc, etc, but I suppose he enjoyed being a sadist.

It was also during this long voyage from Scapa to Ceylon that the squadron passed the liner *Queen Elizabeth* and the battleship *Queen Elizabeth* signalled: 'Snap!'

Leaving this desolate spot behind it once more, with its memories of earlier visits in the 1920s, the fleet continued on to Ceylon (now called Sri Lanka) and, while the rest of the fleet proceeded to Trincomalee, *Renown* proceeded to Colombo harbour direct, escorted by the destroyers *Racehorse*, *Rapid*, *Rocket* and *Roebuck*, arriving at 15.58 on 27 January. Here Sir James Somerville publicly expressed his pleasure at seeing his old flagship once more, while privately recording that, 'she looked very weather-beaten and her drill for entering harbour was distinctly poor.' Admiral Power had to report that the bulk of the new fleet still required a great deal more training to bring it up to first line standards.

Renown left Colombo at 15.43 on 1 February and, escorted by the destroyers *Norman* and *Petard*, and joined by the carrier *Unicorn* and destroyers *Quiberon* and *Roebuck*, joined the rest of the fleet at Trincomalee on the 10th. She started well in her new command by ramming an LCT, which endeavoured to cross her bows as she was passing through the harbour entrance. The officer-in-command of the LCT complained that the sun was in his eyes and he mistook the *Renown* for an island! Actually at the investigation he asked why *Renown* hadn't given way in accordance with the Rule of the Road! Another memory for the old ship. Strangely enough and fortunately, the LCT did not suffer any serious damage.

'The harbour was equipped with buoys to secure the ships fore and aft', wrote Admiral Brooke later, 'anti-torpedo nets were spread between the ships and the sea and in the entrance a substantial anti-submarine net had been moored.'

In this secure berth *Renown* lay snugly enough, even when the south-west monsoon was blowing, in this very beautiful harbour where the waters at that time were clear and very inviting. The ship's company, particularly the captain of the signal staff and the engineers, were pleased to rest at the end of so long a voyage. The ship required painting, small repairs and boiler cleaning. They emerged from this with the ship looking spick and span under her white tropical awnings. There now remained the task of licking the crew into topline form once more under these new, and at first, extremely trying conditions.

The following three months, February, March and April, were therefore mainly spent in working hard and exercises outside the harbour. As there were few attractions ashore and a chronic lack of beer at Trincomalee this mattered less than the fact that they were away from the freezing winds and icy seas of Scapa Flow. It naturally took some time for the Renowns to become acclimatised to the heat, which was particularly trying at night. However the nights became dry and as *Renown* was well supplied with awnings, most people slept on deck when the ship was in harbour. Skin diseases, boils and stomach troubles caused great irritation and occasionally serious cases developed, but the number of hospital cases was fewer than had been expected.

Renown was part of a force that made a sortie toward Ramree Island between 10 and 14 February and the following month came Operation Initial, a sweep into the Bay of Bengal in a show of force between 8 and 12 March. Then came Operation Diplomat, a sortie to protect the India to Australia shipping route. None of these probes brought any contact with the enemy but helped the new Eastern Fleet shake down.

By the end of April the ship's company was becoming rightly proud of itself and morale was high; all departments had reached a high state of technical efficiency and the war in the East was taking a turn for the better; the situation at home was one of expectancy.

Let the *Renowns* themselves again describe how this settling-in period affected them and their shipmates during this early period 'out East'.

G has the following recollections of this time:

We learned we were reinforcing Admiral Somerville's fleet and that our task was to try to smash the Japanese supply lines to Burma where our Army lads were on a hiding to nothing.

Tropical kit was now the rig of the day and seeing each other in white shorts was most amusing, white, pale legs and probably looking like inmates of a sanatorium. But tropical routine was quite a change and we finished work about noon to have the afternoons to swim, sail, play cricket etc, or as many preferred, crash down under our spread awnings and sleep because of the heat.

On shore at Trinco facilities were fully extended after our lot arrived. It had a canteen that was short-lived, because it was burnt down (we always blamed the Yanks for that) but it was only a bamboo structure anyway, a sort of cafe, namely the Elephant House, and various bits and pieces of trading houses where barter was the custom – nothing ever carried a price tag. Certainly a pleasant base in comparison with Scapa but at times uncomfortably hot.

The ship's radio system was now picking up Radio SEAC (South East Asia Command) and from now on we were to be awakened daily, not only by the bugle but also the theme tune of SEAC, 'Moonlight Serenade' by the Glen Miller band.

A new canteen was built, mostly by the craftsmen of the fleet being detailed to work on shore whenever they were available. It was in the canteen where we were to be introduced to dehydrated beer, hardly a sparkling success, and as the water out there never seemed to run cold, it took us quite a long time to get accustomed to it, but knowing jolly Jack, we persevered and won.

Bill Kennelly has similar memories:

Most of the time we operated from Trincomalee and we were able to relax and enjoy our swimming in the safety of the anti-submarine boom, which we also hoped kept out the sharks! We suffered the occasional misplaced sense of humour of some comedian on the fo'c'sle of one of the ships shouting out 'Shark' which was followed by a mad scramble for the shipside ladders.

Beer, or shortage of it, was one of our main problems. It was good when we could get it, mainly Canadian Don or Australian Black Horse and quite good stuff. All hands were rationed to one beer ticket per man as we left the ship, but that didn't seem to limit the enjoyment of a run ashore to the canteen. Naturally Jack soon found a way around the ticket rationing. The coxs'n of the destroyer *Quality* used to take a 'sample' and then pay a visit to the local printers in Durban and return with a few reels of tickets. The return of the *Quality* to Trinco was the signal for a gathering in the canteen. During one such evening a dozen or so of us were seated round a table enjoying our beer when a couple of inebriated sailors came up to the bar. They were carrying a sack, and to satisfy the curiosity of all and sundry as to what it contained, they calmly pulled out a 6 ft snake! Shortly afterwards when we were all still seated around our table in tropical rig, white shirts and shorts, the table suddenly upended with beer flying everywhere. One of our crowd had leapt into the air when a stray dog had passed under his chair and its tail had brushed behind his knees, he, still thinking of the snake, had feared the worst.

The Chaplain, whose Hour was now well established, recollects some memorable gatherings on the *Renown's* forecastle when all the ships were in company.

We had many wonderful evenings and parties from other ships joining us. I remember five different Royal Marine bands giving an astonishingly enthusiastic rendering of *Orpheus in the Underworld,* gallantly held more or less together by the baton of our excellent bandmaster; they had had no time to rehearse! We had hymn singing and a wonderful variety of items by performers drawn from the fleet when possible, but there was always a talk, the Padre standing on a bollard; many chaplains took part, and the evening ended with a simple version of the ancient office of Compline with a thousand men, very often, joining in.

The Padre's Hour was kept to appropriate items for the unusual sort of mixture it was. It had a tremendous atmosphere and was a great source of unity in the ship.

For sheer entertainment I arranged a variety concert on Wednesdays at 8 pm. These were excellent and I am glad to say that we were able to aim at a jolly good standard of performance which meant that although the humour was broad it had to be good, i.e. *really* funny, and so we didn't deal in those seedy double *entendres* which tended to bedevil some ENSA performers of the lesser sort!

In all these activities we had a wonderful assortment of talent among officers and ship's company for in wartime a ship's company has a wide variety of people. In the entertainments John Barron played a leading part; he was later to play a dean in the delightful BBC-TV series All *Gas and Gaiters*. The first violin in the RM band, Musician Dowds, led the orchestra in the Theatre Royal, Dundee and was extremely talented.

The ship was a West Country ship and this suited me very well as I was the son of a West Country parson and had grown up in Somerset and gone to school in Dorset, little did I know that I would become Dean of Cornwall's cathedral. I think this predominantly West County ethos helped to create a spirit of mutual understanding among the men.

The officers were a first class blending of regular and RNVR and the ward-room was really wonderfully happy and harmonious.

The contrast between living conditions in the wardroom and on the lower deck in the warships of those days of course was much more accentuated than in the modern Navy. Among the outstanding young officers was Lieutenant David Williams and I can remember betting him ten shillings (50p) that the time would come when he would fly his flag; he had that admirable humility which is the hallmark of excellence and in due course he has gone to the top, although I have never collected my 10s!

I mentioned the old chapel we couldn't use, I was however able to use it as a store for the magnificent collection of knitted sweaters, scarves and gloves, and of course, Balaclava helmets, which thanks to the anonymous kindness of numerous ladies knitting for the Navy while we were in home waters, I had been able to supply everyone in the ship with; they were now somewhat redundant however! Likewise one was able to collect a vast store of good magazines, which during long periods at sea provided reading matter for men closed up at their sea stations for long hours.

Tom Oliver remembers some special problems of the tropics and some highlights:

Tropical dress (shorts and singlets) was the usual dress but scarcity of supplies, wear and tear and discolouration through intensive perspiration, made the crew look a motley throng after a while.

The Commander, always looking for a diversion from any boredom, decided he would put everyone in khaki. How to dye the clothing? Sick berth to the rescue! Baths of water on the fo'c'sle and a few pounds of Condy's Crystals thrown therein. 'All hands to muster on the fo'c'sle by messes and dye tropical rig.' What a piebald lot resulted especially after laundering, for the dye washed out or at least some of it did!

We had a Special Training Class for backward HO ratings to help them as much as we could, but it was not too popular. It seemed to smack of degrading oneself.

We also had a concert party taken under the wing of Sub-Lieutenant John Barron, RNVR. We had some good efforts, including *Maria Marten and The Red Barn,* our old diehard. Sub-Lieutenant Barron, as officer of the watch, was on duty one day when I took a defaulter before him for a minor affair. Ordinary Seaman John Sharpies, a likable lad, was asked, 'How do you like the Special Training class, Sharpies?' 'Better than your Concert Party', came the reply. 'Commander's Report', said Barron without looking up!

The Regulating Office Messenger (A.B. Hubert Eccles) always accompanied me to Requestmen and Defaulters' table each morning. Our Commander perspired profusely and always brought his hand towel with him to his table positioned outside his cabin. One particular morning pencils were in short supply for some reason and the Commander said to Eccles, 'Pencil, Eccles'. Eccles promptly produced one but, oh no, it was indelible. The Commander had a habit of sucking the end of his pencil while deliberating on a case and thus his mouth grew bluer and bluer and sweat caused it to trickle. Everyone attending the table was spellbound. The Commander wiped his face with his towel – a great smudge. He saw the stain on his towel and his face changed colour again in patriotic fashion, from blue to whiter than white with red tinges!

Admiral Power was driving his ship's company hard in order to prepare them for war against the Oriental enemy and instituted a large number of exercises both inside Trincomalee harbour as well as at sea. The Master-at-Arms recalls one such incident that proved a shade too realistic:

I happened to be in the know but the ship's company weren't. Admiral Arthur John Power signalled to one of the other ships in company to send all men under punishment, including 'second class for conduct' to *Renown* as a boarding party to feign sabotage; a sort of Nipponese type Suicide Squad. The boat arrived alongside unexpectedly with this party of ill-dressed pirates. Even the officer of the watch couldn't make out what was happening. Of course as soon as they were inboard they dispersed making for strategic positions such as the transmitting station and telephone exchange, Flag deck and the like; one did get into the exchange.

When the OOW had gathered his wits the broadcast over the ships inter-corn was 'All Royal Marines report to the quarter deck – Repel Boarders'. The interlopers were unceremoniously rounded up and, struggling and feigning to resist arrest, were herded on to the quarter deck. The Marines still thought it was for real and one poor chap I remember, was held down on the deck against the barbette of Y turret and a corporal of the RM set about his skull with the butt of his .45 Webley. The lanyard swivel in the butt of the pistol pierced the man's skull and blood squirted down his face. He had to be taken to the Sick Bay. It was at this point that Admiral Power arrived and ordered the bugler, who was always a part of the gangway staff, to sound 'Still'. Everything quietened down and the Admiral said his piece and glossed over it all by giving beer all round to the 'boarding party'. It was a good exercise but never tried again! Such was the discipline of Admiral Power. He thought journalists and politicians the lowest form of life and still worse of any publicity.

For many of the old hands the Indian Ocean was a welcome change from the Arctic, as D.G. Anderson remembers:

I think life aboard *Renown* in warmer conditions was much more suitable to me. You could spend more time on the upper deck and awnings were rigged to keep the sun off. Sleeping below decks was very sticky indeed. However, in harbour, it was grand, you could sling your hammock or lay it on the upper deck and sleep in the open air. Painting the ship's side out East was always good for you could 'accidentally on purpose' fall off your Bosun's chair into the warm tropical water to cool off.

During this period of training also, several new members joined the ship's company and quickly became assimilated in the *Renown* family. One of these was Edward Walker:

One day in the spring of 1944 I was seated in the stern-sheets of a harbour launch, which was taking me from the main jetty to rejoin my ship, the *Flower* class corvette *Betony* berthed at the far end of Colombo harbour. Several units of the recently re-formed and reinforced Eastern Fleet were in port that day, including HMS *Renown*. She was commanded by Captain B.C.B. Brooke who later served as Commodore R.N. Barracks Chatham and retired as a Rear-Admiral. She was flying the flag of Vice-Admiral Sir Arthur Power, who was later C-in-C Portsmouth and who commanded the gun carriage party at the funeral of HM King George V before the war.

The harbour launch passed down the length of the *Renown* and I became entranced with her elegance and grace, little dreaming that within a matter of weeks I would become one of her company.

Although as an ordinary seaman I had done my 'CW Seatime' in the minelaying cruiser *Adventure,* my subsequent experience had been in small ships and at this time I was a fairly recently promoted Temporary Lieutenant, RNVR.

Imagine my surprise – nay alarm – when, after a period in hospital at Colombo I was told to travel to Trincomalee to join *Renown*. I was speculating on my likely future when a Master-at-Arms, who happened to be present, reassured me. 'Don't worry, sir', said this worthy man, 'I served in her in 1927. She was a happy ship then and will be a happy ship now.' He was correct of course.

On my arrival at the head of the quarterdeck ladder I was greeted by the officer of the watch – one A.S. Harris, who recently retired as a colonel of the Royal Marines. I later came to understand that I had been sent to *Renown* as some sort of replacement for a sub-lieutenant RN who had recently left the ship on his promotion to lieutenant. This officer is now Admiral Sir David Williams, KCB, ADC, C-in-C Naval Home Command. This rate of exchange was not immediately appreciated by the Commander (Edward Reginald Conder, DSO,

DSC, RN) into whose presence I was shortly ushered. After doubts had been cast as to my probable usefulness I was dismissed gathering that I was on trial, but that if I passed muster I would stay.

I made my somewhat disconsolate way to the wardroom, but was almost immediately joined by the Commander, who stood me a drink (within the meaning of standing drinks in a wardroom mess) and told me a very amusing story of how, as a midshipman, he had joined *Renown* towards the end of World War I, when the sub of the gunroom had been the present Captain.

I was then thrilled to meet again Lieutenant M.M. Balaam RNVR who had been with me at *King Alfred*. He was now Quarterdeck Divisional Officer, who was concerned with the ship's boats and with entertainments. He introduced me to Jim Dobie and before long I found myself admitted to a circle of good friends. We were a large wardroom mess for we also carried the Admiral's staff, but were very integrated, both as to ship and staff and also as to RN, RNR and RNVR. Among many personalities were Commander (E), Kenneth Langmaid, subsequently an author and writer of TV scripts, as PMO, Surgeon Commander Davies, who pre-war had been one of the owners who sailed *Ty-Moh-Shan* home from the China Station, as one of the HACOs,

Temp. Lieutenant John Barron, RNVR, now a well-known actor, and, as Padre, one of the most remarkable characters it has ever been my good fortune and privilege to meet, the Reverend Henry Morgan Lloyd, DSO, who has recently retired as Dean of Truro.

For my own part various niches were found for me and which I thoroughly enjoyed, i.e. Second Officer of the Top Division; Quarters Officer for the forward battery of the secondary armament; sailing boats, of which there were quite a number and, in harbour, on the officer of the watch rota with what was, to all intents a peacetime routine.

Another newcomer was Martin Cain:

I had joined the RN as a 'Hostilities-Only' volunteer in May 1943, serving in the training school at HMS *Raleigh* at Torpoint, moving then to RN barracks Devonport, HMS *Drake*. I was then sent out by troopship to HMS *Assegai* in Durban from where I was sent to join the old cruiser *Caradoc* that we sailed over to Colombo and tied her to the wall to carry the flag of Admiral Mountbatten. I was then based at Lanka barracks where I was put on duty at St Joseph's college on guard as this was Mountbatten's HQ.

On 4 May 1944 I was sent to join *Renown* in Trincomalee and stayed with her until June 1945. When I first joined her I was told that she was a 'scate ship' (which meant that all the crew had done time in detention) and after a time I found out that this was true about a lot of the ship's company but they were a great crowd of lads.

We were based at Trinco and this was noted as being one of the worst bases in the area; it seemed to smell permanently, canteen facilities first-off were non-existent, there being one old canteen which burned down, although later a brick one was built. We used to get an issue of two beer tickets per month; this was Aussie beer and although it was always rated as rubbish, every time we went ashore for our beer issue it used to develop into a punch-up between our oppos from *Queen Elizabeth*, *Valiant* or *Illustrious*, and later all of us against the French *Richelieu* or the Dutch *Tromp* or the Yanks. If we Renowns were not ashore the others used to keep the fun going. I don't know how we managed to work up such energy on a couple of pint bottles of beer but as you will realise we nearly all were very young then, and the boredom was always there in those early days out East.

While the old and new were shaking themselves down the future uses of the great fleet now assembled were under long discussion at the highest levels and there was considerable disagreement. The fleet was now an impressive one and other than the big ships included the 8-inch cruiser *Shropshire* and the Dutch light cruiser *Tromp*, the 4th Destroyer Flotilla under Captain Richard Onslow, *Quilliam, Quadrant, Quality, Queenborough, Quiberon* and *Quickmatch* and the 16th Destroyer Division, *Paladin, Petard, Pathfinder* and *Penn* recently arrived from the Mediterranean, along with the 11th Destroyer Flotilla under Captain De Winton, *Rotherham, Racehorse, Raider, Rapid, Redoubt, Relentless, Rocket* and *Roebuck* and two ex-British 'N' class boats flying the Dutch flag, *Van Galen* and *Tjerk Hiddes*, eleven submarines and numerous lesser vessels. As the only drydock capable of lifting a capital ship was several thousand miles away at Durban the Admiralty sent out a floating dock from the UK in sections to be assembled in India for the fleet. It duly arrived on station early in 1944 and work started on putting it together.

When Lord Louis Mountbatten had first been appointed as Supreme Commander SEAC in October 1943, there were high hopes that his command would be able to go over to the offensive early in 1944. The planning therefore began for a full-scale amphibious operation to land a large force on the north-western tip of Sumatra (Operation Culverin). However when the requirements for troops and landing craft were examined in detail it was found that not enough could be made available due to the commitment of Normandy and so an alternative plan was developed for a landing aimed at the recapture of the Andaman Islands which would sever Japanese sea-borne supply lines to their troops in Burma where a land-campaign in conjunction with the Chinese was also mooted. This operation was codenamed Buccaneer and the Eastern Fleet was to play a major part both in covering the landings and supplying fire support. The operation was planned to take place in March 1944.

But in December it was considered that even this scaled-down attack was beyond the resources available to SEAC and most of the landing craft that had been assembled had to be sent back to Europe. It was decided that the fleet would maintain pressure on the enemy by a series of attacks against his vulnerable flanks, a decision with which Churchill did not agree and fought hard to have changed to a more offensive policy. He tried to get Culverin reconsidered for the autumn of 1944 and much wrangling took place to little avail.

Somerville therefore had to make the best use of the situation as he was presented with it. The arrival at Singapore early in 1944 of a large part of the main Japanese fleet, five battleships, three carriers, eighteen cruisers and two dozen or so destroyers posed a threat to any raids by the Eastern Fleet at this time but the enemy had his eyes fixed on the American advance in the Pacific and had no plans to repeat the foray of 1942. Nonetheless if Somerville's fleet was to operate off hostile coastlines it was felt essential that more powerful air support than that supplied by *Illustrious* and *Unicorn* was necessary. The *Victorious* was still delayed and although the *Formidable* and *Indomitable* were promised later in the year, all that in fact found their way to Ceylon in March were the escort carriers *Begum* and *Shah*. As a stop-gap measure the Americans agreed to loan the big carrier *Saratoga* to the Eastern Fleet for a period and she started off via Australia the same month.

At last the period of training was over and *Renown* was again ready to show her mettle against a new foe having already outfaced the other two Axis partners. The Eastern Fleet sailed in full fighting array on 21 March 1944 under orders for Operation Diplomat.

CHAPTER FIFTEEN

Pounding Nippon

The purpose of Operation Diplomat was to meet *Saratoga* and her escorting destroyers, *Cummings, Dunlap* and *Fanning* (Task Group 58.5) to the south-west of the Cocos Islands but the opportunity was also taken to carry out other important evaluations. Firstly, as operations against enemy-held territory on the other side of the Indian Ocean would always entail long-distance steaming and thereby the paramount need to conduct underway fuelling of both the carriers' aviation and the escorting destroyers fuel oil, this first long-range operation was taken as an ideal opportunity to test this in practice. Secondly, it gave the chance for the fleet to carry out further exercises and for the carrier air group of *Illustrious* to shake down under realistic conditions. Finally, for all the men of the Eastern Fleet it was a test of how well they had adjusted to the new climatic conditions over the previous four months and how ably they were able to steam and fight their ships in this new circumstances.

The fleet oilers were therefore despatched to a prearranged rendezvous escorted by the Dutch cruiser *Tromp* and the main fleet which left Trincomalee and Colombo and consisted of the *Renown* (Flag), *Queen Elizabeth* and *Valiant*, the carrier *Illustrious*, 8-inch cruisers *London* and *Cumberland*, the 6-inch cruisers *Ceylon* and *Gambia* and the destroyers *Quilliam, Quality, Queenborough, Quiberon* and *Pathfinder*, along with the Australian-manned *Napier, Norman* and *Nepal* and their Dutch sisters *Tjerk Hiddes* (ex-*Nonpariel*) and *Van Galen* (ex-*Noble*).

On the 24th they rendezvoused with the oilers in spectacular fashion. *Tromp* had its oilers steaming in line abreast ten cables apart at ten knots. The Fleet met them on the opposite course in similar formation and a magnificent grid-iron manoeuvre followed, with the tankers keeping perfect station. Refuelling followed between the 24th and 26th and then, on the 27th, they met Task Group 58.5. *Sara* made an immediately good impression on the British fleet as she joined up with her ship's company fallen-in in immaculate white uniform on her flight deck. She never lost her reputation for smartness and efficiency from that moment.

The whole force then returned to Trincomalee while the two air groups exercised together for the first time, arriving on 2 April. Somerville determined to make good use of *Saratoga* while he had her. With her experienced air group of Hellcat fighters, Dauntless dive-bombers and Avenger torpedo-bombers she presented a well-balanced force, which the mixture of planes aboard *Illustrious* could not hope to match. They could learn much, however, by operating in company and so an immediate air strike was planned against Sabang, the Japanese naval base that guarded the northern entrance to the Straits of Malacca and the approaches to Singapore.

Before this operation took place further reinforcements arrived on station, the French battleship *Richelieu* on the 9th, the escort carrier *Atheling* the week before.

It was at 11.02 on 16 April therefore that *Renown* again sailed from Trincomalee and pointed her sharp bows to the east to carry out Operation Cockpit. The fleet was divided into two Task Forces for the attack and *Renown* was the flagship of Task Force 70 under Admiral Power, her job being to cover the two carriers, *Illustrious* and *Saratoga* with the heavy cruiser *London*, light cruisers *Ceylon* and *Gambia* and destroyer screen consisting of *Quilliam*, *Quadrant*, *Queenborough*, *Cummings*, *Dunlap* and *Fanning*. Admiral Somerville flew his flag in the *Queen Elizabeth* with Task Force 69, which comprised *Valiant* and *Richelieu*, light cruisers *Newcastle*, *Nigeria* and *Tromp* and destroyers *Penn*, *Petard*, *Napier*, *Nepal*, *Nizam*, *Rotherham*, *Racehorse* and *Van Galen*. As the *Gambia* was New Zealand manned and four of the destroyers Australian, these along with the American, French and Dutch ships, represented a truly Allied force.

On 19th the carriers reached their flying-off positions undetected, and duly despatched their air striking forces – eleven Avengers and eighteen Dauntless with twenty-four Hellcat fighters from *Saratoga* and seventeen Barracudas with thirteen Corsair fighters from *Illustrious*. These duly struck their targets hard and, for the loss of just one aircraft, whose pilot was rescued by submarine, they destroyed three out of the four major oil tanks and bombed the harbour and airfield. The defending Japanese fighters were caught on the ground and hits claimed on the few shipping targets available. One cargo ship was sunk, several damaged and twenty-four enemy aircraft destroyed. The two air groups had co-ordinated their attacks perfectly. Once embarked the fleet headed back out to sea.

A second strike was not considered, and the planned bombardment by the heavy ships had been cancelled. The latter was a great disappointment to the ships concerned of course, and, worse, was later regretted, for as usual the glowing report of the returning airmen on the scale of damage they had inflicted proved highly inaccurate. The Japanese were, however, sufficiently stung into despatching two formations of torpedo bombers against the retiring fleet.

The first wave was intercepted by the Hellcats some 20 miles from the fleet and three of the bombers were promptly shot down during the forenoon. A much more dangerous attack developed at dusk.* The fleet met this with a heavy and prolonged barrage, *Renown* herself firing off 700 rounds of 4.5-inch ammunition in a half-an-hour. Six of the Japanese torpedo bombers were shot down by the ships and no damage was received by the fleet. The barrage was laid down by radar control as Bill Kennelly remembers: 'Our radar detected what was thought to be a reprisal attack by Jap aircraft. We put up a terrific barrage by pom-pom and AA guns, but it was through heavy cloud and in all that time we never sighted the aircraft at all.'

The high-speed dash to the west also provided difficulties down below. After five years almost non-stop high speed steaming in all weathers and in constant action even

---

* It is interesting to note that this major attack is not mentioned either in MacIntyre, *Fighting Admiral* or Roskill, *War at Sea*.

the magnificent engines fitted in *Renown* were beginning to feel the strain a bit, as Norman Hopwood relates:

> Having done our stuff we had to run like blazes to avoid retribution striking. From the engine room department this became difficult for a joint in the main steam system just above the manoeuvring valve blew out and we ERAs could not stay below in those conditions manning the valve for more than an hour at a time. Anyway we eventually arrived back at Trinco in one piece and with no casualties.

Renown returned to that base on 21 April at 09.10. The *Saratoga* was then ordered home to the States for a refit but Admiral King suggested that *en route* to Australia she might launch an air strike against the Japanese base of Soerabaya, and this Somerville was keen to carry out as further training for his fleet. Soerabaya was the main base for Japanese anti-submarine forces operating in the Java Sea and also had the adjacent oil refinery of Wonokromo as suitable targets for such a mission.

There were two problems, which it was felt the Eastern Fleet had to overcome before carrying out this attack (Operation Transom). The first was the great distance to the target from Ceylon. It was felt that, despite the increased proficiency in underway fuelling, the lack of large tankers would mean that instead of this being carried out the fleet would first have to fuel at Exmouth Gulf on the north coast of Australia, before launching the strike. Arrangements were therefore put in hand and tankers despatched there in advance. In all six oilers, and a water tanker were despatched, sailing on 30 April under the protection of the 8-inch cruisers *London* and *Suffolk* (Task Force G7).

The second problem involved the aircraft of the Fleet Air Arm embarked in *Illustrious*. Somerville expected the Japanese to be much more alert after the attack on Sabang and therefore wanted to launch the strike from further out to sea to achieve surprise. The flying-off position, some 180 miles from the target, was beyond the radius of action of the Barracuda bomber. In addition this clumsy aircraft was far inferior in the dive-bombing role compared with proper types like the American Dauntless carried by *Saratoga*. Unfortunately no true dive-bombers existed in the Royal Navy at this time, but the Avenger torpedo bomber was adaptable in a shallow dive and had more than sufficient range to carry out the mission and the Royal Navy had large numbers of these on hand under lease-lend. Accordingly *Illustrious* dumped her Barracudas ashore, re-equipped with Avengers and the fleet was ready.

On 6 May therefore, at 15.37, *Renown* again sailed from Trincomalee on the first leg of the 4,000-mile voyage to start the mission. In company were the two carriers, the 6-inch cruisers *Ceylon* and *Gambia,* and destroyers *Quilliam, Quadrant, Queenborough, Cummings, Dunlap* and *Fanning* (Task Force GG). Next day *Renown* left this force and joined the 2nd Battle Squadron, which again Somerville was commanding from *Queen Elizabeth,* with *Valiant* and *Richelieu,* the 6-inch cruisers *Newcastle, Nigeria* and *Tromp* and the destroyers *Quiberon Quickmatch, Penn, Rotherham, Racehorse, Napier, Nepal* and *Van Galen* (Task Force GS).

On 15 May at 09.13 *Renown* reached Exmouth Gulf and commenced refuelling. G recalls that conditions were rather different from normal here: 'The temperature was much lower than we had experienced for some time and for the first time we were proud to display our goose pimples.'

He also describes life at sea aboard *Renown* during those long voyages across the width of the Indian Ocean:

Naturally, at sea for many days at a time, our food supplies consisted largely of dehydrated vegetables etc and I can assure you that the potatoes of those days bore no resemblance at all to today's modern Smash and the like, even the colour didn't match. However, dehydrated onions were favourite because we all preferred them raw and ate them like potato crisps. It was at times like these when many of us realized that the war at sea was never won by guns and planes but rather by Heinz's fourpenny tins of beans, which were always on sale in ships' NAAFIs and were consumed by the ton, cold and straight out of the tin!

Martin Cain recollects that:

I think that people could never understand the heat that we had to contend with on those ships out there, it was one long sweat day and night, you could never get cool, you were rationed to the drinking water that you got, maybe a couple of cups a day and that was always warm. We did get one cup of lime juice a day; this was supposed to make up for the sweat you lost and keep down the minor tropical diseases but we all used to finish up with prickly heat and toe rot (athlete's foot) which never seemed to leave you. We used to say that when we got home we would never look for the sunshine again.

Peter Elvin remembers also that conditions aboard *Renown* were bad:

We had no air conditioning or air-cooling plants and it was hellish – indeed I established, in conjunction with an RNVR physiologist, that after half-an-hour at action stations we were not an effective fighting unit as far as the gun armament was concerned. The practical research we carried out would be perhaps of no interest today, but was sufficient to cause their Lordships at the Admiralty to move pretty swiftly to install small air-cooling sets in central positions in ships destined for the Pacific War.

The carriers reached their launch positions south of the target undetected at 06.30 on 17 May, south of Java and an hour-and-a-half later had put the two air striking forces into the sky for the long journey to the enemy base, much of it overland. In all forty-five Avengers and Dauntless bombers were sent out escorted by forty Corsair and Hellcat fighters, one group to hit the oil refinery and an engineering works, the other to strike at the docks. The attacks went in at 08.30; complete surprise was again achieved but once more, although great execution was thought to have been done in fact damage was minimal; only a single vessel of 993 tons was sunk and although fires were started Japanese post-war records show that little lasting harm was done to their shore installations, although twelve aircraft were destroyed on the ground.

But their pride was probably hurt and only one Allied aircraft was lost to flak. All the aircraft safely re-embarked and the fleet withdrew to the south-west at high speed but no Japanese counter-attack developed. Churchill signalled: 'I cordially congratulate you and your Fleet . . .', thus scotching a typical signal from General MacArthur claiming that his forces had been involved!

On the 18th the American ships took their departure from the Eastern Fleet, during the afternoon in spectacular style. The Fleet formed one long line, which stretched from horizon to horizon, and *Sara* and her three destroyers steamed down, and were cheered by each ship as they passed by. The signals that were exchanged reflected the mutual goodwill that had been built-up by this short period of co-operation by the Allies.

C-in-C, E. F. from C.T.G.58.5:

On our departure, may I ask that you express to every officer and rating of your fleet the best wishes of every officer and rating of Task Group 58.5. Not only has it been a pleasure to serve with you but it has been an honour. We leave you in the highest regard and we know that great things will be accomplished by you. All of us wish all of you Good Luck, Good Hunting and may God be with each of you in your future undertakings wherever and whatever they may be.

C. T. G.58.5 from *C-in-C EF*:

Your message, which will be promulgated to my fleet, is very much appreciated. You have done grand work with us and we view your departure with great regret. We hope that good fortune will make us fleet mates again in the future. Good Luck and God bless you.

After the sail-past the Americans signalled:

Many, many thanks for the splendid send-off. We shall always remember it.

And even crusty Admiral Ernie King, never a lover of the Royal Navy, sent a signal:

Please extend my congratulations to Commander-in-Chief, Eastern Fleet, and his command on so satisfactorily completing a mission, which inflicted important damage on the enemy.

Although we now know the damage was not lasting, the spirit of close harmony that was set up between the two nations' ships at this time was much more enduring and one that was to stand the test of time in the Pacific a year later.

Renown and the rest of Somerville's command then revisited Exmouth Gulf, on the morning of the 19th, refuelled once more and finally arrived back at Trincomalee on 27 May at 15.06 after a round trip of over 7,000 miles in three weeks. *Renown* was able to give 48 hours' leave at Colombo during a stay there between 9 and 17 June before she again returned to Trinco for the next operation. This was the only overnight leave that she had been able to give for nearly 12 months, and the crew took full advantage of it. Trips were arranged and a special Padre's outing to Kandy took place on the 15/16th. After this break further gunnery exercises were held at sea to continue the process of working up *Renown* to a high pitch of readiness. That this was in fact achieved was reflected in the results of a main armament shoot held around that time and signalled to Admiral Power:

From *Emerald* to VAEF. Following received from *Aimwell* [the target towing vessel]:

> Run 1 *Renown*. Salvos 1,2 and 3 300 yards short; 4-Hits; 5,6, and 7-Stradles; 9 and 10-Stradles; 8-Hit. Average spread 300 yards.

Early on 19 June *Renown* led a small force from Trincomalee, including the *Richelieu*, to escort the *Illustrious* in a carrier raid on Port Blair in the Andaman Islands. Fifteen Barracuda bombers escorted by eight Corsair fighters were flown off on the 21st to carry out Operation Pedal. Poor weather conditions again gave them surprise but although the airfield and harbour were hit results were again minimal and two aircraft were lost. Once more there was no enemy reaction and the fleet was back in harbour on the 23rd.

With all the glory going to the Fleet Air Arm the heavy ships were chaffing at the bit. The dispersal of the heavy Japanese fleet at Singapore due to the great Battle of the Philippine Sea in June, meant that prospects of a surface action were rather remote at this time but they were eager to play a more important role than AA protection for the carriers and finally Somerville relented. Another attack against Sabang was planned – Operation Crimson. This was to be Admiral Somerville's last chance to fly his flag with an active fleet at sea for he was due to hand over to Admiral Sir Bruce Fraser on 23 August. By this time further reinforcements had arrived from the West; the principal units were the carriers *Indomitable* and *Victorious*.

The plan was for the aircraft from the carriers to strike at the airfields first and paralyse any Japanese opposition from that quarter. Then the cruisers were to conduct a shoot from the other side of the island as a diversion while the main heavy units took up their stations offshore and opened fire, with aircraft spotting overhead.

The fleet left Trincomalee at 16.11 on 22 July and three days later was in position off Sabang. Yet again complete surprise was achieved. The carriers *Illustrious* and *Victorious*, escorted by the cruiser *Phoebe* and destroyers *Raider* and *Roebuck,* took up their flying-off positions in the pre-dawn dusk and at dawn flew off a striking force of thirty-four Corsairs. These struck the airfields but found few worthwhile targets to occupy them. The carriers then flew off standing air patrols and spotters while the light cruisers *Ceylon, Gambia, Nigeria* and *Kenya* took up their bombardment positions for the diversion.

Meanwhile the heavy ships moved silently into their prearranged positions offshore, *Queen Elizabeth, Valiant, Renown* and *Richelieu* with the 8-inch cruiser *Cumberland,* screened by the destroyers *Rotherham, Racehorse, Rapid, Relentless* and *Rocket* inshore of them, with the Dutch cruiser *Tromp* and destroyers *Quilliam, Quality* and *Quickmatch* took station in readiness for their part of the operation. Edward Walker later described the scene:

> We went to action stations just before dawn, the main armament was brought to the ready, and the ship was waiting for the order to open fire when we should arrive at the pre-arranged position. At that time I had not been assigned to any particular job, so I was able to go onto the ADP at the after end of the bridge, and so saw as much as anybody, and a good deal more than most.
>
> Slowly we approached the coast, until, again exactly on time, the fleet flagship, with Admiral Sir James Somerville on board, opened up. With a deafening roar our own guns and those of the remainder of the fleet opened fire.

He makes a good point, for it is not always realised that for the bulk of the crew of
Renown such stirring actions were events that took place far above them and nothing
was known of the outcome other than by word-of-mouth messages or infrequent
announcements over the Tannoy system, as this vivid description by G underlines:

> Brookie was no doubt in his element, knowing we were about to knock skittles
> of shit out of the Japs; indeed there was something of excitement for everyone,
> and to see the carrier's flight decks lined with strike aircraft and fighters was a
> sight not to be forgotten, and when you are bang in the middle of enemy waters
> and, being capital ships, obvious targets and no doubt super prizes for any likely
> kamikaze pilot who got through, it made one think; but I didn't feel as fright-
> ened as I'd imagined then.
>
> One thing did frighten me. As shipwrights we were responsible for the water-
> tightness of the ship and to keep her afloat on even keel if possible. This meant
> we played a part in any flooding if hit, so we could quickly flood compartments
> opposite to the side damaged to keep the ship stable. We had to do this with
> the full knowledge that cooks, stewards, writers, NAAFI staff and many others
> were deep in the bowels of the ship serving in the magazines. I dreaded the fact
> that I might have to drown my own shipmates in order to save the ship. How
> I hated this bloody war. This to me seemed cruel. Yes, I wanted to go home.
>
> Then *Renown* opened fire and 15-inch salvos screamed shoreward.
>
> The ship, although perfectly behaved in exercises and practice shoots, now
> seemed in convulsions, the noise, the stench of cordite burning, the heat off the
> engines, the sweat running – God help us.
>
> But somehow when you thought of our lads further north in the jungles of
> Burma and what they were suffering you lost any feeling of remorse for the
> poor bastards on the receiving end of a naval bombardment.

Martin Cain makes the same point:

> When we did the bombardment of Sabang, as you will appreciate, we did not
> see a lot of what was going on as we were in the 15-inch doing the bombard-
> ment, but towards the end we were on the welldeck watching and I saw a very
> large Jap flying boat coming on to the scene. He must have realised too late
> what was happening and then he slowly tried to turn away but the guns blew
> him out of the sky.

In all the heavy ships deluged the harbour and shore installations with 294 15-inch
shells, the *Renown* contributing sixty-three rounds against the Coaling Station alone;
while the *Cumberland* adding 134 8-inch, the other cruisers 324 6-inch and the
destroyers about 600 rounds of 4.7-inch shells; shore batteries and radar and radio
stations were pulverised. Then *Tromp* led Captain Onslow's destroyers into the outer
bay to attack the shipping and coastal installations at point-blank range. As well as
pumping a hail of 4.7-inch shells into these targets the destroyers, as they passed the
entrance of the inner harbour, fired eight torpedoes into it to add to the carnage. Both
Quality and *Quilliam* were hit by a single shell each in reply, which was the only
Allied damage suffered, apart from the loss of one of the Corsairs whose pilot was
picked up.

On the conclusion of this 'spectacular' operation the fleet again assembled and withdrew to the west at speed. During the withdrawal about a score of Japanese bombers approached in a hesitant manner looking for an opening in the defences. They found none and the defending fighters were soon in among them, shooting down seven for the loss of two Corsairs, and driving the rest away before they could attack. Considerable damage was done to Sabang on this occasion; oil tanks, repair shops and port facilities were levelled but only two small ships were sunk in the harbour, which was almost empty at the time. The fleet arrived back at Trincomalee at 13.30 on the 27th in high spirits.

This operation marked the high-point of *Renown's* time in the Indian Ocean and the ship was at a high peak of efficiency, but badly needed docking after this series of long-range operations before renewing the offensive. This they were scheduled to do in August, but then came the saga of Floating Dock 28! *Renown* had a lucky escape from premature retirement in this unhappy episode, as Admiral Brooke had recalled: 'The safe arrival of this dock was a most important matter for it was designed to take our largest ships, which would otherwise have to dock at Durban.'

As related this dock had been sent to India in sections and was then assembled at Bombay and towed to Trincomalee and moored about one mile from *Renown's* berth there.

Admiral Brooke:

> The capital ships were all due for docking and it was suggested that my ship should be the first to dock. We were all slightly suspicious of the dock, which so far as we knew had never raised a capital ship. Eventually agreement was reached that a battleship should be the first to follow the successful docking of a supply ship. The dock was flooded and the ship entered during the day.
>
> A dock of this dimension is moored by heavy chain cables to special anchors securely attached to the bed of the harbour in such a way that the dock's tanks can be flooded until it sinks to a depth which enables the ship to enter. Down the centre of the dock platform there is a row of wooden blocks on which the ship rests when she is centred by wire hawsers and wooden baulks.
>
> The dock pumps gradually expel the water from its tanks and the dock rises until the ship is supported on the rows of blocks. If all is well the process continues until the ship and dock platform are clear of the water by a satisfactory margin.

The trial run with a cruiser was completed satisfactorily, and on 8 August, the battleship *Valiant* entered and the process started. In the harbour life aboard *Renown* was proceeding peacefully.

Admiral Brooke continues:

> During all times of the year evening in the tropics is a blessed relief from the heat of the day. In a ship even setting sun heats the steel until the inside of mess-decks and cabins become unbearably hot. Evening in this lovely harbour surrounded by low jungle covered hills was of great splendour because huge thunderclouds towered over the sea continually lit by lightning. During the

evening we were playing cards and relaxing under the huge awning, enjoying the cool and quiet when a signal lookout arrived in a state of great excitement crying, 'Look, sir, the floating dock is sinking.' We turned to look at a sight I shall never forget.

Before a background of dark hills, surmounted by huge thunderclouds lit almost continuously by lightning, a great deal of black smoke arose. In the tropical gloom could be distinguished the ship's bows risen to an angle of some 20°. The stern appeared to be embedded in the rear of the dock which had collapsed at two thirds of its length with its stern cocked up. There was utter silence.

Other members of *Renown's* crew remember that dramatic moment also. Peter Churchill: 'We watched *Valiant* as the dock broke up under her and she signalled with her 44-inch searchlight, "S.O.S. Dock Collapsing."'

Bill Kennelly:

Trinco was enjoying a quiet tropical evening when there was a sudden uproar all round, bugles and searchlights etc. The dock had failed under the strain, one of its three sections had started to separate and *Valiant* started to slide out. The normal pumps and flood arrangements of the dock were out of action.

Admiral Brooke continues the story:

As I had had the experience of ships being sunk by two-man submarines such a possibility raced through my mind. Sabotage and faulty construction too were reviewed but the overriding consideration was that the stricken ship had all her men on board and was in imminent danger of foundering with the dock.

The Admiral [Power] called for a boat and went to examine the situation while we raised steam, set extra lookouts and took other precautions.

Tom Oliver recalls the incident thus:

Admiral Power again showed his power of leadership in an emergency when the floating dock which had been assembled by dockyard reserve ratings, broke it's back with the *Valiant* in it. The dock had previously been tried out by smaller vessels before attempting *Valiant*. It was an uncanny sight in the semi-darkness with all searchlights trained on it to see the *Valiant* sitting on its stern with bows in the air. Everyone was got off the ship carefully and landed.

Aboard *Renown* the sounding of the alarm bells brought to many the fear of human torpedo attack of the kind that had damaged *Queen Elizabeth* and *Valiant* at Alexandria in 1941 and *Ramillies* in Diego Suarez in 1942 and which the Italians had attempted against *Renown* at Gibraltar in 1941. Martin Cain:

During the night we heard one hell of a bang, we thought that midget Jap subs had got in and torpedoed the dock, but I think then we decided that the dock had just collapsed. Anyway when the bang came they closed up all but main armaments to action stations and they had us 15-inch guns crews at damage control stations. This involved closing most of the watertight doors, but some had to be left open for people to move round, but in the event of a hit on any section of the ship it was our duty to lock those doors when ordered to, no matter who was left in that section.

Also we were set to work blowing up thousands of the blue inflatable lifebelts, throwing them into LCIs with the intention of scattering them in the water around the dock if it collapsed further or capsized.

Admiral Brooke concludes the tale:

The situation raised administration difficulties. The stricken ship was under dockyard control when in dock which was operated entirely by the dockyard as an autonomous organisation. As soon as a ship was received into a dock her Captain had to rely upon the dockyard authorities to operate the dock, about which he had only a rudimentary knowledge and over which he had no control.

When everything had been done for the extra security of our own ship the hours of silent waiting for the next development were filled with the memories of a similar situation: the operations room at Alexandria where we had received a report that, 'two foreigners have been found sitting on the buoy to which the *Queen Elizabeth* is moored.' Further precautions, then more waiting. A cruiser sinking in Norway -after bombing, the time spent watching, watching, the death struggles when nothing further could be done in the deep Norwegian fiord.

The Admiral returned with no idea as to the cause of the tragedy. We waited the dawn. A visit to the dock next day established that difficulty had been experienced in raising the dock and ship the last two feet. After continuous efforts the dock collapsed, the front two thirds holding the ship remained intact, and came to rest, the fractured third having sunk, the front and rear cocked up. The ship slid backwards and came to rest with her propellers buried in the rear portion of the dock while the whole assembly took on a ten-degree list.

Before dawn the dock was corrected in heel by flooding and all apertures in the ship sealed. Sabotage and enemy action were ruled out, the dock was flooded and the much damaged ship worked out. In spite of the vast forces which were involved there were no casualties whatever. The enquiry, which followed, had moments of great drama. The dock having been sunk to enable the ship to be withdrawn, *Valiant's* engine room was only accessible to divers who were unfamiliar with its design. Her engines were out of action.

Regulations for the operation of a dock and on its lifting capacity etc are usually displayed engraved on a plate, which is readily seen and is bolted on to a bulkhead. In this newly arrived dock the engineers could find no one who confirmed having seen it and as the enquiry proceeded it became clearer that no conclusion could be reached without it. Day after day divers searched with no success. Two weeks passed, endless witnesses were examined, until, in the middle of an examination; the missing engraved regulations were brought in.

The Board established that though the dock was capable of lifting the weight of the ship with ammunition, men and stores in total, this would have had to be spread over a greater length of the dock than that of the ship involved.

So *Renown*'s docking was postponed for the time being and they set forth against the enemy once more. *Valiant* mournfully left the Eastern Fleet, proceeding to Devonport via the Cape for extensive repairs, which were not completed until 1946. Meanwhile the new battleship *Howe* had arrived from home waters to form the nucleus of the proposed British Pacific Fleet. Hopes were high aboard *Renown* now that she had proved herself again in action and had the high speed necessary to accompany a modern Task Force, that she too might form part of this fleet and take the war back to Japan itself. But this depended on her refit and, while arrangements were made for this to be carried out, further employment was found in the Indian Ocean. Two further carrier strikes were conducted during August and September, but the *Howe* replaced *Renown* as the heavy ship flagship for both these in order to give her experience in working in these conditions.

In the middle of October *Renown's* chance came again. In the Pacific the Americans were about to re-invade the Philippine Islands by landing in Leyte Gulf. The whole strength of the Imperial Japanese Navy was thrown against this and the result was the largest sea/air battle in history, the Battle of Leyte Gulf. Prior to their sailing for this epic fight the bulk of the Japanese battleship and heavy cruiser forces had again been based upon Singapore near to their oil supplies. In the vain hope of drawing some of their attentions away from the Americans the East Indies fleet sailed to carry out Operation Millet, a combined air strike and bombardment of Japanese positions in the Nicobar Islands. Again the fleet, which sailed from Trincomalee on 15 October, was divided into several groups.

Task Group 63.1 consisted of the flagship, *Renown* herself with Admiral Power embarked as C-in-C, with a screen of three destroyers, *Quilliam, Queenborough* and *Quiberon*. Task Group 63.2 comprised the heavy cruiser division, *Cumberland, London* and *Suffolk* screened by destroyers *Norman, Raider, Relentless* and *Van Galen,* while the carrier group, Task Group 63.3 comprised the *Indomitable* and *Victorious,* the light cruiser *Phoebe,* acting in her usual role as fighter direction ship, escorted by the destroyers *Wager, Wakeful, Wessex* and *Whelp* which had come out from home waters with *Howe* in August. As *Valiant* and *Richelieu* had both gone for refits, *Queen Elizabeth* was docking at Durban and *Howe* was exercising, *Renown* was the only capital ship present. The operation, being designed to draw the enemy fire, involved staying off the Nicobars for several days during which a series of air strikes and shore bombardments would be carried out. And thus it fell out, although both targets and Japanese opposition were meagre in the extreme. *Renown's* turn at bombardment duty came on 18 October.

Edward Walker recollects that:

I, by this time, was OOQ of the forward 4.5-inch and being in the battery saw very little of the action. I was indeed kept very busy as the powers-that-be had allowed us in the secondary armament to open fire, which suited my guns' crews very well. In fact the whole ship's company was very keen to go into action, and always looked forward to what have been termed by the irreverent as 'Eastern Fleet Club Runs'.

This was no doubt originated by the many members of *Renown's* company that had served aboard her during her Force H days. Although opposition was negligible on this operation the fatigue was still present, as Martin Cain's accounts reveal:

I remember the trip to the Nicobars. We all thought at the time we were going down into the Pacific, but were told later that this was not the case. We were closed up at main armaments for a heck of a long while. My job was centre-sight setter on Y turret; it was not a hard job to do, just a boring one sitting there for an awfully long time locked in. The worst part was that I had to crawl between the walls of the turret to get to my position. It used to take a while to get into there and I often wondered what would happen if we ever got hit for I realised that I would never get out.

As I said, it was not a hard or technical job: the dials lay in front of me, I just sat at the stool and turned the handles to follow the needles as they were set by the direction finders. This set the range and direction the turret would be firing. The funny part of it was you never seemed to hear the guns firing when they did. Just a dull thud, the ship would sway and I got covered in grease and oil from the recoil. As we were in the tropics' and wearing next to nothing because of the heat, you can imagine the mess I used to finish up in and to make matters worse I sometimes stayed that way for days.

This was the last time that the *Renown* was to use its main armament against an enemy target however, although the hope that they would join up with the Pacific Fleet that was now assembling in Ceylon remained high at this period. As one of her officers recorded:

Apart from the very real desire to get into closer contact with the enemy, everyone realised that to go home, the probable alternative, would mean a spell of leave and the Eastern Fleet again in another ship. For a hostilities officer to change ships was an uprooting similar in civil life to leaving home and employment and to be avoided at all costs. To leave *Renown* would be a tragedy.

It was known that *Renown* must dock and refit for a period of six weeks; conjecture ran high as to whether this could be completed in time. A suggestion was made to the Admiral that we might go to Sydney and thus be ready when the fleet went East. The ship was on top of her form, little loss of vitality was yet apparent and she was taking a leading part in everything; in appearance, keenness for action, efficiency and morale.

Unfortunately this period was a state of uncertainty preceding the change of Commander-in-Chief, and the formation of the Pacific Fleet and supply train. Only two capital ships were present, *Renown* and *Howe,* and a complete change of administration was about to take place. The *Renown* moreover was waiting to refit in the knowledge that if she did not go soon, she would miss her chance of sailing further east.

Little result could be seen of their efforts afterwards, as Bill Kennelly said: 'We just hoped that the Japs were sailing skywards with the rest of the debris.'

One more visual effect was achieved during the return to Trincomalee soon after the bombardment. An air attack by ten torpedo-bombers had been intercepted by the fleet's fighters, who destroyed seven of them for the loss of three of their own, when over the horizon came a small freighter flying the Rising Sun.

Martin Cain remembers that:

After we had completed this raid we had a buzz going round the ship that all the Japs had been long gone before we had started the attack and that all we had done was cleared the Nicobars and Andamans of monkeys. Well, on the way back a Jap coaster got stuck in the middle of the whole Eastern Fleet and she got blown out the water. We felt better after that!!

Morale, which was high during periods of intense activity, began to be affected when the fleet swung round the buoy in Trincomalee. A fresh repaint of the ship to the new Admiralty Standard scheme had taken place; *Renown* did not look her age, nor was she lacking in efficiency or speed – she still had a two knot margin over the modern *Howe*. But of course it was inevitable that when the final choice was made only the most modern ships would be chosen to go on to the Pacific Theatre and take their place alongside the brand-new ships of the mighty American Task Forces. Although *Renown* might look resplendent in her coat of pale light grey, with a blue panel super-imposed from her forward turret to her muzzles of her after guns, and her main gun-houses themselves the same blue, she was still ill-protected compared with the new battleships, especially for an area of operations where the kamikaze was the most likely missile to put her to the test, against which her side armour could not help her.

Some relief was found from the boredom of Trincomalee and the tension of waiting their fate in August when the ship sailed for Colombo once more. Here she spent a happy period between 18 and 28 August giving leave and celebrating the fifth year of her Commission. A special service was held to commemorate this event and an extremely high proportion of the original crew who had joined her in August 1939 was still aboard her then. One was W. Pittendreigh:

The Commemoration Anniversary Dinner held in the GOH Colombo to mark the fifth year of our being in commission was, for those of us that still remained, having done in fact *two* commissions on a peacetime basis, was something quite special and, as you can imagine, it was quite a night.

After the Nicobar attack however it was back to Trinco and the waiting. Edward Walker described in a lecture later the conditions there:

Life in harbour could be monotonous, but was very well organised. Work commenced at 06.30 and went on till 12.45. After this the non-duty watch could proceed ashore while those not actually on watch were finished for the day except for the routine work that always has to be done.

When we first went there facilities ashore were almost nil. Ratings had to be back aboard by 21.30 and officers by midnight. Beer was strictly rationed. So recreation had to be self-made. Swimming and boating were popular, while many lusty souls played football, cricket and hockey, but usually not until after 16.00.

Everyone slept on deck, and it was very pleasant, as we lay far enough from the shore not to be bothered by winged visitations in the shape of mosquitoes and flies. The bigger ships had cinema facilities, which of course they shared with their more unfortunate brothers.

From October to March the NE monsoon is blowing and from June to September the SW. The worst months were April and May and in April 86%

of *Renown's* ship's company had some kind of skin disease. Prickly heat was with most of us most of the time. We had two deaths due to the climate, one to natural causes and one by drowning.

As well as the Padre's Hour, which was now famous all over the Fleet, a second entertainment grew in strength and popularity with the introduction of the Variety Shows, and *Renown* was lucky enough to obtain permission for Wrens to play the female parts.

Other diversions were found, one of the chief of which was the construction of the Lido and Rest Camp at Sober Island. This again was mainly *Renown's* show, the work being directed by Lieutenant Commander P.M. Ingledew, RNVR, who had been managing director of Tiddenham Chase Quarries near Chepstow in civvy street, with the aid of Maurice Balaam, a peacetime quantity surveyor. The construction of this site, including a bathing pool and refreshment hut, was originally started as a regular naval project but it had to give way to more important work. Volunteer workmen were therefore called for and forty Renowns responded with a will shifting more than 100 tons of sand.

John Roche remembers other small diversions during these dull days: 'A submarine fired a torpedo during tests and sank one of our own tankers, and the WRNS Quarters were burned down', but he does not say whether the two incidents were related!

But at the end of November the blow fell. The decision was taken and, as feared, *Renown* was not included in the list of ships assigned to the newly formed British Pacific Fleet (BPF). Their proposal to refit in Sydney was also turned down.

G remembers:

In November it therefore became generally apparent that we were not any further east. Finally Admiral Fraser came to say goodbye; he informed us that it was intended that *Renown* and *Queen Elizabeth* should remain at Trincomalee as the capital ships of the East Indies Fleet, while the British Pacific Fleet would go further east. Shortly after this Admiral Power spoke to *Renown* on hauling down his flag; after some pleasant and very complimentary remarks, he said that he expected to be in Singapore before Admiral Fraser. This was encouraging.

A signal from the C-in-C East Indies stated that the intention was for *Renown* to sail on 10 February 1945, following her refit, unescorted from Durban to Ceylon.

Admiral Brooke recalls: 'The time soon arrived for my ship to dock and the time was Christmas and so we set sail for Durban.'

CHAPTER SEVENTEEN

Of Admirals,
Presidents and Kings

At 10.37 on 8 December, *Renown* sailed for Trincomalee on the first leg of her long journey to Durban, South Africa. Their first port of call was lonely Addu Atoll in the Maldive Islands, the base that had been Somerville's 'secret' harbour in the grim days of 1942, but which since those times had seen little or nothing of the fleet. Peter Churchill remembers that the first signal request received aboard *Renown* from the shore was, '. . . a bladder for a football!' After a brief refuelling stop here they pushed on and during the forenoon of the 14th raised Madagascar, and put into Diego Suarez harbour.

'The guns of the French fortress were trained on us as we arrived as the French were very trigger-happy at that time.' Recalls Churchill. The Royal Navy had captured that port from the Vichy in 1942, easily breaking the opposition they had put up, but although the place had been officially handed back no doubt that walk-over still smarted! Another refuelling here during the 14th and *Renown* left the surly Frenchmen and pointed her bows toward happier climes. A four-day voyage brought them to Durban harbour during the afternoon of 18 December where a vastly different welcome awaited them.

Everyone who visited Durban has fond memories of the Lady in White who stood on the jetty and sang as each ship entered harbour and the three months spent here was the highlight of the whole long, drab war for most of her crew. South African entertainment for the crew was lavish and sincere. By 23 December half the ship's company had been distributed throughout South African homes by the SAWAS where they had the first really happy Christmas for five years. Many decades of sour propaganda and racially motivated hatred since, have still not dimmed the memories of those who met the people of South Africa at that time.

G recalls:

Here I feel no book would be complete, as far as service men and women were concerned, without some reference to the people of South Africa and what was then Rhodesia. To see and hear the White Lady welcoming us to Durban was a tonic in itself and a great beginning to a break and holiday no serviceman can ever forget. People from all walks of life and all over the Union of South Africa took us into their homes – the hospitality was unbelievable – we were living like lords, feeding like lions, and, to add, drinking like fish!

Bill Kennelly remembers that:

The highlight of our sojourn in the Indian Ocean was docking in Durban and a well-earned spot of leave. The hospitality there was fantastic and the ship's company was soon scattered over Natal and the Transvaal. The rail trip from Durban, up through the Drakensberg mountains to Pietermaritzburg was very memorable; at times it seemed possible to touch the front of the train from the rear as it wound up the steep inclines. Three of us made our headquarters in Jo'burg but we were soon invited to stay at a home near Pretoria.

Captain Brooke recalls:

My whole excellent ship's company was lavishly entertained. For once I knew my ship was safe in a proper dry dock and I could relax and have the holiday of my life with a family in an old farmhouse, riding off daily to fish the wonderful rivers.

For Maurice Balaam the memories included an outing to Uvongo in January and a long leave in February at the caverns in Drakensberg Mountains at Bushams Caves.

While the men relaxed opportunity was also held to give them a really proper medical and some grim realities of life aboard a ship like *Renown,* built thirty years before to cruise in the North Sea, in the tropics were revealed, as Harry Shannon points out:

During our stay in Durban every member of the ship's company had to go to hospital for a chest X-ray. Being screened was the term they used. Well it was an unhappy screening because about 100 or so of the ship's company were picked up as having TB and these had to leave the ship immediately and they were later flown home. Some of these chaps were in a very advanced stage of TB and we often wondered if it was the rats that brought it into the ship. We had a pile of rats on board and we used to set snares with fuse wire on the pipes for them and we always caught quite a lot. Then we had an official rat-catcher who used to go round with a side bag and a torch at night, equipped with leather gloves. His name was Tom Marlow and he could spot a rat or smell him anywhere. After his night hunting he would take his bag of rats out on to the quarter deck in the morning and the Commander would check the number of rats he had caught and pay 3d a tail for small ones and 6d a tail for big ones and enter the amount in his book. At the end of each fortnight the pay office would pay him the money.

Special cards were issued in Pretoria for *Renown's* crew. They showed them and were given free access to cinemas, clubs, restaurants and the like, nothing was really too good for them. The three months passed very quickly indeed.

Meanwhile the very capable dockyard at Durban was attending to their ship. They had originally secured alongside T jetty in Durban harbour and here they remained over the Christmas holiday period. On 10 January however they were moved to the Prince Edward Dock where the ship remained for a month, returning to T jetty on 8 February for further work to be carried out which lasted another four weeks.

Work aboard still had to be done at this time, as Martin Cain recalls:

One thing did happen, when we arrived in Durban, for we were required to de-ammunition ship before we went into the dry dock there. While we were carrying out the 4.5-inch shells they had music playing on the jetty. Halfway down the gangplank the A.B. ahead of me, named Smith, slipped and dropped his shell into the water, the music playing at the time happening to be an American war song called 'You're a lucky fellow, Mr Smith' (Presumably 'This is the Army, Mr Jones'). Needless to say he wasn't because the de-ammunitioning had to stop while divers went down to get the shell and that didn't make *anybody* happy!

In another incident we were lifting out the 15-inch shells and the cordite for them and putting them into rail wagons on the jetty. I was down after in the shell hold slinging shells when one of these monsters dropped out of the sling and fell on the shell room floor. I've never been so scared in my life. The AP cap had cracked and we could do nothing. We had to wait while they moved all the rail wagons on the jetty and this seemed to take forever. Then a WO came down and we moved the offending shell without any mishap.

The alterations were mainly internal during this refit, the machinery was renovated once more and some auxiliary machinery replaced. The boilers were cleaned and general sprucing up took place. Two of the 44-inch searchlights were removed from the after superstructure and their places occupied by a further two Oerlikons giving her a total of sixty-six of these weapons as well as twenty-eight 2 pounder pom-poms. She seemed fit enough with this array to face the most determined kamikaze eager to join his ancestors, but it was not to be. The Type 284 radar set was replaced by the 285 and general attempts were made to lighten the ship for her displacement had increased enormously since 1939 with all the extra fittings and crew members and 'unknown' additions. For example it was estimated in 1944 that her displacement had increased by some 2,315 tons of which 1,621 tons could not be accounted for by known additions! This would have been serious in a general surface action for her main armoured belt instead of protruding 4 feet 6 inches above the waterline as in 1939 now only showed itself 2 feet 9 inches.

At last she was again ready and in good fighting order, and, with some considerable sadness, her crew re-embarked ready for war once more. On 26 February, at 15.53, *Renown* sailed away from Durban harbour with the White Lady singing a farewell song as she left and once more her long bows set course for Trincomalee and the Eastern Fleet. After an uneventful voyage east and north, she arrived at that anchorage again on 7 March.

They now shook down and prepared to take their part in the future offensive operations designed for that command confident of their ability to play their role well. As one of the officers later recalled:

It was when the ship had finished the refit that it became apparent how much vitality had previously been gradually lost in Trincomalee, for the revitalisation was astonishing and everyone was keen to work up the ship to a still higher pitch of enthusiasm. Drills and exercises were arranged to this end and things were going well as we prepared for the next operation.

In the midst of this renewed activity the body-blow was delivered. *Renown* was informed that, on the arrival from home after a refit of the French battleship *Richelieu,* they were no longer required. It was a bitter knock to their enthusiasm and one many felt completely unwarranted.

The Admiralty signal timed at 12.49 on 29 March simply read:

> Ship is urgently required to join Home Fleet. Request you will sail her as soon as possible to UK.

A later signal, timed 11.38 of 3 April, amplified this:

> *Renown* will relieve *Rodney* in Home Fleet.

Captain Brooke recalled:

> We were ordered to embark 500 ratings who had completed a long period in the East and to surrender their equivalent. We were told that we should no longer be considered a fighting unit. We therefore sailed to Colombo to complete the exchange of ratings, a very depressed and disconsolate crew. Whether we remained to steam the ship home or whether we did not, this great ship's company was to be dispersed and the successes with which we had expected to crown our 15 months' great efforts as flagship of the Eastern Fleet, were to fall on other ships.

Her Master-at-Arms, Tom Oliver, was immediately immersed in the problems the transfer of 1,000 men off and on *Renown* involved:

> On leaving Trinco we were ordered to change or rather draft about 500 of our ratings around the command of South East Asia Ships and bring home a corresponding number to the UK, who had been on the station for quite a while and were required for various courses, leave etc. Captain Brooke confided in me a few days beforehand that this was to take place. Had it not been for that I doubted if it could have been done on a one-day operation, as envisaged by the shore staff, before we sailed.
>
> Many of the small drafts that arrived on board were the worst for 'Sippers' (a sip of each of their messmates' tots of Rum) and I had to return one to his former ship with instructions to return him when he was sober. Captain Brooke gave me a free hand with boat routine etc, and the holy of holies, the Admiral's quarters, for my team.

Many old Renowns left the ship at this time; some, like John Roche, had already gone. 'I left *Renown* in December 1944, after five years and four months on the happiest ship that I ever served in,' he related.

D.G. Anderson was another. 'Many of the ship's company were drafted to other ships, including myself, and thus I was standing on the fo'c'sle of the *Woolwich* when the proud *Renown* set sail home.' He was joined there by G:

> We said our last farewells, promised to keep in touch with each other and, as I and many others stood on the deck of HMS *Woolwich* watching *Renown* sail out of Trinco for the last time, we were overcome by silence. I never saw *Renown* again.

In Colombo harbour on Good Friday after this poignant leave-taking, another old Renown came to say his farewells, Lord Louis Mountbatten. He had signalled her as she arrived that she looked so smart that he must visit her, and was good as his word. He later signalled her:

> It was a great thrill going on board the ship in which I served during two of her world tours. We shall all feel the loss of such a powerfully efficient and happy ship from South East Asia. All good luck to you and to all in your ship.

It was then that an urgent signal arrived from the Admiralty, which lifted the aura of gloom from the *Renown* and re-established her pride in herself once more. As Edward Walker recollected:

> On Good Friday, 30 March, a signal was received ordering the *Renown* to England 'with despatch' and at 16.30 we sailed, realising that this could mean only that we might hope to meet the German pocket battleships. All the newly joined officers and ratings, some of them under the impression that they were passengers, were shaken down into their places and again we worked up as rapidly as possible.

Certainly the *Admiral Scheer* and *Lutzow*, along with several cruisers and destroyers, still lay intact in the Baltic and were quite capable of executing one last foray into the North Sea or Atlantic if they wished. This last ditch orgy of destruction might be in keeping with Nazi Germany's fleet, never as supine or hangdog as their Imperial ancestors who, in 1918, had surrendered as tamely as the Italians in 1943. That no capital ship remained in home waters capable of catching them and bringing them to book certainly weighed heavily at this time and the possibility of 'Doenitz's Death Ride' was taken quite seriously. The only other way of sinking them was that the RAF could catch them at anchor, as they did the *Tirpitz*, and blast them to the bottom. However once they put to sea six years of warfare had shown there was little or no chance of the RAF hitting them while they were actually moving.

In fact, of course, both these ships were heavily engaged as shore bombarding ships in the Baltic, holding off the Soviet hordes while millions of refugees fled the Red Terror from the Baltic Provinces. Not until after this vital work was done did they enter dock to refit and here indeed the heavy bombers caught them immobilised and, finally managed to hit them.

But for the *Renown*s the prospect of such an engagement to end their long and distinguished war service was the spur. It also enabled her engineers to show the world that she was *still* the fastest capital ship in the Royal Navy. Admiral Brooke describes the preparations for her voyage home:

> In March 1945 the *Renown* was lying in Trincomalee, Ceylon, when orders were received to proceed to England with despatch. A programme was worked out and she left Colombo on Good Friday.

Renown actually sailed for the last time from Ceylon at 16.30, on 30 March, being cheered by the assembled ships in harbour, their crews lining their decks as the old veteran slid out to sea and quickly worked up to 21 knots.

Suez lay a distance of 3,340 miles to the west.

'There being no danger of attack in the Indian Ocean', Admiral Brooke goes on, 'a direct course was set to arrive there at 06.00 on Friday 6 April, which was the Captain's birthday.' *Renown* cracked on speed and they actually reached Port Said at 20.11 on the 5th, oiled quickly, and sailed again without further delay.

Martin Cain recollects:

> They cleared the Suez Canal for us and I remember thinking in places that we would be jammed on the sides of the canal, it was that narrow. As we passed one such narrow part the soldiers on the banks were cheering us. One soldier sat on the side of the canal in a dinghy and he shouted up at us and asked where we were going. We told him 'Blighty' and threw him a tow line, which he secured to his little dinghy and there was the great 37,000-ton battle cruiser towing him up the canal! All the army lads thought it was great and were cheering their heads off, but our duty officer didn't think it funny so we had to cast him off again, much to his annoyance and the boos of the Army!

They arrived at Port Said, took on 3,500 tons of oil fuel and were off at 10.00 on the 6th. Arrangements were made for practice shoots to be conducted during their 2,233-mile passage through the Mediterranean to Gibraltar without checking their speed. A surface target was laid on from Alexandria and air targets from Gibraltar and full calibre shoots were conducted with considerable success. 'In spite of our 500 changes we were once more ready to sink the enemy.'

The transit of the Mediterranean took three and a half days and they arrived at Gibraltar at 17.40 on 9 April. She oiled overnight while Captain Brooke dined ashore with the Commander-in-Chief and a destroyer escort was arranged for the final stages of the voyage, U-boats still being very active around the British Isles at this stage of the war.

At 09.28 on 10 April, having taken aboard 1,920 tons of oil *Renown* left Gibraltar for the final time, having known that great sentinel intimately during her long life, in peace and war. From now on a zigzag course was necessary with a mean rate of advance of 22 knots for Portsmouth, with the destroyers *Havelock*, *Hesperus* and *Hotspur*, the latter their old friend from *Graf Spee* days and Norway, strung out ahead of her as anti-submarine screen.

The weather in the Bay of Biscay had not changed since they last crossed and re-crossed it and this, and the need to alter course from time to time to avoid convoys, meant reducing speed to 18 knots, even so some of the destroyers could not keep up in the prevailing conditions. Meanwhile her destination was changed to Scapa Flow, and her escort was taken over by the destroyers *Cambrian, Carron* and *Cavendish*. They steered to the west of Ireland. Off the Scillies a submarine contact was reported off *Renown's* starboard bow and, as she turned away, she met a very heavy sea, which came over the fore turret green. Admiral Brook remembers: 'It looked as if the ship would be damaged by the huge weight of water but she shook it off and rose to the next swell with consummate ease. The contact report was false.'

As they neared Scapa it was necessary to ease down still further before first light before completing their 1,980-mile dash from the Mediterranean, but with first light they cracked on speed once more and *Renown* finally nosed her way into the Flow at 07.27 on 14 April. She had covered the 7,600 miles from Colombo in fourteen days, 14 hours total time, or in just 306 steaming hours! It was a grand performance from a 30-year-old ship.

By the time they got home however the remaining German ships had been put out of action and fighting was taking place in the streets of Berlin. The end of the European War was plainly in sight. After a brief stop at Scapa *Renown* sailed at 08.00 on the 15th for Rosyth, entering the Firth of Forth the same evening where she anchored below the bridge. The Commander-in-Chief, Home Fleet had hoisted his flag aboard in Scapa. *Renown* was refuelled above the bridge as she could not pass under without striking her top-mast. Once topped up she was sufficiently low in the water to pass under the bridge and, on 16th at 11.59, she proceeded up the Firth to the buoy immediately above the bridge. Here she lay for the next month, and, at 15.00 on 8 May, received the signal from the Admiralty: 'Immediate. Splice the main brace'; the war in Europe was over.

Renown still had an important role to play however; she was far from finished yet even though her fighting days were clearly at an end. With the war in Europe over the Admiralty decided that the German officers who were to arrange the surrender should do so in *Renown*. This brought more memories for Admiral Brooke as he relates:

> It so happened that the Captain had served in *Queen Elizabeth* when she, at the same berth as *Renown* was lying in 1945, had received the officers who surrendered the German Fleet in 1918. Those who came on board in 1945 were received in the same way, with frigid dignity.

This major event took place on 10 and 11 May. Although this 'Naval Surrender of Norway' is largely ignored by historians, universally it was of some moment in the history of World War II.

The German Naval delegation, headed by Captain Kruger, had been flown in from Norway along with similar representatives of the *Wehrmacht* and *Luftwaffe* occupation forces and then taken to Hawes Pier that evening dressed in full naval uniform. Darkness was falling as the six officers were embarked in the ship's pinnace and their bags bundled in after them. The pinnace then set out across from South Queensferry to the huge dark bulk of *Renown* lying in the stream.

Harry Shannon recalls that historic moment when they came aboard her:

> I remember there was a guard of honour on the quarterdeck, as there was a high-ranking Naval officer in the German staff, and when they came on board

they were saluted by this guard. They were not allowed to walk round and inspect them as in usual circumstances. I also remember the high-ranking officers putting their hands out to shake hands with our Captain, but he refused to do so.

They were shown to the cabins allocated to them and a Marine Guard placed outside.

The Captain met the delegation at the top of the gangway with the Marine guard drawn up with fixed bayonets. Members of the ship's company silently watched from the gun deck. Each German officer saluted the quarter-deck following usual custom and the Captain saluted in return as each officer was piped aboard. 'Their demeanour at this stage', wrote a contemporary observer, 'was one of sullen acquiescence.'

The delegation first proceeded to the gunroom where they were served with refreshments and waited to be summoned to the conference room. Meanwhile the British and Norwegian officers took their places under the president of the British-Norwegian Naval Committee, Vice-Admiral the Hon E.R. Drummond, CB, MVO. They sat along one side of the large oblong table and the German officers duly filed in and sat opposite them. Each officer was asked to identify himself and, this done, Admiral Drummond asked whether the surrender terms had been received and if so when. The German captain replied that they had but he did not know when. Drummond then curtly reminded them that under these terms a party should have arrived within 48 hours after the surrender became effective; why were they late? The excuse was that there was not enough time to get the party together and that flying weather had been bad. Asked about the German representative from the Skagerrak they replied that he would be following later. This party duly arrived aboard a German minesweeper under escort of the old destroyer *Vivien*. Talks on the dispositions of fleet units, U-boats and the positions of all minefields in Norwegian waters continued far into the night and during the next two days.

These details finally established arrangements were made for the return to his homeland of Crown Prince Olav and the re-establishment of the Royal Norwegian Government.

This duty completed *Renown* sailed from the Firth for the final time at 12.14 on 12 May and sailed through the Pentland Firth and down the west coast of Ireland escorted by the destroyers *Carysfort* and *Scourge*, anchoring at Spithead at 21.09 that same night. Next day she moved into Portsmouth harbour and secured at the South Railway jetty in the afternoon, then de-ammunitioned ship.

Arrangements were now put in hand for her to reduce to two-fifths complement and the complicated paying-off procedure was commenced. On 8 June the Admiralty decreed that *Renown* was to remain at fourteen days notice with ⅖ complement, pending Their Lordships decision regarding her future programme. It seemed a refit for future service was still a strong possibility. Two days later a signal from Whitehall stated: '*Renown* will be taken in hand at Devonport about mid-October. Completion date, February 1946.'

The war against Japan was expected to last at least another year, maybe two by most people and so the ships were deemed to be required for service until that time.

Tom Oliver records:

The men we brought home were from all three naval depots and all had varying amount of leave to come. After sending them on leave we prepared to use *Renown* as a transit depot. As they returned they were shown on the victualling sheets and check sheets simultaneously and then presented with a draft note to their respective depots. This, despite the work involved, was very convenient.

Plans were now well in hand for *Renown* to be taken into dockyard hands for a major refit and reconstruction. The Admiralty evidently had post-war plans for her further employment, probably either as a seagoing training ship or perhaps a gunnery training ship. The work was to commence in October 1945, and last for six months. In preparation for this her above-water torpedo tubes had been removed and, as a further saving in top-weight, now deemed vital, the big floating crane at Portsmouth lifted out both forward batteries of 4.5-inch guns. With these six mountings gone the ship had a strangely bare and unprotected look about her and was riding high out of the water.

That a training role was envisaged for her next employment is given weight by the fact that at this time, despite her much reduced complement, she took aboard members of the Chinese Navy for just such purposes. These were trained aboard *Renown* in preparation for their taking delivery of the light cruiser *Aurora* that had been sold to the Chinese Government and was fitting out for them nearby.

This task was not always easy, oriental vanity being quickly upset as Tom Oliver relates:

> The Chinese seemed to take to naval life quite well but many did not care for menial jobs. They were mostly well educated but some were arrogant and nationally aware.
>
> I remember a boxing tournament being put on in the RN barracks and the customary use was made of all available bunting to disguise the gym's utility appearance. The bunting was wrapped around deal planking, which served as the ring-side seating. One piece of bunting proved to be the Chinese flag. That tore it completely. A senior naval officer had to report on *Renown* to the Senior Chinese Officer with a personal apology!
>
> We also had another amusing incident involving our Chinese guests when we gave them leave to various parts of the country. This in itself proved a big undertaking. One of the London group caused a spot of bother with a 'barrow boy' while in town which led to fisticuffs. It appeared the Chinese rating was handling his 'Choice William Pears'. The difficulty arose from the 'choice of words' (forgive the pun), choice being misinterpreted as 'Choose'.

Most of the old Renowns were now leaving the ship in a steady stream. For those that remained awaiting discharge it was difficult to hold back their frustration while thus 'marking time'. This led to the classic exchange as recalled by Bill Kennelly one day:

> One of the 'lads' returned to the ship very drunk and, after being lined up before the OOW, was duly escorted forward to the Sick Bay to be examined. The Duty MO was sent for, a young chap who promptly lectured the offender and concluded by asking, 'Would you come to me in this state if you were in Civvy Street?' and got the well-deserved reply, 'No, Sir – I'd *send* for you!'

On 23 July *Renown* sailed from Portsmouth for Plymouth and on arrival were given urgent orders to 'Paint Ship' and generally to smarten up. The reason was soon made known to them, *Renown* had been chosen as the venue for the historic meeting between His Majesty King George VI and the American President Harry Truman on his way home after the Potsdam Conference. At once work got underway for this great day, codenamed Operation Exodus.

On 2 August 1945, *Renown* lay at her buoys, 'Resplendent in her silver-grey', her fresh paintwork agleam in the first rays of the morning light.

'*Renown* lay silvered in magnificent profile off Breakwater Port,' wrote one observer.

The orders of the day specified rig of the day for her crew as, 'No. 2s with lanyards.' Duty watch was called at 06.00, the quarterdeck was scrubbed and washed and at 08.05 the guns were uncovered. At 10.20 the guard and band assembled and the hands were fallen in by divisions on the fo'c'sle.

President Truman had flown straight in to Yelverton airfield 12 miles from Plymouth. In harbour lay the two US cruisers *Augusta* and *Philadelphia,* the former of which was to take the President back to America on conclusion of the meeting. The King travelled down from London overnight by train and took breakfast beside the River Dart before the Royal Train arrived at the Princess Royal pier in the GWR docks drawn by two 'Castle' class locomotives. His Majesty was accompanied by Lord Halifax and was met by the Lord Mayor and C-in-C, Plymouth, Admiral Sir Ralph Leatham. The King wore the active service dress of Admiral of the Fleet.

The Royal party boarded the *Renown* at 10.20 via the starboard companionway, and was met by Captain Brooke, who introduced him to other ship's officers. The Band of the Royal Marines, Plymouth Division played the National Anthem and, at the same time the Flag of the Lord High Admiral and Union Flag were broken out with the Royal Standard at the Main and the White Ensign astern.

At 12.40 the *Renown's* launch carried President Truman from the *Augusta* where he was duly piped aboard and received by the King. The Stars and Stripes rose along-side the Royal Standard, an historic moment, without precedent, enacted suitably enough within sight of the spot where the Pilgrim Fathers had set sail for New England three centuries before. The two heads of state then adjourned to the Admiral's Quarters for their private conference while the hands went to their messes for 'Up Spirits'.

After their meeting and lunch the two guests walked through the ship to the fo'c'sle where they posed for photographers and the President took his departure at 14.45 and, shortly afterward the King returned his call aboard *Augusta*. On conclusion His Majesty returned to *Renown* and, at 15.15, the two American cruisers sailed from their anchorage off Melampus Bay and headed out to sea escorted by the British frigates *Crosby* and *Holmes*. Before the King finally left *Renown* at the end of this historic day the following signals were exchanged:

President Truman, USS *Augusta* from HMS *Renown*:

It has been a very real pleasure to me to meet you during your all too brief visit to my country today after your recent labours in the great cause to which the Allied Nations are pledged. I send you my best wishes for your homeward voyage and for your safe return. George, R.I.

The King, HMS *Renown* from USS *Augusta*:

My hearty thanks for your generous expressions. It has been a delightful experience to visit you and your country. I feel sure our two nations will co-operate in peace as they are now co-operating so effectively in war. The President.

On his return to London the King had this signal sent to Captain Brooke:

My dear Brooke, The King wishes me to congratulate you on the appearance of *Renown* yesterday, which, in the circumstances, His Majesty considered highly satisfactory. The King was very pleased with the way everything went, and asks me to express to you and your officers his sincere thanks for all the trouble, which had clearly been taken for his visit.

Within a few weeks came news of the surrender of Japan, and the Navy's job was completed as far as combat duties were concerned. However much mopping-up remained, territory had to be reoccupied and prisoners released and cared-for. However VJ Day was celebrated in due style. The *Renown* was dressed overall, 'Splice the Main Brace' was again sounded and special 48 hours' leave was granted where possible. Although training continued aboard, peacetime routine was adopted.

In the resultant celebrations around the world the grim days of 1940 and 1941 were forgotten, as was the vital and unique role played by the great ship lying below Stadden Heights at that crucial time. Admiral Brooke considered that: 'In the first two years of the war *Renown* was our most important ship . . .', a fitting tribute, but though her role subsequently lessened in the years that followed the last of the battle-cruisers was always where the fighting was thickest and the sight of her long, lean bows cutting through the waters, with her great guns elevating and straining to reach the ever-reluctant foe, was a sight that lifted many a man.

And now her last chapter had been reached.

The End, and a Beginning

The brief flicker of hope that *Renown* would continue to serve the fleet in the post-war era was soon snubbed out. There was a new government in power, Churchill had been cast aside. That government had traditionally been opposed to defence, regarding it always as an irritant rather than its first duty to its people, and little sympathy was expected from it for any form of spending in the heady days that followed final victory. Naturally there was a new feeling in the land; the cry was for change and the Royal Navy felt the keenness of the new situation as acutely in 1945 as it had in 1918. All the old lessons of the 1930s were forgotten; it was disarm, forget, scrap. In September came the announcement that *Renown's* scheduled refit, due to commence in October, had been cancelled, and cancelled absolutely. The C-in-C Plymouth was forced to enquire of the Admiralty in a signal timed 20.09 17 October, whether it was confirmed that *Renown* was to be reduced to Category 'B' Reserve, as if he could not believe it himself. It was so confirmed. There was to be no reprieve.

The old ship still found useful employment however. She was moved from her anchorage in Plymouth Sound and taken into Devonport dockyard. On 11 November Remembrance Service was held on the ships fo'c'sle, a service of special significance for the old Renowns who recalled comrades lost over the years. Happily *Renown's* war casualties had been relatively sparse; in that respect, as in others, she had been a lucky ship. Still they remembered the young lad paralysed off the Lofotens; the seamen and officers killed in the 4.5-inch turret by their own fire; the lads drowned in accidents at Gibraltar and Trincomalee, and those that had left *Renown* only to die in action aboard other fighting ships.

On 26 November 1945 *Renown* shifted her berth once more up the Hamoaze to join the many other warships lying in reserve there. She was berthed in sight of the Royal Albert Bridge over the Saltash, just ahead of the veteran battleships *Resolution* and *Revenge,* in their day mighty symbols of Britain's sea power, but now mute and immobile in their dotage, awaiting their inevitable fates, reduced to a training establishment for stokers and known collectively as the *Imperieuse. Renown* joined them as part of this establishment and thus, even in this limited way, continued to serve the nation.

Captain Brooke left the ship he had known so well in two world wars and Captain Maundy took over in command, in readiness for the final degradation, her reduction to care and maintenance in Category C reserve, vessels marked out for early disposal. Already around her, the numbers of salt-caked veterans were dwindling day-by-day as they made their final voyages under tow to the breakers yards. Lofty cruisers which had been the pride of the China Squadron in the 1930s with gleaming white paint-work and embellished brass work now passed *Renown*, rust-speckled and uncared for, on their final journeys. Lithe rakish destroyers, that had torn into action against the Italian fleets, whose guns had spat defiance at the German Stukas off Dunkirk and Crete and in a thousand epic fights, made the same melancholy trip along with frigates and corvettes that had won the Battle of the Atlantic, the only battle that really counted for Britain's survival, and little minesweepers that had doggedly carried out their unrewarding task for six long years around the shores of the land and as far afield as North Russia and Okinawa.

All were destined for the same fate. Here lay her old Indian Ocean companion *Unicorn*, and once passed a ship brand spanking-new and proud, the *Vanguard*, last of the battleships, setting forth to sea in defiance of the new era of jet aircraft and atomic bombs.

Renown still lay here a year later, in September 1946, and the opportunity was taken for a final farewell from many of her old crew members with a party to celebrate the thirtieth anniversary of her first commissioning at Fairfields on the Clyde, two wars and a whole generation ago in time. Two hundred guests came aboard and, for the last time, her wardroom rang with the talk and laughter of naval officers and their ladies.

In 1948 the Government pronounced final sentence, and, in a typically ham-fisted political way, gave the reasons for scrapping *Renown* as, '. . . due to the lack of speed for service in the modern fleet.' As John Stuart remembered, this gaff caused some comment among knowledgeable persons:

> I received a letter at that time from *Renown's* wartime Engineer Officer – who was then Deputy Engineer-in-Chief of the Fleet, Rear-Admiral Iain Maclean, to the effect that such an announcement was a bit steep since *Renown* was still the *fastest* capital ship in the Navy!

On 19 March 1948 it was announced that *Renown* had been sold for scrapping. On 1 June came the final paying-off and also the last ceremony to be held aboard the *Renown*. Commander D.T. Dowler was now 'In Command' of the old ship and Tom Oliver was with her to the last as Master-of-Arms. Together they arranged for a final paying-off ceremony to mark her passing with some dignity. The C-in-C came aboard at 18.10 and the band played a selection of marches used by HMS *Renown* during past commissions. Then the assembled company recited 'The Evening Hymn'. At 18.30 the Royal Marine Buglers sounded off 'Sunset', followed the 'Last Post' then 'Reveille'. The company then sang the National Anthem before being marched off. The C-in-C left the ship while the Senior Officers left for the *Unicorn*. The *Renown* finally ceased to be His Majesty's Ship after a period of service to crown and country that lasted for thirty-one years and nine months.

Shiner Wright was among the veterans of 1939, like Tom Oliver, who had stayed with the old ship right through to the end. Shiner recalled:

> What a grand finale to a marvellous life was the very sad day when the White Ensign was lowered for the last time. I can hear it all now as plain as if it were

yesterday, 'Sunset', being played by the Royal Marine Band, but not to the present well-known background hymn of 'The day though gavest, Lord, is ended' but to a much more appropriate hymn for the occasion, 'Now the day is over'.

The day was over for her and what a glorious end to such a gallant ship and for the thousands of men who had passed through her, slept in duffle coats and sea boots, cursed her when she bucked in rough seas. I can remember standing between the 15inch guns on the quarterdeck during the final ceremony. Beside me was a civilian of advanced years. After the ensign had been lowered for the last time I turned to him and asked him what his interest was in *Renown*. His reply was somewhat unexpected, 'I was the first Master-at-Arms when she commissioned during the Great War and I have come up especially for today.' The spirit of *Renown* was set that far back.

Her end was now not long delayed. In July she left Plymouth, under tow of tugs, *Englishman, Masterman* and *Seaman,* on her last journey north to Faslane in the Gareloch for breaking up, and here she was moored awaiting her fate.

In October she was visited by a reporter from *Scottish Field* at the yards of Metal Industries Limited, the firm who were busily engaged in scrapping other veterans, *Resolution, Malaya* and *Iron Duke,* all of which lay in various dismal stages of devastation. *Renown* was still, at that time, intact, her once gleaming hull and upperworks blotched and stained with rust. Her big guns were still intact, hooded and cowled and impotent, as were her after four 4.5-inch turrets, but all else had gone, no ship's boats, no radar, no life. She lay a barren hulk. The reporter, Edward Scouller, wrote:

The layman, looking at her great, graceful, sinister bulk and thinking of the vast sums of money she has cost, may doubt the prudence of breaking up what looks still a useful vessel. He may wonder whether even an old ship is not better than no ship at all.

He also added the reflection that:

Apart altogether from the wisdom of disarmament in the Molotov era, anyone who loves ships must feel like turning his eyes away from the humiliation of her conversion to piles of scrap. Presumably that consideration has been weighted by their Lordships of the Admiralty; and we may console ourselves with the reflection that only by the scrapping of the old is room made for the new. But the *Renown* is a bonny ship all the same. It's a pity.

Few saw her go, but among those who witnessed her passing was one *ex-Renown*, CPO T.J. McCafferty who had served aboard her as Chief Mechanician from September 1943 to June 1946 who remembered her as the finest ship he had ever served in:

In 1948, being then stationed in Faslane aboard HMS *Mull of Galloway, I* watched a number of ships being towed up the Loch to the breakers yard which was but a few yards away from where we lay; merchant ships in particular and also a few small carriers. These ships seemed to be broken up and despatched at great speed. Then one day I saw a number of tugs towing up another ship destined for the yard and I recognised HMS *Renown*. I remember saying, 'Oh no, not her', but yes she ended up in the floating dock used for the purpose. I felt very sad indeed and I relived so many moments in a flash of time. And so day by day I watched her becoming smaller and smaller. The breaking up of ships at this time was done purely by cutting away sections with oxyacetylene torches. The sections then being lifted off with the huge cranes situated there and literally dumped into waiting trucks on the railway. Turbo and diesel generators I saw being lifted out and dumped. Deck by deck was removed until all that was left was the huge keel that also finally disappeared in a matter of weeks, and then *Renown* was no more, just truckloads of scrap. To me it seemed such a waste when her machinery was in so good a condition. Nostalgia stayed with me for some while after.

And so she went to her grave her long story ended. And yet . . .

Many years were to pass before another ship bearing her proud and illustrious name joined the Royal Navy. When she did it was to a Navy and world that *Renown* herself, and even more so her old creator, Jackie Fisher, would not have recognised. Far from being the major seapower Great Britain has sunk to a middle-class one, and hard put to even maintain that profile too. The great Empire had followed the Great Ships into the same oblivion and so has her voice in world affairs. Far from exercising a benevolent influence upon the world for good and order, the nation was just concerned with basic survival at all in an era dominated by hostile 'Super-Powers', while for her people, who once ruled a third of the globe, the burning topics were 'Top of the Pops' and the 35-hour week. But in order just to survive at all, as a fallen giant in a world of force, Britain had to create new ships of war and destruction, ships the like of which the world had never seen.

Great glistening monsters of the deep, the four Polaris missile submarines were fuelled by nuclear power, remained submerged for months and carried, in each of their sixteen nuclear-tipped missiles, more power than all the battleships of the world throughout history could conceive. With the advent of such machines the war at sea took on a new aspect. They were obviously the capital ship of the day and were given battleship names, and one became the tenth HMS *Renown*.

Thus the name was handed on as in ages before. Although the ships and their crews had as little in common as the battleships that preceded them had with the first *Renown*, the common link that binds them remains in the name. Perhaps also, after all, Fisher might have seen some merit in them. They could certainly fulfil his stricture to 'Hit Hard', although they would never 'Hit First' nor 'Go on Hitting', their function in life was to deter war in an age when might seems the only reply to the ambitions and selfishness of mighty powers seeking world dominance. Until such times as sense returns to such nations, and peace towards men is a fact and not a political catchphrase, such ships remain, as before, our only bulwark against enslavement and worse. We can therefore only pray that they *will never* see action for if she does her whole purpose has failed and with it civilisation. But perhaps it was ever thus?

As I write even this monster has now herself long gone to the breakers yard and has become a fading memory also. The achievements of the ninth *Renown* should not go unrecorded however, despite these sentiments. She herself failed to deter war but she played her full part in seeing that the result of that disaster was that the people of Great Britain remained free. It is not an inconsiderable achievement.

APPENDIX ONE:

Battle Honours of
HMS *Renown*

GABBARD	1653
SCHEVENINGEN	1653
USHANT	1781
EGYPT	1801
NORWAY	1940
ATLANTIC	1940
SPARTIVENTO	1940
MEDITERRANEAN	1941
Bismarck ACTION	1941
MALTA CONVOYS	1941–42
ARCTIC	1942–3
NORTH AFRICA	1942
SABANG	1944

APPENDIX TWO:

Commanding Officers of
HMS *Renown* 1916–1947

Captain Hugh SINCLAIR
Captain A.W. CRAIG, CB
Captain E.A. TAYLOR
Captain The Hon. H. MEADE
Refitting
Captain Norton A. SULIVAN
Captain Sidney R. BAILEY
Captain A. TALBOT
Captain G.F. EDWARD-COLLINS
Captain G. LAYTON, DSO
Captain Henry R. SAWBRIDGE
Refitting
Captain C.E.B. SIMEON
Captain R.R. McGRIGOR
Captain C.S. DANIEL
Captain W.E. PARRY
Captain B.C.B. BROOKE, CB
Captain H.M.S. MAUNDY, DSC

Renown's Predecessors

There have been *Renowns* in the Royal Navy since the mid-seventeenth century, and they have carried the torch of freedom around the world ever since. Appropriate enough then was her badge, a fiery torch surrounded by a golden wreath of honour, and appropriate enough also was her ship's motto, *Antiquae Famae Custos,* Guardian of Ancient Renown.

No fewer than eight ships had proudly carried that name in battle before her and had upheld its honour and that of the unique service she was born to serve.

In fact the appearance of the name *Renown* in the Navy List was first connected, as with so many equally famous vessels, with a prize capture. The French ship *Renommee* was taken by the British vessel *Nonsuch* in 1651 and added to the Royal Navy as a Fireship. She rated as a 20-gun man-o-war in this capacity and was too small for front line service. However she was present at the naval engagements with the Dutch Fleet at that period, winning for herself the battle honours Gabbard and Scheveningen in 1653. She was sold out of the service in the following year and for a long period the name lapsed in the Navy List.

The second vessel was also a prize, the 32-gun French frigate *Renommee,* being taken in 1747. In September of that year she fought a classic frigate duel with the British *Amazon* and was subsequently taken prize by the British fourth-rate, 50-gun *Dover.* She was repaired and joined the Royal Navy as the frigate *Fame.* However the following year her name was changed to *Renown* and this began an almost unbroken period of two centuries in which such a ship has served Great Britain.

She served initially with the Channel Fleet without undue distinction and it was not until a decade later that she achieved her first notable service in wartime during the Seven Years War. In 1758 she took part in the attack on Cherbourg; together with the fourth-rate *Rochester,* the *Renown* effected the capture of another French vessel at this time, the frigate *Guirlande.*

Renown then sailed for the Leeward Islands and there became part of the British fleet operating in the area whose operations culminated in the capture of the French island of Guadeloupe. She saw no further active service and was subsequently broken up in 1771.

She was almost immediately replaced however, when a fourth-rate ship-of-the-line, or battleship in modern terminology, was launched as *Renown* in 1774. She was a 1,000 ton vessel rated as a fifty-gunner. She first commissioned in 1775 and her first cruise took her to the North American station where she joined the flag of Sir Peter Parker whose fleet was engaged in helping to suppress the American revolutionary forces. The first actions in which the *Renown* took part in this theatre were the attack on Rhode Island and on Natagansett Bay, which were both successfully completed.

The third *Renown* continued to serve in the Royal Navy for a further thirteen years before she in turn was broken up in 1794. But she saw no further action in war during this long period. The story of *Renown* is complicated during this period by the fact that there were, in effect, two ships of the name serving in the fleet for much of it. For another French frigate named *Renommee* had surrendered to the Royal Navy, and this latter vessel had been duly added to the British fleet under her own original name. She was taken in 1796 and, as HMS *Renommee,* served until 1810 before being scrapped. She is recognised as the fourth *Renown.*

Before she left the Navy List another *Renown* had joined the flag. She was a 2,000-ton battleship, a third rate, one of the famous British '74s' after the number of guns she carried. Henceforth the name *Renown* was to be carried exclusively by capital ships in the Royal Navy, the term in this context being taken to mean the most powerful ships in the Navy.

This new battleship was launched in 1798, just in time to participate in the long-drawn out struggle against Napoleon.

The French did finally venture to sea in 1801 and *Renown* was part of a British squadron that gave chase and followed them south into the Mediterranean, a sea in which her successor almost a century and a half later was to earn undying fame. Here she took part in the naval operations off the Egyptian coast that saw the termination of the Emperor's dreams of an Eastern Empire to add to his European conquests.

On conclusion of this episode *Renown* joined the fleet under Nelson then blockading Toulon, a thankless endurance test that was to last for two years. The Navy was patient and were ultimately to be rewarded with the victory of Trafalgar, but *Renown* was denied participation in this great battle having earlier been withdrawn to another squadron. She paid off in 1806 but remained in reserve at Devonport and this gallant old veteran did not finally take her final trip to the breaker's yard until 1853 after a life span of almost sixty years.

Those seaman who sailed her off Toulon were long since in their graves when the next *Renown* appeared. Those sixty years had seen the supreme fulfilment of sea power vigorously applied and the Royal Navy elevated to a supreme and unchallenged position as the maritime power. Under that shield and cloak the power of the nation waxed steadily to its peak, but changes at sea in respect of fighting ships and tactics changed but little until the mid-nineteenth century. Then the advent of steam at sea, of armour plate and huge long-range guns and the like, caused a half century of turmoil with ship design changing, almost annually, in an effort to keep pace with technological advances the like of which had never been known. Not surprisingly then the sixth *Renown* had a much briefer life than the fifth.

She was a second-rate battleship launched in 1857. She was a 3,000 tonner, in some respects little changed from the wooden walls and broadsides of old, but she had steam engines as well as a full spread of sail and had screws to drive her through the water. She was a compromise warship produced by a conservative Admiralty, and after a two-year commission in the Mediterranean her day was done; she was surpassed by the advent of such vessels as the ironclad *Warrior* and

Black Prince and their myriad successors. Her hulk lay idle until 1870 when she was sold for disposal.

A quarter of a century later sail had vanished from the major ships of the fleets of the world and the mass of 'one-off' experimental designs had finally somewhat stabilised into a fairly constant battleship type following the building of Sir William White's majestic *Royal Sovereign* class ships in the 1890s.

Sir William himself always expressed himself against the construction of 'second-class' battleships holding out that wherever a British battleship might come up against a foreign one it should always be superior in size, armament and protection, but this wise judgement was overruled and the parrot cry of the time was for 'moderate dimensions'.

The seventh *Renown* was therefore laid down at that yard in the February of 1893, launched on 8 May 1895 and finally completed in January 1897 at a cost of £709,706, showing a large saving on the *Royal Sovereign* type. However to achieve that saving she carried a main armament of four 10-inch guns, against the 13.5-inch weapons of the latter class. These were supplemented by the usual smaller batteries of ten 6-inch quick firing guns, 12- and 3-pounders together with five torpedo tubes. She had a complement of 674 officers and men.

Although designed for 18 knots *Renown* excelled herself on trials reaching 19.75 knots with a mean hp of 12,901. She was always regarded as a pretty little ship with a marked sheer fore and aft, paired funnels side by side and heavy fighting masts. Small and graceful for a battleship, her fighting power was small compared with the front-line vessels of the same period and finding useful employment for her had there been a major war would have been difficult. However she did incorporate several new features in her internal layout and armour protection disposition and watertight battle integrity and this proved a useful test-bed for future development. She also won the hearts of those that served in her, and was particular favourite of Admiral John Fisher. He had been the Director of Naval Ordnance when she was first projected and was later to hoist his flag in her. He was to play a major part in the story of the ninth *Renown,* as we have seen, but even at this time he was making his name with improvements in gunnery and the like.

As her employment was to be in tropical waters one unique feature of the *Renown* was that her hull was sheathed with wood and copper to minimise the effects of frequent docking in those distant waters. On completion she passed into reserve and then was commissioned in June 1897 as the flagship for Queen Victoria's Jubilee. This duty completed, the *Renown* hoisted the flag of Admiral Fisher on the North American and West Indies Station in August that same year, serving there for two years and then transferred with Fisher to the crack Mediterranean Fleet.

In 1902 she was fitted out as a Royal Yacht and carried the Duke and Duchess of Connaught to represent the Queen at the Delhi Durbar.

In 1905 she conveyed the Prince and Princess of Wales, later King George V and Queen Mary, to India with Commander H. Tyrwhitt as her captain. Escorted by the big cruiser *Terrible,* both ships were specially painted up once more for the voyage, having white hulls with a broad green band around the upper edge. This marked the last distinguished service this battleship was to play. After a life of only twelve years, eight of which were in commission, she was relegated to dockyard service, using her own engines for the last time in 1909. She lingered on in this lowly capacity painted a dull grey and used as a stokers' training ship – a far cry from her Royal patronage!

She lay at Portsmouth harbour for a number of years, the only event that deserved her dotage being the mortifying one of being rammed by the water tanker *Arid* on 26 September 1911 and damaged. She was handed over to care and maintenance on January 1913 and in the December of the same year was towed up to Motherbank, sold in 1914 and broken up on the eve of the Great War.

APPENDIX FOUR

Ships Profiles

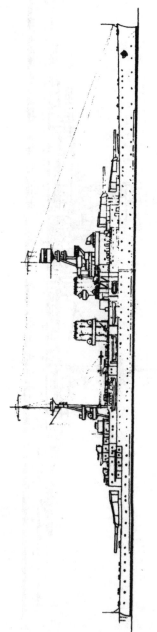

Profile of *Renown* as in 1916. (John R Dominy)

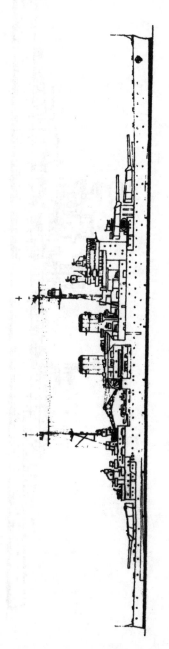

Profile of *Renown* as in 1946. (John R Dominy)

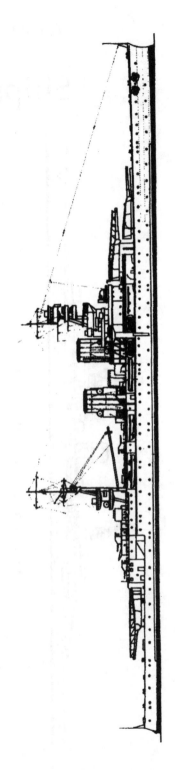

Profile of *Renown* as in 1917. (John R Dominy)

Profile of *Renown* as in 1919. (John R Dominy)

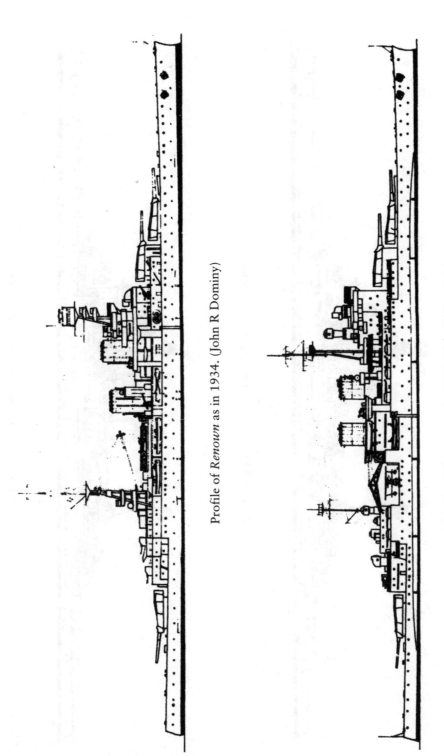

Profile of *Renown* as in 1934. (John R Dominy)

Profile of *Renown* as in 1939. (John R Dominy)

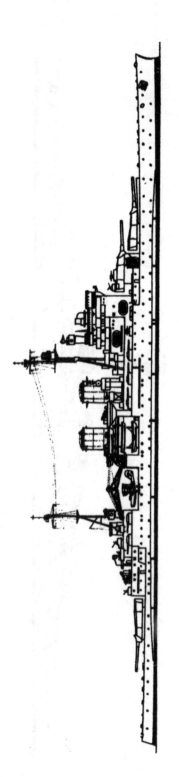

Profile of *Renown* as in 1942. (John R Dominy)

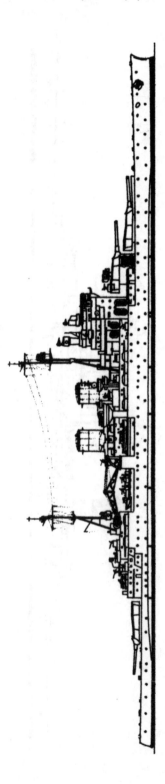

Profile of *Renown* as in 1944. (John R Dominy)

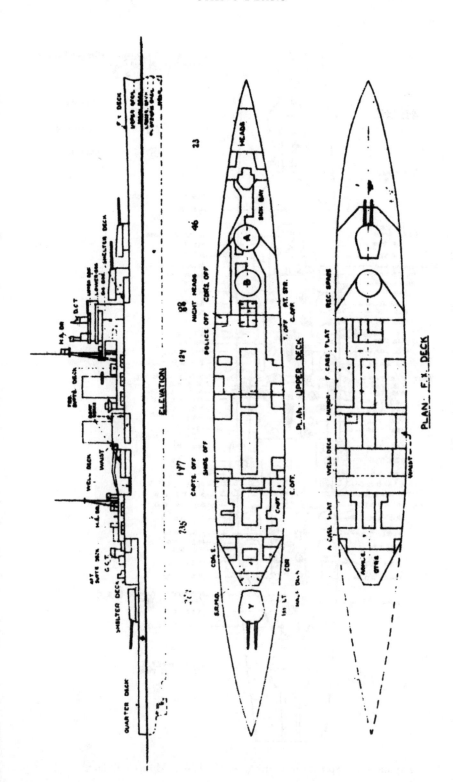

Plan of HMS *Renown*, 1944. (Maurice Balaam)

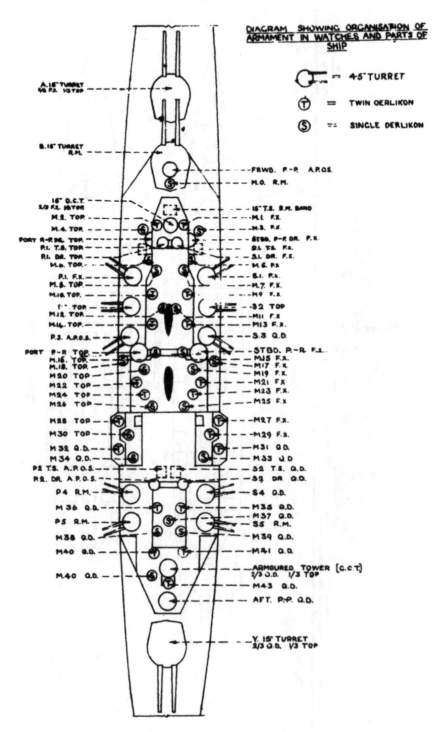

Layout and disposition of armament in 1944. (Maurice Balaam)

Abbreviations Used in Text

AA	Anti-aircraft.
'A' arc	Position of ship relative to target when all main armament guns will bear (as in broadside position for example).
AB	Able Seaman.
ACNS	Assistant Chief Naval Staff.
ACQ	Admiral Commanding, Battle-cruiser Squadron.
ADO	Air Defence Officer.
AFCC	Admiralty Fire Control Clock.
AMC	Armed Merchant Cruiser.
AP	Armour Piercing.
APA	Australian Press Association.
APC	Armour Piercing Charge.
AT	Admiralty Telegram.
BC1	Officer Commanding First Battle Cruiser.
BCS	Battle Cruiser Squadron.
BL	Breech Loading.
BM	Bravery Medal.
BPF	British Pacific Fleet.
CB	Companion Commander of the Bath.
C-in-C	Commander-in-Chief.
CPO	Chief Petty Officer.
CR	Cruiser.
CS	Cruiser Squadron.
(D)	Senior Officer of a Destroyer Flotilla.
DB	Double Bottom.
DC	Damage Control.
D/C	Depth Charge.
DF	Destroyer Flotilla.
DNC	Director of Naval Construction.

DNI	Director of Naval Intelligence
DNO	Director of Naval Ordnance.
DR	Destroyer.
(E)	Engineer.
E-boat	i.e. Enemy boat (British name for S-boats, German MTBs).
EF	Eastern Fleet.
ERA	Engine Room Artificer.
(Flag)	Ship carrying Senior Officer, Commander-in-Chief of a Squadron.
FO	Flag Officer (i.e. as above).
GOH	Grand Oriental Hotel.
GWR	Great Western Railway.
HA	High Angle.
HACO	High Altitude Control Officer.
HACP	High Angle Control Position.
HACS	High Angle Control System.
HE	High Explosive.
HF/DF	High Frequency/Direction Finding. (known as 'HuffDuff' homed in on the radio signals of German submarines and cross-plotting could reveal their positions so they could be attacked or the convoys routed to avoid them).
HMS	His Majesty's Ship.
HO	Hostilities Only.
hp	Horse Power.
HP	High Pressure.
HT	High Tensile steel.
HRH	His Royal Highness.
KC	So-called Krupps Armoured plate. ('Krupps cemented', after process).
KG	*Kampfgeschwader*, German bomber unit.
LA	Surface firing weapons. ('Low Angle').
LCI	Landing Craft for carrying infantry.
LCT	Large landing craft for carrying tanks.
LL Sweep	Anti-Magnetic Mine Towing Device for minesweepers.
LTO	Leading Telegraph Operator.
MO	Medical Officer.
MTB	Motor Torpedo Boat. ('PT' Boat in American, 'MAS' boat in Italian, S-Boat in German etc, etc).
(N)	Navigator.
o.a.	Length overall.
OOQ	Officer of the Quarters.
OOW	Officer of the Watch.
P1	No. 1 mounting of the secondary armament on the port side of ship.
PMO	Principal Medical Officer.
P and O	The Peninsular and Orient Steam Navigation Company.
PP	Length between perpendiculars (i.e. *excluding* rake of bow or stern).
psi	per square inch.
P.T.	Physical Training.
PTI	P.T. Instructor (Licensed Ship's Torturer).

RDF	Radio Direction Finding (Radar).
R/F	Range Finder.
RFA	Royal Fleet Auxiliary.
RM	Royal Marines.
RN	Royal Navy.
RNR	Royal Naval Reserve.
RNVR	Royal Naval Volunteer Reserve.
RPO	Regulating Petty Officer ('The Crusher' – from the size of his boots!).
S1	No. 1 mounting of secondary armament on starboard side of ship.
SAP	Semi-Armour Piercing.
SAWAS	South African Welfare for Armed Services.
SEAC	South-East Asia Command.
Sm.79	Savoia Marchetti 79 – Italian bomber and torpedo bomber.
SHP	Shaft Horse Power.
(T)	Torpedo Specialist.
T/B	Torpedo Bomber.
TRH	Their Royal Highnesses.
TS	Transmitting Station.
USN	United States Navy.
USS	United States Ship.
VAEF	Vice-Admiral, Eastern Fleet (Vice-Admiral Power).
W.O.	Warrant Officer.
W/T	Radio Equipment ('Wireless Telegraphy').
WTC	Wireless Telegraph Control.

Index

An index of operations and ship's names follows the general index

SHIPS

OPERATIONS